TEACHING GENERAL MUSIC

TEACHING GENERAL MUSIC

Action Learning for Middle and Secondary Schools

Thomas A. Regelski

SCHIRMER BOOKS
A Division of Macmillan Publishing Co., Inc.

New York

Collier Macmillan Publishers
London

Schirmer Books
A Division of Macmillan Publishing Co., Inc.
866 Third Avenue, New York, N.Y. 10022

Collier Macmillan Canada, Ltd.

Library of Congress Catalog Card Number: 80-5561

Printed in the United States of America

printing number

3 4 5 6 7 8 9 10

Library of Congress Cataloging in Publication Data

Regelski, Thomas A.
    Teaching general music.

    Includes bibliographies and index.
    1. School music—Instruction and study—United
States. I. Title.
MT3.U5R43   780'.7'2973   80-5561
ISBN 0-02-872070-9

This book is dedicated to the memory of my mother, whose own musical talents and interests provided my first music education, and who helped me keep at it through the "problem years" even though I was more difficult and troublesome than most adolescents. The major model and goal for this text is the hope that others may similarly be turned on to music and nurtured to a lifelong interest in it.

CONTENTS

Acknowledgments

The author wishes to acknowledge his gratitude to the members of the original Manhattanville Music Curriculum Project (MMCP) and the College Music Curriculum Project (CMCP, based upon the premises of the MMCP) with whom he was fortunate enough to work, who inspired many of the teaching suggestions contained here. Acknowledgment is also due to those undergraduate and graduate students and teachers who have encouraged and stimulated—with their perceptive challenges, questions, and suggestions—development of and research on the rationale presented here; and finally to those teachers whose ideas have been subsumed here as though they were new and original with this author. So often the collective efforts of many people, of many sources, fall to one mind to organize and present. It is hoped that justice has been done here to these diverse sources, but the final responsibility rests solely with the author.

Introduction

WHAT DOES THIS TEXT HAVE TO OFFER THE PRESERVICE AND INSERVICE TEACHER?

SCOPE

The early or preadolescent is a great mystery to just about everyone. This book is intended to remove much of the mystery of working with this kind of student in general music classes. *Early adolescence* involves young people ten to thirteen years old in grades six through eight. This level of schooling is described by a variety of names throughout this country. The terms middle school and junior high school, however, are used to describe the most characteristic institutional arrangement. *Middle school* often connotes the inclusion of sixth grade along with seventh and eighth, but sometimes the fifth grade is also included. *Junior high school* usually refers to a seventh and eighth grade arrangement, but in many locations it also involves ninth grade.

Middle School	Junior High School
5-6	7-8
6-7-8	6-7-8
5-8	7-9

Preadolescence involves those youngsters who have not yet succumbed to the physical growth spurt that marks the onset of puberty, yet who *do* exhibit many of the learning, growth typical, and behavioral traits of early adolescents. Because of these traits, this text is equally relevant for this age group, which may involve children as young as eight years, but certainly those nine and ten years old. Thus the scope of its relevance begins as early as the fourth grade, and for that reason it makes a definite and original contribution to general music instruction for what, in some localities, may be called the *intermediate grades* or *late elementary school*.

Primary Grades	Intermediate Grades
("Early Childhood")	("Tweenagers")
K-3	4-6

As long as the level of difficulty or sophistication is appropriate for the abilities and interests of these childdren, there is not one word, idea, method, approach, theoretical rationale, or research-documented conclusion in this text that is not readily workable with this group. They are sometimes called "tweeners" or "tweenagers" in referring to their often precarious position somewhere between childhood and the onset of adult development that is marked by the beginning of puberty, the point at which adolescent social role-playing becomes pronounced.

Such young people, then, still exhibit some of the endearing traits of children, but are already burdened with some of the problems and growth needs of early adolescents. The approaches recommended and explained in this text are very effective in dealing with this *transitional stage* marking the first clear departure from childhood. These approaches are easily combined or worked in with conventional methods—singing, playing classroom instruments, etc.—used traditionally with these ages.

The special character of the approaches and activities developed in this text are also especially useful in minimizing many of the special problems of motivation and intellectual challenge that often appear at the preadolescent stage—the point at which fundamental changes in brain organization, development and, capacity are taking place. Thus their use in combination with conventional methods can rescue instruction from the somewhat sagging enthusiasm for singing, etc., that this age sometimes can exhibit (especially if the methods of instruction used by the teacher are almost exactly the same kinds used in the primary grades).

Too many teachers of general music today are unaware of the special problems of this transitional stage and are unprepared or unwilling to adapt their instruction to the needs of the "tweenage" and early teenage groups. Many teachers attempt simply to continue almost exactly the methods used with children in the earlier grades. Others, vaguely recognizing some difference, try to make general music class into a "respectable academic subject" with "content units" and "unit quizzes and tests" on notes taken during lectures and lecture-demonstrations; with notebooks graded for neatness and completeness; and where a final grade is awarded as reward or penalty for acquiesing or not to the institutional expectations. The imposition of this format for *emphasizing verbal information* as the basis of general music education runs afoul, especially with adolescents. The resulting discipline problems can be overwhelming and the percentage of verbal information forgotten within minutes, days, and weeks is overwhelming too!

While misbehavior may not be as flagrant with most youngsters between the ages of nine and eleven, there often is, nonetheless, too much of it. And however much there is, it results in some interruption of the process of learning. A net result is typically a growing disenchantment among these youngsters with the concerns of general music classes. This by itself is often a large part of the problem of teaching in grades six through eight: teachers at these levels inherit the accumulated frustration, disenchantment, and negativism of young people who, beginning in fourth and fifth grades, become increasingly resistant to the use of teaching methods and materials better suited to the primary grades.

General music teachers and programs can no longer afford to ignore the important impact of this age group on the success of instruction in the secondary schools. We have the immediate need of regarding the period that begins in the late elementary years, preadolescence, as a time of special concern. It requires such special methods as those recommended in this text at least in combination with whatever approaches can be continued effectively from the early elementary years.

In the same manner, and for similar reasons, the ideas explored and exposed here are exceptionally suitable as the basis for a meaningful and very successful program of general music study in high school (usually grades 9-12 or 10-12). This instruction is easily worked into so-called music "appreciation" classes, specific high school level general music classes, as well as theory or musicianship classes of a general or college-preparatory nature. In fact, a coherent program based in the recommended methodology that runs from fourth or fifth grade through high school (see Appendix A) is guaranteed to be much more effective than a program where the basic instructional strategies are greatly disjunct between each of the three levels involved.

In place of a series of greatly dissimilar approaches to instruction and "content," this text outlines a general methodology and a psychological and philosophical framework of thinking that is to teaching what a theme and variations process is to extending, expanding, enriching, and enlarging upon musical ideas latent with great potential awaiting some medium for actualization over time. Thus *the basic methods recommended here are "themes"* that are to be used consistently with ever-varied, expanded, and refined musical content of the duration of a program's unfolding between preadolescence and the end of high school. In this text, then, the term "middle school" will be used to refer generally to the age-group that ranges from fourth through eighth grade, and "high school" will retain its usual meaning. With an appropriate adjustment of the challenge or difficulty of the learning and the learning experiences themselves, the methods, materials, and ideas suggested here are fully applicable across this entire expanded version of secondary school.

A fugue or song written in the fifth grade prepares the way for an even more advanced fugue or song written in the eighth grade. And for those choosing to continue into high school—as certainly more will do who are "turned on" by the enjoyment and challenge of manipulating musical materials meaningfully—songs and fugues written, arranged, and rearranged in general music type of classes will be correspondingly more advanced, more capable, and more satisfying. The process is not unlike the learning of basic mathematics. After basic arithmetic is learned in the primary grades, approaches to mathematics are established in the late elementary years that form the basis for continuing refinements, extensions and applications throughout the remaining school years, including the various forms of advanced mathematics taught in the last years of high school.

PRACTICALITY WITHOUT PRESCRIPTIVE RECIPES

In addition to the qualities already described, this text seeks to distinguish itself by steadfastly *avoiding the recipe or cookbook approach* that in so many other texts amounts to nothing more than a limited compendium of prepackaged lessons. *It does, to be sure, contain literally hundreds of practical teaching suggestions, ideas, and gimmicks.* But these are presented in a manner that avoids an invitation to imitation while *encouraging inexhaustible variation and adaptation.* A collection of recipes followed mindlessly presents problems to the teacher just as readily as to the homemaker or cook.

Certainly teaching, just as creative cooking, involves more than following the specific step-by-step directions of a recipe. Always involved in both is a knowledge of how to make adjustments, additions, deletions, adaptations, and variations necessary to specific needs. Even an isolated successful recipe does not insure a successful "complete meal," and certainly it does not insure a week or month-long "menu" that is balanced, sufficiently varied, and reasonably practical enough to achieve efficiency and consistent effectiveness. In teaching, as well, the ability to implement a prepackaged lesson is not the same as an ability to develop a fully successful curriculum or program that has sufficient balance, variety, and practical efficiency to merit praise as being successful music education.

None of the recipe books for music education contain, in any case, enough recipes to sustain teachers for very long. Ultimately they are left with only the model of the "canned" lessons, but with no real understanding of the factors involved in conceiving and planning original lessons. Creativity in teaching is just as rewarding as creativity in any undertaking. For that reason, this text also avoids a prescriptive approach to teaching where the reader is left without an understanding of the principles or rationale underlying the suggestions made.

In place of a "canned" approach, the text seeks to develop in the reader a comprehensive background in such factors as *why* we teach music, *what* we should teach out of all that is available to be taught, and how to recognize *whether or not* we have achieved our purposes. Also important in clarifying *how* best to teach will be the related question of which general view of education best suits the needs of music in general education, *where* or *when* in "real life" music learning can be relevant and useful, and *who* is responsible for each of the necessary phases of effective musical learning, the teacher or the student.

With this kind of background woven in and through all segments of the text, it is expected that the reader will be able, and in fact will most certainly want, to devise *endless variations of the basic activities and approaches* recommended and exemplified throughout. This will render the act of teaching general music itself a creative activity of great personal satisfaction, and should similarly contribute to the overall effectiveness of such instruction.

MINIMIZING DISCIPLINE PROBLEMS

Another distinguishing trait of this text is a central concern for the *discipline problems* that are all too often associated with teaching general music to pre-and early adolescents. While this is not regarded as an inevitability or an indictment, the author's considerable experience observing instruction in schools all over the country reveals a real concern among general music teachers (and their administrators) for the difficulties of dealing with this age group. General music in the middle or junior high school is often not an elective course, and many students are not entirely aware or certain of the reason why they are in these classes. It is in recognition of these and related problems that this text is oriented especially *to minimize discipline problems* by heading off their causes, causes *often stemming from the continued use of certain traditional approaches* (or approaches better suited to the early elementary years) after they have lost their relevance or effectiveness for the special needs and characteristics of this age group.

Psychologists of learning have discovered the early adolescent years to be a most pivotal stage for learning. Developmental psychologists have emphasized again and again the importance of certain developmental tasks that should be successfully fulfilled during these years. And social psychologists and sociologists are increasingly concerned with the special problems and plight of adolescents in our society. It is generally known that the onset of adolescence has gradually been occurring earlier than ever before. The preparatory period for adolescence, called pubescence, is likewise occurring earlier.

At the other end of the spectrum, educational formats in schools, especially high schools, are changing in the direction of flexibility and greater relevance to "real life." While recently this has resulted in some states in an emphasis on competency tests, generally less emphasis is being placed today on tests and grades as part of the regular program of instruction, while more is being placed instead on educating for adult life—what some have called "teaching for the real world."[1] Thus a major intent of this text is to assist the teacher in *understanding and dealing with the causes of student misbehavior, resistance to learning, and similar common problems* in dealing with adolescents.

"Real world" applications of music learning, whether during or after the school years, cannot be predicted if students and teachers alike come to predict a constant struggle, an incessant tug of war that uses the general music class as its arena. Simply put, the most enduring thing a student can learn in a music class that will incline him or her toward a richer life-long involvement with music is *a positive attitude* toward music.

The development of this positive attitude is a major *goal* of general music instruction. But it is often ignored that nurturing such an attitude is also a prime *means* by which a significant level of such a goal is reached. A student generally cannot be expected to have a positive attitude toward music if his or her attitude while studying it has been negative. Learning is not some neutral "medicine" shoved into unwilling students who then are enabled by it to achieve a new "healthy" state of mind.

One of the major problems leading to "unhealthy" states of mind among students in general music classes in the middle and secondary school years is the fact that public school education has largely been a matter of acquiring *verbal control* over one's interaction with the environment, including other people. Words, thus, have come to stand between person's perceptions and their actions. They have formed a kind of semantic web that filters raw or pure experience until, as one writer puts it, a "normal lunacy"[2] results around the time of adolescence. While this is one of the sources of everyone's concern with reading problems and verbal skills generally, it is of special importance to general music teaching because of the discipline problems often brought on by this process of acculturating children verbally.

As Piaget has taught, the stage of *operational thought* which occurs prior to adolescence allows the child increasingly to collect, combine, and transform data from reality "in his head." Schooling is intended to fully maximize this trait. It also does so, however, in the culturally accepted direction of converting "direct reality to semantic reality."[3] This tendency of increasingly representing direct or "pure experience" in semantic form is of special importance for music education.

While the general music teacher must *use* language, music itself *is* a different kind of language. It deals at its own level and in its own way with "pure experience." While it does not communicate as literally or functionally as actual language does, it is well suited to dealing with subjective qualities. Music of any kind is an interpretation or symbolic transformation of reality as experienced, captured, and projected in its "felt life" by composers and performers. Therefore music is a major vehicle the child and early teenager can use to deal with reality. It is especially central in its relevance to the volatile reality of feelings and anxieties that accompany adolescence.[4]

When the child's ability to think abstractly develops during the "tweenage" years, so the ability to deal effectively with the abstractions of music also grows. When with the full bloom of adolescence more complete powers of abstract thought become possible—Piaget's *stage of formal operations*—the youngster is now ideally ready for an adult-like relationship with music. This is a period at which a young person's fullest creative capacity can give up its latency[5] in favor of actualization.

Unfortunately, the demands of society, the creative needs of the individual, and the need for developing those skills required in actualizing creative potential are almost immediately in conflict. Society requires just the opposite of the "natural state" in which young people deal directly with reality without the intermediary of words. Society requires children and young people to be able tc "control" themselves, to outgrow the "natural" tendencies which society considers to be roughly equivalent to the behavior of animals.[6] Creativity without well-developed skills (training) is considered by society as expression without apt form, and therefore is discouraged. The skills, they hold, must come *before* rather than *through* creativity.[7]

Finally, in the face of all this, the adolescent grasps tenaciously to the very same "naturalness" that society wishes instead to limit and control. Adolescence—and a long period of time it can be, running on into the college years—becomes the "last gasp" effort of the individual to retain spontaneity, a natural and direct responsiveness unmediated by intellectual or social "filters." Thus some rebellion or resistance during these years is natural and predictable. As the later years of high school approach, however, more and more youngsters become increasingly influenced by the restraints on their responsiveness and by the responsibility (or response-ability) society considers to be acceptable. Thus the youngster is unlikely to seriously attempt anything outside the parameters of culturally defined consensus realities.[8]

As a result, of course, young people who have not yet had the opportunity to apply their nearly adult minds to significant musical pursuits are often lost for good to the subtle yet no less valuable benefits of music. Their creativity and natural responsiveness to the arts are cumulatively diminished by the demands of a society which has created no secure niche for the arts, save for an elite few professionals; a society that is still so enmeshed in sex-stereotyping that men and women alike in the arts suffer cruel barbs and taunts for daring to be creatively different. While the process of socializing children is, in fact, necessary to some degree in order that we have a smoothly functioning society, it is too often done at the expense of the individual—particularly creative individuals. Thus it is the direction and degree of such socialization that is the problem, and nowhere is this truer than in schooling.

It is inevitable that a tension comes to exist between the demands of society and the culture it supports, and the demands of the individual who to one degree or another attempts to retain the spontaneity, the freedom, the joyfulness of childhood. This tension too often results in a struggle between the individual student and society's representatives and functionaries in the schools—the teachers and other authority figures. So from age six, when school begins, some inevitable conflict arises for most children. The kindergarten child begins school freely open to most of the possibilities of life: anything is equally possible and equally valid. But within months, school teaches an awareness of some of society's prescriptions for valuing some things more than others:

> Kindergarten children interviewed in September, and again in October, used the categories of work and play to create and describe their social reality. Their responses indicate that the first few weeks of school are an important time for learning about the nature of work in the classroom. In September no child said "work" when asked what children do in kindergarten. In October half of those interviewed responded with the word "work." All of the children talked more about working and less about playing in October than they had in September. The teacher was pleased with the progress of the class during the first weeks of school and repeatedly referred to the children as "my good workers."[9]

For such children, now all things are *not* equally possible or valid! And it must be remembered that the word "play" is the operative concept in the activity of "playing" music. No one has ever called it "working" music! So with this initiation into the social dimension of schooling, the child learns not so much the "manifest" or publically explicit curricular goals. It is the "latent" or "hidden" curriculum that is impressed on the consciousness of youngsters without their awareness:

> The content of specific lessons is relatively less important than the experience of being a worker. Personal attributes of obedience, enthusiasm, adaptability, and perseverance are more highly valued than academic competence. Unquestioning acceptance of authority and the vicissitudes of life in institutional settings are among a kindergartener's first lessons.[10]

Some things such as work, then, come to be seen by school children as more valid or valuable, while others such as play are seen as less important, less culturally sanctioned. And while this may seem relatively harmless at this early age, it is precisely the youth, and thus the vulnerability of such children that establishes life-long attitudes and values. It will not be for another four or five years that they begin to be conscious of the imperviousness of social forces and prescriptions. In fact,

> somewhere in the general vicinity of puberty . . . comes a moment in the subjective life of the individual which I speak of as the "Existential Moment." It is the moment when the individual first discovers himself as existing. It is the abrupt onset, the charged beginning, of awareness of the phenomenon of one's own presence in the world as a person. Prior to this point there is no such awareness. Children do not know what they are; they do not even know *that* they are . . . the transition [from "pre-Existential" to "Existential"] is perhaps more profoundly turbulent than the well-advertised string of adjustments we attach to adolescence and teen-agery."[11]

Thus at this age, just prior to adolescence, resistance to acculturation—to the "semantic network" of schools and their organization—may begin in earnest.

Since "the preadolescent begins to function according to cultural logic (or begins really to respond as a 'reality-adjusted' person) somewhere around nine or ten years of age"[12]—roughly fifth grade—teachers can expect a burgeoning of resistance around this time. In fact, if there is no evidence of the onset of the "existential moment," if the child shows no sign of independence and subjective affirmation against external pressures, this is a more abnormal state than the more typical "storm and stress" state, and such children may be on their way to a variety of maladjustments that can cause real problems later in life.

Piaget, among others, considers preadolescence to be the beginning of true maturity, as society understands that term. Children from this time on are generally expected to be more responsible, more responsive to societal demands and norms. Before this time, "children cannot be 'held responsible' for what they do because they are not yet 'existential,' that is, self-aware subjectivities capable of *feeling* a sense of responsibility. The Existential Moment is the beginning of the sense of being responsible." From the Existential Moment forward, the child is expected to be responsible for everything that happens, yet "the world that opens out . . . after this remarkable event, is baffling and difficult . . . an 'encounter with meaninglessness'".[13]

Unfortunately this increasing sense of being held responsible, of being self-aware, and of meaninglessness or unreasonableness often results in increased resistance to the *readymade meanings* society is inculcating through the schools and other social agencies of education (e.g., church, courts, etc.). Children are expected to accept these meanings without understanding the reasons for them, yet often they perceive more clearly than many adults do the inconsistencies, inanities, and ineffectiveness of many ready-made social meanings and prescriptions. The increasing incidence of autistic children in

Europe and America is often attributed to the refusal or inability of some exceptionally perceptive children to make this adjustment in an increasingly demanding and complex society.

The resulting incidence of discipline problems, misbehavior of all kinds, crime in the schools, and the "testing" of themselves and their capacities, as well as the "probing" of social strictures for weaknesses, these all testify to the fact that young people of this age are being pushed to new extremes of resistance in order to adapt somehow to the ever-more contradictory times in which they live. Teachers, parents, and law enforcement officials are the representatives society has chosen to represent them in the front-line trenches, so to speak. Without doubt, any typical teacher can testify to the resulting dilemma: the more our society tries to dictate or control *arbitrarily* the reality by which young people will live, the more complex are their techniques of response. And so, they raise the ante. Teachers (and parents) need to learn how to break this escalating problem rather than further contributing to it.

In school *an emphasis on direct experience* that bypasses the culturally sanctioned semantic grid or the semantic filter that society uses as a weapon of control stands a good chance of breaking this vicious circle. It is not that the semantic function is denied altogether; but it should be placed *after the experience,* not before it. And it should progress in the *student's own terms,* wherever possible. Without the semantic function, neither culture nor the individuals constituting it could survive. But when the semantic grid is placed *between* the child and the reality—especially when the reality is music—all kinds of problems arise. By placing it afterwards and, furthermore, by allowing it to be formulated more in the student's own terms, society's needs are served generally and the conflicts are reduced to more manageable limits.

Language is not needed before learning, before the intellect can be developed. Research with children deaf since birth (who thus have no access to language) shows that "conceptual thinking develops through living contact with the environment regardless of the presence or absence of a ready-made linguistic system."[14] But to the degree that social maturity is considered the ability to function according to the verbal consensus of society, young people will experience some significant conflict between their "nature" and verbal presentations of society's norms and demands.

> The intellect develops by activity. And a system designed for interaction with a real world of living process finds interaction with abstractions [*viz.,* language; semantic abstractions of reality] more difficult and less attractive. . . . The child adopts consensus thinking largely through fear—but he must be *motivated,* which means literally *driven,* to adopt the abstractions of our current literate and abstract orientation.[15]

In place of such "driven" forms of external motivation and control, general music teachers must promote ways of using the real, direct experience teenagers crave because it is in tune with their true "nature." This text is oriented to assisting the teacher in just this quest. Students taught according to the recommendations given here are not *trained* to know *about* music (i.e., learning about someone else's concept in *their verbal terms*), they are *led* to *know music* directly (i.e., the concept *is* the experience), and to act on or with it. With this approach there is no serious need for external motivation to drive students against their will. Music becomes increasingly its own reward. It is self-validating, just as it is for virtually all people in natural life settings.

ACTION LEARNING

This brings us to the central distinguishing feature of this text, the unifying and motivating theme of the variations which constitute the actual recommended methods and approaches. Without a proper perspective and understanding of this aspect of the text, the reader is in danger of perpetuating the very problems the "activities approach" suffered at the hand of vast numbers of teachers. These problems resulted from placing an emphasis on the activity *for its own sake* rather than emphasizing the *goals* or *ends* of instruction (the purpose of the lesson; what is to be learned and why; what a student is better able to do or know; and what difference such knowing or doing will make in his or her life) which activities serve as the *means* of attaining.

The *activities approach* is by now jargon used to refer to learning by doing, learning through active involvement rather than passively taking in information dispensed by the teacher. It implies a type of class where the students are at least mentally active, if not also physically active in their involvements with music. This type of approach sought to distinguish itself from the teacher-directed approach where the teacher "tells" or demonstrates the learnings to a passive class which, it was imagined, "soaks" up the learning and reproduces it on periodic examinations. The activities approach was especially central in moving the music education field toward a stance of *teaching concepts* rather than teaching separate bits and pieces of facts or skills. Rather, active involvement with music was to result inductively in broad concepts of rhythm, pitch, form, and so on, which would form the basis of later refinements and skills.

All of this was healthy for the field of general music teaching. However, texts dealing with the activities approach rarely made mention of exactly how this process was to be conducted. This is a problem, for in an activities approach, individual learners must somehow personally sort out the individual experiences that are the result of each activity, and then relate those that are similar through some process of insight. And by a similarly unexplained process, such texts imply that these concepts cumulatively and developmentally expand and embrace subsequent similar experiences. The resulting ability to generalize from all related experience with, say, rhythm amounts to "the" concept of rhythm. Because these texts fail to detail in psychological terms how this complex process is supposed to be facilitated by teachers, cohesive and enduring results of any tangible kind were infrequently observed, even though children might seem to be enjoying individual activities immensely.

The activities approach did lend itself to a situation where individual activities might seem to be brilliantly taught by teachers and gratefully appreciated by students, but where any two or more activities did not seem to fit together in any cohesive plan or curriculum: they did not seem to lead anywhere! Often, at best, children came out of such instruction with good feelings about music *class*; often that was all they had gained!

Music teachers at subsequent levels, or in the instrumental programs at the same level, often complained—with justification it would seem—that nothing tangible or concrete was the result of such classes. Parents and administrators have made similar observations, and this alone accounts for some of the threats of cutbacks that face such music programs throughout the country.

Again, it is necessary to point out that this situation is not so much the result of the use of activities for instruction, but rather that two conditions too easily cropped up as the result of teachers lacking detailed knowledge of how concepts are learned:

1. Too often teachers fall into the bad habit of *teaching an activity for its own sake* instead of using it as the *means* for reaching *predefined curricular goals or ends*. Thus a teacher might "teach" a sound composition as the sole purpose of a lesson, instead of "using" a sound composition activity to teach a clearly defined and clearly recognizable goal or end result.

2. Authors of most commonly used texts embracing the activities approach have very little to say about how activities taught for their own sake are to achieve any unified, collective impact. Thus teachers are largely uninformed about how they should proceed in organizing any sequence or succession of activities that could predictably result in tangible evidence of conceptual learning.

Individual activities are not necessarily at fault, nor is the idea of active involvement. What promotes the difficulty is the inability of teachers (and textbook writers, workshop clinicians, and the like) to control the process by which individual experiences lead to collective results (concepts). In fact, there is often a kind of quiet despair that just *assumes* that a certain number of similar experiences will automatically or necessarily lead to a concept.

Furthermore, even if conceptual learning seems to be successful, there does not seem to be any clear idea or directive to teachers of how, when, where, or under what circumstances such concepts might be useful to a person "in life." Again it is *assumed* that concepts will automatically transfer to real life listening, performing, or composing situations. The operative word among such teachers in informal discussions is "hopefully": "Hopefully the student will be able to perceive music more accurately," or "hopefully the student will appreciate music more."

Most seriously, textbook writers are guilty of inferring or directly asserting that a concept is single, invariable, and absolute. Thus they often refer to student learning *the* concept of rhythm, or whatever, as though somehow a single preordained concept pre-existed each student. Further, it is often implied that concepts are *verbal* statements or generalizations, and thus that students should be led *to experience concepts* in order to arrive at the same verbal formulation which provided the teacher's beginning point for the activity. One source, for example, states concerning concepts that the child "should be able to verbalize about them in terms meaningful to him." The same source illustrates this with the following types of verbalizations that children are presumably to be able to provide:

"Melodies move up, down, or straight ahead."

"The rhythm of music is organized in patterns of long and short sounds and silences."

"Chords differ in sound and feeling."

Certainly there has got to be more to music than "discovering" such "concepts" via an activities approach! Besides, "the" concepts learned can only be "the" teacher's concepts, and these may themselves be confusing or unproductive.[16] It is difficult to imagine how statements such as these can lead to an understanding of music, let alone to a greater feeling responsiveness or an appreciation of it. Those statements are clearly verbalizations empty of any practical or significant meaning.

The perceptual and psychological fact is, of course, that concepts vary somewhat from person to person, if only because people have had different experiences, and have experienced these through sensory organs that vary perceptual content from person to person, even if only slightly. Concepts, thus, do not arise from language but, rather, are primarily *non-verbal*. Direct experience—in our case directly with music, musical problems, musical thinking—*precedes* any verbal formulation of what initially are non-verbal concepts. A "concept can't be experienced, it *is* the experience."[17] *Concepts are experience!* They are not verbal rules, statements or definitions that are exemplified, illustrated or taught *by means of* experience. They *are* the experience itself; the tendencies, values, choices and attitudes by which we interact with, actively organize, and act upon reality.

Thus *concepts are not taught* directly: they do not precede learning or the learner. But *they are learned*, and are the unique formulations of each learner *based upon direct action with or on musical materials*. To openly admit this fact throws an entirely different light on the use or mis-use of the activities approach. It is seen that there is great confusion afield concerning virtually *every* stage of the approach. So very often, then, teachers can be observed "teaching *the* concept of rhythm" as defined in some text, song series or scope

13

and sequence chart, "by teaching a rhythmic activity" that is somehow, mysteriously, supposed to lead to the child's eventual ability to verbalize or at least realize the original definition/verbalization. And whatever or whenever results were forthcoming, teachers of this kind can seldom specify in terms that can be behaviorally observed or evaluated whether learning has indeed occurred. Thus they cannot count on such learning—supposedly the focus for a given activity—as the basis for subsequent learning.

Yet for all of this, the activities approach "loosened up" general music instruction and made possible the kinds of advance represented by the Manhattanville approach to developing concepts and creativity. But the logical extension and improvement over the activities approach represented by MMCP requires a knowledge of psychological learning processes, and of music, that often seems to exceed the abilities, interest, or energies of many music teachers. Then too, vagueness of results, even in the presence of vital and enjoyable involvement on the part of students, is too often a liability. But mainly, MMCP represents an attitude toward instruction rather than a systematic approach.

This text stakes out a somewhat different territory, one that in effect includes some of the basic conceptions of the activities approach with some of the basic spirit and creative thinking or inventiveness of the Manhattanville movement. It regards both of these as effective *means* of carrying out or orienting instruction, but it seeks to go further. It seeks to specify in some useful detail a psychological approach to understanding more effectively how concepts are developed, and to what significant ends they may be put. It emphasizes a variety of *means* by which learning occurs (learning *activities*) *and* it proposes certain specific *ends* (curricular goals and realistic uses) to which these newly applied or updated means can be put.

The conception serving as the underlying premise of this text has something of a long and distinguished history in education, philosophy, and scientific research. It has been called *Action Learning*,[1] and has some well-developed traits that characterize it. First and foremost, however, it is not to be confused as being synonymous with the activities approach, even though it includes many general means of learning that are on the surface similar to the activities approach.

To begin with, the *theory of action* in which Action Learning originates (along with action research in science) is rooted in the distinction between *what passively happens to a person,* against or without his or her volitional input, and *what an individual actively does* or causes to happen *for* some sought *goal.* Beyond this, Action Learning is rooted in the attempt by philosophers and scientists earlier in this century to formulate a science of the practical. It is especially this sense of concern with the *practical* that most characterizes action concepts. Even in common parlance, when someone is regarded as a "person of action" the strong implication is of a person who does things, who gets things done, who acts definitively rather than tentatively.

Philosophers have consistently echoed this common sense understanding by emphasizing the central conception of action in human existence. For example, contemporary existential philosophy, the inspiration for much of what is in the United States called humanistic psychology, is predicated on this concept of action. Jean Paul Sartre, perhaps the best known European existentialist, wrote, "the real world is revealed only by action . . . one can feel himself in it only by going beyond it in order to change it."[18] Additionally, "human reality is action and that action upon the universe is identical with the understanding of that universe as it is, or, in other words, that action is the unmasking of reality, and, *at the same time*, a modification of that reality."[19]

Even the more gentle oriental philosophies center on the relevance of action. A contemporary western interpreter has written: "All action is concerned with linking a present situation with a past situation, giving some continuity to that past." He adds, "To live is to act."[20] And a modern philosopher of science writes, "I regard knowing as an active comprehension of the things known, an action that requires skill."[21]

Modern brain scientists have also echoed this refrain just as strongly from their perspective. Leading contemporary researcher Karl Pribram writes:

> Symbols are representations that refer to the world within the organism. The symbols are produced, just as are signs, through action, but it is the remembrance of the effect of the action that produces the symbol. Symbols are thus context-sensitive constructions that take meaning from the history of their *use* and the current state of the organism using them.[22]

The brain systems involved in producing the signs and symbols so central to human functioning—among which are language and music, just to mention a few—Pribram calls "the action systems."[23] In a related point very relevant to music education, Pribram states:

> When the variety of perceptions exceeds . . . the repertory of action available to the organism, he feels "interested" and is motivated to . . . extend this repertory. . . . Emotion is likely to occur when the probability of reinforcement from action is deemed low.[24]

A researcher specializing in work with deaf and dumb children describes in the clearest possible terms the relevance of action concepts to the concerns of general music instruction and thus of this text: "thinking [is] an activity, an internal action which corresponds to the sensory-motor schema of the previous period [of a child's development] and is habitually associated with or accompanied by observable organismic events."[25] He adds further, "action is the source and medium of intelligence and the reality of concepts must be sought in the actions of thinking which can become embedded in a symbolic medium."[26]

Finally, perhaps the most noted child psychologist of them all, Jean Piaget, in his germinal book *Science of Education and the Psychology of the Child,* sums up a central tenet taken throughout this text:

> Knowledge is derived from action, not in the sense of simple associative responses, but in the much deeper sense of the assimilation of reality into the necessary and general coordination of action. *To know an object is to act upon it and to transform it,* in order to grasp the mechanisms of that transformation as they function in connection with the transformative actions themselves. To know is therefore to assimilate reality into structures that intelligence constructs as a direct extension of our actions."[27]

What is more, Piaget affirms that "intelligence derives from action," and "consists in executing and coordinating actions, though in an interiorized and reflexive form." And even though the actions have been interiorized—have in other words become purely mental rather than external—they "are still actions nevertheless" and constitute the very essence of human intelligence.[28]

Several related themes run through these and similar expressions about action-related human functions:

1. that one acts *on* the world, as opposed to *it* acting on a passive recipient;
2. that acting on the world in someway modifies, transforms and personalizes what is acted upon;
3. that such action links past and present through the continuous creation of the mind in comprehending;
4. that our symbolic behavior (music) arises through action, and is meaningful to the degree that the symbols are used in further actions;
5. that human motivation is a matter of the potential of situations and stimuli for meaningful action;
6. that thinking and knowing are internalized actions which nonetheless transform or actively manipulate what is thought about or known.

In sum, then, one sense of Action Learning used as a central guiding principle of this text is that *knowing and learning are actions* whereby *the mind reaches out and acts on the music in coming to know it.* In such actions, *the mind personalizes what is known.* This *personalization provides a motivation toward subsequent action with or on what has come to be known.* Future behavior with regard to this learning, thus, is not a matter of passively being acted upon by, in our case, music. Instead it is a matter of *actively seeking future practical (actual) uses of such learning* and of actually *creating ones own responses to and uses of music.*

A person then does not relate to music passively, as in the case of Muzak, where music is encountered casually and unintentionally. Rather, the person's intentionality comes into play and actively seeks musical contacts which are then participated in actively, even in the capacity of a listener. Action Learning in general music, then,

1. *seeks to inspire an actively positive attitude* toward the benefits of musical involvement during and after the school years;
2. *provides the learning and skills* needed to most productively benefit from such present and future involvements with music; and
3. uses the kind of teaching/learning activities that are *closely modeled on the musical realities life has to offer the ordinary citizen* who is not considered to be a "trained" musician, but who is nonetheless gratified by musical experiences.

It is in these ways that the goals and processes of action learning for general music education are *practical* and realistically down to earth.

In educational labeling, Action Learning has been the term used to describe the kind of *educational experience that closely duplicates real life experiences.* According to one writer, Action Learning involves programs of instruction that enable young people "to participate in productive adult activities and to assume real responsibility for what they do; the kind of curriculum that vitalizes and strengthens the educational experiences developed outside [school] walls."[29]

In some forms it has involved on-the-job training. In other versions it involves actual apprenticeships. Still in other programs it involves in-school simulation of out-of-school roles, or "games" designed to provide students with the opportunity to become actually involved in the *thought processes of adults* in a variety of occupations and professions.[30] In one school, for instance, a high school psychology/social studies teacher has students "live" a simulated marriage. They actually go through a mock marriage ceremony, then encounter and practice handling typical problems and dilemmas faced by newlyweds in the community at large. Plenty of community resources are called upon to add to the realism and pertinence. In another school, computer and other forms of "games" enable students to interact with one another in solving the very same problems encountered, say, by international financiers and business persons. They do not study *about* economics; they *live* and *experience* it as closely as can be approximated in a school setting.

It is in the spirit of such applications as these that the basic premise of Action Learning stated above can be applied to the needs and concerns of general music education in the middle and secondary schools: "Initial objectives should be those that students at the time see are interesting and/or meaningful for them to learn. . . . As they gain greater understanding of the relevance of what they are learning, they will see the meaning of and develop interest in objectives that stimulate them to further study."[31]

Such a sense of meaning or relevance with adolescents is inevitably tied to their ability to prevision some present or potential *use* for the learning that they regard as somehow contributing positively to their lives. *Any potential use is assured when the kind of real life use to which a learning or skill is functionally related is also the major means by which it is acquired in the first place,* or at least closely approximating it:

> This means that learners must see the way in which the things they learn can be used, and they must have the opportunity to employ the learned behavior in the various situations they encounter.[32]

> The failure to transfer what is learned in school to situations outside of school is a problem that has long been central to educational psychologists. Schools are established to help students acquire behavior that is important for constructive out-of-school activities. If something is learned in school that is not used by the student in relevant situations outside of school, most of the value of learning has been lost.[33]

To summarize this facet, *Action Learning seeks the closest possible connection or relevance to a student's life.* Learning *activities* in which early adolescents take part *should as closely as possible resemble the potential they have for being musically active* outside of school and later as adults. It is concerned with learning from within *reasonably realistic real life musical experiences,* and with *realistic application of learning to approximations of real life settings:* "Learning experiences can be designed that involve many situations like those outside of school and students can be encouraged and asked to use what they are learning *in* school to relevant situations *outside* of school."[34]

There is, however, one more sense in which Action Learning for general music is derived from philosophical, psychological, and educational precedents. It is based in a *problem-solving mentality* where music study and learning are applied to practical musical "problems" or potential uses. It is not the purpose of Action Learning to develop a *theoretical understanding* of music *in general.* Rather it is a personal, individual, and specific impact on each student that is sought. Solutions to the musical "problems" posed actually involve *doing something;* actively manipulating or transforming something musical, if only mentally, rather than learning *about* music in some passive, impersonal sense. In essence each student develops his or her *own* "theory" of music and a "theory" of its importance or relevance to life generally, and his or her life in particular.

In this sense, then, with Action Learning students come to appreciate the immediate application or relevance of skills and learnings for they are able to see the results of their class efforts *now;* they do not need to be motivated to look forward to some indefinite time in the future. They need not be told, "You'll be glad someday you learned this information!" Instead, the musical actions that constitute learning are done *by* the learners, the doers, and are *not* done *to* or *for* them. Thus, Action Learning so conceived is clearly *student-centered*.

Rather than a *teacher-directed* style of teaching, as in lectures or lecture-demonstrations, or even in the kind of activity approach where the student only follows directions of the teacher and never has the opportunity to choose freely the use made of musical materials, Action Learning stresses *the responsibility of each learner for the specific nature of his or her own learning*. It is not predicated on, but does help to foster intelligent self-direction and self-discipline—to the degree, at least, that *students come to discover that learning itself is a creative act or process,* that listening to music and performing it are just as creative as composing it, and that composing music (manipulating musical materials) is a constructive process that leads to the kinds of learning that are self-validating. Such learning, thus, is its own reward because it is seen as leading to greater pleasure in continued efforts of a similar nature.

Action Learning, then, is a key conception of this text. It is not some new-fangled or revolutionary idea, but rather one that has had currency in social science and education since the 1930's. It is not some idealistic, theoretical, or technical buzzword, but rather it amounts to a businesslike attitude of *systematically pursuing a practical course of action*, both in the sense of the *efficiency* and *effectiveness* of individual lessons and in the sense of *personal relevance* and *potential use* that is afforded the student by such an approach.

Whenever mention of Action Learning is made throughout these pages, you should remind yourselves of these key ideas. It may even be helpful to copy them on a separate piece of paper for reference as you read because they will be assumed and not re-explained.

Action Learning involves:

1. acting on and with musical materials;
2. personalizing or individualizing what is learned;
3. increased inclination or motivation toward continued action with music in some form;
4. learning activities that are closely modeled on real life musical experiences;
5. the student's own sense of relevance in the relation of musical learning to his or her own life, now and in the future;
6. relating activities to present life circumstances and to reasonably predictable adult experiences shared by ordinary people;
7. acting from within a problem-solving mentality that poses musical (but realistic) problems for students to solve actively;
8. an orientation toward immediate and tangible results as the major vehicle for maximizing long term, future results;

9. a concern with what the student does or is able to do, more than what the teacher does or has to do in order to nurture student progress—it is student rather than teacher-centered;

10. encouraging ever-greater self-responsibility and self-discipline as the practical personal rewards are appreciated by the learner.

Also remember that Action Learning should clearly be separated from much of the current practice stemming from the activities approach where activities are taught as self-sufficient ends, with little regard for where a succession of such lessons is leading in the way of goals. It is especially important that the reader remember these facts at every point in this text:

1. One does not *teach* a sound composition, or a listening lesson, or some other activity. One *uses* such activities in reaching certain prespecified goals.

2. In Action Learning, all such *goals are determined and defined by the key ideas listed above*, 1-10.

3. These are the basic guides for choosing both goals and the activities used to reach these goals, and a teacher is, thereby, well enabled to promote positive and significant learning in most students, in most school situations.

4. One's program is *automatically unifed* through the impact of *personal and practical relevance and application* that Action Learning facilitates.

5. Such a program effectively and consistently pursued, naturally generates *tangible and concrete results* which are noticed by students (who are thus increased in their motivation), by other music teachers, administrators, and parents.

Learning activities such as those advocated in the activities approach should be regarded as *specific strategies*, the use of which are governed by the general learning principles and goals of Action Learning outlined here and throughout the text at various points.

Action Learning is a step beyond the activities approach and capitalizes on or encorporates the advantages of activities while minimizing or eliminating most of the disadvantages and liabilities that frequently characterize such programs. In another way of thinking, however, one could say that currently successful programs governed by an activities approach are, in effect, Action Learning programs *if* they promote a sense of relevance among students, and result in *tangible* progress that has clear practical application "in life."

So not very much new is proposed in organizing a course of studies around an ideal of Action Learning; rather, it is the difference in the way activities are used and the goals toward which they are employed that determines whether or not Action Learning becomes a reality. Action Learning does not exist if there can be no observed pragmatic effect in the desired direction!

EVIDENCE AND RATIONALE FOR RECOMMENDATIONS

One final distinguishing feature of this text should be mentioned if the reader is to derive full value from it. Most of the activities, materials, and rationale recommended are based upon *contemporary empirical research* from various social and behavioral sciences, as well as being drawn from certain *central philosophical premises and tenets.* Even though these ideas have been derived from the practices of successful teachers, they are substantiated and supported by reasonably objective evidence as well. Other textbook publishers have been content to ignore this vital margin of confidence, as the following statement from a noted publisher of music education materials points out. The editor wrote in a letter:

> The material needs points made with little or no elaboration or justification. This kind of student will accept statements as being authoratative [sic].

This view is an insult and an affront to serious musicians in education who respect the musical art and the problems of teaching young people too much to believe seriously that authoritative pronouncements can or should be accepted blindly or mindlessly.

Instead, this text is written in the expectation that experienced college and public school teachers, preservice and student teachers will appreciate, need, and profit from a thoughtful, reasoned, explanatory approach to teaching. Therefore, throughout the text, as you have already seen so far, the recommendations made will be *supported by reference to research* and *to acknowledged practice* where that is possible or, where agreement is not uniform or where no unequivocal research data exist *a full explanation of the rationale will be provided for the reader's own judgment.*

Thus the text presents not only a wealth of practical suggestions for actual teaching methods. It also deals with the many and varied factors that such methods bring to bear on instructional problems. *This supporting evidence and rationale has a direct bearing on the success or failure of the suggestions made.* It is wise to remember that *methods do not work* automatically and inevitably: *teachers must make them work!* These variables are relevant:

1. The teacher's own musical, pedagogical and personal predilections, strengths and weaknesses.
2. The specific nature of the local teaching situation.
   a. physical environment
   b. instructional resources
   c. characteristics of students and community
   d. educational philosophy of the school and community

Therefore, it is *always necessary* for a teacher to:

ADAPT . . . all teaching methods, ideas, or gimmicks to the conditions prevailing in the local situation.

PERSONALIZE . . . the methods, ideas or gimmicks by developing a personal understanding, insight or "feel" for the methods that is rooted in the teacher's individual traits.

ADJUST . . . all of the above applications based on the feedback provided by continuous evaluation.

All of this amounts to, in effect, a remaking of methods and ideas in terms of the teacher's own thinking. In effect, the approaches become the teacher's own creation. The teacher is not mindlessly implementing someone else's ideas, but rather is creatively actualizing the potential inherent in those ideas by bringing them to reality in a given context. This process could be called "action teaching."

The practical recommendations and the supporting evidence and rationale are both necessary to this process. In part, the absence of such information has been a major reason for the problems encountered with the activities approach: too often only the activities were described, and the teacher was left uninformed as to the underlying rationale or evidence (if there was any) that would be necessary or useful for the implementation and integration of the activities. For example, a leading educator has lamented *The absence of a clearly established valid knowledge base* for professional practice"[35] in education. Another writer adds: "It is probably no exaggeration to say that the average teacher makes little or no use of learning theory in his day-to-day classroom activities."[36]

This text seeks to remedy this condition by presenting both practical "how to" ideas along with the theoretical underpinnings necessary to implementing teaching ideas effectively. For the reader's convenience, both are easily identified visually by being presented in contrasting print. The reader, thus, should first read and study *the entire text* with special attention to understanding the rationale, theory, and evidence. Then, once the reader has achieved his or her own general "theory" or understanding, it is a simple matter to pick out visually the abundant practical teaching suggestions by referring back through the text when searching for specific teaching ideas to use on a daily basis. Approached in this manner, it is intended that this text can continually be used by inservice teachers to provide daily inspiration for teaching ideas, and as a reminder, wherever needed, of the supporting concepts or evidence. This latter is especially useful when, for reasons not immediately apparent to the teacher, the "methods" do not seem to be succeeding (which usually means the teacher is not properly taking some relevant variable into consideration). On such occasions the teacher will find it useful to restudy the supporting concepts before once again attempting the methods in question. Use the *checklist guide* at the beginning of each chapter to quickly locate the practical or theoretical ideas you need at a given moment.

The college methods teacher will doubtlessly wish to augment the activities and approaches recommended here with additional favored ideas and practices, especially those idiosyncratic for that teacher or region. In addition, it is useful to assign projects and activities from the text for application in the methods class. The author has discovered through preliminary use of this text, however, that *it is imperative to probe students constantly and energetically as to the specific musical GOALS of an Action Learning nature that are supposed to be at stake.* It is vital that preservice teachers can articulate the Action Learning goals they seek! The methods class teacher *cannot be forceful enough* in this, both in the methods class and in student teaching. This practice will assist immeasurably in preventing another generation of teachers from singlemindedly "teaching activities" instead of teaching music *through* activities.

Teachers who are informed as to the human nature and needs of early and young adolescents will teach lessons that are more sensitive to the realities of working with this age. Teachers who are attuned to the feedback provided by these young people will be able to adapt, personalize, and adjust instruction as the situation requires. But teachers who expect only to follow ready-made recipes or plans are doomed to encounter all kinds of difficulties, not the least of which are discipline problems of varying degree of severity.

An expenditure of interest in the human dimensions of teaching and a creative imagination with regard both to music and teaching will serve well to inspire similar interest and creativity on the part of students. The alternative is, at best, student apathy and, at worst, student misbehavior. So we can now begin with a setting of the scene in terms of the basic growth-typical characteristics that provide the basis of any successful program of instruction for pre- and early adolescents.

NOTES: INTRODUCTION

1. Asa G. Hilliard III, "Near Future Imperatives and Educational Leadership," *Educational Leadership*, vol. 35, no. 3 (December 1977), 164.
2. Joseph Chilton Pearce, *Exploring the Crack in the Cosmic Egg* (New York: Pocket Books, 1975), p. 46.
3. Ibid., 49; see also William James, *Essays in Radical Empiricism and a Pluralistic Universe*, Dutton paperback (New York: Dutton, 1971), pp. 15, 224-26.

4. See, Thomas A. Regelski, "Aim for the Inner Life: Teaching Early Teens," *Music Educators Journal*, vol. 65, no. 9 (May 1979), 24.

5. See, Howard Gardner, *The Arts and Human Development* (New York: Wiley, 1973).

6. For example, "That sixth grade behaved just like animals today." "You have to whip these kids into shape or else they'll eat you alive." This point of view was dramatically epitomized in William Golding's novel—and the movie based on it—*Lord of the Flies*.

7. See Michael W. Apple and Nancy R. King, "What Do Schools Teach?" in *Curriculum Theory*, ed. by A. Molnar and J. A. Zahorik (Washington, D.C.: Association for Supervision and Curriculum Development, 1977), pp. 108-26, especially pp. 121-23.

8. Pearce, *Exploring the Crack in the Cosmic Egg*, p. 49. Counsellors, clinical psychologists, and psychiatrists will advise adults to be more spontaneous, more child*like* (not childish), and more "in touch" with their natural inclinations and needs. What acculturation and socialization have put asunder (in an attempt to make "normal" people) must be retrieved by mental health functionaries whose "norms" often describe an entirely different picture than common sense does.

9. Apple and King, "What Do Schools Teach?", p. 122.

10. Ibid., p. 123. In the noted book *Schooling in Capitalist America* (Basic Books, 1976) the authors, economists Samuel Bowles and Herbert Gintis, argue persuasively that schools teach the inequalities of the capitalist economic system. What is learned, they point out, is how to know and acquiesce to authority and the roles appointed for people by others. Schooling is prime in teaching people to "work" upon demand for extrinsic rewards (grades) rather than pride or self-satisfaction, and for teaching people how they compare with others in the competition for rising up the academic and economic ladders of success.

11. Van Cleve Morris, *Existentialism in Education* (New York: Harper and Row, 1966), pp. 112, 113.

12. Pearce, *Exploring the Crack in the Cosmic Egg*, p. 51.

13. Morris, *Existentialism in Education*, pp. 113, 115.

14. Pearce, *Exploring the Crack in the Cosmic Egg*, p. 201; see also, Hans Furth, *Thinking Without Language* (New York: Free Press, 1966), which explores concept-formation among deaf youngsters and cites conclusive findings that language is *not* a precondition for concept-formation.

15. Pearce, *Exploring the Crack in the Cosmic Egg*, pp. 52-53.

16. For example, from the same source cited in the text, the statement is made that "rhythm may move fast or slowly." This is clearly confused, or even wrong. Tempo (the speed of the "tactus" or "main beats") has qualities of fast or slow; meter might be thought of as contributing to impressions of speed; but rhythm, considered by the same authors as "patterns of long and short sounds and silences" is difficult to measure in terms of speed. It is measured in terms of long and short, but not fast or slow. Is $\frac{4}{4}$ 𝅘𝅥𝅭 𝅘𝅥𝅮𝅘𝅥 𝅘𝅥𝅮𝅘𝅥𝅮 fast or slow? Is it faster or slower than $\frac{4}{4}$ 𝅘𝅥𝅮𝅘𝅥𝅮 𝅘𝅥𝅮𝅘𝅥𝅮 𝅘𝅥𝅮𝅘𝅥𝅮 if 𝅘𝅥 = mm60? Both have the same tempo, and thus neither "rhythm" is fast or slow. Sometimes an impression of apparent

speed is created by squeezing more notes per main beat into the rhythm. Thus ♩ ♫♫ ♫♫ might seem to be fast while might ♩ ♩. ♪♩ ♩ not seem fast. But even this belies the fact that fast and slow, high and low, and similar "concepts" are not absolute qualities, but rather are relative. Thus something can be only faster or slower, higher or lower than something else.

17. Pearce, *Exploring the Crack in the Cosmic Egg,* p. 224.

18. Jean Paul Sartre, *What Is Literature?,* trans. by B. Frechtman (New York: Philosophical Library, 1949), p. 60.

19. Jean Paul Sartre, *Literary and Philosophical Essays,* trans. by A. Michelson (New York: Criterion Books, 1955), p. 213.

20. Robert Powell, *The Free Mind* (New York: Julian Press, 1972), pp. 3, 118.

21. Michael Polanyi, *Personal Knowledge* (Chicago: University of Chicago Press, 1962), p. vii.

22. Karl Pribram, *Languages of the Brain* (Englewood Cliffs, N.J.: Prentice-Hall, 1971), p. 365.

23. Ibid., p. 369.

24. Ibid., p. 212.

25. Furth, *Thinking Without Language,* p. 177.

26. Ibid., p. 197.

27. Jean Piaget, *Science of Education and the Psychology of the Child,* trans. by D. Coltman (New York: Orion Press, 1970), pp. 28-29 (italics added).

28. Piaget, *Science of Education,* p. 29.

29. Ralph W. Tyler, "Desirable Content for a Curriculum Development Syllabus Today," in *Curriculum Theory,* ed. by A. Molnar and J. A. Zahorik (Washington, D.C.: Association for Supervision and Curriculum Development, 1977), p. 43.

30. See National Association of Secondary School Principles, *25 Action Learning Schools* (Reston, Virginia: NASSP, 1974).

31. Tyler, "Desirable Content for Curriculum Development," p. 38.

32. Ibid.

33. Ibid., p. 39.

34. Ibid., p. 40.

35. Hilliard, "Future Imperatives," p. 16.

36. Chester A. Lawson, *Brain Mechanisms and Human Learning* (Boston: Houghton Mifflin, 1967), p. xi.

1

Setting the Scene: The Play, the Actors, the Stage

☐ * Children and Music

☐ What Music Is and Is Not

Music Is a Personal Event
Not the Stimulus, but the Response
Musical vs. Verbal Action

☐ Music as Serious Play

☐ What Music Education Is

☐ What Music Education Is Not

☐ The Importance of Understanding Preadolescence and Early Adolescence

The Physical Nature of Adolescence
The Psychological Nature of Adolescence

☐ The Traditional Administrative Units: Elementary and Junior High Schools

☐ The Middle School as Administrative Unit or State of Mind

* Check off each section as you read it; check sections of special importance to you for further reading, future reference, or other purposes.

CHILDREN AND MUSIC

All children seem to gravitate toward music. Should the teacher intervene in such a natural process? No, if the result is to *diminish* the natural regard children have for music. *Young people find music a rewarding activity when done for its own benefits.* Parents and teachers are often guilty of making work and drudgery of the things children otherwise crave.

The initial learning of most children is inductive: it is freely exploratory and unconcerned with right and wrong. Teachers and adults introduce such abstract absolutes. *Children are motivated by the thing itself.* In music, this involves the acts of creating, listening, moving, singing, or playing. Their initial inclination is to pursue it for its immediate rewards.

Many teachers assume, as a result, that given free rein children will seek only those musical contacts that are in some way self-gratifying, and that they will not seek to extend their capacities for a musical response. Adults, generally in response to psychoanalytic "folk wisdom," assume that childhood is an animalistic, primitive state corresponding somehow to an early stage in the evolution of man. Thus it is often assumed that children must learn to repress their instinctual drives and that education must take children beyond these natural, "primitive" inclinations to a more "intelligent," higher level of understanding. From this idea comes the questionable practice of teaching music as a discipline: as an accumulative body of facts, information, and skills required of the "generally educated" person. There is no quicker way to destroy a child's natural curiosity for music.

No, music should not be taught in any form if it will cause young people to love it less. Nor should it be taught as a discipline. It should be taught only when the child can see the joy and beauty that can result from musical learning. In this way the teacher can enhance the child's ability to "feel" music, and thereby "feel" success—"feel" good, unique, and worthwhile. When this condition is attained, a child's musical horizons do not have to be broadened by force. They will grow naturally through the child's personal experience with music.

WHAT MUSIC IS AND IS NOT

It is not unusual to find a music class in which no music is heard. It is plain, then, that *such a class is not studying music as music.* It is studying verbalisms *about* music and other nonmusical behaviors. Music in the strictest sense is a phenomenological experience, that is, an event that must be *personally experienced.* The uniqueness of each mind is responsible for the unique reception and perception of musical phenomena. Musical behavior involves interaction between the individual mind and the musical stimuli provided by the teacher.

MUSIC IS A PERSONAL EVENT

Music, therefore, is not those static notational symbols on paper. That is a musical score. A score is only incidental to certain kinds of music in that it facilitates performance. Music consists of tones, having varying degrees of audibility, that convey an apparent or illusory motion in time. For typical purposes, music is sound and silence organized for and by human intelligence and purposes.

In addition, music exists in what is called a *phenomenological field.* Such a "field" consists of *all the factors in the individual perceiver* (i.e., perceptual acuity, personal history with music, the age or era in which the person lives, etc.) *and the environment* (i.e., "live" or recorded music, nature or size of the room, aliveness or deadness of the acoustics, nature or size of the audience, etc.) *that influence a person's perception of music.* Because of constant changes in the phenomenological field, *music has an ever-changing apparent reality.* According to the variables in the perceiver and his environment, music is perceived somewhat differently by different people, just as people perceive colors with qualitative differences.

On separate occasions music will be perceived somewhat differently by the same person. The personal history of the perceiver changes over time, as does his or her perceptual acuity. Environmental factors usually change as well. There are so many stimuli that make up even the simplest musical composition that it is very difficult, if not impossible, to focus aural attention on the same stimuli in exactly the same manner for each subsequent hearing. Consider the fact that individual musical stimuli combine into certain musical elements, and that these musical elements are capable of interacting in various ways depending on the features that command attention, and you can see how complex and variable the phenomenon of music can be.

A great advantage of this condition arises in our ability to listen to a composition many times and still maintain interest. Each such occurrence is an added measure of musical growth that infers the likelihood that our personal musical history—and thus our perceptual acuity—will be slightly altered for all subsequent musical experiences. Thus our subsequent perception of all music is slightly altered by those changes in the phenomenological field that constitute the musical experience.

NOT THE STIMULUS, BUT THE RESPONSE

When regarded as a phenomenon, music is not the **stimulus.** *It is the* **response** *of the human organism. It is the* **experience** *of the stimulus.* It is not the musical score. It is not the source of the sound. *Music is the* **experience** *of the sound as perceived by the individual person.*

Granted, the musical score and the way in which it is executed each has its own historical development. Music often results from such dynamic forces, but *it is not the same as those forces.* Public school music education, therefore, is not the study of the theory of music or the history of music, but the study of the experiencing of music. It is a sharpening or focusing of a person's perceptual apparatus within this particular phenomenological field called music.

It must be admitted that the study of the experiencing of music sometimes profits from the knowledge of certain information. Usually this knowledge "informs" the intelligence and assists it in directing perception; that is, information *can* direct selective attention. *Information has no value unless it has been preceded by and derived from the personal experience of the listener, and unless it is applied to the perception of music.* Many teachers make the mistake of proceeding in exactly the opposite manner. They try to define or explain musical phenomena to children, and then illustrate their lectures with examples. Rather than using information to direct musical perception (i.e., selective attention), they use the musical example to explain the "meaning" of verbal information *about* music. No emphasis is placed on the inner "meaning," or the experiencing, of the music—that is, on the child's response to the music perceived. The music serves only as a proof or example of abstract or symbolic ideas that are not, in their strictest sense, the same as the musical experience itself.

MUSICAL VS. VERBAL ACTION

What results are *verbal actions* (by the teacher) rather than *musical actions* (by the students). It is assumed that these verbal behaviors will function in the future to enhance musical behaviors, but this is seldom true. Information (i.e., cognition) is acquired only after repeated experience with and use of musical principles. Only information that leads to present or future *action* (use) in a musical experience is relevant. Only then can it "inform" or direct intelligence, and thus sharpen the perceptual acuity of the perceiver. Whatever can enhance the learner's musical *actions* is what should be taught.

Musical *actions* are the result of activity, inner and private (covert) or outward and observable (overt). They are purposive behaviors, and may be more or less complex. They are *goal-directed*, therefore, and *conscious*. They involve perceiving, striving and willing, or desiring, and therefore manifest *intentionality*. In Action Learning the "content" is a result of the *processes* of such covert or overt actions, and is determined by them. Therefore, "content"—the degree of learning, how much is learned—will vary according to the student's ability to *act upon* the stimulus situation or the musical environment the teacher creates in the form of learning activities.

Learning activities provide the occasion for *acting upon or acting with musical knowledge and skill.* But it is the process of this action that is important: students can progress only as quickly and as far as their readiness for learning permits. By emphasizing action, the teacher starts in motion those mental processes that can grow and change under their own impetus, and therefore continue to act on behalf of the individual throughout life. While "content" (specific information) can and will be forgotten, the processes, the actions of "learning how to learn" with music, can and will continue as a lifelong influence (just as we can always ride a bicycle after many years simply by calling upon long-dormant processes developed in our younger years). It is the action pattern or structure that is retained and that can be revived or relearned.

The increasing ability, therefore, *to act with* music knowledge, *to act upon* musical stimuli or materials, is the goal of a successful music education. It is not a matter of "remembering content" (specific facts and information) about music. In this sense *MUSICAL BEHAVIORS (actions) are the goals of instruction in music education.* The very nature of music as a phenomenological field demands that if verbal behaviors (information, concepts, etc.) are to have any merit at all, they must be acquired through and applied to active experiences with music. Thus, when musical behaviors are analyzed and discussed (i.e., when verbal labels are attached to these experiences or when children are encouraged to verbalize their active experiences with music), verbal behavior *can* be acquired. This verbal behavior may then be put to the service of directing the selective attention of the children in subsequent musical experiences. *Verbal behaviors,* then, even when they deal directly with a musical experience, are not the *raison d'être* of music education.

MUSIC AS SERIOUS PLAY

Much of a child's education is verbal. This is why reading is stressed, and why there is a high correlation between reading ability and intelligence. But since music (and indeed all arts education) is sought for its value *as an experience*, there are important differences between it and other studies. These are very much of the same character as the differences between *experiencing* a sunset or a flower garden and knowing in terms of verbal learning how or why the sunset or flower garden came to be what they are.

Music, like art or play, is an activity worthy of pursuit for its own sake. No young people need a "reason" to play. They do it for the *intrinsic interest* and *immediacy of results* at the moment. Psychologists have always noted the importance of play for various kinds of personal growth in children.[1] The relationship between such free play carried on universally by children and the fact that we "play" music should not be ignored.

Participation in music should have the same qualities as play:

1. It must engage the attention immediately.
2. Many of the rewards or effects of such activity must *seem* relatively *immediate* rather than distant.
3. The immediate benefits should have immediate *interest* and relevance and be *self-validating*.
4. It is often better if activities or benefits can be *shared* in some way with others.
5. Participation should not require sustained inactivity or forced attention.
6. Finally, it should have positive *growth benefits* that are relevant to the child grown into an adult.

There are those who believe that the human being should be defined as *homo ludens* (literally translated: "man who plays") rather than *homo faber* ("man who works or makes"), for it is the play element in human culture that allows a person to experience life most fully.[2]

Some readers may wrongly conclude that what is recommended here is simply mindless "fooling around" with music. This could not be more removed from the truth. Play is a very serious business. Just notice a child at play sometime. Notice how often there is complete concentration on the matter at hand, no matter how long or short the activity might be. Notice, too, that the child seems to have a purpose, an ultimate objective in mind.

Children play with the intent of realizing a goal, overcoming a problem, discovering how something works or how it is put together. They play games with the expectation of succeeding and deriving gratification. Consider, too, the play of adults as they pursue their "hobbies." Who can deny the seriousness, yet the pleasure, of the weekend gardener, the amateur photographer, the stamp or coin collector? The seriousness of such "play" is seen in the fact that often such so-called amateurs become true experts.

It is in this spirit of the hobbyist that music education finds its proper perspective. We do not seek necessarily to prepare professional musicians or critics, or even dilettantes. We do seek to discover and nurture potential musical talents. But above all we seek to bring music to all people as an engaging and rewarding activity worthwhile for its own sake. In a sense, music education seeks to make music a rewarding, lifelong "hobby" for everyone. This is the seriousness of the play element at its best.

WHAT MUSIC EDUCATION IS

1. *Music education is the semiformal attempt to facilitate positive, broad musical growth through contact with music as a phenomenon.* This act is semiformal because the teacher does not have total control over young people during all their waking hours. They do learn musical behaviors outside the school day. The process is called facilitating because the teacher can only *guide* students through or to musical environments in which musical stimuli are featured. The teacher has neither the practical ability nor the ethical imperative to "brainwash" students by inculcating the values of "good" music (as defined, generally, by the teacher). On the other hand, music educators do encourage students to develop, refine, and sustain individual value systems. This is inevitable. Usually, however, the values and attitudes students hold with regard to *music* are confused with their attitudes towards music *instruction* (in school, private music lessons, etc.). Teachers must realize this and seek a more positive musical value system.

2. *Music education is the invention (creation) and establishment of musical and pedagogical environments, situations, and events for the purpose of inducing fruitful musical actions.* Here "inducing" should be understood as stimulation, not as a musical force-feeding of students' attitudes and preferences. It is assumed that students' informal contacts with music, however profound, still warrant stretching in the more formal setting. Also implicit is the idea that a wide variety of music should be encountered. In other words, music education seeks to *broaden* the musical contact beyond what an individual ordinarily encounters in the home or community.

3. *Music education is a process of building upon the natural foundation of musical interest that every child seems to have.* Just as youngsters are not always predisposed to play, and when forced to do so can only "fool around," they cannot always be expected to be well disposed to musical pursuits. But just as adults can enhance a child's "play" by providing ample opportunity, an environment (playgrounds), and objects to play with (toys, etc.), so too can music education enhance and build upon the student's natural inclination to "play" with music. From such a process, significant musical learning can result.

4. *Music education is the action of building upon the psychological, physiological, and physical bases of the human organism's natural response to the forces of music.* Infants are entranced by a pendulum swaying within their field of vision. Similarly, children naturally move to music. It is almost a com-

pulsion. Music, it is said, captures the dynamic flux of life more fully than the other arts because it is predicated on time and movement. Thus it is also said that "music sounds as feelings feel."

Music can present a simultaneity of "feeling" events very similar to the often-diffuse welter of impressions and feelings we have daily. The difference is that music can make these available to our consciousness for contemplation when we have the "mental time" to reflect upon such feelings. In our daily affairs, our mind sorts out only those impressions and feelings that are of immediate practical importance. In daily life, then, our selective attention to practical matters causes us to miss much of life, especially our "inner" life.

Music re-creates for our contemplation, awareness, and concentration the dynamics of life with its moments of despair or *exhilaration, its moments of frenzied emotions* or calm, peaceful relaxation. And music moves well between these aspects of life, flowing as it does either smoothly or with alarming suddenness from one to another, just as we experience life daily. Music captures and "distills" all of the facets of life and presents them to our consciousness for concentrated and abstract reflection (mental action). We are better able to "feel" our feelings, are more aware of our "awareness," and think more about our thoughts. In this sense, music takes a slice of life and returns it to us when we are more able and inclined to attend to it and appreciate it.

It should never be forgotten that *life is not an object.* It, too, is a *phenomenological field* that must be *experienced, consciously* and with *awareness of its and our "being,"* in order to have meaning. This is probably the difference between merely being alive and "living" life fully. Music education builds on this aspect of existence and seeks to enhance the "living" of life by increasing our awareness of its full dimension of "feeling." In this way each person constructs her or his own "life" by a continuous process of growth in which the "self" (me) is constantly evolving by the personal redefinition that results from each new experience.

5. *Music education is the development and use of students' full sensory apparatus for the perception of musical events relatable or relevant to their present and future lives.* The dual content of music education is *music* and the *child.* We deal in musical instruction with the phenomenon of music as it is perceived actively by the child. Thus we deal directly with music and the feelings it brings to the awareness of the perceiving child. It is our task to direct the student's attention to his or her own feelings and thoughts; to enable each child to become more aware of his or her uniqueness and indefinability. This is the eventual benefit of the musical experience whether it is viewed as generating "expression" or as creating "formal patterns." The responses it engenders are unique to the experiencing being. Such responses thereby affirm the uniqueness of that individual being. But they can do so only if they

are related to the child's present life experiences, and if they can be extended as the child gradually grows into a more complex person.[3]

WHAT MUSIC EDUCATION IS NOT

1. *It is not simply performing music by playing instruments or singing.* Without "feeling" and a sense of significance, these acts have no more "meaning" than do those of the child whose behavior is exemplary out of fear of punishment. Let there be no doubt—musical performance can be one of the most rewarding kinds of musical actions. But it is only *one* kind! Not all children necessarily derive the same benefits; nor can we expect all children to become equally proficient. Music education is the exploration of the musical experience in *all* its many dimensions (creating, listening, and performing). In this way, every child can find some avenue of fulfillment, some measure of success and meaning.

2. *It is not lecturing on facts and information about music, or other such ways of "giving" musical concepts abstractly.* Music education must always flow from the experiencing of music. Such experiences must be frequent, action-laden, varied, and well chosen for their appropriateness. *Each learner must personally discover the fundamental structure or principles of the musical art* through productive and progressively differentiated interaction with *music as phenomenon.* The child must, as a result of instruction, be increasingly able to assimilate and synthesize experiences in solving common musical problems. Such solutions are quite naturally in line with each child's physical, mental, and environmental endowments. This process, as Jerome Bruner has said,

> requires something more than the mere presentation of fundamental ideas . . . it would seem that an important ingredient is a sense of excitement about discovery—discovery of regularities, of previously unrecognized relations and similarities between ideas, with a resulting sense of self-confidence in one's abilities.[4]

In this sense, the child must discover "meanings" or "relevance" for himself. Thus *intentionality* — goal-directedness: the search or desire for meaning—is the most basic attitude or value in any learning experience. It also explains why the hobbyist is a useful teaching or learning model, since intentionality is precisely the quality all sincere hobbyists possess. It is their unique sense of relevance. "Meaning," therefore, cannot be "told" or "given" by teachers to students. Such verbal processes only further the chance for failure, and no child will develop self-confidence through repeated failure.

It is very possible to arrange musical experiences so that no child comes to believe that music is "hard," or that he or she has no "talent" for it. Many people have been "turned off" to music because they have, in the truest sense, *learned* in school that they could not master it. They say, "I like music but I can't carry a tune" or "I like music but I'm not very good at it."

3. *Music education is not the breeding of failure by establishing circumstances that emphasize absolutes.* In such circumstances, learning is made to seem absolutely correct or incorrect. Instead, situations can and should be devised in which such absolutes are minimized or eliminated altogether. Music is quite naturally suited to this, since virtually no absolute value judgments are possible. There are no circumstances in *music as phenomenon* that are absolutely true or false, absolutely good or bad.

But many teaching techniques do foster such absolute judgments. Having to perform the correct notes, with good tone, in the correct rhythm establishes absolutes that can induce failure in those children who have difficulty with any one or more of these aspects. When students create their own music using their own notational symbols and criteria, they can forge positive learnings without undue fear of failure. Their works may be more or less satisfactory, but they will always contain some elements that prevent attaching the label "bad" or "failure."

The development of self-confidence—the inner conviction of future personal success—is of vast importance to continued growth in music. Self-esteem, too, arises from an ongoing pattern of more successes than failures. *Success is its own motivator!* Success breeds its own intentionality. Success is its own value. Adolescents, especially, realize this. The teacher must not only realize it but take steps to insure it.

4. *Music education is not the employment of a "method."* No single method or strategy is necessarily the best for any teacher, child, or school system. No teaching approach can be transported intact from one place and one teacher and used with equal success in another situation by another teacher. Teaching methods must be in accord with the nature of the children, their readiness, the instructional format of the class or school, and the personality, inclinations, skills, and weaknesses of the teacher.

The many "methods" propounded as panaceas to cure all ills generally can be criticized for their inability to meet the diverse needs and abilities of a heterogenous group of children. The more a teacher uses varied approaches, the more likely it is that the teacher will be able to "reach" each student. The more diverse the approaches, the less predictable instruction will be for the children, and therefore the more interesting such instruction can be.

Avoiding predictability is one of the most demanding tasks of the teacher, especially as middle school children grow closer to the more problematic adolescent years. But at any level, variety will lend a certain degree of interest that monotonously similar teaching formats cannot. Varied approaches lead to varied kinds of pedagogical results and musical products. This, too, has its advantages in preserving a sense of adventure, excitement, or discovery.

When activities are predictable, the end is already known and music class becomes as interesting as watching summer reruns on TV.

5. *Music education is not anything that will cause a child to love music less because of the manner in which musical instruction is implemented.* It has been said that "the medium is the message." Never is this more true than in teaching, and in music education in particular. If instruction in music is excessively verbal, is usually boring, and often results in failure, then students will take from your classes enduring learnings and attitudes that are negative. If, on the other hand, instruction involves musical actions and experiences that are usually interesting (even if not always exciting), and often result in self-confidence, then learners will profit from it through the favorable attitudes and values they attach to the music they have encountered. If instruction in music is only information *about* music how long can you expect students to remember such information? And what practical use can they have for it? How can it become an integral part of their lives?

When instruction in music involves fruitful *experiences with music and actions upon music,* you can feel more confident that your efforts hold the potential of lasting benefit in the lives of your students. Thus, if the medium or "method" of teaching music is musical actions and involvement with music (composing, listening, performing), then the message or result of such instruction will more likely be a continuing active involvement with music—after or outside of school and into the adult years. Music education, then, is concerned not simply with musical actions during music classes but also with the carryover of these actions into the out-of-school life and later adult life of each student. Music education at its best is and always has been Action Learning.

THE IMPORTANCE OF UNDERSTANDING PREADOLESCENCE AND EARLY ADOLESCENCE

In order for teachers and the educational establishment in general to be able to serve that troublesome stage (to both students and adults) of human development we know as adolescence, it is useful to understand the *growth-typical behavior* of this age group. Once we know what is typical for this group we can understand even better what constitutes problem behavior. Arrived at in this way, a teacher's *patience* becomes a crucial element in avoiding or dealing with so-called discipline problems. In this sense, then, patience is not the capacity for calm endurance, suffering, or passive resignation as suggested by some dictionaries.

Patience is determined by what a person expects from a situation. Thus, *patience can be learned!*[5] It is not, as some people imagine, a quality you were born with once and for all time. Nowhere is this realization more important than for teachers. Teachers of youngsters with learning disabilities are trained to recognize and deal with the behavior characteristics of a certain disability. Other teachers and adults often wonder how these teachers can "put up with" learning-disabled children, yet the seemingly inexhaustible patience displayed by such teachers is simply due to their *expectations* — i.e., what they know is *typical behavior* for their students.

Similarly, successful kindergarten teachers have certain expectations as a result of experience with and study of five-year-old children. Their patience with all the squirming, energetic, erratic behavior and with unpredictable outbursts of enthusiasm simply results from their realistic expectations of this age group.

In the same way, teachers of pre- or early adolescents must know and understand (even appreciate) the growth-typical characteristics of the age group in order to be "patient" with normal or expected behavior and more accurately discern the nature and extent of any aberrant behavior (true "discipline problems").

It will be maintained here that most teachers create their own problems, their own disciplinary crises, through their ignorance of and unwillingness to make an effort to learn the factors that stand behind much of the behavior of this age group.[6] Such teachers simply cannot recognize perfectly natural and healthy growth signs. They misread certain behaviors and end up creating their own unceasing stream of problems. Thus all teachers who are working with this age group or contemplating doing so can begin to enhance their "patience" and increase the effectiveness of their efforts by studying the following summary of adolescence.

THE PHYSICAL NATURE OF ADOLESCENCE

In the progression known as childhood, there is eventually a stage of development in which the body and physical processes of childhood begin the evolution to the body and processes of physical maturity (adulthood). This new developmental stage is called *puberty*,[7] and the process of arriving at puberty is called *pubescence*. Upon completing this process, the youngster becomes an *adolescent*.[8]

The *primary sex characteristics* are those features of anatomy that allow us to distinguish between boys and girls at birth. At the onset of adolescence, roughly eleven to thirteen years later, the *secondary sex characteristics* develop. Specifically this entails the maturation of the sex organs, the resulting production of hormones, an increase in body size and weight, and corresponding changes in the psychological frame of mind.

Of special importance is the fact that "on the average, girls begin puberty two years ahead of boys," though there is "a fair amount of individual variation." Nevertheless, "girls commence well ahead of average boys and complete their physical development correspondingly earlier."[9] There is a great range of chronological age when the process of puberty may begin. In rare cases, it can begin as early as fourth or fifth grade or as late as the first or second years of high school. Therefore, biological age or puberal maturity is important in any assessment of adolescents.[10]

Even when actual physical maturation is not present, prepubescents often begin to adopt pubescent and adolescent behavior patterns and mannerisms, presumably in imitation of older brothers and sisters or the models of older children in the school or community with whom they are acquainted. For this reason, even fourth and fifth grade teachers are likely to encounter some of the symptoms of adolescence.

Seldom, however, do they have to contend with the actual physical changes of puberty. Once the process of physical maturation begins in a child, a chain of growth events is set in motion that will take from two to four or more years to complete (and even then the body is not the one the person will inhabit as an adult in later years). Typically, a *growth spurt* in body height, sitting height, weight, and muscle and bone development *occurs around mid-puberty.*[11] Most parents and teachers mistake this growth spurt for the onset of pubescence, when in fact the onset of pubescence occcurs sometime before the actual growth spurt of mid-puberty.

In boys, aside from the growth spurt, puberty is announced by the appearance of facial hair ("peach fuzz") and the enlarging of the larynx with its corresponding deepening of the voice. "Also at this time the auxilliary sweat glands enlarge, giving rise to the characteristic adult odour."[12] In girls, "budding of the breast is usually the first indication. . . . The physical growth spurt begins at about the time of the breast bud."[13] Menarche usually occurs six to twelve months following the growth spurt.[14]

With the differentiation of the secondary sex characteristics, other evident sex differences arise at puberty. The boy catches up with and surpasses the girl in physical size (e.g., body measurements, weight). Girls "have rather more subcutaneous fat before adolescence and a great deal more after growth is completed."[15] Boys become stronger, and a divergence of physical strength is steadily more evident.

The arrival of puberty may be affected by economic factors (e.g., nutrition), and "in general, during the past one hundred years in Western-type societies, the age of puberty has been decreasing three to four months every decade."[16] There is also "an inverse relationship between family size and both body size and physical maturation."[17] That means that children from larger families may tend to reach puberty later than those from smaller families. Some evidence also suggests that the IQs of children from larger families tend to decrease with the addition of each child. Thus, the oldest child in a large family will often have a higher IQ than the youngest.[18]

Climate seems to have little effect on the rate of physical development, although "both boys and girls grow more in height in the spring and more in weight in the autumn, but there are wide individual differences," and this "seasonal effect is reduced in well-nourished children."[19] With puberty, the blood pressure rises and levels off at different points for boys and girls. Pulse rates fall steadily during childhood and stabilize just before puberty.

Due to hemoglobin production and metabolic rates, there is some tendency for boys to become anemic, and therefore to display certain chronic symptoms: a pallor of the skin, weakness or general lethargy (sometimes appearing as apathy), dizziness, easy fatigability, or drowsiness, ringing sounds in the ears, or spots before the eyes. There can also be difficulties in breathing, digestive complaints resulting from a higher amount of gastric acidity in boys than in girls,[20] and problems of nervousness.

Girls, on the other hand, are more prone to obesity than boys.[21] Acne is a problem for both boys and girls, but "due to estrogen-androgen imbalance, it is more common in males than females and may continue for several years."[22] Problems with vision, particularly myopia, increase strikingly at this age, and vision should be tested at this time,[23] especially since it can influence school work (e.g., reading—how far away from the chalkboard or overhead projector the student can sit and still see without strain). Existing vision problems increase in severity at this time as well.[24]

Generally, experimental evidence indicates a tendency toward more or greater psychological problems for late than for early maturers. Late maturers "are more likely to have negative self-concepts, feelings of inadequacy, strong feelings of being rejected and dominated, prolonged dependence needs and rebellious attitudes." The early maturers tend to be more "self-confident, independent, and capable of playing an adult role in interpersonal relationships." Furthermore, later maturers have been "rated higher in sociability, social initiative (often immature) and eagerness. Their peers [have seen] them as more attention-seeking, restless, and bossy, but less grown-up and less good-looking."[25] And early maturers seem to display a higher mentality before, during, and after puberty.[26] It seems, as well, that some of these differences continue into adult life.[27]

THE PSYCHOLOGICAL NATURE OF ADOLESCENCE

Most prospective teachers study the above-described developmental characteristics of adolescence while in college. They are repeated here to emphasize the exceedingly important role that they can play in the educational process. It is obvious from this description of the growth-typical characteristics that the middle school years are a pivotal time in the development of each person and personality. The impact of these physical changes on young people, how well their parents, teachers, and community help them to deal productively with these changes, and the influence of the peer group are all crucial. Each teacher should be aware of these changes and take them into consideration in planning and executing instruction and in handling the inevitable "discipline problems" that arise.

The term *adolescence* is most fruitfully regarded as involving the psychological and sociological results of puberty, and the individual's success or failure in dealing with the accompanying physical changes. These consequences have a topology[28] of their own that is also growth-typical and is equally deserving of each teacher's most sincere attention.

First of all, it should be noted that our complex industrial society has, for all practical purposes, *invented* adolescence (but not puberty; that is a biological given). Most primitive societies have no middle stage between childhood and adulthood. When boys and girls reach puberty, they are initiated automatically into the adult society. Confirmation, the Bar Mitzvah, eighth-grade graduation exercises, and so on—these are all remembrances of simpler times past. In primitive societies the postpubescent youngster becomes a warrior, or fills any of the other functions provided for men in that society. Women become eligible for marriage, motherhood, or other roles assigned to them by the society.

Our society, probably without intending to, has invented adolescence as a kind of transition for children in adjusting to our more complex social functions, particularly in terms of jobs and vocations. Unfortunately, the result is also, in part at least, a psychological limbo: the adolescent has many of the same problems as do other adults in the society but has been given little preparation in the way of knowledge, skills, or opportunity to deal with these problems. Such problems as sexual drive, romance and love, employment while not in school, leisure time, and crime and violence—all of which are also problems of the so-called mature adult society—plague the adolescent. This is a very insecure time for the adolescent, and *excesses of compensatory bravado are common.* On the other hand, such behavior really does not help the youngster to solve these problems—even temporarily for the immediate present.

The adolescent turns, then, for security to others who share similar problems. Thus the *peer group* assumes increasingly major importance in psychological and social development at this age. The peer group is much more likely to sympathize and empathize with such concerns than are the suspect representatives of the adult establishment—parents, *teachers,* law enforcement officials, and others. In dealing with an adolescent, it is almost always necessary, or at least helpful, to consider the relationship of the individual to the peer group.

Here is a clear example of the Gestalt principle that *not only is the whole more than the sum of its parts; the whole determines and controls the parts.* Trying to understand an adolescent outside of the peer group is as fruitless as

41

studying the typical behavior of a fish by removing it from water, its natural milieu. Much behavior—good and bad—encountered in the classroom is similarly influenced by the peer group; or, more precisely, by the interaction and sometimes mixing of the various subdivisions within the peer group known as *cliques*.

Every class or musical ensemble contains many smaller cliques. Membership in a clique is small and often exclusive (rather than indiscriminately inclusive); but the total number of cliques can be large. Usually each clique will try to distinguish itself through some means or other: dress, interests, conduct, speech patterns, etc. Cliques also overlap in a variety of ways.

The desire, even need, for *peer-group approval is perhaps the most important growth-typical trait of adolescents.* Most of their anxieties and drives are social (or interpersonal) in nature. Intrapersonal (psychological or psychiatric) problems often depend on how well or whether the adolescent is able to deal with social problems. Hence the concern with appearance (clothes, acne, obesity, performance in sports) and with "losing face" to authority (parents or teachers) that preoccupies so many adolescents.

A major growth need at this time is for self-esteem, self-respect, self-identity: "Who am I? What is my evaluation of my Self? In what ways am I unique or different from everybody else?" Abraham Maslow[29] asserts that a positive self-image, a true self-esteem (being favorably impressed with one's Self—having attained personal and physical security) is the major requirement for continued psychological growth. Only when self-esteem of this kind is achieved can the individual go on to heights of achievement involving understanding, aesthetic awareness, and other such "peak-experiences."[30]

Sociologist Edgar Friedenberg points out that some self-image is bound to arise no matter what adults and other people do or don't do. His plea is for adolescence to be a time when young people are allowed to discover their identity for themselves.[31] True, they need some guidance in order to avoid calamity. On the other hand, adults can introject themselves in unhealthy ways into the lives of adolescents and thus complicate already complex problems. This is especially true when adult intervention places adolescents in the position of not knowing whether they can take personal credit for certain accomplishments or for the version of Self that they finally discover: "Am I me, or am I the creation of my parents, teachers, and society? How responsible am *I* for this Self I find I have?"[32]

Renowned anthropologist Margaret Mead calls for what she identifies as a "psychological moratorium,"[33] in which adolescents are given certain freedoms to experiment with roles, with potential vocations, with their feeling-world, etc. This freedom should be of such a nature as to allow the adolescent to profit from success *and* mistakes. The adolescent is the action agent; that is, he or she is largely in charge of personal self-development and is correspondingly less *acted on* by outside forces (parents, teachers, adult society in general). Put another way, the adolescent is regarded as a "subject" having an inner life of feelings, rather than as an "object" to be manipulated without regard for inner meanings.

While this may seem to be a subtle distinction, or perhaps even a potentially dangerous one, it has some very important consequences. When you are directing the acting, *are the actor in your own life,* it is more possible to come to understand your Self as *subject.* When you are *acted on* (whether by adults, government operation, or anonymous computers) the "self" soon can become regarded only as an *object.*

On the other hand, it is obviously necessary to provide adolescents with minimal guidelines and protections from serious or long-lasting harm (drug abuse, pregnancy, etc.), for they otherwise have very little to go on in solving major life-crises by and for themselves. And, in general, *adolescents prefer the guidance and security of minimal rules,* if only because total freedom is difficult for anyone—adult or adolescent—to deal with in our complex times.

Someone has said, "The main business of the adolescent is to stop being one." And while that is usually true enough, it is also necessary to point out that if we solve all teenagers' problems for them, if we intervene too often in their lives, if we introject our values, our life view, or our authority too strongly, adolescents are denied the growth possibility of personally confronting, acting upon, solving, or otherwise coping with the dilemmas of the human condition. Thus the adolescent is denied the potential of self-directed growth for which he or she in large part deserves the credit (i.e., growth that is "inner-directed" rather than "other-directed").

Denied this opportunity, adolescents are literally nothings, neuters, until around age twenty-one when society finally allows them (or even forces them, ready or not) to take charge of their lives. If denied a real adolescence, individuals arrive at this point in life ill-prepared to assume this awesome responsibility.

In summary, then, adolescents *are* aware of impending adulthood, mainly through its problems rather than its advantages—maybe too aware for some parents or teachers! They like to *feel* relatively free and independent, and therefore *react well when given options and choices.* But since they require the security of minimal rules of behavior or action, adolescents usually allow *the teacher (or parent) to control the nature, direction, or number of choices.*

It helps, though, if the teacher (or parent) is fair and flexible, and allows periodic forays into untested or previously untested territory. Such occasions can always be controlled or supervised to some degree by the teacher without totally neutralizing the situation or force-feeding *introjected* values under the guise of "Socratic" (leading question) learning. Adolescents should come to be able to understand their limitations. The one thing they resent the most is direct interference in their personal affairs. In this sense, they resent invasions of their privacy at home, and invasions of their personal lives on the part of teachers.

As half-children and half-adults, it is not unusual that adolescents exhibit many paradoxes in their behavior: they are only trying to outgrow the older things of childhood and cope with the coming things of adulthood. Sometimes they seem aggressive, yet they are not really self-confident—especially if the school situation minimizes success and maximizes the potential of failure. This violates Mead's prescription for a psychological moratorium.

Some adolescents, or all adolescents at some time or another, seem highly sympathetic or empathetic in regard to others—peer groups and adults. At other times they can appear unfeeling, hardened, stoic, or just outright contemptuous of the feelings of others. Is the naive and guileless feeling-state of childhood giving way to the neurotic suppression of feeling (e.g., "Men aren't supposed to cry") that many adults have learned in the process of enculturation?

Adolescents' interest or *intentionality* can vacillate between the two extremes of self-direction and apathy. They often resent authority (especially when it seems arbitrary or exercised for its own sake by adults), and yet at other times can be almost neurotically submissive. This submissiveness can be confused with the not-infrequent moments of lethargy when they literally do not have enough energy to misbehave! Similarly, the lethargy can be misread by teachers as apathy.

According to Piaget, puberty brings with it the *stage of formal operations*. Prior to this, in the *stage of concrete operations*, children can reason and perform mental functions as long as they have tangibly (concretely) before them the elements they are to analyze, manipulate, etc. Now, however, they become increasingly able to think in totally abstract (formal) terms. It is at this stage that all the many particular experiences they have had are synthesized as concepts and begin to function effectively as an interdependent network. Now, in addition to the continuing need for inductive learning, deductive reasoning becomes a more suitable teaching approach than in earlier years.

As children approach adolescence, they become increasingly good at dealing with generalizations. Abstractions such as questions of quality and value can be dealt with successfully from this stage onward, and the abstracting abilities relevant to creative activity and creative expression can now be put to particularly good use (if, that is, these capacities are not stifled by the threat of failure, particularly failing grades or other ways teachers have of informing the peer group of someone's failure). The active imaginations of adolescents, while not as given to the fanciful fantasies of childhood, do find pleasure and an outlet in constructive and manipulative activities that deal with aspects or products *they* consider to be relevant. However, they have a *marked aversion to monotonous drill and other repetitive behaviors*, or to any activities in

44

which a relevant or at least interesting goal is not apparent or immediate gratification is not provided. Their abstracting ability thus fails with regard to long-term goals, and they cannot be motivated by such exhortations as "Someday you will find this relevant" or "Someday you'll thank me for this."

The often rapid and radical physical changes of puberty can have psychological implications that influence an individual's ability to take part in or profit from class activities. For example, a student can be poorly co-ordinated for a while and thus clumsy. This may be true especially for some boys and girls whose growth spurt is so great that they take a longer while to learn to control all the new amount of body, legs, arms, and feet.

Nothing is more amusing in this regard than some high school freshmen on the Junior Varsity basketball team: they are all limbs, and lack the graceful motor control of the Senior Varsity models. Early adolescents are known to trip occasionally while walking along a perfectly empty hall.

The factors that contribute to anemia in boys (and sometimes in girls) result in periodic fatigue, apathy, and total lethargy. Unless students in such states are stimulated by the teaching-learning environment in some way, little interest or enthusiasm (or even willingness) for cooperating in class activities can result. On the other hand, if these students are "pushed," they can muster enough energy to defend their "honor." *It is the unwise teacher who gets into a situation from which there is no graceful or "face saving" exit for either the student or the teacher.*

Adolescents are extremely sensitive and concerned about their appearance. Both sexes are now very interested in their newly developing secondary-sex characteristics and derive increasing self-esteem from their approach to physical adulthood. Both boys and girls often flaunt their new physiques for one another, and the gamesmanship of courtship and romance is awakened from its childhood hibernation.

On the other hand, some children react with alarm, fright, or shame to physical changes for which they are psychologically unprepared. For girls, such responses can often arise with the onset of menstruation. For boys, these responses usually involve the changing voice; but boys can also begin to experience guilt or worry about their awakening sex drives, especially when these manifest themselves at unexpected times, or without there being any apparent way of control. Either kind of response can be expected from many children in sixth grade, and for others earlier or later.

In these ways and others, the emotions of adolescents are distinctly variable and paradoxical.[34] Combinations of anxieties and frustrations give way to pride in impending adulthood. Emotions occur in response to what teenagers think but are also influenced at preconscious levels by the physical changes (especially hormonal) that are taking place. Adolescents need to express their emotions, and at times they profit from such expression—verbally or otherwise. Outbursts of enthusiasm, seemingly uncontrollable, can be frequent. But at other times, they are very protective of their feelings, especially with regard to "romantic interests" (or among boys, romantic subjects. Yech!).

Overemphasis on conformity in expression, or repression of enthusiasm and other forms of adolescent energy, can impede the developing self-concept and can have deleterious and long-lasting effects on the personality and behavior of the individual in adult life (i.e., what the Gestalt therapists call "unfinished business"). Keep in mind that teenagers are now capable of and inclined to the formal thinking involved in truly creative and imaginative activities, and these go a long way in meeting many an adolescent's need for self-expression.

Adolescents of any age usually develop a language of expressions uniquely their own. Adults can seldom think in these terms, and are laughed at (secretly, most often, but also openly on certain occasions) when they attempt to talk in the clichés and vernacular of the peer group. And even within the larger peer group, you must remember, each clique is likely to distinguish some "in-group" expressions of its own. Even adult cliques play this little game. Mutual language, interests, and life-problems are generally the glue that keeps peer groups and cliques together in the face of considerable challenges from the adult world.

Many adolescents will choose friends on bases related to the peer group rather than on similarity of background, taste, or aspirations. And the cliques often reflect this extreme heterogeneity with all kinds of combinations that teachers and parents cannot begin to understand. Still, keep in mind that the peer group or a particular clique represents each individual's need for security, esteem, accomplishment, and "belonging."

These personal relationships will change as often as the individual's perceptions of his or her needs. Therefore, cliques are far from permanent (no more so than "going steady" is for most youngsters at this age). They are constantly in a state of flux—sometimes growing larger, then splitting off into several smaller, more exclusive groups, each of which may grow larger again, and so on.

Preadolescents, especially, can be intensely curious and generally have many (often very diverse) interests competing for their attention. Initially, they are not usually likely to be very responsible in following any *one* of these competing interests. Some interests, like fads, come (for an intense while), then go (overnight). While this determined dilettantism and amateurism mystifies teachers (who can never predict what will be found interesting with classes) and parents (who usually have to support these phases), it is usually a positive, growth-inducing development in the adolescent. It is related again to Mead's psychological moratorium. Here, it involves experimenting and experiencing a variety of life's offerings, and at the same time attempting to uncover that synthesis of responses that will later be regarded as the Self.

46

THE TRADITIONAL ADMINISTRATIVE UNITS: ELEMENTARY AND JUNIOR HIGH SCHOOLS

The junior high school concept originated after developmental and educational psychologists began to study and propound the importance of adolescence as a developmental stage. This took place roughly between the years 1892 and 1918. By 1920 the junior high school was a standard feature of the educational establishment. Originally its program was designed to meet the various special characteristics and growth-needs of adolescence that have been outlined here. It also helped to "institutionalize" the problem. In our society, naming and isolating a factor (as when a doctor diagnoses an illness) makes everyone feel more secure. It leads us to believe that we have increased focus or control over the problem. Hence, the nature and structure of the junior high school was set up to correspond to the onset of puberty and its accompanying psychological and sociological implications.

Adolescents were given an increased responsibility and freedom in comparison to elementary school. The self-contained classroom of the elementary school gave way to changing classrooms and teachers for each subject. This also permitted an increase in the specialization of teachers, both in the "core subjects" and the host of "special subjects" now offered. These latter subjects were offered in order to accommodate the sudden new interests characteristic of early adolescents.

These courses—usually music, art, home economics, "shop," and physical education—were supposed to allow and encourage exploration and experimentation with new interests (vocational or avocational, as was the case with music and art classes); or they were intended to prepare children for certain life functions or roles. In this sense, homemaking and shop ("industrial arts" in fancier schools) coordinated beautifully with what today is called "sex stereotyping": girls were being prepared to be housewives and mothers, cooking and tending to domestic matters, while boys were prepared to be the handyman around the domestic dwelling. Physical education was supposed to improve body development, fine-muscle control, coordination, and general health.

Junior high was also the time when "clubs" were emphasized more than they had been in the elementary school. These were usually after-school or "activity period" groups, devoted to special interests of either the extra-curricular kind (e.g., scouting, chess, photography, or stamp collecting) or the co-curricular kind (e.g., intramural sports, musical ensembles, international relations club, journalism club) as potential vocations or avocations. In these clubs students were supposed to be able to explore the nature, depth, and breadth of their interests and competences. Clubs like these were sometimes found in sixth grade as well.

The structure and the nature of junior high school served a real need for a while, although it never entirely satisfied many of the requirements of the adolescent stage. Youngsters were notably unreliable in beginning their physical maturation. Some began the process in fifth or sixth grade and were already quite physically mature as seventh graders. This was often true of girls. And as was noted earlier, the onset of puberty kept occurring earlier and earlier.

Depending on the physical plant available to a school, the junior high school concept existed in middle ground, a no-man's-land. If placed in buildings with elementary school youngsters, the eighth graders got "totem pole-itis": they were the "top of the heap," only to become "low man on the totem pole" as high school freshmen. Under this arrangement, their behavior rubbed off on the younger children. When placed in buildings with high school students, they were at the bottom of the pecking order and displayed the unfortunate tendency of picking up the habits and attitudes of their older models.

The junior high school curriculum also created its own problems. The function to be served by the "special subjects" never was straightened out very satisfactorily. Few schools were able to contend with the problem of how to give grades in studies that were supposed to provide the opportunity to *explore* interests and capabilities! "Pass-fail" systems were not yet employed. The option of not giving grades either did not occur to anyone or if it did it was dismissed as removing motivation (which was what the courses were supposed to uncover or discover for students in the first place!). So schools and special-subject teachers struggled with the varying levels of student interest, and with a strange grading system that usually gave grades but *did not require that such courses be passed* in order to move on to the next grade level (unless, in severe cases, a student "failed" two or more special subjects; then he—and it often *was* a boy—might be failed, especially if it was determined—how?—that he would never amount to much anyway).

There were other curricular problems too. The unequal physical maturation of pre- and postpubescent youngsters—particularly among boys—made contact sports in physical education and intramurals a significant problem. Girls' *physical and mental ages* were on the average two years ahead of the boys', yet grouping was still done by *chronological age*. This made for very uneven accomplishment in academics. The girls' earlier development made them physically bigger than most sixth- and seventh-grade boys (and some eighth-grade boys) and allowed them to outperform boys in academic classes. "Tomboys" (how will the new women's consciousness deal with this sexist label?) would even, on occasion, out-muscle boys in sports or in an infrequent fight.

This was degrading for boys, to say the least. It didn't contribute to their self-esteem and self-concept at all (although perhaps some men spent much of their later years getting even).

Music class, often called "general music," posed special teaching and scheduling problems. It was intended originally to be a kind of survey course sampling many different kinds of music, skills, and the like. It often degenerated into boiled-down music theory and history, and became just another "subject" to not like or to be "no good" at.

There was more time given to general music than in elementary school, but otherwise many teachers taught it in much the same way as in the late elementary years. In fact, junior high specialists were often shocked to notice that many if not most youngsters had learned and retained very little during the earlier years of elementary school music classes. They had only experienced some hardening of the attitudes. In particular, *boys often equated music class* (not music as such, you should notice) *with singing.* Singing was the prime vehicle of music development in the elementary music class then, and to a large degree is still so today.

Now, this causes boys a special problem. Adulthood—as embodied by their fathers, sports figures, older brothers, and other "hero" figures—does not provide appropriate models of the male involved in singing; not, at least, models boys will accept. Somehow, in their haste to rationalize their discontent with singing, boys can conveniently overlook the fact that most of the most popular music stars are men! Those students who do enjoy singing activities in the elementary school often are in a fifth and sixth grade chorus. Others are in the elementary band or orchestra, or take piano lessons. Many adolescent boys, however, find little satisfaction in such pursuits and tend to equate music classes with childish things.[35]

The real complicating factors, though, are the physical changes and the resulting voice change that occurs in boys at or around this age. As the body grows bigger and stronger, so does the larynx. This results for most boys in the noticeability (depending on their build) of the so-called Adam's apple. It is one easily recognized sign of both impending voice change and other physical developments connected with puberty.

The voice change can be very disturbing to some boys. Its major manifestations are all troubling to the insecure pubescent youngster.

1. The voice "cracks" in speaking and singing.
2. It loses the flexibility it had in elementary school.
3. The pure sound it had in elementary school gives way to a strained, "bleating" sound.
4. Several years of elementary school experiences designed to train youngsters to "match pitches" (i.e., sing the correct pitches in the appropriate vocal register) may have been counterproductive, for the boys' voices drop an octave or more at this time. With this change of range, matching pitches becomes a problem once again.
5. What used to be a relatively easy feat is now hard work, since in order to sing it is necessary to retrain or at the very least expend much energy in controlling the clumsy, uncoordinated vocal apparatus. In adolescence energy is often expended with extreme economy; singing usually suffers from this stinginess.

There are far too many disagreements about what really happens during the voice change and what music teachers ought to do about it (if anything) to argue this out here. What can be noted, however, is that music classes were advanced at one time as being of particular use in assisting the pubescent boy to adjust to his changing voice. With the proper supervision by the teacher (although, as mentioned above, what that entailed was never settled by the experts), the boy could be kept singing and nursed through this period to a postpubescent stage when he would no longer have vocal problems or poor attitudes.

It seldom works out that way, and the scheduling of music classes often compounds the issue. In most elementary schools, fifth- and sixth-grade boys might have music class once or twice a week. In grades seven and eight, when the problem can be even more crucial, a variety of formats is used. A common pattern is to have general music (and the other special subjects often follow this pattern as well, with the exception of physical education) for a block of weeks (often ten to thirteen), five days a week. Then the classes switch and move on to another special subject. In another pattern, general-music class meets for two days a week, or every other day for a block of approximately twenty weeks, before the rotation. Some students have general music once or twice a week for forty weeks.

None of these is entirely satisfactory for all purposes. The last-stated plan does not facilitate transfer of learning or a continuing sequence of studies from one class to another. Because classes are so far apart, much of the achievement in the first class is lost by the next class. However, this is the only format that is adequate to keeping track of the boys' changing voices *all year long.* A voice is not going to accommodate itself to schedules and conveniently change during a certain ten- or twenty-week period. It will change when it will change, and it will take varying amounts of time to fully develop its potential for growth (some high school sophomore boys still have unchanged voices).

So the situation has never been a satisfactory one for the purposes of the general-music teachers who have to deal with *all* youngsters at one time or another during the year. In fact, depending on unique local circumstances, it can be just plain counterproductive. Discipline problems can be severe, and to many teachers authoritarian teaching seems to be required. This teaching response to student behavior just adds fuel to the flames simply because adolescents, you recall, can respond securely to the order and control of authority but reject authoritarianism.

The more authority wielded in this way, the more resistant becomes the peer-group spirit. Diverse cliques can work together to weigh in the students' favor the "gamesmanship" that develops as an adversary relationship between the teacher and class. This all too common situation is neither healthy nor educationally suitable for anyone involved. It would be unfair not to point out that many of these conditions and circumstances still prevail in many schools today and in some ways are worse than ever.

Not all the problems involve the elementary or junior high school as an administrative convenience. Many—perhaps many more—stem from inappropriate teaching means and goals. Most often these problems arise when the general methods of elementary school years are carried over into the junior or senior high years. This practice does not take into adequate consideration the growth-typical behavioral characteristics of pre- and early adolescents. *This is always a serious mistake.*

Conflict and confrontation inevitably ensue. They take form as a continuous struggle between the adolescents, in continual search for self-identity and other growth needs, and the teachers, who see every student act as defiance, deliberate misbehavior, and scapegoating (with the teacher as the goat to "get"). These situations are often so severe that some teachers conclude that "the kids are out to get me" in a sense far more serious than scapegoating. These teachers often end up genuinely disliking and distrusting adolescents and often refer to them as "animals." For their part the students see in this situation a confirmation of their suspicion that adulthood is not something one simply reaches, but *something that has to be won in direct confrontation with adults* (teachers, parents, etc.); i.e., to the victor belong the spoils!

The "self-fulfilling prophecy" works all too well for both groups. Students' behavior often turns out to be as bad as teachers expect it to be. Students, expecting the worst, see teachers as the "enemy," obviously out to make life miserable for kids. Teachers beat the school buses out of the parking lot at the end of the school day and make full use of their allotted sick and personal days each year (recouping lost physical and psychological energies). Students frequently take out their accumulated aggressions and frustrations by damaging school property, one another, or various symbols of the adult establishment.

This is just one among a host of other problems that call out for a change in the point of view toward the educational arrangements needed to deal effectively with this most problematic, yet crucial, stage of human development. As parents and churches increasingly hand to the schools more and more of the responsibility for "character development," "socializing," or "citizenship education" (that is, inculcation of social values, enculturation, conformity, docility, etc.), the need for a new approach becomes more and more pressing. Thus was born the idea of the middle school.

THE MIDDLE SCHOOL AS ADMINISTRATIVE UNIT OR STATE OF MIND

The junior high school took several forms. Most usually it included grades 7-8 or 7-9. While almost every school had some administrative unit called the "junior high school," few evolved a local philosophy of what it was supposed to achieve, and according to some experts, local variety was considerable.

At best, the term junior high school (sometimes also called the intermediate school, the junior school, and the departmental school) simply described that this arrangement was established to suit the needs of adolescents and to meet the criticisms of the traditional system that poured forth from the 1890s to 1920.

Various grade organizations were determined by particular local purposes. By the close of the first decade of the twentieth century, the junior high school was not a definite institution but rather a state of mind, an attempt to attain an ideal.[36]

During the 1960s, a new wave of discontent swept over the educational establishment and many of the unsatisfactory aspects of the old elementary and junior high schools were criticized. These criticisms, however, did not evolve into a single "middle school" arrangement or format which could be defined in terms of the grade levels it encompassed. Rather, the middle school involves extremely varied patterns of grouping according to the already existing physical plant available or according to the ability of communities to support new building programs.

In some communities, what is *called* the middle school involves the grouping of grades 6-8. In other communities, grades 6-9 are incorporated. Some schools have created two middle stages between the elementary (primary) level and senior high: a 4-5 middle school plus a 7-8 or 7-9 junior high school. Some systems have a 4-5 or 4-5-6 intermediate school and a 6-8 middle school. So it is obvious that *as a name* "middle" does not describe anything even as singular as was the elementary or junior high school.

Well, what do middle schools have in common, and in what ways are they different from the idea of an elementary or junior high school?

The middle school is a philosophy and belief about children, their unique needs, who they are, and how they grow and learn.[37]

The middle school, therefore, is a state of mind, a point of view, *an ideal* that tries to tailor the school to the individual child *at least* for the early and middle stages of pubescence, when the youngster needs the most attention and when special needs are greater, perhaps, than at any other time. Thus, it can relate most directly to the needs of students from grades 4 or 5 through 8.

Without this commitment to tailor the school, its function, and even its physical nature around the needs of preadolescents it is all too easy to slip once again into a junior high school or "upper" elementary school in disguise simply by calling it a middle school so as to sound up-to-date. Without doubt, this happens not infrequently with some schools that are *called* middle schools.

The main distinguishing characteristic of the "ideal" middle school is *flexibility*. Middle schools should be flexible enough to accommodate the wide differences among students—their interests, learning styles, abilities, and so on—and flexible enough to accommodate social changes as they manifest themselves in local communities. One published rationale is summarized here as illustration of the bases of the middle school philosophy.

1. *Continuation of the school's role as an agent important in the transmission and modification of the culture.*
2. *Intensification of efforts to individualize instruction beginning at an early age and expanding rapidly as more maturity is gained.*
3. *Implementation of techniques for helping early adolescents to become problem solvers and creative thinkers.*
4. *Provision for balance in educational experiences.*
5. *Utilization of various patterns of instructional organization.*
6. *Integration of the efforts of the total school personnel responsible for the educational program.*
7. *Growth in technological aids.*[38]

1. The old functions of school in both passing on our cultural heritage and challenging it in order to keep up with ever more rapid changes—all this is retained. Culture shock need not result from the implementation of the middle school concept. However, given the next six factors, it is very likely that this first function will result in more self-directed, self-motivated, and self-actualizing individuals than was the case with previous educational concepts, which placed emphasis on enculturation or even indoctrination. The results may be the same, in effect; but today's public school graduate should know where and how he acquired his view of the culture. Values should no longer be inculcated without the student realizing that such "programming" is taking place.

2. Individualized instruction should become a reality, and not just a philosophy on paper. This need not be understood as independent study or even as mediated instruction (i.e., use of media). It *will* mean *more grouping of students according to ability* and a greater tailoring, in general, of their program to their individual weaknesses and interests.

3. Public school graduates should be able to think for themselves. In fact, taking this one step further, students should learn how to learn, how to grow, and to want to learn. In doing so, the individual takes on increasing responsibility for his or her own learning. In recognizing the importance of decision making and problem solving we also recognize the fact that since we learn what we use, we should be able to use what we learn. This helps overcome questions of relevance and tends to bring the student some immediate gratification (this is in keeping with the need of adolescents for immediate results and reinforcements; i.e., they are somewhat shortsighted at this age). At the same time, the knowledge or skill in question is being reinforced for permanent inclusion in the learner's repertory of behaviors for use after graduation.

4. Balanced programs try to *avoid making intelligent but dull* human

53

beings. All work and no play is not the motto or view of secondary schools articulated here. In addition to work—the skills, cognitive abilities, attitudes, and values needed by every student—there should be provided an opportunity for balance along the lines of Margaret Mead's psychological moratorium. In other words, middle school students should be encouraged and given ample opportunity to explore a wide range of interests and possibilities. High school students, in turn, must have the chance, the choice, to develop the human and personal aspects of human existence along with the academic aspects. No poorly adapted geniuses here!

5. In using many different patterns of instruction the school will recognize the fact that students have different learning styles. "Cognitive mapping" will help identify the instructional means best suited to each youngster. The school will be able to provide sufficient instruction in accord with each student's learning style to maximize success and, more importantly, to minimize failure. More generally, this attitude accepts the reality that no one instructional organization will suit all students. This is true whether the method in question is traditional or the latest innovation.

6. The middle school teacher will be unique.

Bringing together in one school teachers with the different training experience and attitudes typical of teachers certified to teach "elementary" and "secondary" schools tends to have salutary effects on both groups as they come to understand one another's point of view.[39]

This new point of view will be applied as a much closer cooperation in the best interests of each student than heretofore has been characteristic of education for early adolescence.

7. As technological aids become more common and less expensive, multiple forms of mediated instruction should be used to facilitate some of the aforementioned goals, particularly numbers 2 and 5. In addition, school buildings need to be constructed to suit the specific needs of the new curriculums, instructional styles, and physical requirements.[40] Therefore, commitment to the middle school concept cannot be simply a matter of philosophy put on paper. It costs money. *Most middle schools will cost more in the long run than most conventional elementary and junior high schools.*[41]

The increased specialization of equipment, facilities, and teachers, and even the smaller classes, all make a commitment to the middle school concept a true investment. Once seriously undertaken, it is difficult to back away, although if it is undertaken in "name" only, nothing is lost—but, then again, nothing is gained!

The middle school concept attempts to accommodate the needs and problems of pre- and early adolescence by means of *flexibility*. In comparison, the typical elementary and junior high school tended to be—whatever form it took—more rigid in its approach. Junior high school especially took on an "institutional" character, a propensity for slipping into one rut or another. The middle school seeks to escape this by systematically adapting the school to the clientele. Of course, this does not make the middle school "immune" to the disease of ruts. It does, however, indicate a particular sensitivity to the danger of institutional ruts that midddle schools seek to avoid.

Because of the importance of the growth-typical characteristics of pre- and early adolescence for any teacher, and especially because the *true* middle school is determined largely by these characteristics, the reader is strongly urged to review and study the early sections on the physical and psychological traits of adolescents several times while reading this text, and periodically thereafter. And, of course, exploration of other sources is highly encouraged. There is no way one can ever know *too much* about the adolescent in contemporary society. Teachers have everything to gain from being the specialists for society in "applied" adolescent psychology. This is one area in which teaching ability can be improved by the direct application of "learning" to that "inborn" skill good teachers are supposedly graced with at birth.

THE HIGH SCHOOL

Over the years, the high school has shown little signs of major change either as an administrative unit or in its programs. Outside of the variety of "alternative schools" that became somewhat more popular in the mid-1970s, much of what happens today in most high schools is more different in *degree* (amount of emphasis on traditional programs, schedules, teaching methods) than in *kind* (new, innovative programs) in comparison to the past.

As before, a major purpose of the high school is to prepare youngsters to enter the adult world. Today vocational education enjoys a new emphasis that has come in part as a consequence of the debunking of college as the only route to a well-paying job. High schools today manage to offer a greater variety of studies in pursuit of the independence needed by their graduates in the world outside of school. More "specialty" high schools exist to prepare students for ever more technical post-high school employment. And there seems to be a movement toward the regional or cooperative high school; schools are pooling their resources to provide specialty programs or instruction they could not otherwise afford to offer their students.

There is today, however, a new emphasis on "competence." This movement has amounted to making the high school accountable for the skills and knowledge a graduating student should have. It is partially a result of previous tendencies among educators to allow the "social promotion" of students regardless of their actual achievement. This practice of moving students ahead with their age groups for reasons of social adjustment resulted in high school graduates who could not read, write, or do basic arithmetic. Today, increasingly, state-mandated criteria force schools to insure that students graduating from high school do indeed have those most basic skills necessary to economic and social well-being after graduation.

Related to similar needs for after-graduation competency are Action Learning programs, and programs with related or similar intent or practices. Most involve giving the student at least a taste of the requirements or nature of post-high school employment or careers. Many actually go further by placing students part-time in a variety of apprenticeship positions that give them the opportunity to actually learn and apply a sampling of skills they would be called upon to perform were they to continue in that line of pursuit. Still other programs provide on-the-job training: in addition to taking basic courses in the enabling academic subjects (reading, writing, etc.), students spend a significant portion of each school day or each school term learning a job skill out of school actually on the job.

In the latter type of program, students often enter such emploment directly after graduation. In the former types, where some degree of preliminary "tasting" is provided, students can make more realistic choices for post-high school training or education than students lacking this opportunity. With a clearer idea of what is involved in their prospective careers, students may attend college or seek other kinds of technical training in their chosen field. Thus it can be said that these programs generally provide students with a preview of and some significant preliminary involvement with pursuits that will make up an important part of their adult lives.

It is in this spirit that Action Learning in music should be understood. It is for this kind of experience, although in most cases within the school and school day, that all middle school Action Learning should aim: the involvement in musical responding, musical behaviors, that as closely as possible approximate the kinds of musical pursuits to which the typical adult will be most predictably attracted, or the kinds which are most available. Thus, while there is some opportunity for musical performance upon graduation from high school (most notably in church choirs and community performance clubs), the kinds of musical pursuits most accessible to the typical adult are those which stem from general music activities in the middle and high schools.

An Action Learning program of music education, therefore, seeks to prepare adolescents with the musical skills and knowledge that will allow and encourage them to be musically active to a significant degree in their post-graduation years. To this end, and beginning in the middle school, musical activities and learning should have a distinctly "practical" or "functional" application not only for the immediate present (since adolescents of all ages are notably shortsighted) but for the long run as well.

Even more than this, though, general music opportunities must be made available to high school students. Too often general music instruction all but ceases in many typical high schools. Aside from an occasional music theory course for the college-bound student musician (who thus needs it least since the training in music theory will be done best in the particular format of symbology, etc., used by the college or conservatory itself) and a watered-down music history and rudiments course called "music appreciation," high schools all too often ignore the general music needs of the vast majority of students. Since it is typical for no more than 20 or 25 percent of all high school students to be involved in performance ensembles, that leaves at least 75 percent of all students in high school who are functionally cut off from any guided or serious musical pursuit of the kind that could serve to enhance their lives after graduation. It is no wonder that many taxpayers consider music programs to be elitist!

It is difficult to tell whether the status of high school general music is the result of any philosophical disposition against such courses in the high school by principals, school boards, or communities in general or whether one result of some of the ineffective traditional style of teaching general music in the middle school is an inability to interest students enough to fill elective courses in the high school. Since the more expensive performance classes *are* offered in almost all high schools, it seems as though officials and parents have no particular philosophical bias against music as such. If there is a bias it would seem to be against general music, and probably for the same reason that even college-level music majors can affirm: hardly any adults can remember enjoyable or profitable general music experiences when they were in school. Beginning in the middle school, most children can report nothing very positive about their general music experience.

Society in general seems to feel this way, and most musicians are not exceptions. It is not at all rare to find instrumental music teachers (inservice or in-training) lamenting the likelihood of their being "stuck" with a general music class. This is all the sadder since more and more instrumental specialists find themselves in that position because of the diminishing support for music programs in these days of educational cutbacks. The most frequent reason given in support of cutbacks in music programs is that they are not "relevant." Since performance ensembles enjoy a certain amount of public relations value in the minds of school administrators, it has been the general music programs that have suffered under economic pressures. Classes have gotten larger and supporting materials have gotten older or shorter in supply, and the effect of such instruction thus contributes even more to the continued poor health of general music.

Further contributing to the problem has been the manner in which music instruction is offered in most states. Typically, in most states music activities in the elementary school are integrated by the classroom teacher in the self-contained classroom. In these states music specialists assist the classroom teachers in preparing such instruction. But in the junior high schools, the music specialists often direct the performing ensembles and teach the general music classes. Since these specialists themselves have seldom had good models of general music classes during their own public school years, and because such specialists are often well-trained musicians, many music teachers working in the middle school and by far the majority of those working in the high school *prefer* to devote their care and effort to the performance ensemble because of the musical rewards available and because such ensembles are elective. Finally, when the public visibility of the ensemble is compared to the general anonymity of *any* classroom teacher, a corresponding lack of interest is noted on the part of performance-oriented music teachers for general music teaching in the middle and high schools.

All told, then, an Action Learning program, by emphasizing the nontrivial musical pursuits of adult society as a whole can begin to reestablish the central importance of general music for *all* students, even and especially for those youngsters who are in performance ensembles, for it is they who seem more naturally inclined toward and able to profit from musical involvement. Only with the removal of the childish associations that are too often held over from elementary school music activities (which, not to demean them, *are* necessary for *that* age group but are increasingly problematic thereafter) can even the performance-oriented music specialists begin to see the essentially musical benefits that argue for their own involvement as well as their students' involvement in general music. Only with that switch of interest will the general music program in the middle and high school begin to approximate an effective Action Learning program—that is, one that most breeds true musical activity and continuing use of music in the lives of increasing numbers of adults.

Once again, the key to beginning such a transformation is the change of attitude and approach recommended here for general music instruction beginning no later than in the middle school. Only after several years of success with instruction at this level will the effects and benefits begin to be felt in the high school. And only then will it become possible for a music education program to reach a progressively greater number of high school graduates; only then will it be possible for music education to influence in a long-term way the lives of high school graduates. New support will be forthcoming for such music programs at all levels, but especially for enriching even further musical instruction at the high school level in order to bring it in line with the historically greater support accorded elementary and middle school instruction in music. Only then—and it is a program requiring patience and perseverance—can Action Learning in music be said to have been successful.

MUSIC FOR PREADOLESCENTS AND EARLY TEENS

Since the later elementary, junior high, and middle school years deal with roughly the same age group, and thus with the same problems, many aspects of a successful music program are applicable to any of the administrative units, regardless of how they are labeled. However, there are so many more possibilities in the more expansive and flexible middle school concept. Therefore, in order to present the reader with the greatest number and variety of possibilities, this text will detail the middle school approach to the early adolescent and its follow-up in general music programs in high school. Among other things, this allows for a more coherent *program* from roughly fifth grade all the way through high school.

But whether the reader is or will be teaching in a middle school, late elementary school, junior high school, or high school program or setting, most of the practical teaching ideas and their supporting principles are equally applicable in each of these contexts. Some special efforts may be required to adapt some of them to the usually less flexible junior high school. But ideas to guide the reader will be provided at appropriate points in the description of the methods in question.

One last matter needs to be taken up before the scene is finally set: the unique attributes a music program *can* have in an educational setting that involves only pre- and early adolescents or at least a majority in this age group. The most obvious connection is that never before has a generation of young people been so "turned on" by music—and by such an increasing variety of types, styles, and idioms. This truly is "music's generation."

Some adults, parents and teachers alike, are concerned that young people's musical tastes are too singularly oriented to the "pop" or "youth" music of the time. A thesis can be advanced to explain this, that at the same time provides some insight into the special relevance music can have for just about anyone.

"MUSIC SOUNDS AS FEELINGS FEEL"

If, as it has been said, "Music sounds as feelings feel," then it should not be too difficult to understand why all people, and particularly teenagers, are addicted in one way or another to music. Music embodies or captures human feeling. In this sense, it does not really "communicate" feelings as much as it collects, sorts out, abstracts, and purifies them. The composer, in the way he or she organizes or presents musical ideas, can heighten certain feeling-tones and the connections—subtle or sudden—between contrasting feeling-tones. As a result, we can be brought to a greater awareness of our Self; of that unique being who is responding to this piece of music at this particular time in this very specific way.[42]

We cooperate in this venture, first by seeking out musical contacts or by being open to them when we encounter them unintentionally. Thus, we have the attitude or state of mind that is suited to contemplating and *feeling* the music. We are not (or should not be) distracted by the problems and actions of our mundane existence. We can focus our full attention on the music as a "symbol" carrying human significance or human content in the feelings it embodies or evokes.

Sometimes it seems that *the music acts ON us,* as though we are objects and "it" is the acting subject. Then (using very misleading language) we say loosely that music "makes us" tap our foot, "gives us" a chill or response of some kind, "tells us" a story, or "paints us" a picture. As casual talk between adults this is probably not very harmful. But when this language is used in instruction with young people it is very counterproductive. It slowly brainwashes them into thinking that music *must, invariably does, or is supposed to act ON them.* They come to believe that they are passive and the music is *active;* that all they have to do is receive it and the music will work its special magic.

As preteens grow up with this semantic confusion, they begin to notice that more often than not much of the music studied in music class does *not* "make," "give," "paint," "tell," or "do" anything *to* them. It doesn't act *ON* them either. They conclude, quite logically it seems, that either the composer and his music failed (and are therefore deserving of no more attention) or the teacher has chosen a poor piece of music for instructional purposes.

On the other hand, there are numerous times when *we reach out to and act upon the music.* This is again where Action Learning comes in. We project our Self toward, in, or through music. We are the acting subject, and the music is regarded more as "object."[43] In this frame of mind, *listening is active rather than passive.* Through our action, we survey and experience our own Self, our uniqueness as a result of our contact with music.

In a real sense, we create our own response to the unique significance music has for us at this moment, much in the same way we do when responding aesthetically to nature. And in this active response, we affirm that we exist and have feelings and a uniqueness of perceptions, conceptions, and awareness that no other creature has or will ever have had.

This latter more active approach to music is far more successful and also far more satisfying than the passive kind. It is the one teachers of early adolescents ought to emphasize, although both types are found in adolescents' responses to popular music.

There are times when teenagers seek out music in order to let it "work on" them. They are in a blue funk, and they seek to rise above it by listening to happier music; or they masochistically decide to wallow in self-pity by playing "funky" blues. At other times they project their own problems, their growing Self, their fears, apprehensions, and other feelings toward the music. They are pleased then to find that the music parallels, echoes, expresses, embodies, reflects—whatever you want to call it—the very same kinds and qualities of inner life they experience during this very feeling-laden time in their lives. They come to regard it, especially, as one form of reality they can experience without the prior intervention of society's "semantic grid," which always verbally mediates "pure" experience. They find that they can experience the reality of music directly, unfiltered by society. Unhappily, they assume that they are thus avoiding or resisting society's manipulation.[44]

And that is an important answer to why early adolescents are involved so heavily in musical pursuits, and also why musical experiences in school—handled correctly—can have a special importance for them. At no time in life, perhaps, will they have a greater need to be in *direct* touch with their feelings; will they need to express their joyous feelings, fears, anxieties; will they need the confirmation that somewhere else out there in life others have experienced these same feelings and survived (i.e., that's how such feelings got "into" or are gotten "out of" the music in the first place). At no time will their feelings be so pressing and crucial. This is the time that basic personality traits can solidify and can determine the degree of neurosis or mental health the individual will experience in adulthood.

And music, as perhaps the most directly acting of the arts, does not require verbal intellectualization in order to profit these listeners. That is perfectly evident to them. They have very little music learning, but they have no difficulty in responding to their preferred style of "youth music." Teachers who try to semantically intellectualize music—youth music or otherwise—and make of it a mere disciplinary study for memorization and testing are not greeted with open arms, nor are they often granted cooperation. Such an approach by a teacher too often results in a tug-of-war where the teacher endeavors to motivate, control, or "discipline" the class, while the students resist and subvert such efforts. Eventually the students usually win. In this way there is far more "training" of teachers by students than many teachers prefer to acknowledge.

If you agree that somehow, some "thing" in or about music can pierce the emotional armor of adolescents, or can cause them to lower the drawbridge in order to willingly venture into the land of feelings on the other side of the fortification; if you agree that this corresponds in general to your own experiences with music, or your experiences with early adolescence (your own or that of others), then you also know intuitively why all people value some kind of music. Their experiences with certain kinds of music are satisfying, rewarding, or relevant precisely because they always find or project at least a little and sometimes a lot of themselves in or onto the music.

Whether we consider that music *acts on us* or *we act on it*, we can all agree that *the "meaning" of music resides in our connection, our inner relationship, with it.* There is no single, absolute, finite "meaning" *in* a composition (i.e., a performance or a score). The meaning is *in* (or a result of) our contact: the aural/mental "touching" of our mind/body with the music/feeling. This action is a musical (and human) *experience.* It is in the experience—by whatever means people will always argue—that the "meaning" of music is found.[45]

When you consider that all stages of adolescence are a pivotal time for the emotions, self-esteem, and self-confidence of the individual, you should not underestimate the importance of music as it enriches the meaning of life and as it benefits young people in much more direct ways. Music, thus considered (and taught with these goals in mind), has special credentials that recommend it as a vital part of an educational program for early adolescents. Any educational program that does not take their feelings and emotions into serious consideration is doomed before it begins. Any program that is rooted in the realities of the inner life of young people has an excellent chance of producing a real and long-lasting impact. A music program *can* be organized in this way and *can* serve up such benefits.

EXTRINSIC BENEFITS OF MUSIC INSTRUCTION

There are even some other, more direct benefits that are extrinsic to the musical art but nonetheless are potential factors in the involvement of preteenagers with music.

1. As has already been noted, music instruction at this level *can* (with planning and luck) *rescue many male voices* that would otherwise go the way of sex stereotypes that prevent men from any display of emotions of a "sensitive" type (such as those evoked by the arts or by "girls").

2. Musical experiences, in general music classes and performance classes, can contribute to the *development of small-muscle or fine-muscle control.* On the other hand, without a real understanding of the coordination problems that surface at the time of the growth spurt,[46] music teachers can unintentionally turn off more students than they rescue. Witness how many students studying instruments privately or in school give up—or almost give up—studying music (i.e., practicing, which is the same thing to some teachers) during the early years of adolescence.

3. Music can be well suited to the youngsters' *increasing intellectual interests, imagination, and creativity*, all of which are becoming capable of much more abstract operation. Thus, musical experiences can simultaneously draw on and stretch such mental activities.

4. Music, by its very nature—and if taught with regard to its inherent nature—involves the *uniqueness of each individual* and each response, and thus can contribute to or facilitate the process of individuation that is ongoing. On the other hand, insensitively taught it can be used (abused, misused) to enforce uniformity and conformity. The "sublime" is turned into the "ridiculous." If anyone claims to you that there is a singularly "correct" response to a certain piece of music, ask that individual whether this holds true for a sunset as well.

5. Music does provide for *peer-group activities and participation in group processes.* The resulting benefits—in addition to hoped-for musical ones—in-

volve weakening the overinfluence of cliques; cutting across other social boundaries; widening the circle of social contacts; deemphasizing sex stereotyping; developing a sense of responsibility that is larger than Self because it is due to the group; and, finally, recognition and achievement.

6. This last point can be extended to affirm that music can be an area in which *every person can experience considerable success* no matter how much difficulty he or she may be having with "academic" subjects. It is one of the few areas in life that admits this possibility of achievement without fear of failing (Who worries in group "sings" around a campfire?). Yet some teachers, in order to "motivate" their students and to "raise" the status of music in the eyes of other students and other teachers, make of music a difficult study as a "discipline," as a "subject," as a "content area" to be "covered." This inevitably works against the best interests of the teacher, the students, and the music. It is the *musical experience* in which students find sustenance and continued "life"—not the musical information that they inevitably forget through lack of use.

7. However, music also has this uneasy quality of existing as *skill and knowledge* required in programs that lead to careers as a musician or teacher. Since this is the model with which most teachers are familiar, they have difficulty getting back to music as experience, music as a unique phenomenon in the mind of each responder. And since many music programs—especially those of instrumental-music teachers—involve musical-performance instruction, it is all too easy to impose a watered-down conservatory atmosphere. That atmosphere may seem to work well enough for professional training. It has *not* been demonstrated to work well for most aspects of an *avocational education.*

All the above mentioned benefits can accrue to students and teachers alike—whether in general music classes or performance classes of virtually any kind—if emphasis is placed where it belongs: on the human experiencing of music. As often as possible students should have the opportunity to experience and act on or with music. If the prospective or inservice teacher never loses sight of that one simple prerequisite, the music program in its many aspects can significantly serve the early adolescent, and—as is testified to daily—even harness the often-misdirected and thus wasted human potential of the age group and turn it to good use.

Now the scene is set. The actors have been described and are about to move into their places. Do you still want to be the director-perceiver-critic of this educational event? There is a lot at stake: the heritage of music, and the feelings and emotions of generations of early adolescents-grown-into-adults. On the other hand, the rewards are enormous! It is particularly satisfying to succeed in work with young people of this age if only because it is demanding work. But it is also an extremely important formative period in the development of any individual. This is why and how it gives the teacher an added impact in contributing to the quality of life our students-grown-into-adults establish for us and our progeny.

NOTES: CHAPTER I

1. Jerome Bruner, "Play Is Serious Business," *Psychology Today*, vol. 8 (Jan. 1975), p. 80.

2. Johan Huizinga, *Homo Ludens: A Study of the Play-Element in Culture* (Boston: Beacon Press, 1960). See also Susanna Millar, *The Psychology of Play* (Baltimore: Penguin Books, 1973).

3. Thomas A. Regelski, "Self-Actualization in Creating and Responding to Art," *Journal of Humanistic Psychology*, Vol. 13 (Fall 1973), p. 57.

4. *The Process of Education* (New York: Random House, Vintage Books, 1960), p. 20.

5. George Mandler, *Mind and Emotion* (New York: John Wiley & Sons, 1975), pp. 171-72, 205.

6. "Imperfect knowledge of growth typical physiological changes in the second decade of life may lead to errors in interpretation of major aspects of the life situation of a person."—H. Bouterline Young, "The Physiology of Adolescence (Including Puberty and Growth)," in *Modern Perspectives in Adolescent Psychiatry*, ed. John G. Howells (New York: Brunner/Mazel, 1971), p. 3.

7. From Latin, *pubertas*, "an adult," and *pubescere*, "to become downy (hairy)"; *os pubis*, "pubic bone." Thus, the covering of the pubic area with hair.

8. From the Latin, *adolescens*, present participle of *adolescere*, "to grow up"; the past participle of *adolescere* is *adultus*, "grown up."

9. Young, "Physiology of Adolescence," p. 3.

10. Ibid.

11. "Practically all tissues, except the brain, seem involved in the adolescent growth spurt period. In most cases the growth is positive, that is, there is a spurt but in a few cases . . . there is a decrease."—Ibid., p. 7.

12. Ibid., p. 8.

13. Ibid., p. 9.

14. Ibid., p. 10.

15. Ibid.

16. Ibid., p. 13.

17. Ibid.

18. Robert B. Zajonc, "Birth Order and Intelligence: Dumber by the Dozen," *Psychology Today*, Vol. 8 (Jan. 1975), p. 37.

19. Young, "Physiology of Adolescence," p. 13.

20. Ibid., p. 16.

21. Ibid., pp. 19-20.
22. Ibid., p. 20.
23. Ibid.
24. Ibid.
25. Ibid., p. 22.
26. Ibid., p. 23.
27. Ibid., p. 22.
28. A descriptive process that deals with behavior in the context of an individual's life.
29. See, for example, Frank Goble, *The Third Force: The Psychology of Abraham Maslow* (New York: Grossman, 1970), pp. 40-41.
30. Ibid., p. 50.
31. Edgar Z. Friedenberg, *The Vanishing Adolescent* (New York: Dell Publishing Co., 1968), pp. 3-16.
32. Recall from the brief explanation in the Introduction how the demands of society for a semantic consensus contribute to the child's conflict as he or she struggles to remain "natural" and nonacculturated; see pp. 9-10.
33. Rolf E. Muus, *Theories of Adolescence*, 2d. ed. (New York: Random House, 1968), p. 178.
34. Herbert Hendin, *The Age of Sensation: A Psychoanalytic Exploration* (New York: W. W. Norton & Co., 1975); a probing of the emotional lives of young people in America today.
35. As in Paul's Epistle (I Corinthians, 13): "When I was a child, I spoke as a child, I understood as a child, I thought as a child: but when I became a man, I put away childish things."—*The Bible: Selections from the Old and New Testaments*, ed. Allan G. Chester (New York: Holt, Rinehart, & Winston, 1962), pp. 392-93. However true this may be, it is unfortunate that in growing up we are not able to preserve more of the freshness, spontaneity, and natural or pre-sematic-grid aspects of childhood, so that we can be "in tune" with our basic nature. Bill Bradley—athlete, Rhodes Scholar, and politician—has been quoted as saying, "Think as adults, but feel as children."
36. Joseph C. DeVita, Philip Pumerantz, and Leighton B. Wilklow, *The Effective Middle School* (West Nyack, N.Y.: Parker, 1971), p. 17.
37. Ibid., p. 25.
38. Ibid., pp. 30-32.
39. Ibid., p. 66; citing "Middle School Costs in New York State," State Education Department, Division of Educational Finance (Albany, N.Y., 1968), italics in original.
40. DeVita et al., chapters 4, 6, 8, 9, 10.
41. Ibid., (citing "Middle School Costs in New York State"), p. 17; italics in original.
42. Regelski, "Self-Actualization in Creating and Responding to Art," p. 57.
43. In the sense that it has taken human feeling and *object*-ified it for contemplation by others (not in the sense that a musical score results as a tangible object).

44. In fact, they perhaps more than anyone else are shaped in their tastes by the commercial forces that determine the popular music to which they listen.

45. Similarly, it could be said that the "meaning" of life is found in our conscious contact with our environment, including other human beings and their works—such as art; and that education in the arts, with emphasis on its human content, its "feeling-tone," is a prime means for increasing depth or refinement in appreciating or creating the "meaning" of life.

46. There are three mental factors involved in *musical performance:* the *intellectual readiness* needed to learn; the *attitudinal* and *motivational* factors promoting difficult practice sessions; and the *kinesthetic ability* to spatially locate (by feeling) one's limbs in space. The latter is especially difficult during early adolescence, but all are demanding, sometimes more than adolescents can handle.

2

Action with Sound:
The Music of Yesterday,
Today and Tomorrow

☐ The Creative Action Potential of Adolescents

☐ General Advantages of Creative Activities

☐ Beginnings: Exploration of Sound

Environmental Sounds
School Sounds
Body Sounds
Classroom Sounds
Home and Community Sounds
"Found" Sounds: Tape Recording

☐ Sound Compositions

Advantages of Sound Compositions
Types of Sound Compositions Briefly Compared
Improvised Compositions with an "Outline Plan" Considered in Detail
Freely Improvised Sound Compositions
Improvised Sound Compositions Summarized
Notated Sound Compositions Considered in Detail
Potential Problems with Notated Sound Compositions
Advantages of Notated Sound Compositions

☐ Notational Systems and Sound Sources

☐ Symbols and Scores

☐ Sample Notated or Composite Sound-Composition Projects

☐ Summary: When to Use Notated or Composite Sound Compositions

    Concept-Areas Covered in Employing Sound Compositions

    General Activities Derived from Sound Compositions

☐ Chapter Notes

THE CREATIVE ACTION POTENTIAL OF ADOLESCENTS

Adolescents will seldom cause problems for the teacher if they are kept productively busy with significant activities of interest to them. The teacher's best defense against disciplinary disturbances is a good teaching offense. Now, this is not to say that the goal of teaching is to survive the school day without any behavioral flareups. But it is true that no productive learning can occur at all if these young people are misbehaving. And a major cause of misbehavior with early adolescents is simply that they are bored.

We have seen that all adolescents are deeply involved with music in some way or another, so it is unlikely that they are bored with music as such. They may be bored, however, with the kind of music that is studied in music class. In particular, they are easily bored by teaching methods that have little or no action potential and thus do not involve considerable participation on their part.

The *lecture* or *lecture-demonstration* is especially responsible for a large majority of problems with early adolescents. In this kind of class the teacher is the active element and the students are passive. Filling notebooks with musical information does not necessarily imply students' involvement (action). In fact, it often insures that there is *no* productive participation on their part at all. As many people have noted, a lecture is the quickest way to get information from the teacher's head into students' notebooks without touching anything in between. They become stenographers; they copy information down but do not think about it.

They may "study" it for a test, but this usually means that they try to memorize it. And we all know that memorizing (recalling) information is not the same as understanding. Memorized information is quickly forgotten, especially if it held little personal meaning for the student in the first place.

"Enriching" a lecture with visual aids, diagrams, or other demonstrations has very little bearing on improving the success of the lecture for early adolescents.

It also has been said that a lecture is talking in someone else's sleep. This is a clever way of noting how little inclination there is for students to "pay attention" and "think" when the lecturer-teacher is doing all the work. It is exactly this practice that gives students the notion (as an unfortunate byproduct of the "hidden curriculum") that teachers are supposed to *teach* with or without their cooperation. Everyone comes to feel that *learning* is something teachers *do to* or *for students* rather than something that they do *for themselves* (i.e., by intending to learn and working hard at it) — or, at the very least, that learning is a *cooperative enterprise* with the teacher.

When students do not do well in a subject (i.e., do not get "good grades"), they say that the *teacher* was not "good," that the *teacher* "didn't get the information across," was not "interesting"[1] or did not "motivate them," or that the classes were not "relevant." Does all this sound familiar? It should. These same complaints are voiced just as often by late adolescents[2] in college as they are by adolescents in the middle and senior high schools.

Students come to equate the quantity of notes they take with the amount of learning they acquire. Teachers often reinforce this by checking and grading students' notebooks according to such criteria as neatness, organization, and comprehensiveness.[3]

If it isn't already apparent to you now, it will be so the minute you step in front of a class of early adolescents and begin to talk *to* them (i.e., lecture) *about* music. *They are just not interested in information about music!* Their interest stems from their involvement *in* or *with* music, whether through composing, performing, or listening to it. Thus the music class for early adolescents simply must be built largely around *active involvement* with music, with musical *experiences* of one degree or another, with music as a *phenomenon* that is somewhat unique in quality to each person.

Music-education texts and articles, as well as writings in general education, are usually full of exhortations for "creative activities." Many teachers are "turned off" by the platitudes and jargon that often abound in such theorizing. It is very difficult, therefore, for the present writer to deal with these ideas without using language that has been overused and abused, and which thus sounds shopworn. This text seeks to spare the reader as much of this as is possible. All activities described here have worked for and are being used by successful teachers across the nation (though never in exactly the same form). They represent the vanguard of music education, not its panacea.

The creative activities dealt with in this text should be qualified before we begin to outline them.

1. They are creative in the sense that they involve the *creation by students* of musical products or responses.
2. The products or responses *created* by students *may or may not be "creative"* in the "ar-

tistic" sense (i.e., original, unique, "inspired"); they may or may not result in increased artistic creativity on the part of the students.

3. Here creativity is equated with *problem solving* and *decision making* as the two major factors in a program of Action Learning through active involvement with music. Thus the creations of students will be judged first and foremost by specified criteria and not by standards of artistic creativity or originality.

4. In other words, these creative activities need not result in "a work of art"; they are learning actions, and artistic creativity or its development will be a *beneficial byproduct* for those students who have (or are developing) creative skills employed musically.

5. Thus no fancy claims are made for *developing* the "artistic creativity" of students, although this certainly will happen for some. The claim made here is that the activities described and suggested *can* have significant results for students' *understanding* and *appreciation* (however defined) of music.

All the activities dealt with here and in subsequent chapters ought to be thought of principally in terms of *active involvement in or with music by creating musical works* (i.e., scores or performances) and *actions or responses* (i.e., while listening). Such activities are well suited to the nature of adolescence and correspond in many respects with the rationale cited in chapter 1.

Such creative activities involve the inter*action* of musical knowledge and skill with the multiple interpretations, combinations, and possibilities brought into the student's range of consideration by the problem solving and decision making required in an activity. A classroom involving creative activities is neither a "workroom" nor an artist's or composer's "studio." It is a gestation center for knowledge and skill in the service of creative discovery. The results of such an involvement will be multiple (i.e., vary from student to student, or with one student from occasion to occasion) and often unplanned or unexpected. Thus such classroom activities deal with the development of knowledge and skill without either eliminating or planning for serendipity. It will arise, and when it does it can be that aspect of class that breeds the degree of interest and excitement that is needed for a program to be successful.

GENERAL ADVANTAGES OF CREATIVE ACTIVITIES

1. Creative activities are largely *inductive* (i.e., personal actions), and that is the main way children and adolescents learn.

2. Students come to class with *varied readiness levels* (i.e., ability to learn based upon the success of past learning and experience—more about this in chapter 5), and creative activities are easily adjusted to suit the resulting individual needs.

3. Creative activities are individualizing and humanizing because they permit *multiple results* based on student needs, interests, and abilities. They thus avoid the dehumanization that results from conformity and uniformity.

4. Creative activities encourage *discovery learning* (when each student learns in his or her own terms) and *problem solving* (when students learn to use what they have learned).

5. Creative activities *facilitate transfer of learning* by encouraging the student to *seek relationships* between past and present experiences.

6. Creative activities provide for *integrating learning into life* (both after school and after graduation) by focusing on *what the student is able to do* as the result of musical instruction.

7. Creative activities are *summational* in that they facilitate the *synthesis of otherwise separate musical learnings* by drawing on the *sum* of a student's learning in the solution of a musical problem.

8. Provision for the *music of the future*—the music today's students will encounter as adults tomorrow—occurs in those creative activities that deal with nontraditional sounds and sound-structures.

9. As with all activities that involve an overt, assessable outcome, creative activities *facilitate the teacher's evaluation of student learning* (and simultaneously the efficacy of the teacher's instruction!) and provide *tangible evidence* for administrators, parents, and children of a productive program.

10. Creative activities can actually *nurture individual artistic creativity* for those children who are interested or talented in music.

As a rule of thumb, *these advantages of creative activities should be the major results of such activities.* Therefore you should seek to realize all of these advantages as the major goals of your music-education program.

BEGINNINGS: EXPLORATION OF SOUND

Music consists of arrangements of *sound* and *silence.* Silence is to music as a frame is to a painting. But silence is also interspersed with sound in establishing the actual "body" of a musical composition. It is logical, therefore, to begin by exploring sound and its many dimensions. Fortunately, it works out that adolescents very much enjoy this kind of activity, probably for at least two major reasons.

1. It allows their imaginations full scope of operation.
2. It is not predicated on prior musical learning. Therefore the chance of failure is minimized and the incidence of success (even if only defined as "no failure") is maximized.

Activities involving the exploration of sound can be done with individuals or small groups (specific information on the formation and use of groups is found in chapter 5) or as full-class projects. *All activities should initially be large-group (full-class) projects.* They are easily set up and run. The only requirement is that the teacher approach these explorations imaginatively enough to generate student involvement. As students become increasingly involved, and as they demonstrate they understand the general purposes and processes of an activity, then small-group and individual activities can be pursued—*carefully at first!*

ENVIRONMENTAL SOUNDS

Begin with activities in which students recall sounds encountered in their everyday lives—e.g., at home, going to and from school.

1. What qualities do these sounds possess?

2. What "expressive value" *do* they have? For example, sounds at sporting events or in a factory, sounds of fire trucks and other emergency or rescue apparatus, sounds of aircraft (airports).

3. If we could extract these sounds from their actual context and only hear the sounds alone, what expressive value would they have then? Is the expressive value associated with the "pure" sound, or with the former context?

4. What physical properties do sounds have? Are they "higher" or "lower" (pitch)? What do we mean when we use the words "higher" and "lower" regarding pitch? How and what is measured? Do the sounds last for a longer or shorter time (duration)? Are they louder or softer (intensity and amplitude)? Are they unique in quality depending on the timbre of the sound-producing source?

5. Does the order in which we hear *consecutive sounds* make a difference in how we react to those sounds? For example, arrange the following sounds in different sequences and explain how they can tell a different "story" (i.e., have a different meaning or significance) depending on their order: a police whistle; an automobile tire squealing; a siren; a voice crying "Help!" over and over. Stage and act out your plots to make the meaning more graphic.

6. When sounds are combined at the same time (*simultaneity*) do some sounds tend to stand out? Or do we tend to hear one massive sound newly created out of the combined sounds? Does it matter in terms of expression which sounds are combined? Which sounds stand out more?

7. What is the *role of silence* in the way we perceive and react to environmental sounds? If there were no such thing at all as silence, would we tend to notice combined sounds more or less? The same? Not at all? Is silence the *total* absence of sound or the *relative* absence of noticeable sound? In other words, is silence really very soft sound? Is silence really *empty*? Or is it *full*? Does silence have any dimensions similar to those of sound? Does it have duration? Are some silences more "intense" than others? Does silence create a different effect depending on whether the sounds on either side of it are loud or soft? Give examples.

8. Is there any difference between *noise* and *sound*? Does each word have a different meaning for you? Should it?

Questions and activities such as these should be pursued at various times during early adolescence. Certainly it is useful to deal with many of these questions at the beginning of studies, but it is also useful to deal with them at increasing levels of sophistication right through high school. That way the teacher and the students can see the increased refinement and subtlety of class responses.

Above all, however, *these questions should not be approached as though they had correct, absolute answers!* They are explorative questions or *ventures.*[4] They are designed to stimulate thought and to provoke discussion. Discussion should be based on a "What do *you* think?" premise rather than on a "What is the teacher after?" premise. The teacher, at most, should contribute his or her point of view *during* the discussion at various points, and *not* at the end. If the teacher gives his or her insight at the end of the discussion, it is inevitably "read" by students as *the teacher's summing up.* This they take for the "correct answer," or the one the teacher is "after." They will tend, therefore, to try and remember (take notes on) the teacher's summary. Hence, the teacher should comment on and participate in the discussion itself, then should simply move on to another question or activity when the discussion starts to wind down or become redundant.

During the discussion, the teacher should jot down ideas contributed by students. These ideas may be the basis of more specific activities later on. Similarly, when a contribution made in these early ventures is reaffirmed later on by experiences or activities, the teacher should attempt in some way to bring this relationship to light.

SCHOOL SOUNDS

Another source of environmental sounds to be explored is the school itself. These sounds will often be the most immediately available and expressive of any the students can explore because they can be heard right now in the present. They are not the sounds observed or recalled and talked about. They are present experience.

1. As a class activity, listen to the "composition" *4'33"* by John Cage. (Don't rush out to buy the record, though. The piece consists of four minutes and thirty-three seconds of whatever environmental sounds are heard.) What is heard? Does what is heard mean something different for each listener? How do we know when the composition begins or ends (or does the composer even really want it to have a beginning or an end—is he just taking a "slice of time" on either side of which is the ongoing business of life?) If we cover clocks and watches (and this *is* recommended), how do we judge how long (in terms of actual clock-time) the composition lasts? If one person is assigned to watch the clock and to signal when the composition is over, did the *experience* or *feeling* of the passage of time (i.e., the "created time" of the composer) seem to be longer or shorter than the "actual" clock-time?

2. What sounds can we hear from the halls? From outside the windows at this moment? (Focus on one or the other at one time.) Can we tell what is happening simply by listening to these sounds? Do these sounds *feel* "good" or "bad," or are they neutral? Why? How? When sounds are judged "good," is it because of their qualities, or because of something in the hearer, or both?

3. Have the members of the class close their eyes (and, if necessary, shut off the lights). Silently choose students to walk loudly (but otherwise naturally) across the back of the room several times. Can the class identify them by the rhythm and accents of their footsteps alone?

4. Bring several students (ones who often are verbal in class) to the back of the room. Members of the class are directed to close their eyes. Ask each student you have chosen to say something (one at a time) while disguising his or her voice. Can the class identify the speaker, even with the disguise of vocal timbre? When they are able to identify the speaker, how do they do it? By the rhythmic nature of their speech? The inflection? What other qualities are involved in our recognition of vocal sounds?

Repeat the activity without disguising the voices and have the class identify the speakers. How was it possible to do this? Could we compile a list of words that describe a person's voice so that a stranger could read the list, listen to several voices, and pick out the person described in the list? Try it! Get a "guinea pig" (a student from another class, another teacher, a teacher's aide, a janitor, or whomever you can) to study a list of vocal characteristics (made up by the class) that describes the voice of one student. Have the "guinea pig" listen to something read or said by five different students and try to determine which of the five the list pertains to.

The last two groups of suggestions work especially well in helping students experience what has been called "tacit knowing"[5] or "qualitative intelligence."[6]

This mental quality is fascinating for any area of arts education, but it is especially important when dealing with early adolescents. It is precisely this kind of mental activity that characterizes much of the thinking and worrying that transpires naturally at this stage of their lives. When their attention is directed to it, they can instantly "feel" it work.

It involves the fact that "we can know more than we can tell."[7] Whether with adults, children, or adolescents, it

> is exercised whenever qualities are selected, organized, and experienced in whatever areas of life one functions within. How we choose to dress, the style with which we express our thoughts, the environment we create in the homes in which we live are products of qualitative thought . . . . In countless ways the selection and rejection of qualities are made as we function in life.[8]

It is the kind of "knowledge" (i.e., "intuition" or "insight") that allows us to recognize the features of a person—even after many years of separation—although we could never say *how* we "know" (recognize) the person or what the qualities are that elicit our response. This kind of "knowing," in which we deal intuitively with *qualities,* cannot be satisfactorily explained, rationalized, or justified in a logical way. We can recognize voices, faces, etc., without having any clear idea about how or on what bases we accomplish that feat. When given a pitch from the piano, most people can—on cue—instantly whistle that pitch. How do we do that? How do we "know" what size and what kind of lip aperture will produce that exact pitch? There are many other kinds of "tacit knowing" and students should be encouraged to seek them out. Special emphasis on our response to sound (music) is a fruitful exercise of "qualitative intelligence."[9]

5. How do we "know" that such-and-such a sound was being produced by such-and-such a source? Can we make a list of qualities we find in that sound? Will that list "mean" anything to someone trying to "find" that sound by using our list? Is there, therefore, a kind of reality that must be experienced directly, because it cannot be captured (indirectly) by any other means (say, for instance, by words)? Is music such a reality? What are some other such realities in your lives? Are the qualities you "feel" in music related to specific types of realities in your life?

6. Is there anything you can *say* that would give a deaf person the same *experience* of a composition that you had? What can you *say* to a blind person that creates the same *experience* as a painting or a sunset?

Whenever possible raise these questions again on occasions that arise in the future. Give yourself and the students an opportunity to see how their views have matured.

BODY SOUNDS

Another stage in exploring sound can focus on "body" sounds. How many different kinds of sound can we make by using our bodies both as the *object* from which the sound arises and the *subject* that conceives of the sound initially?

1. What are some *interesting* sounds we can make using our bodies from the neck down? (N. B.: this removes the possibility of using the voice, mouth, etc.) Invent several sounds *you think are interesting* and several *you think are not.* Can you explain the difference between the two? Now do the same thing again, but without explaining which group you think is more interesting. Let's see if the class can determine (and discuss) which group of sounds is more interesting.

After several such experiments: What do you think are some of the qualities of sound that we have tended to find more interesting than others? Can these same qualities be reproduced by musical instruments or other sound-producing objects? If so, which ones? How? Why? Why not?

2. Think up some *interesting* sounds that use only your voice, mouth, lips, and tongue. Are some naturally soft (e.g., popping the lips open and closed)? Which ones are louder? What is or is not happening that makes some louder than others? Does it make a difference (in the volume) if the sound is supported by an air column from the lungs? In what ways are the human vocal cords and head cavity similar to parts of a guitar or violin? What is the function of the resonating chambers of each? Is the loudness or softness of the sound influenced greatly by the resonating area? Where would the resonators be in the head? (Forget about the chest resonators for now.)

3. In what way is an *acoustic* guitar different from an *electric* guitar? Are there two kinds of human head: an "acoustical head" and an "electric head"? In replacing natural resonating chambers, does electric amplification give us additional expressive possibilities for sound (i.e., from an "electric head" using a microphone, or from any electrified instrument)? If so, how? If not, why not?

The first mention of electric instruments can bring a ripple of new interest (if interest has been marginal or fading); or it can become a monomania that many adolescents would like to focus on exclusively. If it is the former, stick with it for a while. If it is the latter, defer detailed follow-up until appropriately planned opportunities in subsequent classes. Spread out this interest over many lessons. Do not let it burn too brightly right away and thus quickly burn itself out!

CLASSROOM SOUNDS

Explore the classroom (or, if possible, the school building and grounds) for objects from which interesting sounds can be coaxed by various means. Insist that the sound sources should be portable, generally available to most people, and repeatable.[10]

1. After allowing a few minutes for all the class members to settle on interesting objects, ask each person to find *five different ways of producing an interesting sound on his or her "instrument."* After each student has demonstrated an instrument, discuss the results.

2. Then have the class *select those they especially liked.* In order to have enough with which to work, yet not so many as to be unwieldy, it is useful to aim for a list numbering about half the total number of students in the class (e.g., if the class has 30 students, work toward compiling a list of about 15 preferred instruments). Whatever you do, *do not make it sound as though the unchosen instruments or sounds are "bad" and the chosen ones "good".* There should be no "failure" possible from this activity. To prefer chocolate ice-cream is not a criticism of all other flavors.

3. As a group, have the class *classify the instruments* according to similarities: e.g., metallic, wood; scraped, shaken, etc. Using these classifications, have the class compose a short composition in a predetermined musical form. For example, an ABA form could have all the

metallic instruments playing various rhythmic patterns for the A sections and all the wooden instruments playing the B section. Or the difference between the A and B sections could be the manner in which the sounds are created (scraping vs. shaking).

4. *Create a "standard orchestra"* out of all the various new "instruments" that the class has invented or discovered over the course of several lessons. Specify how many of each instrument the orchestra will have as its "standard" and who among the students will perform in each section. These permanently assigned performers will be expected to be "proficient" on their instruments, but from time to time they can also free-lance when needed on ever newly invented instruments.

5. Do not seek the same "orchestration" in each class. Let each class you teach evolve its own preferred instruments and performance practices, and thus its own musical personality. In the middle school, assembly programs or concerts can serve to allow each group its deserved recognition and exposure. If you regularly tape-record the compositions/performances of each group, these recordings can serve well as listening lessons for other groups (see chapter 4 for detailed information on listening lessons).

6. Periodically aim certain compositional activities at the use of this "standard" orchestra, or various elaborations of it:

   a. Evolve a "standard" notation for each instrument.

   b. Set compositional problems that explore such aspects of music as timbre, form, mood, and "sound effects" that must imitate sounds from life programmatically.

More about these activities follows in this chapter.

7. Evolve other, *smaller and more "specialized"* ensembles. For example, just as an orchestra has a viola section, or just as there are string quartets or woodwind quintets, so your class can invent smaller groups. This should always be done according to some musical rationale, and not because friends simply want to work (fool around?) with one another. These small groups can be more or less "standard" or they can be invented as needed. In either case, they are important enough to deserve *roughly half of the activities* you use. Why? Because it is useful to have small groups perform while the remainder of the class listens. When the entire class is the orchestra, no one can listen attentively to the "expressive whole" of the piece. This is particularly true for untrained listeners, who will not be able to divide their attention appropriately between performance and listening.[11]

HOME AND COMMUNITY SOUNDS

Have students *explore their homes or community for sound-producing objects* they find particularly interesting. Make sure you remind them to secure their parents' permission if they bring something from home, and whatever they bring should not be dangerous (such as certain power tools, electric carving knives, etc.).

1. Most of the activities outlined in the section on classroom sounds can be achieved using these new and (because of the greater potential for choice) presumably more interesting instruments. It will not be possible to evolve a "standard" orchestra, but that turns out to be an advantage in this instance.

2. The "standard" orchestra, as with anything else involving adolescents, will become boring if overused. This is an additional reason (see item 7 above) for variety in ensembles. The occasions on which new "instruments" are brought from home hold forth ever-new expressive possibilities.

3. In general, keep some kind of written record—or better yet, let a volunteer student keep a record—of all the "instruments" (sound sources), performance means (how the instruments are played), and classifications (see item 3 above) established by the class. This can be kept in a

notebook, but the easiest and most useful way is to put the information on $3'' \times 5''$ cards so the entire class has access to a central source of information. File each card according to a system that keeps track of all three aspects: sound source, performance means, and classification.

4. These records can serve several purposes: (a) to assist students with particular needs for solving an assigned problem; (b) to generate ideas for your use in the future with other classes (i.e., the card system aids *your* memory over the years); (c) to have some tangible evidence for principals, parents, school boards, etc., that significant results are being achieved in your classes.

"FOUND" SOUNDS: TAPE RECORDING

Finally, and especially relevant to many adolescents, are projects that involve "found sounds" captured on cassette recorders. More and more students have access to small, inexpensive, portable cassette recorders, and excellent use of them can be made by the inventive music teacher.

1. *First determine how many of these recorders are available to your students.* Assign groups, if need be, so that *every* student is in a group with a person who has access to a recorder. Where possible let friends combine in groups, even when the groups end up being of unequal size. Many of these activities will involve out-of-school work, and it is to be expected that friends usually live in the same neighborhood or can get to see one another conveniently. The simple fact that friends usually know one another's addresses is of major assistance in guaranteeing the success of these activities. But when grouping by friends is not entirely successful in involving everyone with a tape recorder, feel free to assign people to groups on some other realistic basis.

2. *Initiate a "name that sound" contest.* This is not intended to breed competition, or to invent a game with points, winners, and losers. It is calculated to draw upon the natural competitiveness of early adolescents. It requires "cleverness" and "guile" on their part, and they get a real "charge" out of working very hard to trick their classmates. A successful "trick" is its own reward for them. The assignment involves recorded sounds "found" (wherever) and captured by the tape recorder and played back for the class. For this latter phase, the students need only bring the cassette if your classroom is equipped with a cassette player.

3. Assign a *"sound collage"*[12] *as an out-of-school project,* with the length of the composition and the amount of time before it is due limited to suit your instructional plans. You probably should require a "score" to accompany the tape at these early stages.

Such a "score is worked out in advance. It is simply a verbal listing of sounds, their order of occurrence, and the approximate length of each. Once this has been worked out, the group can then set about making its tape.

It also helps, at first, if the assignment has a special requirement, such as a *musical form* the composition is to manifest, or a *title,* or something else to serve as a guideline. Remember, early adolescents prefer some minimal guidelines. To leave them totally free and just say "Compose!" generally causes problems, if only wasted time and effort on their part. The "name that sound" task can be carried out while the class listens to these small-group projects; or if a form, title, story, etc., was required, the listeners can try to determine this as well.

4. Since the previous activity dealt only with the patterns of successive sounds, it is useful to devise activities that involve simultaneous sounds. These can be of two varieties:

    a. Using two or more tape recorders, or auxiliary record players and television or radio at home, groups can combine several sounds on the tape by playing sounds (collected on one or more other cassettes, or, selected from records, radio, etc.) simultaneously and record them on the "master" recorder.

Master tape is running ⟶ while ⟶ multiple sources are combined and recombined in several ways.

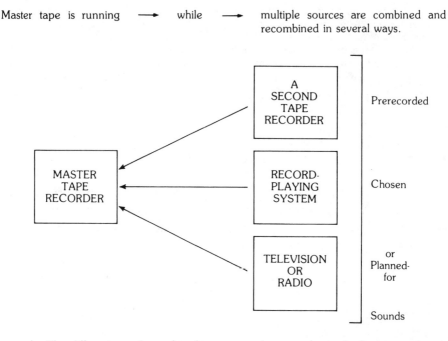

b. The different members of each group produce vocal sounds, body sounds, or invented "instrumental" sounds simultaneously while recording them on one cassette recorder. For this activity, in other words, the group creates a *Sound composition* and records it on tape for playback to the class.

5. These tape activities in general have several advantages over "regular" sound-composition activities done in class:

a. The simple addition of the tape recorder makes them vastly more attractive propositions for some students (especially for boys).

b. Much class time is saved. The time used to compose a piece is usually saved when groups can be gotten to work together outside of school. Time is saved as well in organizing and executing a performance of a composition.

c. Finally, some students who are embarrassed (for any of a million reasons they can think of) to perform in front of the class will be able to perform on the tape. A related advantage stems from the fact that there are no "visual disturbances" associated with the tape playback, as there can be with a live performance (e.g., "cutting up" and "showing off" in any of a hundred ways).

The exploratory activities described here should *not* be thought of as an instructional "unit." While they can provide a certain focus or emphasis, the unit-approach to planning tends to chop up music into falsely self-sufficient pieces. And, as with Humpty Dumpty, it is very difficult, if not impossible, to reestablish the *whole*. This "whole" of music is the major concern. As was emphasized in another context earlier, the whole is not simply the sum of or even more than the sum of its parts. *The whole determines and controls the parts.* And whereas certain activities can emphasize specifics, we must not lose sight of the forest by being overconcerned with one or two trees. We are interested in the total, unified experiencing of the music, and not in any piecemeal approach that emphasizes one element to the exclusion of the infinite other possibilities that exist in the simplest of compositions. (See Appendix A for hints on planning a program.)

Therefore the foregoing activities are well situated in the middle school, where they prepare the students for the more ambitious projects associated with full sound compositions. But—and this is important—they should not be ignored in high school elective classes. Most of the questions and issues raised in these experiences are important enough to be considered at every step along the road to musical literacy, even in college! Just adjust the level of the challenge involved.

It is strongly urged that the teacher return again and again to these issues, always refining, always reformulating the questions and answers anew. This facilitates *transfer of learning* from an early experience to a later one and tends to enhance the student's ability to retain or even use such well-integrated learning.

Now we leave temporarily the general exploration of sound and silence as an area of emphasis and move on to specific activities that refine, reinforce, and extend this initial learning. With some organization and luck, and singleminded determination, the teacher will find that virtually all adolescents are to some degree most capable of and even interested in the act of musical composition. Many a teacher has found his or her own limits of understanding challenged by the accomplishments of typical adolescents. These are the kind of problems a music teacher ought to have instead of problems related solely to discipline.

SOUND COMPOSITIONS

Sound compositions involve just what is implied in the name. Various kinds of sounds from a host of sources are "composed" or organized into various kinds of sonorous structures. They are compositions in every sense of that word. They involve many of the very same techniques used by trained composers and pose the very same compositional problems. There exist only two qualifications that can be considered to distinguish these student compositions from those of recognized composers.

1. Most obviously, they will not involve the refined artistic conceptions or technical execution evidenced by trained composers.
2. They will not employ the elements of music in traditional idioms; that is, they will not use melody, harmony, rhythm, form, and tone color in the manner of compositions which fall roughly between Renaissance and early-twentieth-century styles.

In considering this second qualification, some people are inclined to the opinion that such "compositions" are *not music* as such. This begs several questions. First, there are many, many fine, recognized composers in this century—and not even necessarily ones who can be considered avant-garde—whose compositions are similarly nontraditional. To disclaim students' sound compositions because they use nontraditional sounds, compositional techniques, or forms would similarly disclaim much highly regarded music composed since World War II. Music as much as the other arts continues its own internal development, and this has increasingly been going in directions that are very much comparable to these student products which here we call "sound compositions." In fact, students making sound compositions actually *use* (act upon or with) the musical techniques, processes, "sounds," and compositional philosophies of much of the music of the present. Many of the sounds and techniques used in sound compositions are easily related or compared to similar techniques and sounds used in a variety of popular music styles and idioms. There is little doubt among serious musicians—popular or "classical"—that music is evolving more and more in this direction. Therefore the present experiences early adolescents have with this kind of music also prepare them better for their inevitable encounter with the music of the future. In other words, it generally fits the rationale of the middle school to prepare students to deal with the future in productive ways.

A final point should be made. If some people simply refuse to accept these arguments in spite of all the evidence that can be used in support of regarding sound compositions as music, the success of sound compositions as teaching can still be defended. The techniques to be suggested in this section have many advantages.

ADVANTAGES OF SOUND COMPOSITIONS

1. *Students are actively involved* in productive learning as they act on and organize sound in a variety of ways.

2. The suggested techniques are virtually the only available means for inductively (i.e., experientially) learning many of the most important aspects of the musical art;[13] that is, sound compositions allow *learning by doing or acting*, which is the best way of achieving long-term learning.

Regardless, then, of whether or not you consider sound compositions to be "real music," they are of great pedagogical use. By acting upon the same problems and using the same techniques and processes as real composers, adolescents are able to discover and as a result understand the musical art more completely. Learning in this way is far more productive and long-lasting than copying information in a notebook and studying it periodically for tests.

The kind of learning that is possible as a result of working with sound compositions is what some might call "permanent" learning.[14] It is the kind of learning that is not forgotten, because it involves *acting* with concepts (ideas, principles, etc.) and not information.[15] It is the kind of learning that is integrated into a person's life; that is, it is Action Learning and will always be, therefore, an active factor in the person's attitude toward music. This kind of learning is more properly called *understanding,* and as such it can be applied to many diverse musical encounters in the future.[16] Finally, because of this applicability to many different kinds and styles of music, it is well suited to early adolescents.

3. They consider it to be *more relevant,* or at the very least more interesting, because it provides immediate gratifications, applications, and other benefits related to their present musical involvements or personal lives.

4. It is a tangible kind of learning. It results in *overt evidence of learning:* performances and scores or tapes are the products of such learning. They represent tangible (and immediate) evidence to students of their learning progress, and that is important for this age group. Ancillary benefits involve similar evidence of learning for parents, administrators, and school boards, all of whom are responsible for the financial health of a music program!

With these factors in mind, you are encouraged to complete samples of these activities for yourself and with classmates. If you share the fruits of your labors with classmates and friends who also have been attempting these activities, you soon will see the specific nature of what here has been called *multiple results.* You will notice that the sound compositions (or, if you prefer, soundscapes or sound products) you complete *can all be different* in significant ways, yet *correct or valid in different ways or to different degrees.* You probably will also experience some sense of achievement, perhaps even the satisfying feeling of success.

TYPES OF SOUND COMPOSITIONS BRIEFLY COMPARED

Sound compositions include an infinite variety of methods for organizing and performing sounds. The sounds available for sound compositions are equally limitless. Virtually all sounds can be used, but it helps if the sounds can be repeated, and if more than one type of sound can be derived from a sound-producing source. This is a bit more economical than if every sound required an entirely different instrument.

Generally, sound compositions fall into three types: improvised; notated; and composite.

1. *Improvised* sound compositions are freely invented, but are not usually as fully spontaneous as, say, jazz improvisation.[17] While they are not strictly notated, student performers do profit from working from a kind of "outline plan" that is worked out or agreed to in advance of the performance in order to focus or organize their otherwise spontaneous creation. As students gain in experience and confidence, improvised sound compositions may eventually become more totally free and performed "on the spot."

2. *Notated* sound compositions involve some kind of fully notated score. It can employ either student-invented or standard notation, and sometimes both.

3. *Composite* sound compositions combine both notated and improvised aspects. Usually this means that the major elements of the composition, and the performance of it, are controlled to some degree by notation. Additionally, performers are given a certain latitude in executing the score: for example, they may be given the chance to improvise a rhythmic or melodic pattern, but the exact sound source and the time limit for the improvisation are controlled by the notation provided by the composer.

81

IMPROVISED COMPOSITIONS WITH AN "OUTLINE PLAN" CONSIDERED IN DETAIL

This type of sound composition is employed: (a) when *time is limited* (i.e., it takes much more time if a composition has to be fully notated); (b) when the need for *an exact repetition is not important* to your teaching goals (i.e., these compositions can seldom be repeated with the same results); (c) when *broad concept-areas* are at stake (i.e., when the intent of the lesson is *not* to emphasize specific detail).

The teacher has many options in controlling the various facets of an activity.[18] For example, you can control the amount of *time* you will allow students for preparing their outline plan and practicing from it. You can also assign the class to use certain kinds of *sounds*; a *title* to be programmatically interpreted; a musical *technique*; or a certain musical *form*. The following behavioral objectives serve to exemplify several of the kinds of activities that can be dealt with in this kind of sound composition.

Title: Given the title **"space ship"** and ten minutes for preparation, each group of four students will freely interpret that title by planning and performing an improvisation and being able to discuss its interpretation with the class.

Form: Given its own choice of sounds and ten minutes to prepare, each group of four students will demonstrate an understanding of **Simple binary form** (AB form) by planning and performing an improvisation in that form and discussing it with the class.

Texture: Given a choice of any sentences from one of their texts and ten minutes for preparation, the four students in each group will use their comprehension of **Imitative counterpoint** by planning and performing an improvisation with the texture of a canon or round, and will discuss with the class the appropriateness of their comprehension.

Compositional technique: Given a choice of any previously notated sound composition of its own to elaborate and ten minutes for preparation, each group of three students will plan and perform an improvisation of at least two different **variations** on a segment of the original and discuss with the class how it was done.

Timbre: Given only a choice of sounds from wooden and metallic objects and fifteen minutes to prepare, each group of two students will differentiate and synthesize **timbres** by planning and performing an improvisation in which the organization and expression depends heavily on their use; after the performance, each group will be able to discuss its intent with the class.

These activities should not be construed as busywork. They should advance your instructional intent and your curricular structure. For example, the first behavioral objective above emphasizes a feeling response. Feeling responses are the result of personal values and therefore no "objective" criteria are present in the objective. The remaining four objectives emphasize cognition. With these, the students must be evaluated in terms of how well they achieve the content specified for the activity (i.e., the part of the objective given in bold-face type). Even so, it is difficult to totally "fail" one of these projects. Usually, some aspect of the effort will be satisfactory enough to deserve some positive comment. For example, in the objective that emphasizes timbre, the students may come up with several very interesting timbres but not put them to particularly appropriate use in making the organization of the composition clear to the listeners. Notice, too, that there is still considerable freedom (and therefore "feeling" elements) involved in these cognitive objectives. Varied results can be expected, and because of this diversity it is likely that *some degree of feeling response* is confluent with the *cognitions* that are emphasized.[19]

The kinds of outline plan that students can devise will not be, nor need to be, very complicated at all (see Fig. 2:1). In fact, the students' compositions will not be very complicated at first. As they acquire more experience, their compositions will become correspondingly more complex. Over a period of several years of middle school the teacher can expect that adolescent compositions will become ever more refined and subtle. Around the eighth grade (i.e., when students are thirteen or fourteen years old), some teachers

FIG. 2:1

A student plan for the "Form" activity might look like this:

A	B
Sandy & Ralph: Scrape metal book-binder for 10 seconds with pencil, then for 10 seconds with comb; use long strokes	Scrape combs with pencil for 20 seconds using short, quick movements.
Seymour & Sonia: Blow short tones in two soda bottles 1/3 full of water for 20 seconds	Blow long, sustained tones in two soda bottles filled 1/2 to 3/4 full

A student plan for the "Texture" activity might look like this:

Sandy, Ralph, Seymour, and Sonia use the first sentence from our science-book chapter on —.
Sandy begins reading; Ralph waits until she says "it," then he begins. Seymour waits until Ralph says "it," then he begins. Sonia waits until Seymour says "it," then she begins. Everybody except Sonia stops at the end of their sentences.
When Sonia comes to the end of her sentence, she immediately begins to read it backward. When she says "they," Seymour begins to read his sentence backward; when Seymour gets to "they," Ralph begins his sentence backward; when Ralph gets to "they," Sandy begins her sentence backward. Everybody stops when they get to the ends of their sentences.

themselves often begin to feel really challenged by their students ac-complishments.

Outline plans are easily put together by students who can already read. Even young students or poor readers can do this by using only key words they can already recognize. In many circumstances *activities using words as sound material can be used easily as part of a language-arts lesson*. In order to familiarize students with some of the ways of doing outline plans for im-provised sound compositions, you can begin by working from prepared hand-outs similar to the plans shown in Fig. 2:1.

Instead of names, provide blanks. After dividing the class into groups, let each group fill in their names as *they* decide who will do what. In this way they are initiated by performing from plans devised by the teacher. The class discussions that follow should emphasize the musical content of the performances (e.g., What were the differences between the two sections of the compositions?). Over several lessons, some attention should be devoted to the different pro-cesses that can be used for the outline plans of improvised sound compositions.

Many different plans should be assigned to a class. Then the performances will not be repetitive and boring, and several different concept areas will be en-countered by all students as performers or listeners.

FREELY IMPROVISED SOUND COMPOSITIONS

Unlike the planned variety, these usually have no outline (see Fig. 2:2). They usually involve the entire class or large groups within the class, and thus make efficient use of time. The teacher should "conduct" the first few com-positions so students can get an idea of what the conductor's responsibilities and opportunities are. They can start to learn some of the physical gestures and facial expressions that are helpful in realizing a piece.

Commonly, half the class listens to the other half perform. Then their roles are reversed for the next composition. This insures that each student is fully engaged in performing or listening. In this regard, however, the teacher should plan quite carefully how these initial experiences with teacher-directed improvisations will be followed up (see Fig. 2:3). *This step is very important.* Far *more benefit results for the students from the ensuing discussions than from the compositional activity itself or from the actual performance.* Later, when the students function as composer-conductors, the benefits of the per-formances become of more direct importance to them. But even then, the follow-up discussion should be considered as at least roughly half the total ac-tivity.

When dealing with freely improvised sound compositions, the teacher or student conductor-composer may begin with a sketch *in mind* such as is described in Fig. 2:2. The main idea, however, is eventually to feel free enough to elaborate spontaneously on the basic plan once the performance is

84

1. Conductor divides the performing half of the class into thirds: Groups A, B, and C.

2. Group A is directed (verbally) to say "oo" on a rising and falling pitch (which is reinforced by a physical gesture: the hand going up and down to establish the timing of the rise and fall). Group A begins.

3. Group B is directed to hum, starting very softly and then growing gradually louder. Group B begins.

4. Group C is directed to say "tat-a-tat–tat-a-too," with a loud emphasis on the second "tat" and on the "too." Group C begins.

5. Now all performers are in action.

6. The conductor turns to Group A, and using hand gestures makes its fluctuations of pitch wider and wider, louder and louder.

7. Quickly the conductor turns to Group B, encouraging it to become louder still.

8. Turning to Group C, the conductor directs them all the slap their knees on the second "tat" and on the "too."

9. General attention is directed to all groups to become still louder until they are almost shouting.

10. Group C is told to repeat just the syllable "too"; then the other groups are cut off (i.e., stopped). By means of the conductor's hand gestures, the third group is gradually quieted and slowed down until it is almost whispering.

Fig. 2:2. Description of a freely improvised sound composition. This is not an outline plan. It merely describes one possibility.

under way. When the students are conducting a free improvisation, teachers must be on their toes and listening keenly in order to be able *to devise appropriate questions for the follow-up discussion.* There is seldom an occasion when the teacher has much time to think about such questions in advance. And with freely improvised compositions, there is no score the teacher can look at for reference.

As problematic as this may seem, it usually turns out to work in the students' best interest. Of necessity, the kinds of questions a teacher can come up with on the spot, so to speak, are precisely the kind that the students are best able to handle. Listening lessons for which the teacher has ample time to study the score or listen to the recording several times can end up being way "over the heads" of most students at this age level if you are not careful (for more on this kind of listening lesson, see chapter 4).

The first several times some teachers attempt this kind of activity, they really feel under the gun, as though they will look dumb if they cannot come up with a dozen very significant questions. When in doubt, refer back to some of the same questions pursued in the earlier lessons (pp. 72-77) when the broad dimensions of sound were explored. Another "emergency procedure" you

The half of the class that has been listening is asked to "describe what you heard" and a class discussion ensues on the musical elements used in this piece:

Timbre: the "oo" sound; the humming; the "tat-a-tat–tat-a-too" sounds.
Q. "What did you like about those sounds?" (Rather than, "Did you like those sounds?")
Q: "What other sounds might have been good?"
Q: "Did you hear one mass of sound, or did you hear three separate layers of sound, as in a cake?"
Dynamics: the variety in loudness and softness.
Q: "Was this piece loud or soft, or both?"
Q: "If it was both, did it grow louder or softer?"
Q: "Both again? Well, which came first: the growing loud or the growing soft?"
Q: "What do you think it would have sounded like if the louds and softs had been reversed? More exciting, less exciting, or just different?"
Rhythm (periodicity): the feeling of pulse or regularity in the various parts.
Q: "Which of the three parts had no feeling of pulse or regularity?"
Q: "Were you able to feel pulse or regularity in the 'oo' or humming parts?"
Q: "How were you able to feel it in the 'tat-a-tat–tat-a-too' part?"
Q: "If you were to replace those sound with the words 'short' and 'long,' what would the pattern say?"
Q: "If 'short' equals a quarter note, what kind of note wold 'long' be?"
Q: "Is there any aural difference between ♩♩♩♩|♩♩♩♩ and ♩♩♩|♩♩♩ ?"

Fig. 2:3

can use until you build up your skill in devising questions is simply to *ask whether the intent of the assignment* (i.e., the assigned form, title, musical technique, etc.) *was fulfilled by the performance;* if so, *how* or *in what ways;* and if not, which aspects *were or were not* successful?

Where possible, *freely improvised and all other types of sound compositions should be tape recorded.* It is especially useful if the music room (or classroom) has a tape recorder permanently installed for just such occasions. It need not be a sophisticated setup. Even a simple cassette recorder will do; in fact, its ease of operation is a decided advantage. The important point is to have the microphone(s) in place at all times so that all you have to do is turn on the machine. If you have to fiddle around with the microphones each time you want to tape a sound composition, you will soon be tempted to become lazy and to forego the taping. Five minutes of preparation done once can eliminate this problem and can provide a definite teaching advantage.[20]

Aside from the benefits of tape recording for the teacher, there are positive effects for the students. They are usually delighted to listen to tape recordings of their compositions. Perhaps it gives them a sense of achievement, the pride of having accomplished something tangible. It is not unusual to have a student bring in her or his own cassette and request that the teacher record the performance so that it can be taken home to play for parents and friends. This kind of result is especially to be welcomed by teachers. It is the kind of tangible evidence of significant learning that has so often been missing from general-music curriculums at all levels.

Performance groups have always had public visibility and are generally well supported. Never pass up the opportunity to increase the visibility of your general-music program. This is not to say that you should go out of your way in promoting public relations. It merely means that the activities recommended in this text generally result in some overtly tangible "product," and that this can enhance the credibility of general-music programs in the eyes of the public and school officials.

The quality of the recording (i.e., its high fidelity) is not as important as the ease of hearing the composition again in relation to questions asked by students, or in order to verify conflicting opinions or answers that may arise. A final benefit arises from the fact that you can use some of these tapes to practice your own listening skills and ability to devise questions.

Improvised sound-composition activities (including, remember, the follow-ups) are directly effective in enhancing students' musical ideas and in furthering their understanding of many of the major aspects of the musical art. They can be of value also in other ways. For example, they are useful for *exploring the relative highness and lowness of vocal sounds* (see Fig. 2:4) *without embarrassment* after the result of the tone-matching "games" that are usually used in conjunction with singing activities. Used in this way, these activities are suitable for all ages. If used with younger children (K-4), they should be "conducted" by the teacher. When used with preadolescents they may be led in whatever the normal manner has become.

This type of activity is especially good for those children or early adolescents

Fig. 2:4 Sample activity for exploring the relativity of pitch

The improvisation consists of vocal sounds and tones that are high and low. High hand gestures will mean high sounds, and low hand gestures will mean low sounds. Students are directed to go up on tiptoe when making high sounds and to crouch when making low sounds. Each of three groups will be given a pattern of high and low sounds. When all three are involved in performing, the teacher will manipulate the relative dynamics of each group. The piece will end as it began, with one group at a time dropping out.

who are having difficulty managing their voices in singing activities. Some children enter school with the ability to match pitches; others have not learned this skill from their informal, preschool experiences with musical pitches. In sound-composition activities, students are spared being singled out for special attention (generally in front of the remainder of the class).

You should recall that the adolescent's changing voice brings with it a host of potential vocal problems. The use of activities such as are suggested in Fig. 2:4 (with modifications to suit the age group, "hang-ups," interests, or preferences of the individual class involved) can go a long way in preventing some of these vocal problems from arising in the first place and can attenuate such problems when they do eventually arise. In other words, these activities provide an effective means for attending to the changing voice by means other than, or in addition to, singing (in which some boys may or may not prefer to engage).

Finally, as the middle or high school teacher you should encourage the elementary or primary school teachers to employ as many of these same activities as possible in the earliest years of schooling. With appropriate allowance for and variation of (a) the levels of difficulty of the skills or learning in question and (b) the preparations for getting the activity underway,[21] young children take very naturally to sound compositions of all kinds. In fact, when started in kindergarten, children take to these activities much more readily than early or late adolescents, and one hundred percent more readily than adults. They have not acquired as yet the labeling and dichotomizing straight-jacket of most adults that makes them judge everything to be either good or bad, music or not-music, fun or not-fun, happy or sad, etc. As with almost everything else in their lives, children are moved by the experience itself and not by a compulsion to qualify and label it.

It can be somewhat of a different story with older children or early adolescents. Because they have had more practice with the adult way of thinking and the resulting introjection of values, they sometimes feel silly at first doing sound compositions. However, your persistence, open discussions with them, honest optimism, and particularly the many other activities that are closely related to these (e.g., notated sound compositions or listening lessons in which popular music is studied that features sound composition-like elements) can help overcome this initial reluctance. In fact, one of the over-riding advantages of sound compositions is that inhibitions loosen as competence develops. This proves to be healthy both in musical and personal development.

Things do work much more smoothly when children experience these kinds of activities from their earliest years. And if they reach middle or junior high school after several years of experience with sound compositions, the musical horizons available to them as adolescents are greatly expanded, and often significant *musical* expression can result.

IMPROVISED SOUND COMPOSITIONS SUMMARIZED

1. *Improvised compositions with an outline plan*
   a. An outline plan is developed and serves as the organizing basis for improvisation.
   b. As a rule, these are most successful as the initial improvised activities.
   c. With experience and competencce, improvisations may become increasingly free of any predetermined plan.
   d. The teacher can control many facets of these sound compositions:
      (1) Time allowed for preparation and length of performance.
      (2) The title, form, musical technique, etc., that the improvisation is supposed to manifest.
   e. Nonetheless, the improvisatory aspects of these activities involve considerable freedom for students to make personal responses.
   f. This is ideal in that it provides the minimal guidelines that adolescents often desire and simultaneously the opportunity for personal expression which they need.
   g. Having few absolutes insures the likelihood that no student can be totally unsuccessful (fail).
   h. Teachers can initiate these compositions by providing the first few outline plans for students to work from; these are the models which the students will increasingly learn to follow.
2. *Freely improvised sound compositions*
   a. These have no, or very sketchy (a few words at most) outline plans.
   b. The first few are usually conducted by the teacher.
      (1) Students learn the function of the conductor and some of the gestures that the conductor can use.
   c. Usually half the class performs while half listens; then the groups alternate for the next performance.
   d. Follow-up activities (discussions, etc.) are just as important as the performances.
      (1) The teacher must devise questions or other activities to fruitfully engage the class in the follow-up.
      (2) The aim of follow-up activities is to insure that understanding has been successful, or to refine, reinforce, or extend the learning in question.
   e. It is desirable to tape record these and all other sound compositions.
      (1) A permanent setup, no matter how primitive, is recommended.
   f. These improvisations and those with a plan are useful in exploring pitch with children and adolescents who have some vocal difficulty in matching pitch.
   g. Activities such as these should be encouraged among primary-level

89

teachers in order that students entering middle or junior high school are prepared to go on to significant musical achievements.

3. *When to use improvised compositions with an outline plan*
   a. When the time you can allow for preparation is limited.
   b. When specific details of compositions are less important than the broad handling of musical elements.
   c. When some type of plan functions as a minimum guideline in helping adolescents organize their efforts.
   d. When your class or specific students are inhibited about freely improvised sound compositions; or when they do not yet have the necessary readiness or patience for fully notated sound compositions.
   e. When you want to give emphasis to free "feeling responses."
   f. When you are about to explore for the first time the usability of notation for long, complicated, or precisely controlled compositions; the need for notation is often discovered in this way.

4. *When to use freely improvised sound compositions*
   a. When you want to illustrate a musical principle or technique for the first time without lecturing; this is followed by Socratic questions of the kind illustrated in Fig. 2:3, which inductively prepare the student for subsequent activities emphasizing the principle at hand.
   b. With younger children or poor readers who cannot create or read a plan for a sound composition.
   c. With children or adolescents who are having difficulty using their voices flexibly to produce higher or lower pitches.
   d. When time is especially limited, and you cannot afford even the time for the planning stage of "planned" improvisations.
   e. When you especially want to allow children to give free and immediate vent to their feelings: this benefit accrues to the student "conductors" who *volunteer.*

In general, then, improvised sound compositions often have the advantage of saving time and thus more immediately involving students in productive activity. As such they serve well as an initiation into fully composed or combined sound-composition techniques. They are useful also in those situations or on those occasions when large-group work is necessary. They also make it easy for large groups to be broken down for the first time into moderate-sized groups without "all hell letting loose."

NOTATED SOUND COMPOSITIONS CONSIDERED IN DETAIL

The major difference between notated compositions and free or planned improvisations is that some sort of musical score is the result of the former and serves as the basis for performance. For purposes of these activities, a musical score will qualify if it meets all of the following conditions in some general way.

1. It includes some *words* as performance directions. The fact that words may also be used as sound materials is not at issue here.

2. Graphic symbols are used to represent sounds. These may be literal symbols (e.g., a drawing of a hand to indicate clapping) or abstract symbols that are arbitrarily assigned to certain sounds.

3. The score should be conveyed on paper, or some substitute writing surface (e.g., acetate for overhead projection). This contributes a degree of permanence and reusability.

4. A performance of the notated work can be repeated; or it can be interpreted by performers other than the composer(s).

Initial attempts at notated compositions may *not* meet all of these qualifications; that would be unreasonable for beginners. But after sufficient experience with a variety of musical/notational problems, a useful score should generally meet all four conditions. Each condition has a rather specific educational and musical intent.

1. The *words* that provide performance directions are intended to cause the composer(s) to think carefully about specifics of the performance. Some of these might include tempo, dynamics, "interpretative markings" ("lightly," "warmly," "with intensity," etc.), and other nuances. Dealing with these qualities helps insure that students are considering seriously all aspects of their composition, and often results in much more sensitively rendered works.

It should be noted that classes will have to be given much "assistance" in learning the expressive possibilities of *dynamic levels other than loud,* and in appreciating *the value of silence!* Usually their beginning compositions are loud, overly "busy," "gimmicky." Part of the teacher's responsibility will be to suggest or draw out all the expressive potential of sound and silence beyond the conventional ideas that too easily satisfy students initially. They need considerable challenge and prodding to surpass these naive beginnings.

2. The use of *symbols* to represent and control sound encourages economy of operation in the act of composing and in the performance of a work. Early attempts at devising symbols will almost certainly result in quite literal representations of the sound-producing object itself! Rather than automatically *forcing* students to adopt the more useful abstract symbols, it is often wise to *wait until their expressive ideas exceed their notational inventiveness.* Then by Socratic questioning you can draw from them some alternative possibilities. Once one group moves in this direction, other groups quickly see the "wisdom" and follow suit in inventing their own set of abstract symbols. Some ideas for notation are suggested for your benefit later in this chapter.

3. The score should be conveyed on paper or some substitute writing material. This allows it to be studied by the teacher and class or to be executed by many performers. The purpose of notation is not primarily to facilitate memorization of a score for performance, although this sometimes happens in the natural course of composing. What is more, the notation should not simply serve as a "reminder" of agreed upon sounds or events; it should fully convey all relevant performance instructions so that it is playable by other than the individual or group composing it.

It is a very economical and successful idea to pass out acetate sheets (usually 8″ × 10″) with or without a cardboard frame. If the students use black china marking pencils, or better yet, the felt-tip pens designed especially for writing on acetate, each group can project its score using the overhead projector. Since notated sound compositions exist in part for the possibility of such score study, this turns out to be the most efficient way of doing it.

Of course there are many times when students can be allowed to produce (usually at their request) their own score. You should permit this, but it is recommended that you ask them to make it poster-sized in the event that you might want to hold it up in front of the class for discussion or analysis. Caution! Students at this age level can often become overly engrossed in the visual aspects of such scores, and can even tend to make them a work of visual "art." While this is certainly not undesirable, it should not be allowed to so overwhelm the composers or the teacher that the *musical or notational aspects under consideration are ignored or glossed over.* There may even be, without your caution, an inverse relationship between the visual beauty of the score and the appropriateness of the composition.

4. Finally, the performance from a suitable score should generally be *repeatable.* This, of course, is subject to the same kind of "exactness" as any notated piece. Some variety in performances is expected and is often considered desirable. That is one reason why "live" performances are often preferred to recorded ones.

In the case of *aleatory*[22] music such repetitions may result in compositions that sound entirely different. This is useful, however, and is not always to be avoided. Sometimes it should be sought. Occasionally highlighting points such as this help to point up the inevitability that each performance of a work is in a way a new composition. It is the joint product of the composer, who created the score, and the performer(s), who must realize a score as a sound product that is slightly different for each performance.

Much choice is left up to the performers, although the composer still controls the overall nature of the composition (see Mus. Ex. 2:1 below).

MUS. EX. 2:1 "Xenakis"

XENAKIS is an aleatoric composition for five or more performers of undetermined instrumentation. If more than five performers are used, no more than two performers should play the part for Performer 4 at any time during the piece.

All timings (|——— ca. 30″ to 40″ ———|), are approximate. ("ca." is the abbreviation for circa, meaning approximate.)

▼▲● = a short duration
▽—┤ = a long duration, sustained until cut off
▲ = a very high note
● = a mid range note
▼ = a very low note
▽ E♭ = sustain the lowest E♭ concert possible on your instrument
O F♯ = sustain the mid-range F concert on your instrument

△ F♯ = sustain the highest F♯ concert possible on your instrument

INSTRUCTIONS FOR PERFORMERS

1st Line
Enter one at a time (1 through 5). Begin in a soft, sparse manner in a very low register. Gradually build to a high degree of virtuosity, increasing volume and using the entire range of your instrument up to the release point ①.

At Ⓐ, enter in the same frantic manner as at the release point ①. Execute a complete retrograde of the opening section, dropping out one at a time in reverse order (5,3,2,1). Performer 4 continues in a soft sparse manner from ② through the entrance of Performers 1 and 2 at ③, stopping at the entrance of Performer 5.

2nd Line
At Ⓑ Performer 4 should use the entire range of his

instrument, including non-conventional sounds. He should think more in terms of timbre than conventional melody and/or harmony. Incorporate silence into the solo. The solo should develop from simple gestures to complex, frantic brilliant playing at Ⓒ.

After the soloist enters at Ⓑ, Performer 5 is to create as much energy on the E♭ concert as possible. To do this, alternate between straight tone and vibrato (vary the speed of vibrato). Also vary attacks (accent, staccato, legato), bend the pitch (quarter tone), employ < and >.

3rd Line

At Ⓒ all join the soloist playing wild frantic gestures[1] as at Ⓐ. However, choose a register where you can play virtuosically at both the loud dynamic at Ⓒ and the *subito pp* at ①. The order of release is obvious and not strictly timed in seconds. The soloist, Performer 4, is the last to stop, after all others have released.

---

1. Gestures — A musical action or collection of musical actions (i.e. — a fast four-note figure, a trill, a glissando).

Xenakis

Don Owens

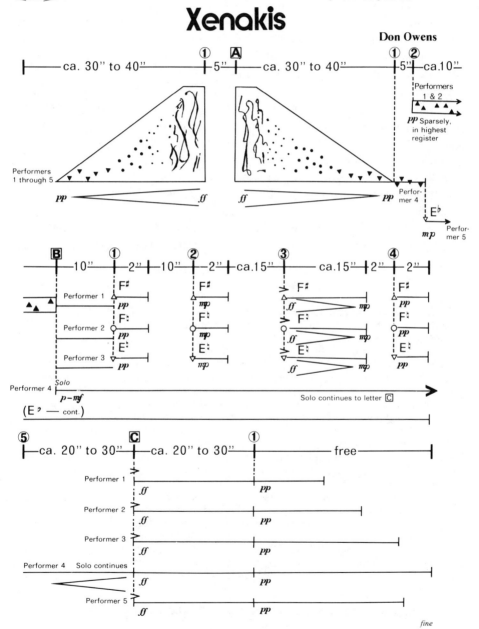

fine

In traditional music it is customary that the performance does not vary widely from the manner in which the composer is believed to have performed it himself. However, in many cases this is only speculation. We often have very little objective evidence about the composer's intentions. There is no doubt that certain "traditions" have become standard in virtuosic performances that go well beyond the composer's original intentions. These are all excellent questions to challenge the minds of adolescents.

Consider, for example, that most rock music is never notated and probably never will be. If various groups or subsequent generations ever perform this music, it will have to be learned and worked out "by ear." This approach does not foster accuracy. But it does parallel the "aural tradition" by which most authentic (as opposed to "composed" or "urban") folk music is learned generation after generation. Each succeeding generation in the past learned a given song with a small "mistake" or variation, and hence the songs would be varied and changed slowly over the years. Because they continued to evolve, they often were "kept alive" or were more relevant for each generation. It is only when the ethnomusicologist notates traditional songs that they become frozen for all time. Fortunately, the "folk" versions often continue in the aural tradition.

Here are some questions adolescents usually like to tackle, and they should be encouraged to do so by teachers who are equally fascinated by the implications:

1. Does notation, or its lack, influence in any significant way the longevity of music?

2. Does notation directly determine the nature of the music it notates? That is, is the expressiveness of music limited to the notational systems composers are able to invent? Is the medium the message?

3. Is music notated in other cultures throughout the world? How is music different in societies not having a notational system?

4. What are the implications for music when—as is happening today among composers—each composer invents his own notational symbols which are often different for each composition or from those of other composers? An international conference of composers has tried to cope with this very same question, with the hope of agreeing to some greater standardization of notational systems.

5. In what ways are rock, jazz, and folk music performances—the kinds where notation is not and never has been a factor—producing a "new" kind of music? How much like "electronic music" are they when the efforts of the composer-performer produce a composition only in the form of the recording that results? The composer-performer's work is not subject to "interpretation" or "misinterpretation" by performers if the composer and performer are the same person. So, what advantages and disadvantages does this kind of "electronic composition-as-recording-a-performance" have for the composer-performer? For other performers? For audiences? Why must so many pop and rock singers do "lip synch" (silent synchronizing of lips along with a recording) when they sing "live" on TV? Which recording stars and groups cannot, do not, or prefer not to perform "live" because they cannot do without studio manipulation of the performance-composition? Etcetera, etcetera, etcetera.

Questions such as these, and others you should be able to think of, fire the newly developing imaginations of early adolescents. If anything, they become too fired-up by these questions and prefer to talk about similar things all of the time. So again, you have a "good problem." You allow and guide such discussions; but eventually you should have students *apply their learning, act upon their insight,* in their own compositional efforts.

Notated sound compositions are particularly useful for most instructional purposes, and are just as easy as the improvised type to create. For example, the five suggestions for improvised sound compositions described on page 82 can also be used for notated compositions. The behavioral objective for each lesson would specify that a notated score should serve as the vehicle for the performance.

Thus these works are often repeatable; or the scores as well as the performance can be analyzed in the follow-up activities. This is especially useful when the performance of a student composition does not at first or clearly seem to "make sense" to the teacher or class in terms of the assignment.

POTENTIAL PROBLEMS WITH NOTATED SOUND COMPOSITIONS

1. Notated sound compositions tend to require *more time* for two reasons. First, it simply takes more time to prepare and produce a notated score for performance than it does to prepare an improvised sound composition (either free or planned). Also, notated sound compositions tend to be *more intricate or longer.* In fact, notated scores are a distinct advantage when the musical problems at hand are complex. Compared to improvised sound compositions, which are useful when dealing with broadly applicable musical principles, notated sound compositions can deal more adequately with specific refinements and other nuances. This does tend to result in longer compositions, but this too can prove to be an advantage since it shows that some form of notation is useful or necessary when dealing with long or multi-movement forms of music.

On the other hand, notated sound compositions can sometimes use no more time, or even less time, than improvised compositions. In some instances, for example, previously notated scores can be used for new purposes. Scores can be collected and studied by the teacher. Score preparation can take place also outside of class.

2. Another potential problem with notated sound compositions arises from the need for students to devise symbols to represent their musical ideas. Since the invention of visual symbols is not strictly a "musical behavior" (i.e., it is not unique to music, nor necessarily inherent to music), this can degenerate into a session on graphic inventiveness rather than on music learning. But once again, if the teacher is aware of the potential difficulty, sessions devoted to devising notational systems can arise from and be applied to musical needs.

This can become an advantage, since it encourages students to consider the purposes of notational systems, and can have direct bearing on other work with standard graphic notation. Some teachers have found that their students know something about traditional notation from their singing experiences in the early elementary school. While they are seldom "turned on" to learning this notation solely for the purpose of music reading (singing), there sometimes seems to be some interest on the part of early adolescents in learning it for the purposes of sound compositions. So it is not unusual for such students to ask the teacher to teach them standard notation, especially the rhythmic/metric aspects, which they find most useful in notating sound compositions. Once again this possible disadvantage is turned to a probable advantage.

It is very likely that the notational symbols invented by students will vary among individuals and groups, and thus will not be usable in a "standard" way. Students' early attempts at invented notation, as has been mentioned, are usually very literal. As they gain in experience, more use is made of abstract graphic symbols. But the additional step of "interpreting" the symbols, or of reading the composer's "code" for using these symbols, can take up time.

It is not unusual, however, for this process to continue for a while and then, of its own accord, turn around. The students, seeing that some systems are more workable than others, often start to adopt certain symbols more frequently and hence move toward standardization. It is often around the time of this reversal that students become most naturally interested in learning standard notation.

3. A final difficulty should be noted, although it is the easiest with which to deal. Paper and writing implements of some kind are usually necessary. Given the propensity of students of all ages to forget their materials, the teacher should always have a supply on hand.

ADVANTAGES OF NOTATED SOUND COMPOSITIONS

1. As implied earlier, notated sound compositions *can deal with more detailed or specific musical ideas and techniques.* The notation allows the composer(s) and performer(s) more control over more of the musical aspects of the composition. Notated compositions, thus, allow greater sophistication and can bring students ever closer to authentic compositional problems.

2. Related to that advantage is the fact that *the teacher can study the scores* of students as evidence of their learning. This is especially helpful when time does not permit a performance of each composition. However, students' compositions should be performed regularly, even if it is just for the teacher after or before school or during the activity period. As an alternative, try having students with cassette recorders pretape their compositions outside of class for hearing during class. Without these performances, students' efforts will be abstract, mechanical, sterile, and of increasingly less relevance to them. *Students must hear,* very frequently, *the aural results of their compositional activities* if their music education is to remain musical rather than "academic."

3. The score study by the teacher, however, can also *follow* a performance. Requiring two scores (one for the performers and one for the teacher) or notating directly on acetate for the overhead projector allows the teacher to follow the score *during* the performance. When the teacher does collect a score, *it should not be for the purpose of grading students' compositional and performing efforts.* (This holds true for any compositional efforts). If they are graded regularly, students will "play it safe." Their work will become uninspired and commonplace. Some will begin to cheat. All will begin the "gamesmanship" in which students try to guess what the teacher "is after" with a particular assignment. According to this process, the best students turn out to be those who "understand" the teacher best and not necessarily the music studied.

Regular grading of creative activities *always* degenerates into *extrinsic motivation* such as the fear of poor grades or the desire for good ones. This diminishes the *intrinsic motivation of the musical fulfillment* represented in the activity. When grades become the factor that controls what students do or do not do, most of the opportunity is lost for significant *musical learning for its own satisfaction.* Lost is the very significant discovery that *involvement or action with music is self-validating.*

4. It is possible, however, to employ sound compositions in your assessment procedures. This is usually done simply enough by assigning a sound composition (or more than one) as a "test" of students' applied understanding. Such an assignment should have quite specific criteria, but you should not call it a test, and the conditions under which it is carried out should in every way possible resemble similar conditions in the past. This will generally be done only around the time that grades are due and not as a regular daily or weekly practice. There should be only one difference between these "tests" and regular classes. They should be *summational;* that is, they should be structured to *cause each student to draw on the sum of his or her musical knowledge, understanding, and skill.* This kind of test is *fair* (it evaluates what you have had

your class learning), *realistic* (it involves *using* learning and not simply regurgitating it), and *less intimidating than formal exams* because it is undistinguishable from regular class activities, the only difference being the grade itself. This kind of test also satisfies those principals who insist on a "unit test" at the end of each "marking period."[23] Finally, this kind of assessment most closely meets the goals of Action Learning.

5. A special advantage of notated sound compositions is that *students can revise their scores according to subsequent learning.* Similarly, they can refine and improve their own notational systems as they learn the inadequacies of their initial systems. Much use ought to be made of this advantage. *Reuse of previous compositions or notational systems on a planned basis by the teacher facilitates transfer of learning and fosters growth-centered Action Learning.* In other words, through such activities students learn to diagnose and improve upon earlier weaknesses. This is especially helpful and healthy when it contributes to a student's sense of progress: "I did this myself!"

Quite often teachers will follow a sound-composition activity with a specific activity of this kind. After class discussion of solutions to a compositional or notational problem, the students are given the opportunity to revise their first versions in terms of new insights gained from the discussion. This can be done before or after a piece is actually performed and discussed, but before the score is handed in to the teacher (for diagnostic comments, not grading). This shows the teacher the nature of the changes made, and whether these changes represent significant understanding.

6. Notated sound compositions can be assigned as *individual or group homework and as independent or group study* during times other than music class. This is especially useful in any of the varieties of "open" education that are becoming increasingly evident (if not yet popular). Whether the compositions are done as homework or as independent study, the teacher will have to prepare the directions, procedures, etc., carefully for students to follow. Every attempt must be made to eliminate time wasted in completing assignments poorly or incorrectly because of incomplete or vague directions.

The directions should be spelled out clearly step by step, and the criteria for evaluation (if any)[24] should be just as clear. In-class assignments are best handed out on a 3" × 5" card (see Fig. 2:5). Retain these cards, and update and improve them as experience with them dictates. Out-of-class homework can be assigned on a handout that is fully explained, and questions answered, before students leave the class. Independent study projects done at various times during an "open" school day can be done as part of activity corners, learning contracts, goal cards or independent learning packages[25].

7. Another advantage of notated sound compositions is that students learn through personal actions *which musical elements notation controls.* Therefore the importance of notational systems in the musical art are better understood. Ordinarily, early adolescents see very little reason to learn *any* kind of notation. But when notation is studied in relation to their own creative efforts, the problems and advantages of notational systems take on more meaning for them. This holds true equally for either standard or newly invented notation. A generation of students taught in this manner will be the first one that is not only prepared to deal with the traditional notation needed to perform the standard repertory but also sufficiently experienced with new notational systems and practices to function effectively as musicians in the future.

8. The *tangibility of the score* itself is another advantage of notated sound compositions. To adolescents this can represent *tangible achievement* and can be a source of real pride. The score (and also the taped performance) is available for comparing early and late efforts, and as tangible proof of learning: some *thing* has been accomplished! Students can even take the score home along with art, shop, or homemaking projects in answer to the question, "What did you learn in school today?"

9. In this regard, but also a special advantage in itself, is the fact that notated sound compositions have a *special value for musically interested or talented youngsters in nurturing their creativity.* You should recall that "creativity" in this sense is not the first or paramount goal of these activities. Too many people just are not suited for creative accomplishments in music. Their talents or interests may range, for example, from motorcycle maintenance to dancing, woodworking, or cooking, and although everyone probably has some "creative potential" in

NOTATED SOUND COMPOSITION

1. In ABA form.
2. Using only "wooden" sounds.
3. No longer than 1 minute performance time.
4. You have 15 minutes to prepare, notate,
    and rehearse your composition.
5. Each member of the composing team must
    take part in conducting or performing the piece.
6. Be prepared to discuss all the compositional
    techniques and ideas you used.

This activity card could be used in a music class or in a media corner as an independent project. It has specific criteria, yet leaves much freedom to the composers (e.g., the specific wooden sounds to be used). The task involved is one of finding a way to produce the variety called for in section B and the interest needed in the A sections when the timbre is restricted. Thus students will have to explore all the other musical elements besides timbre: pitch, dynamics, rhythm/meter, texture, etc.

Fig. 2:5

many areas of endeavor, this does not seem reason enough to justify a program for developing everyone's creative potential in *music*, however meager that may be. These activities *do* serve, on the other hand, the creative needs and growth potential of students who *do* have special interests and talents in music. Such activities often can represent a major step on the way to a musical vocation or avocation.

10. Finally, notated sound compositions *require no previous readiness*. No special musical skill or learning must be acquired beforehand. Virtually all the specific "information," such as musical forms or compositional techniques, *arises from doing sound compositions*. The information is *not* doled out in advance, with the sound composition employed as a "test" activity to determine how well the lecture has "sunk in." There is no need for this. A well-organized teacher will proceed with determination in a step-by-step program of activities in which this *information is acquired through use, through action*.

This is accomplished, generally, in two ways. First, assignments are given that direct students in their compositional activities in such a way as to result in a sound product which the teacher wishes to emphasize, not only for the composing group, but for the entire class:

"Compose a notated sound composition using the diagram on p. 99. For the space marked "A" use metallic sounds; for "B" use wooden sounds. Try to make each section as interesting as possible. To end the piece, repeat the "A" space so that you will have an overall pattern of ABA. You should limit the piece to no longer than 45 seconds. Perform the piece yourself. You have 10 minutes to work on, notate, and practice your piece."

The resulting composition will be, of course, in ABA form. The teacher can then use the oppor-

A	B

tunity of its performance to emphasize (preferably through questions) the usefulness of this form. In any event, the activity can be concluded with the direction, "From now on, when I ask you to compose a piece in ABA form, you will use this pattern: statement—counterstatement (contrast)—return (unity)." In this way, or at least after several more such activities, the way is prepared for each student to develop a concept of ABA for repeated use and refinement in subsequent class activities. It has been done without prior or follow-up lectures, and since it is being used regularly, it will become a "permanent" learning for the class.

Secondly, serendipity can be a major factor in "discovering" information. Untutored as they may be, these young composers often make use "accidentally" (i.e., without conscious intention) of standard compositional techniques. It is the teacher's responsibility to be on the lookout for such occasions, and when they occur, not only to praise the "discovering" group, but also to emphasize or highlight the effectiveness, usefulness, or other aspects of the techniques used.

For example, two seventh graders doing their *very first* sound composition in accordance with the directions below came up with the score shown in Mus. Ex. 2:2 (p. 100).

Note the "A" section involved five sound events performed by Joe. The "B" section, in order to be contrasting, involved five different sound events performed by Bob. Quite by accident, the two composers decided not to repeat the initial "A" section literally to complete the ABA form assigned. *They specified that it would be performed backward* (i.e., in reverse order). Not only are the events reversed, but also, in the case of sound event 3, the "melodic" direction is reversed as well. This backward repetition of the "A" section is a clear case of *retrograde motion*. The teacher failed to notice this important accident, but fortunately a group of observing student-teachers did pick it up and brought it to her attention. She then made an appropriate to-

---

Notated Sound Composition

1. Interpret the title "Sunrise-Sunset."

2. Use some form of notation.

3. Your piece should be no longer than 3 minutes.

4. The piece is to be performed by the composer(s)—so rehearse it.

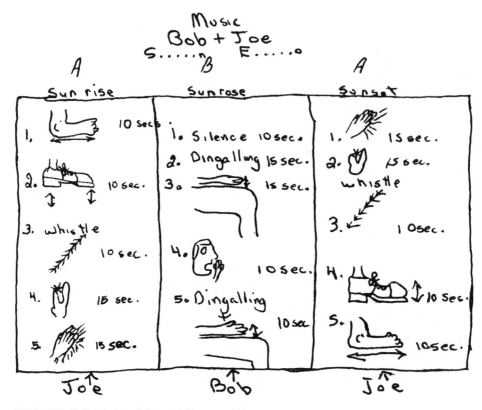

MUS. EX. 2:2. Notated Sound Composition

do about this exciting discovery and its usefulness. There seemed to be little doubt that the composers were delighted at their inventiveness, and that the class was impressed enough to employ the same technique in their own efforts in the not-too-distant future.

Many other "information items" arise in this manner. Students often use *augmentation* or *diminution* unwittingly when they double (augment) or halve (diminish) the duration (time) values of a previously stated sound event. Often, after ABA has been emphasized for several lessons, some adventuresome student will strike out and "invent" ABACA form, not realizing that this is a *rondo form*. Many other information items arise in this natural, non-force-fed way.

Using assignments that have specific criteria; and being alert to serendipity is to be preferred to lectures, note taking, etc., as dictated by the teacher *before* the activity. These are the recommended paths of generating information. Information learned through or from experience will enter permanently into the musical actions of your students. It will not be forgotten the way information studied only for a test invariably is forgotten. If you reflect on it for a moment, you will find that most of the valuable information that guides the day-to-day conduct of your life was first encountered not as a lecture but in the natural exploration of your environment through the same kind of trial-and-error action learning. In any event, *your classes will learn only that information they use.* Thus to the degree that you employ these activities their learning it *from*, and using it *in* sound composition activities insures that it will be a permanent, lifelong influence in their musical behaviors as performers, listeners, or composers—whatever the future may hold in store for them. This, you should recall, is the essence of Action Learning.

Prior readiness, prior information, prior learning, prior talent are not prerequisites for sound compositions. This is a very important point for you to consider. The higher up the ladder of education a student goes, the more his or her readiness is called into question or applied. At each successive level it is expected that new learnings can be added to or based on old ones supposedly attained at earlier levels. This expectation does not apply, however, to music classes based on the kinds of learning activities illustrated here.

Notated sound compositions make an asset out of what otherwise is a liability of instruction in general music: extreme variation in students' musical preparation. Sound compositions actually *thrive* on this diversity, as is illustrated by the multiplicity of responses to a particular assignment. Students profit from the most unexpected variations in their musical products. Bright students who otherwise have very little formal musical training often catch fire and easily outdo students with some musical background. Less academically gifted students can succeed as well as and sometimes better than the more gifted students. Their goals are often less ambitious and more realistic, and thus they can often achieve what they set out to do (or, in many circumstances, what the teacher has tailored to their abilities). Brighter students frequently want to go out on a variety of "limbs" and resist the more conventional solutions with which their less-gifted classmates are more than pleased.

11. The final advantage of such sound compositions is that they *match the growth needs of early adolescence*. To detail this match-up would require more space than can be afforded here. It can be said, however, that their needs for self-expression, self-esteem, positive self-image, imagination, peer-group relations, minimal guidelines in conjunction with considerable freedom,[26] tangible results and immediacy of satisfaction, and energizing tasks that shake off lethargy are all satisfied to some degree by the very nature of sound-composition activities. Therefore it is safe to conclude that these activities are among the most suitable for minimizing such typical behavior problems of early adolescents while simultaneously maximizing the healthy satisfaction of their developmental needs.

Putting the shoe on the other foot, sound compositions also minimize the teacher's problems and maximize the impact of instruction. They allow the teacher to emphasize virtually any musical concept-area and make of it material for actual and productive involvement on the part of students. Even the elements of melody, harmony, and rhythm/meter can be dealt with in their expanded, contemporary sense. The resulting products often bear a striking resemblance to the efforts of major contemporary composers (although some readers may not see that as a point in favor of these activities), and can be vastly more interesting for the teacher than lecture-demonstration teaching methods.

With the techniques suggested here for implementing sound-composition activities, students can deal inductively with virtually any musical style, element, principle, or concept-area they will ever have reason or need to know. Most beneficially, once a healthy program of these activities is started, the incidence of behavior problems ("discipline" problems) arises in inverse proportion to the degree of success the teacher has been able to achieve. Teaching under these circumstances is rewarding and satisfying, and that is as it should be.

NOTATIONAL SYSTEMS AND SOUND SOURCES

While no attempt is going to be made here to delimit the teacher or student to specific notational systems, some suggestions can be given based upon the experiences of many teachers.

There are only three sources of sound available for use: (1) vocal sounds; (2) body sounds; (3) sounds from objects.

Vocal sounds are all made by the vocal mechanism. These include vowel sounds and other sounds sustained on a column of air from the lungs, and sounds made with the mouth, tongue, and lips (e.g., buzzing or clicking sounds). *Body sounds* are generally made by having the limbs strike the body in some manner. This results in clapping, slapping, tapping sounds, etc. Sounds derived from *objects* involve real instruments as well as those made by striking, blowing, shaking, etc.

Teachers should not shy away from using real instruments. Their use enhances the transfer value of learning for students who are in band and orchestra. Similarly they enhance other students' interest and their sense of the legitimacy of sound composition. Standard instruments can be used in their intended way of playing. However, strikingly "new" (at least to students) and intriguing sounds can be discovered if students are encouraged to use their instruments experimentally.

Some ideas such as the following can be suggested to start the students' imaginations at work:

1. "Popping" the finger keys on flutes, clarinets, and oboes.
2. Using only the mouthpiece of brass and reed instruments.
3. Removing the slide section from a trombone and playing while holding a jar or can over the open end of the slide tube.
4. Using small mallets to bounce on the strings of stringed instruments; this also works inside the piano.
5. Using a "prepared piano": this involves placing small objects *on* or *between* the strings of a grand piano. With an upright piano you are limited to objects (e.g., aluminum foil, paper) placed between the strings or held between the strings and hammers.
6. Playing instruments directly into (or from behind) the sounding board of a piano while the sustaining pedal is depressed.
7. "Muting" brasses or woodwinds by (gently!) stuffing a variety of (removable!) substances (fabric, paper, etc.) in the end of the horn; by wrapping something around the horn (e.g., a towel); or by playing into larger resonating objects (e.g., a wastebasket).
8. Plucking strings (guitar, violins, etc.) while turning the tuning peg (carefully!)

Be very sure that you constantly remind and caution students to be careful. Some ideas—such as putting a trombone mouthpiece in a trumpet—can ruin the horn (in this case the larger mouthpiece may get stuck in or may stretch or expand the diameter of the smaller tubing). Reasonable care will avoid these occurrences.

These three sources of sound result in sounds having three general types of duration: (1) sustained; (2) fading; (3) short.

Sustained sounds will be vowel sounds, those achieved by blowing (as with wind instruments), and other sounds that have a duration of their own (e.g., from an electric drill, pencil sharpener, or whistling tea kettle). Sounds that *fade* usually come from instruments or *resonant objects* that are struck, vibrate (ring), and then gradually die away. *Short* sounds usually arise from objects that are not very resonant and therefore do not vibrate (ring) very much when struck (e.g., a wood block). Such sounds as clicking made by the lips are also short in duration.

The sounds produced from these sources will fall into three general categories: (1) sounds having a definite pitch; (2) sounds of indefinite pitch; (3) nonpitched sounds.

Resonant objects that result in a *regular pattern of vibration*[27] will have a *definite pitch*. Aside from standard orchestral wind and string instruments, instruments of definite pitch include classroom chimes, tone bells, step bells, tympani (kettledrums), xylophones, and marimbas. Certain "non-instruments" also qualify in this category: pieces of resonant metal, old brake drums, tuned glasses or bottles, etc.

Sounds of *indefinite pitch* have vibrations that are uneven. These usually involve such standard percussion instruments as the bass drum and snare drum, cymbals, castanets, tambourine, and gong. It is possible to describe the bass drum's pitch as low and the snare drum's pitch as higher, but the sounds in this category do *not* have the *definite* degrees of highness or lowness that pitched instruments or objects do. A continuous sound that constantly rises and falls in pitch might be included in this category (e.g., sirens).

The final category of *nonpitched* sounds expands as more and more sounds are deemed suitable for musical purposes. Once upon a time the sounds in this category would have been called "noise." Today "anything goes" as long as it serves the composer's expressive or formal intent. Sounds in this category include such things as rattling paper, objects being dropped,[28] and many body sounds. Many "sound effects" also fall into this category: sounds imitating nature (except for birdcalls of certain types), machinery, etc.

In addition to their various sources, durations, and pitch characters, sounds have a certain distinctive quality that is often referred to metaphorically as *tone color* (*timbre*, pronounced "*tam*-br" or "*tam*-ber"). This quality results from the nature of the sound source (its construction materials) and its unique vibratory characteristics. Tone color allows us to differentiate between two different instruments—say, a trumpet and clarinet—when both play the same pitch. It is, therefore, one of the most important of musical elements.

Composers employ tone colors for both expressive and formal purposes. Many of the experiences at the very beginning of this chapter were designed to heighten students' awareness of the expressive and formal potential of tone color.

In addition to the compositional use of *single* tone colors, various *combinations or groupings* of tone colors are possible. Sounds of similar tone color—all metallic sounds, for instance—can be combined. This can be boring, so interest can be provided by varying other aspects of the sound: pitches, durations, combinations of pitched and nonpitched sounds, etc.

When *sharply contrasting* tone colors are put together—say, metallic sounds with wooden sounds—some attempt can be made to decrease excessive contrast by seeking similarities where possible: using similar pitch levels, similar durations, similar patterns, etc. *Mixed* tone colors result when a variety of tone colors are combined and result in an overall effect that is distinctly different from similar or contrasting groupings. This is the kind of grouping that students find the easiest to handle at first. Until they begin to think specifically about and plan tonal combinations for specific reasons, most of their efforts will result in mixed qualities.

When *similar* tone colors are used, the tonal effect is one of *unity*. Too much unity can be as bad as too little. Therefore the compositional problem often associated with using similar tonal grouping is to provide some kind of *variety*. On the other hand, when *sharply contrasting tone colors* are used, the result can be one of too much diversity or *variety*. This presents the compositional problem of finding or creating *unity*.

Mixed tone colors combine certain similar tone colors (unity) and certain contrasting ones (variety). The resulting unity *and* variety is generally easier to handle at first than homogeneous groupings (using only similar or contrasting sounds). On the other hand, too much of it can become static and dull. Its inherent blend of unity and variety can become bland, undistinctive, uninteresting. The eventual compositional problem that can be established for such mixed groupings is to create unity *in* variety.

Unity *in* variety results when a musical element performs two functions: it *unifies at the same time as it provides variety*. Consider these equations:

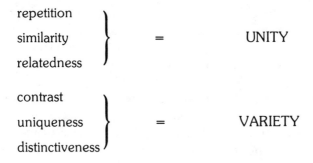

Thus to the degree that elements seem repeated, similar, or related, unity results. The closer the relationship or similarity (up to the point of exact repetition), the stronger the unity. Contrast, uniqueness, and distinctiveness result in variety. The greater the degree of difference, the greater the variety exhibited.

"Unity *and* variety" is mostly an either/or proposition. Either an element is a factor in providing unity *or* it is a factor in providing variety. "Unity *in* variety" combines these two aspects in order that an element can simultaneously unify and provide variety. There are many ways in which this can occur. When an instrument or sound-producing object is consistently played in one way, the result is unifying. However, when that instrument or object is played in a variety of ways, unity *in* variety results. For example, if a brake drum is always struck with the same hammer, the results will be unifying. But if it is struck with a variety of objects, each of which produces a qualitative difference, a timbral nuance or refinement, then unity *in* variety is the compositional result.

When you add to this the possibilities presented by other musical elements, an even greater array of compositional alternatives opens up to you. For instance, using that same brake drum and performing on it with a number of different strikers generates an unlimited number of possibilities when combined with the similarity or contrasts of rhythm/meter that can be used.

The progression of events in an instructional sequence should generally follow the order of presentation given here. *Begin with similar (unifying) tone colors* (or similar rhythmic/metric patterns, etc.) *and devise compositional problems that require variety (contrast).* After sufficient work with that, challenge students by giving them *sharply contrasting tone colors* (or rhythmic/metric patterns, etc.) *which they must devise ways of unifying in the composition.* Then, after sufficient experience with that, you can move on to the problems of unity *and* variety, and unity *in* variety as described above.

A final kind of grouping arises from the possibilities of the *simultaneous* combination of tone colors and the *alternating* combination of tone colors. Simple forms can easily arise from alternating tone colors: one section (call it A) consisting of patterns played on wooden instruments; another section (call it B) consisting of patterns played on metallic instruments.

However, the question of simultaneous combinations is one of searching for "shadings" or "intensities" of tone color. This can be compared to the activity of the painter in mixing colors on the palette. Mixing one part of this color with two parts of that color results in a certain subtle variation of color quality. We might refer to such varied qualities as shadings or tints, as bright or dull, or as light or dark.

Similarly, musical sounds used in simultaneous combination can create subtle variations of tone color that enhance the expressive potential available to the composer. This is, however, a pursuit that is relatively sophisticated. It should be held in reserve until students have had ample experience with similar, contrasting, mixed, and alternating groupings of tone color, and until they have significantly explored many of the possibilities available in those groupings.

Figure 2:6 summarizes the many possibilities for choosing and using sounds in sound-composition activities.

105

Source	Duration	Character
1. vocal sounds	1. sustained	1. definite pitch
2. body sounds	2. fading	2. indefinite pitch
3. sounds from objects	3. short	3. nonpitched

Timbre Grouping ⟶	Provides ⟶	Requires 29
1. similar tone color	unity	variety
2. contrasting tone color	variety	unity
3. mixed tone color	unity *and* variety	unity *in* variety
4. a. alternating tone color	unity within sections	variety within sections
b. simultaneous tone color	varied tone color nuances	effective expressive or formal use

Fig. 2:6 Sounds for Sound Compositions

SYMBOLS AND SCORES

Sustained sounds can often be symbolized by a line or broad bar running horizontally, with ups and downs representing highness and lowness of pitch:

Sounds that are *short* can be symbolized with a single symbol of one kind or another. Virtually any geometric shape will suffice:

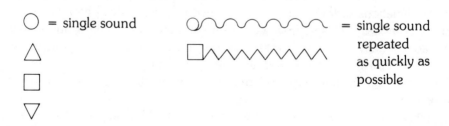

One shape can serve several uses if it is filled in a variety of ways:

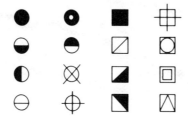

Or if it is added to in a variety of ways:

Sounds that fade can use the same kind of symbol as short sounds, but with an additional line to show that the sound rings for some short duration of time:

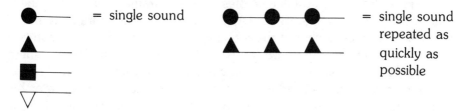

Young children are inclined to invent symbols that are very literal in their pictorial qualities. A hand will be drawn to symbolize hand clapping, a foot for foot tapping, and so on (remember Mus. Ex. 2:2). While this is somewhat useful in the beginning, it is very helpful to gradually encourage the use of totally abstract symbols such as those shown above (or any others you may suggest). Eventually students can become accustomed to the totally abstract, graphic nature of standard musical notation.

Middle school students and adolescents who have been working for quite a while with both original and standard graphic notation often can combine both types in the same composition. Composers often do this when standard musical instruments are used along with other sounds, or when specific rhythmic patterns are involved (see Mus. Ex. 2:3, page 112).

Scores also have to control the temporal element: how long a sound should last or how many times it should be repeated. There are two general ways of doing this, although any you or your class may invent are fine if they

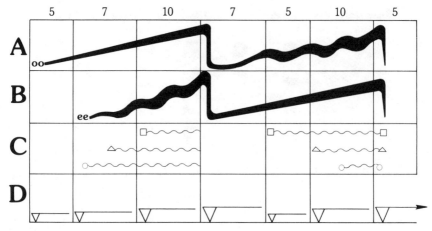

A and B: mixed voices. C: pitched instruments (high-middle-low).
D: gong-like sustained sound. Volume = size or thickness.
Height within box = pitch.

Fig. 2:7

work. A score can be divided into vertical lines that represent specified time intervals, usually seconds (see Fig. 2:7).

In Fig. 2:7 each vertical line creates boxes, or frames, for each of the four individual parts (labeled A, B, C, D). The duration for each frame is indicated in seconds by the number at the top: the first should last for 5 seconds, the second for 7 seconds, the third for 10 seconds, and so on. The thickness of the lines or relative size of the symbol can indicate relative volume. How high or low each symbol is placed within its box can indicate the relative highness or lowness of pitch. At the end of part D there is no vertical line indicating duration, so the gong-like instrument will be allowed to ring until it fades away naturally.

It is possible to have a group perform such works by reference to a large clock with a sweep-second hand should there be one in the room. However, this often divides the players' attention among the score, their instruments, and the clock. It requires a sophistication more suited to high school students. Otherwise, time factors are best controlled by a central source in the form of a conductor. The conductor makes a gesture (perhaps merely a downward "beat") to indicate the beginning of each new time frame. Thus only the conductor needs to refer to a wall-clock, wristwatch, or stopwatch. Or the relative length of each frame can be left up to the approximations of the conductor.

In either instance it may work better if the seconds are notated in only the conductor's score. This is recommended either for younger students or for students of any age doing this kind of activity for the first time. The children can have in their score "cue numbers" placed at the point of each vertical line (see Fig. 2:8). In first rehearsing or performing such works, the conductor can even shout out the cue number or point to it on the chalkboard (or overhead

cues

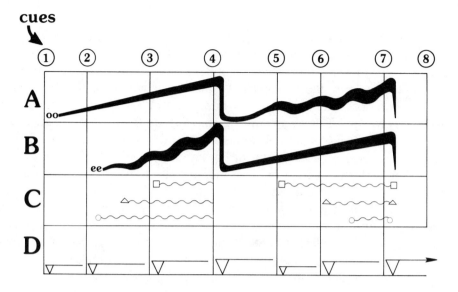

Fig. 2:8

projector if the score is notated on acetate) to be sure all the players are aware of where they should be in the score. Later they can learn to watch the conductor to keep track of their cues.

Sometimes an even more ambitious conducting arrangement can be used if necessary. It has the dual advantages of making performance contingencies even clearer and of involving more than one conductor, thus affording more conducting experience for everyone. The "master conductor" (see Fig. 2:9)—who could be the teacher at first—stands at the rear of the room, facing the backs of the class.

Fig. 2:9

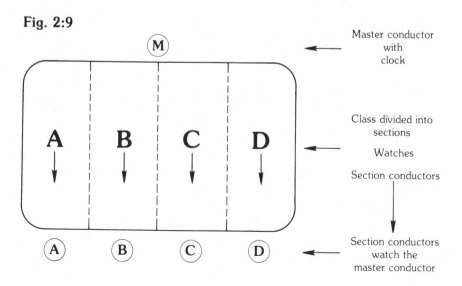

In front of each separate section there is a separate conductor for each group. Each "section conductor" is responsible for cueing and directing his or her own group. The four section conductors (in this instance) watch the master conductor for the gestures that signal the beginning of each time frame or other compositional unit. They, in turn, cue or direct the members of their group accordingly. This also permits them to guide the section in performing the specific musical or sound elements within the box. For example, the conductor for section A could use his or her hand to coordinate the slowly rising pitch. Conductor B could coordinate the fluctuating "waves" of pitch for section B. And so on for the other sections.

Remember, all four section conductors watch the master conductor at the rear of the room in order to coordinate themselves. Thus the entire performance can be very well coordinated, and as noted previously, will give several people the opportunity to conduct. The more conducting of this kind they do, the better they will be as the master conductor themselves, or as the solo conductor in an improvised sound piece.

There are, of course, many other ways of organizing scores for sound compositions. For instance, specific rhythmic patterns can be entered directly in the appropriate boxes, as can standard pitch notation if the composition calls for specific pitches. Eventually, standard dynamic markings can be used directly in the boxes, as can *rests* and other standard devices that are useful. *Eventually, the boxes and vertical lines can evolve into measures and measure lines, respectively; then into standard notation.* This possibility is enhanced when songwriting activities (covered in chapter 3) proceed at a parallel pace.

By the means suggested throughout, students are able to organize sound in a variety of ways, according to a variety of criteria. They are able also to perform their works, as well as those of their friends. All important musical concepts can be undertaken inductively since all the standard features of traditional music—pitch, duration, volume, form, timbre, etc.—can be encountered initially in the relatively unencumbered format of sound compositions.

Initial *ventures* work best when they are highly organized and directed by the teacher. For example, instead of soliciting notational symbols from the class, have them choose from among several you have devised or presented to them. Those suggested or illustrated here provide a good starting point and are quite flexible. *You* should consider conducting the earlier compositions until enough students have had some experience to take over that role in increasing numbers.

The very first sound compositions undertaken by a class (especially a young group) probably should deal with a single linear part composed by the teacher and performed by the entire class (see Fig. 2:10).

In this instance, the class might be divided into three groups: those with wooden sounds that are short; those with ringing, metallic sounds (including, perhaps, tone bells), and those who will perform the vocal sounds. During the

110

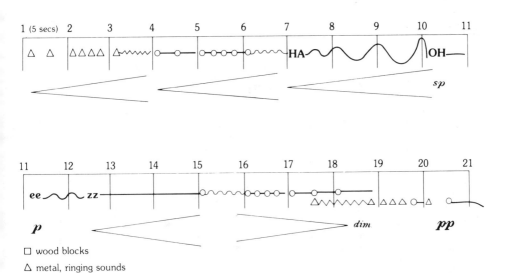

□ wood blocks

△ metal, ringing sounds

Fig. 2:10

performance, each group must watch for the entrance of its part. Each group must keep track of what is happening with other groups in order to reenter.

Toward the end of this example, at the beginning of time frame 18, there is a momentary overlapping of two parts. You should gradually extend simple activities like this to include more and more two-part work, then three parts, and so on. This familiarizes beginning students with the technique of *following a score,* and with *keeping track of their location in the score by listening to the other parts* when they are not actually playing themselves. This parallels what is known as a "coversation song," in which different groups of children are assigned to sing different segments of phrases of a song. Sound compositions are better, however, since in conversation songs children will often follow only the sense of the words rather than the notation.

Thus most of the most difficult aspects of score reading can be accomplished simply through a student's own efforts in (a) composing sound scores, (b) analyzing sound scores,[30] and (c) performing them. This is true not only of musical ideas and techniques that involve standard notation. Sound compositions perform the same function with regard to listening to all kinds of music; by improving aural perception they heighten the potential for a feeling response.

There is perhaps no other type of Action Learning that is easier to implement than sound compositions. Similarly, sound compositions are among the most effective techniques for the successful learning of virtually all major aspects of music. They can be effective without so simplifying or watering down a principle that it no longer bears a significant relationship to the musical art. Very little, if any, prior learning is required. The teacher gradually prepares all students in the minimal orientations necessary to maximize success. Finally, this pedagogy is largely based on students' active involvement as composers, performers, and listeners. These are all *musical* behaviors, musical *actions.*

When the techniques and activities of notated sound compositions are combined with freely improvised elements, or are paralleled with similar activities

111

Mus. Ex. 2:3

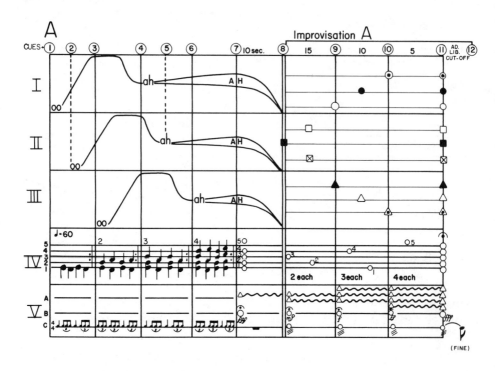

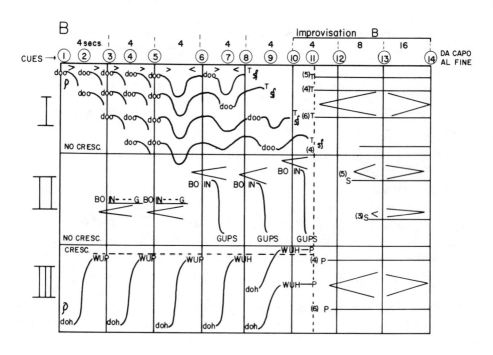

Performance Directions

Parts I, II, and III are composed for vocal sounds throughout. Part IV involves five melody instruments such as tone bells, step bells, and metalophones. Part V consists of three kinds of nonpitched percussion instruments: A = 4 castanets or a mixture of any 4 instruments that are shaken; B = 1 bass drum, or a gong or similar long-ringing instrument; C = hand drums, snare drums, bongos, etc.

Specific pitch is notated for part IV. Parts I, II, and III have pitch notated as relative to the highness or lowness within the box. Volume is indicated by the thickness of the lines.

In Improvisation A, a middle-range vocal pitch should begin in part II with the symbol marked "2". This sound is repeated only twice: beginning on cue 8 and once more at the performer's discretion. Of the next two different sounds, the higher one should be slightly higher in pitch, the other slightly lower in pitch; each is performed only three times (thus the "3") at the performer's discretion. Sounds marked "4" should be a little higher and lower, respectively, and are performed four times at the player's discretion; and so on with sounds "5" (still higher and lower, performed five times) and "6" (one very high, one very low, each performed six times). Each of these sounds is cued by the conductor (even the ones in between cues 8 and 9, 9 and 10. Each sound is performed once on cue 11.

In Improvisation A the melody instruments enter in the order indicated. Regardless of where they enter, they play only the number of pitches indicated (two, then three, then four per measure) at their own discretion. In part V, only A and B play: B as the symbols are located, and with the dynamics indicated. The A parts begin with two instruments, then three, then four shaking together.

In the overall ABA form, the B section has only parts I, II, and III performing. Improvisation B calls for mouth and tongue sounds made as often as indicated by the numbers accompanying each in parentheses: T = "tih"; S = the "s" of gups; P = "pih." All of these should be done without using the vocal cords—using only exploded air. Repeat the whole A section again, including Improvisation A.

N.B.: If band or orchestra (or piano) players are in the class, they can be assigned to parts IV and V to play their own melody and percussion instruments. Non-instruments can perform parts I, II, and III.

and techniques involving composition of more traditional music (chapter 3), a synthesis of all the conceptual possibilities of music is even more likely. The old and the new work hand in hand to provide an inductive, conceptual basis that furnishes the greatest opportunity for transfer to all kinds of future musical experience.

When sound compositions use both notated and freely improvised techniques, the resulting *composite sound compositions* synthesize the advantages of each (see Mus. Ex. 2:3). Some elements are notated, and others allow the greater performing freedom of the improvisation. As students gain experience with both of these approaches to sound composition, and as they acquire a working knowledge of standard notation by working with the *songwriting activities* dealt with in the next chapter, composite sound compositions will include all three elements: standard instruments, rhythms pitches, etc.; "invented" notation to deal with newly created "sound" factors; and improvisation (free or "planned").

While this usually presents some complicated compositional problems, it often results in a quite complex synthesis of musical concepts. It is precisely this kind of synthesis that prevents musical learning from being chopped up into little pieces by constant emphases on this or that factor. It is a synthesis of concepts that is most likely to stay with students and to exert a continuing influence on their understanding and appreciation of music.

A discussion of some other ways in which sound compositions and songwriting activities can be related or extended is found at the end of chapter 3. You are urged to study Mus. Ex. 2:3, pp. 112-133 to find the various notational and compositional techniques employed. It will be useful, too, if you can gather together the instruments and people to perform this work and the variations suggested.

Mus. Ex. 2:4 shows an integration of invented and standard notation.

Mus. Ex. 2:4

Prelude and Dance

for Voices and Hands

Lloyd Pfautsch

Notation:
▼ Pitch level of voice as low as possible
▲ Pitch level of voice as high as possible
◄⊕ Inhale audibly
⊕► Exhale audibly
⊰ Click tongue
Ᵽ► Pop lips like a cork popping out of a bottle

♪ Vibrate lips
Also ~~~~~~~~~~~~~~~ Glissando
♪ Whisper
J× Speak, following various pitch levels where indicated
↑ Shout
⊎ Slap right fist into open left hand

Pronunciation Guide:

EE as in He	AH-OO as in Now	SH as in Hush	P as in Keep
OH as in Ho	AH-IH as in Night	K as in Hook	T as in Hot
AH as in Hah	EH-IH as in Day	FT as in Left	S as in Hiss
AYE as in Hate	IH-UHR as in Ear	CH as in Touch	F as in Cuff
OO as in Hoot	EH-UHR as in Care	BR roll or trill	B as in Rub
EH as in Head	AH-UHR as in Far	the consonant R	D as in Rod
IH as in Hit	AH-OO-UHR as in Our	BL as in Black	G as in Rug
AW as in Haw	AH-IH-UHR as in Tire	PL as in Plow	L as in Hill
		CL as in Cloud	NG as in Sing
OH-OO as in No	TS as in Hats	M as in Mum	What pronounced
OO-UHR as in Sure	ZZ as in Buzz	V as in Vow	as HW
AW IH as in Toy	VM as in Vim	N as in Noon	

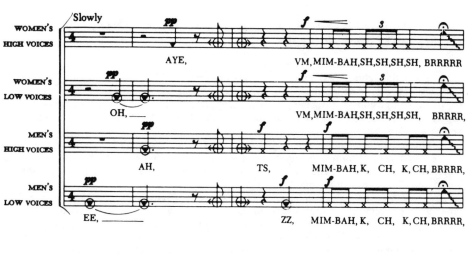

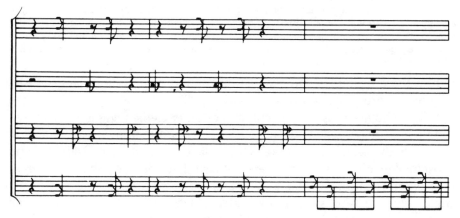

115

SAMPLE NOTATED OR COMPOSITE SOUND-COMPOSITION PROJECTS

1. Given their choice of a reproduction of a painting and 15 minutes, students, in groups of four, will *interpret their feelings about* the relative *brightness and darkness* of the painting's colors by composing and notating a sound composition whose timbres they think are appropriate to the painting; the composing group will perform its work and explain its interpretation to the class.

2. Given their own choice of sounds and 15 minutes, each group of three students will *synthesize* its concept of *form and rhythm* by creating and notating a work whose form is determined mainly by rhythmic and metric factors; each work will be performed by the composing group and discussed with the class.

3. Given their own choice of sounds, forms, and original notation, 10 minutes' working time, and a limitation of 1 minute per performance, each group of four students will *understand* the elements of notation well enough to create a work notated so that *another group* can perform it successfully; each performing group will have 2 minutes to study the score before attempting the performance; discussion of the success of each notational system will be carried out by the performing group and a list will be derived of criteria for successful notation.

4. Given the use of school tape equipment to collect "found" sounds in the school environment, a student will *decide* which sounds work well together in producing a tape collage in *second rondo form* (ABACA); playback will be during the next class, when the class will try to determine the form of the piece and will discuss it with the composer.

5. Given their own choice of sounds and symbols for notating those sounds, the class will *perceive* the contrasts between the *timbres* of metal and wooden objects by completing and notating an ABA sound composition that uses this principle; after suggesting the sequence of sounds and notating them on the chalkboard, the class will perform as the teacher tapes the work; discussion will follow based upon repeated hearings of the tape played back at all three speeds.

In example 1 above, students can experiment with "bright" and "dark" timbre qualities. They also will be encouraged to express their feelings freely. In example 2, two previously separate concept-areas (form and rhythm) are brought together, perhaps for the first time. While the focus is cognitive, the results will also reflect students' personal creativity and feelings. In example 3 the students can begin to discover the qualities required by a successful system of notation. Whatever list of criteria you might draw from the class by Socratic questioning will surely be applicable to standard musical notation. Example 4 is obviously intended for a student whose interest and ability warrant this kind of activity, and who might not be sufficiently challenged by the majority of activities done in class. Example 5 involves a large group-project suitable for any age or ability level. Through Socratic questions and solicited suggestion, the teacher can easily draw out an ABA form in which the B section has a contrasting timbre. All the other ideas will be entirely student-generated. This is combined with an electronic manipulation of the simplest kind, and reused as a listening experience.

From these examples you can see that sound compositions can serve virtually any instructional purpose (see the outline of concept-areas on page 117). If you have a musical concept-area or other element in mind for study, a sound-composition activity usually can be devised that involves students actively with the learning at stake. Not only do sound compositions permit almost total involvement on the part of the students but they also permit *multiple results* in terms of individualization and *multiple products* in terms of useful variety. Multiple results serve the varied abilities of early adolescents. The resulting variety not only stems boredom, but also expands the range of conceptual growth over a greater number of particular inductive experiences. This facilitates transfer and thus encourages the rapid growth of concepts.

SUMMARY: WHEN TO USE NOTATED OR COMPOSITE SOUND COMPOSITIONS

1. As individual projects for youngsters done as independent study or homework from goal cards or contracts placed in a learning center or "corner."

2. When specific detail is important in addition to the large outlines of a project: for example, when in addition to having two contrasting sections (AB), you require there to be some *unity*, some similarity or relationship between the two sections (i.e., unity *in* variety).

3. When you cannot possibly afford the time to hear all compositions, you can collect the remaining notated scores to evaluate student accomplishment.

4. When reusing or revising a sound composition seems useful or desirable, have it notated rather than improvised. On some occasions it is useful to have students notate a previously improvised composition.

5. When you are emphasizing the purposes and criteria of notational systems, students can discover for themselves what it is that musical notation controls, preserves, and facilitates. Such discoveries will lend substance to the singing and playing activities in which students will be learning to perform from standard notation.

6. When, aside from "interpreting" someone else's notation, you want a practical use of notation by students in a creative or constructive manner of their own.

7. When tangible products of student growth and accomplishment seem desirable. Students and parents respond well to such tangibility, as do school administrators.

8. When, as is usual, it is useful to get students immediately involved in creating and performing music and thereby learning musical concepts from the very beginning, composed sound compositions are very useful, since they require no prior learning or performing ability.

CONCEPT-AREAS COVERED IN EMPLOYING SOUND COMPOSITIONS

Sound compositions are very useful in facilitating an understanding of:

1. *Musical forms:* binary, ternary, rondo, theme and variations, sonata, fugue process, concerto principle, suite and other combined forms, etc.

2. *Techniques, qualities, and processes:* the goal is to know what one hears and only then, perhaps, to learn its name.
   a. Unity and variety: repetition gives unity; contrast gives variety.
   b. Unity *in* variety: a single musical element can provide *both* unity and variety by being related to some elements (i.e., similar) yet different from other elements.
   c. Symmetry vs. asymmetry: balance and proportion; how much "weight" each section has in relation to others; relative length or importance of sections.
   d. Impression of time: the impression of time moving faster or slower can be created by including more or fewer sounds in a given time span (i.e., "created" time).
   e. Responsorial: a musical statement by a *soloist* answered by the remaining performers.
   f. Antiphonal: a musical statement by *one group* answered by the remaining performers.
   g. Augmentation: a stretching out (e.g., doubling) of the time values of an earlier musical idea.
   h. Diminution: a shortening (e.g., halving) of the time values of an earlier musical idea.
   i. Fragmentation: breaking up into pieces a previously "whole" musical idea.
   j. Inversion: turning a musical idea upside-down so that what went up now goes down and vice-versa.
   k. Retrograde: refers to a musical idea that is ed backward.
   l. Retrograde-inverted: refers to a musical idea that is used upside-down *and* backward.

117

    m. Klangfarbenmelodie: distributing, one at a time, the individual tones of a "melody" among many instruments rather than one.

    n. Development: all those music techniques (such as the previous nine) that allow composers to expand a musical idea for its latent expressive potential.

3. *Styles*: baroque, classical, romantic, impressionistic, modern (jazz, rock, folk, popular); the "styles" of individual performers or groups playing the same piece; the "styles" of arrangers and composers that distinguish one from another within a style period; national or regional styles, etc.

4. *Textures*
    a. Monophonic: a single line of melody unaccompanied by harmony; not influenced by how many performers play that single line of melody or by rhythmic accompaniment.
    b. Polyphonic: two or more melodies or melodic lines combined, as in a canon or round; listening involves keeping track of the individual melodies.
    c. Homophonic: a single melodic line, accompanied by some kind of vertical harmonic structure.[31]

5. *Traditional musical elements:*
    a. Melody: the succession of tones and their relationships.
    b. Harmony: combining tones into vertical relationships, as in (though not limited to) chords.
    c. Rhythm/meter: the organization of tones into temporal units and relationships that aurally aid perception.
    d. Form: the sense of "wholeness" or "completeness" resulting from a composition. (See "Musical forms" above.)

6. *Timbre*: the "tone color" of sounds; their *formal value* in creating musical forms; their *expressive value* as interesting, pleasing sounds, or their ability to evoke certain moods, feelings, or impressions; the uniqueness of individual sounds and the "composer's palette" that blends these sounds into combinations that result in new tone colors; the exploration of our environment for new and interesting sources of sound; the use of electronic media to capture or change sounds.

All the concept-areas listed, while not inclusive of all possibilities, should provide more than ample "content" for music classes. The items listed are especially susceptible to treatment by sound compositions, although many also will be undertaken in other areas of your curriculum as well, thus facilitating transfer of learning and serving as continual reinforcement and refinement of your students' developing concepts. Remember: each activity involves *creation* for some and a *listening lesson* for the remainder. See Appendix A for a hypothetical program based on these concept-areas.

With these advantages in mind, the following suggestions are not meant to be inclusive or restrictive. They serve to point out the wide range of activities that can be derived from the sound-composition approach. The teacher's personal creativity and instructional goals will determine the extent and nature of such follow-up activities that are invented.

GENERAL ACTIVITIES DERIVED FROM SOUND COMPOSITIONS

1. *Use of the voice: sound compositions are particularly useful in dealing with concepts of pitch, especially with youngsters who have difficulty in matching pitch.* The linear designs used for sustained vocal sounds, as they rise and fall (as in Fig. 2:7), provide the kind of *tangible aid* that provides readiness for actual singing. However, since pitches are seldom specified, the *stu-*

dent is not stigmatized or made nervous by the spectre of failure. All students who have pitch-matching problems can be put on the appropriate parts along with some who do not have this problem. They can stand at the chalkboard and trace the line with their hands; this can be one way of conducting a sound composition—the section follows the course of the conductor's pointer as it traces across the line representing the sustained sound. Other, similar activities with pitched sounds can be derived from sound compositions.

2. *Readiness for standard notation*: when classes are inventing their own graphic notation, they often will have difficulty devising symbols that everyone can understand. Slowly you can *suggest and introduce simple standard devices.* As these are used more, students are more prepared to deal with standard notation. When sound compositions are paralleled with songwriting activities (which always use standard notation), a more complete integration of notational systems becomes possible. Sound compositions also have the advantage of emphasizing duration in very visual terms. When time frames are used, the passage of time seems more tangible; activities emphasizing such features can be derived when *a sound piece is re-notated somewhat, using measure lines instead of time frames, and pitches on a staff instead of indefinite pitch references in the original score.*

3. *Playing: sound compositions provide ample opportunity for playing instruments.* Sound compositions can use all available standard and invented instruments. *Some use can be found also for accompanying, chording instruments* (guitar, autoharp). *Melodies* (as in part IV of Mus. Ex. 2:3) *can be performed also on melody instruments* after the performer, perhaps in conjunction with the instrumental teacher, has learned to transpose his or her own melodies for his or her own instrument.

4. *Arranging and rearranging: works done by individual groups can be organized in a variety of combined forms or textures.* Sound compositions can be combined into suites, symphonies, etc.; shorter ones can also be made into larger forms, such as rondos.

5. *Stylistic variations: sound compositions in particular, are suitable for dealing with the very difficult concept-area of style.* An individual sound composition can serve as the "theme" for a theme-and-variations form in which each variation is a stylistic manipulation of the original theme. Students can "romanticize" their compositions, "jazz them up," make them "swing," or make them "rock," just to name a few possibilities.

6. *Reorchestration: sound compositions can be reorchestrated for differing combinations of timbres,* or with other expressive purposes in mind (i.e., stylistic variation). *Even songs written by the class as part of songwriting activities* (chapter 3) *can be orchestrated, using classroom instruments as accompaniment.* Different groups can suggest different sound composition-like "orchestrations," and several can be tried.

7. *Refinement of original work:* by far the most useful derived activities involve *reworking sound compositions to improve or change them in some way according to criteria* established during discussion, analyses, and listening. As this becomes a more regular (though not an invariable) concluding phase of creative activities, subsequent creative efforts by students will come more under the control of their new understanding and will be, therefore, increasingly competent. These kinds of activity are central in importance. They can be largely responsible for most initial learning. They also provide reinforcement and review of cognition acquired at an earlier time.

These suggestions should serve to remind you that *the ultimate value of creative activities does not end with the initial creation. What the teacher is able to "do," what the teacher has the students "do" with these creations often is more important to the total success of these activities.* Sometimes—particularly when the cultivation of students' feelings is at stake—creations serve as *self-sufficient* ends. Most of the time, especially when cognitions are emphasized, the composition functions as a *means to other ends.* These other "ends" are the further cognitions that can be developed through subsequent activities, discussions, and analyses.

NOTES: CHAPTER 2

1. This writer once heard this short conversation between two college music majors and immediately jotted it down for posterity: Student A: "Music history sure is a boring course!" Student B: "Yeah, I know! But at least [the professor] tries to make it interesting for my section." Notice that the *teacher* "tries" to *make* the course interesting even though the "subject matter' (whatever that is) is not. Implied here is that the teacher of the other section has not really succeeded in enlivening classes with entertainment beyond the boring "subject matter." Also interesting is the notion that the teacher is attempting to *make* the subject interesting *for* this class. This illustrates the contention that many students really believe that learning is done *to* or *for* them *by* the teacher. The teacher tries to lead the horse to water to make it drink for its own, sometimes reluctant, benefit.

2. No one has satisfactorily defined when adolescence ends; it ends presumably with adulthood, but there is no generally accepted definition of that growth stage either.

3. This trend can be so pervasive that it becomes a habitual state of mind for some people. The author had a student in a college-level music course for non-music majors complain about a class which featured a "live" recital by an internationally famous pianist. The student complained that the class was worthless because no lecture notes were given. This student, brainwashed by the system and equating notetaking with learning, evidently missed the entire musical experience that constituted the lesson.

4. *Ventures,* from ad*venture,* meaning to speculate on or confront or explore something unknown—as in "to venture into unknown territory."

5. Michael Polanyi, *The Tacit Dimension,* (Garden City, N.Y.: Doubleday & Co., Anchor Books, 1967), pp. 3–25.

6. " . . . A conception of intelligence that appears to me to describe more adequately the intellectual processes dealing with the creation and appreciation of affective life . . . . the production and appreciation of objects, events, images, and relationships among men are subject to the controls exercised by human intelligence, and as such are capable of being expanded through appropriate experience. Because the subject matter of such experience and the use of such intelligence, especially in those forms we normally associate with the arts, are qualitative in character, this mode of intellectual functioning can be called *qualitative intelligence* . . . . those aspects of thinking that are borne with and by qualities."—Elliot W. Eisner, "The Intelligence of Feeling," in *Facts and Feelings in the Classroom,* ed. Louis J. Rubin, (New York: Viking Press, 1973), pp. 201–2 See, too, Sam Reese, "Polanyi's Tacit Knowing and Music Education," *The Journal of Aesthetic Education,* Vol. 14, No. 1 (January 1980), 75.

7. Polanyi, *The Tacit Dimension,* p. 4.

8. Eisner, "The Intelligence of Feeling," p. 204.

9. The psychological bases for this mental action are described more fully in chapters 4 and 6. See, also, the description of the processes of the right cerebral

hemisphere of the brain in Thomas A. Regelski, *Brain Research and Arts Education* (Reston, Virginia: MENC, 1978), *passim*.

10. These criteria generally steer students away from considering breakable, valuable, or nonreplaceable items.

11. This, in fact, is one of the flaws in the argument that says membership in performance ensembles makes better listeners. Performers in school groups are seldom sophisticated enough in their listening skills to be able to "listen" to the piece with the same perspective they would have if they were in the audience. If they did have the necessary qualities (and, it is possible to argue, even professional orchestra players cannot really do this), they certainly would have no need of playing in the ensemble to improve their listening skills!

12. A collection and blended arrangement of a mixture of recorded sounds.

13. "To *discover* the phenomena revealed in music, painting or any other order of art, one has to know what *problems* the maker of the symbol encounters and how he meets them. Only then can one see new forms of vital experience emerge" (italics added).—Susanne K. Langer, *Mind: An Essay on Human Feeling*, Vol. 1 (Baltimore: Johns Hopkins University Press, 1967), p. xix.

14. In point of fact, there seems to be little justification for trying to separate "permanent" learning from "temporary" learning. There can never be an agreement on such questions as: How long must learning last at a minimum to qualify as only "temporary"? Of what value or purpose is any "temporary" learning (however defined)? If "temporary" learning is forgotten over time because of disuse, then why should it be learned at all if it is not something people can use or profit from in some way or another?

15. If the student is interested and understands (i.e., has a concept), information can be located from reference books as or if it is needed.

16. This kind of learning, as it applies to music, is dealt with in more detail in chapter 6.

17. This kind of spontaneity is distinguished from compulsion or mere "fooling around" by the degree to which past experience is reflected in a performance. Thus it is a "practiced" craft.

18. Teacher controls over activities, and behavioral objectives for music learning, are dealt with separately in chapter 5, pp. 283-295.

19. It is this kind of wedding together of affects (feelings) and cognitions (understanding; comprehension) that is referred to by the increasingly used term "confluent education." This is of special importance in all areas of arts education. See George Isaac Brown, *Human Teaching for Human Learning: An Introduction to Confluent Education* (New York: Viking Press, An Esalen Book, 1971).

20. Only two steps are needed. (1) Locate the tape recorder in or near the area you usually occupy while listening to sound compositions; plug it in. (2) Locate the microphone (two of them if the recorder is stereo) in a central position relative to the area used by students to perform. Either put the microphone on a floor stand of some kind or hang it from the ceiling or wall (janitors love to help!). A clever audiovisual specialist or a local electronics repairman can improve this setup for

you by adapting the microphone input for two or more microphones (stereo or monaural) and longer patch cords. This allows you "global" coverage of the room, which is an advantage when the entire room is used for a performance (e.g., a "quadraphonic" piece using all four corners). Strangely, its permanent advantage is that the students who are the "listening audience" often learn to be quieter when the entire room is covered by the taping system. In other words, they soon learn that their extraneous sounds can be picked up along with the performance.

21. Obviously, the younger the student, the more elaborate your plans for implementation should be. This includes the fact that everything must proceed at a much slower pace, and in a much more step-by-step manner. Otherwise there is absolutely no reason whatsoever why children five years old cannot profit immensely from all kinds of sound composition. In the first place, it is perhaps the most natural and spontaneous means of musical expression for them. Just put a five-year-old child in front of a piano and you will not have to wait very long before the first strains of the budding composer come banging out of the piano. Except when the piano is in jeopardy, this should not be discouraged. In fact, if more experience of this kind were gained before and after starting formal piano lessons, far more children would be likely to continue their lessons.

22. *Aleatory* music (increasingly called "aleatoric") involves "chance" or unpredictability ("indeterminacy") in composing a work, performing it, or both. Throwing dice (John Cage), picking letter names of notes at random from a bag (Marcel Duchamp), using telephone numbers randomly chosen, or other such techniques are employed in composing the work. Elements of performance also can be left to chance by permitting the performers to make certain choices, such as selecting the sounds or the sequence in which they are heard. The aesthetic principles behind this music generally involve questions of the process of "becoming" rather than the definite fixity of "being." It is held that art—like nature—should evolve, grow, change, from one performance to another; or should be "created" (composed) from the same kind of "natural laws."

23. Especially if you announce that your test is based on "summational, long-term behavioral objectives designed to measure each student's acquisition of musical behaviors and his or her ability to apply such acquired behaviors to significant musical problems with a view toward integration of learning for the student's in-life and continuing musical benefit and growth." Principals who think that testing is the sole or major function of education can usually be buried under or hoodwinked by such a barrage of clichés and educational verbiage such as the sample given here. You are allowed to invent your own, or to quote or elaborate on this sample.

24. Remember, for *affective responses*—that is, feeling or subjective responses—objective criteria are usually *not* specified.

25. For more detail, see Rita Dunn and Kenneth Dunn, *Practical Approaches to Individualizing Instruction,* (West Nyack, N.Y.: Parker, 1972).

26. Elsewhere I have used the term "permissipline" to describe this balance of teacher control and student freedom. See Thomas A. Regelski, *Principles and*

Problems of Music Education (Englewood Cliffs, N.J.: Prentice-Hall, 1975), pp. 115-19, and chapter 5 of this text.

27. A regular vibration pattern is one that can be measured electronically. The number of complete vibrations (i.e., a *cycle;* vibratory movement from and back to the point the object occupied when at rest) that occur in one second is recorded. Thus pitch is measured in terms of cycles per second (CPS).

28. As long as the objects are not dropped *on* resonant objects or instruments. For example, a basketball dropped on a kettledrum would produce a more or less definite pitch; that same basketball dropped on the bottom of an overturned metal garbage can would result in a nonpitched sound (noise).

29. Teachers should structure ample activities around these requirements. For example, restricting students to the use of wooden instruments and specifying a particular form (e.g., ABA or ternary form) will cause them to confront the problems and techniques of achieving variety by means other than tone color.

30. Aural analysis with the score as a visual aid is common for young or beginning classes. With experience, though, some visual analysis can be done *before* the score is performed. This encourages "hearing" the score with the "inner ear."

31. In sound compositions, these three textures usually involve dissonant kinds of tonal combinations in which instruments or voices are used tonally without regard for "key" or standard "chords," etc. Thus these techniques can be used without regard for prior knowledge of music "theory" or rudiments. These skills are learned in *songwriting activities,* and in the later stages they *can be used* in sound compositions.

3

"Song" Writing: Dealing with Traditional Music

124

TOWARD A TOTAL ACTION RESPONSE TO MUSIC

In the last chapter activities and procedures were suggested for involving early adolescents and teenagers actively in the exploration of the raw materials of music considered in their broadest sense: sound, silence, and time. Remember, all aspects of music can be subjected to student involvement through the various sound-composition activities.

Sound compositions are most useful in dealing with broad instructional aims. *They are not as easily directed toward first experiences with specific learnings related to standard notational practice and the more traditional musical practices that are controlled by that notational system.* You saw, however, that students often *can* apply standard musical elements to sound compositions and indeed often reach a point where they see the direct relevance of such practices for sound compositions. At these points it is not unusual for them to *ask* to learn more about these standard elements.

This is, of course, one of those "ideal" conditions that seem too good to be true. Nonetheless, it happens, and it is more likely to happen when the teacher also implements "song"-writing activities that focus on traditional musical practices and the standard notational system.

Such activities are not intended to "supplement" sound-composition activities, nor are they supposed to "reinforce" other learnings. It is not even really a case of "paralleling" on a separate "track" the studies and concerns taken up in sound-composition activities. A successful music program will inextricably wed *all* musical activities in the pursuit of certain instructional goals. Sound compositions and nontraditional notation, etc., are not a "unit" that is followed by another "unit" on standard notation and songwriting. Nor are listening activities, although they are treated here in a separate chapter (chapter 4), some "special" activity relegated only to "listening days" or to "units" on rock music, jazz, folk music, etc.

All activities should be blended together in a seamless fabric of student actions that involve the problems and practices of music in all its aspects (see Appendix A). *But you can do only one thing at a time.* Therefore those activities

125

that most completely involve all three musical behaviors—creating, performing, and listening to music (however defined)—are those which enhance the synthesis, the singularity of the musical experience. Such activities can minimize or eliminate the *atomism* that results when specific musical elements are emphasized to the point that they can only be experienced as fractional parts, or "atoms," of music. With an *atomistic approach*, analysis, perception, identification, comparisons, and other such techniques are used for reducing music to its supposed component parts, to labels and verbalized compartmentalism—and thereby the musical "whole" is lost.

Music is meant to be perceived, to be experienced in its total or unified whole. Any emphasis should always move from the whole to any part. In other words, *music should be studied in some kind of authentic musical context.* Some teachers do this quite intuitively, and often do it well.

Many teachers however, do not *move back to the whole* after briefly studying the parts. Thus the expressive or formal context from which the momentary focus stemmed is lost. Such brief emphasis of a part is intended to heighten students' awareness, understanding, and appreciation of that element. But students' responses to any musical whole cannot grow richer if no opportunity is given that allows studied parts to be applied while responding to a total work.

We must devise programs of study that sensitize students to a wide variety of musical qualities. This can be achieved most effectively through the nontraditional approaches of sound compositions AND the more traditional approaches of songwriting activities. Neither is seen to be better or worse, harder or easier, more or less interesting, or—most importantly—more or less "musical" than the other.

Thus *both* can enhance students' ability to "hear" more, or as much of the total musical whole as is possible, realistic, or necessary to understanding and enjoyment at adolescent levels of personal and intellectual maturity. Students, thus, will not simply "hear" a *melody*—the emphasis given during songwriting activities. Students will "hear" the melody AND the instrument, the melody AND the rhythm/meter, the melody AND the harmony—all together in a kind of musical ecology, or wholeness, that nonetheless allows the listener to be aware of and respect the various interdependent elements.

Now, you should be cautioned that this is the "ideal." Your students, even if you were a "perfect" teacher in all regards, would approach this ideal to different degrees and in different ways. The important point at this stage is for you to appreciate that all musical elements, aspects, facets, questions, problems, techniques, and what have you—all these should be approached in a never-ending, determined synthesis of sound compositions, songwriting, and listening. Listening activities are what might be called the final synthesis.

After musical emphases have been pursued through sound compositions and songwriting, the two-sided viewpoint that is developed is further blended in a synthesis that largely determines what the nature of our total musical response can be at any given moment. The synthesis of listening is the *musical action* most available to all people whether they are professional musicians or non-musicians.

The more that is made of it, the more "total" can be the student's possible response to music and the more *confluent* can be the total response. Cognition (understanding) and affect (feeling) work most naturally when emphasized *together*, and the student neither wallows in a shallow "emotionalism" nor struts like a professorial peacock with elevated "intellectualism."

Sound compositions and the songwriting activities to be taken up in this chapter are a means for heightening awareness of certain aspects of music. By themselves, these activities are not the *goal*. They are the *means* for assisting students in profiting most richly from a fuller and more natural experiencing of the musical art.

ADVANTAGES OF SONGWRITING ACTIVITIES

The "songs" involved in these activities include those with and without words. Basically, songwriting activities involve composing melodies in a homophonic texture (i.e., melodies supported by chords). It is more customary to compose songs with words in the initial stages of these activities. Poems or other words can be used as a tangible aid in the development of rhythmic concepts, to make the songs more interesting and to allow you to use student-composed songs for singing experiences. Words can be chosen— by the teacher or by the student(s)—that are of special importance to early adolescents. Working with such relevant words is a great inducement for all young people. It seems unarguable that relevant words set with appropriate music—both of which express or capture adolescents' feelings—are a major factor that attracts this age group to the variety of popular music.

As with sound compositions, there are several special advantages in using songwriting activities.

1. *Songwriting activities are the major means for developing concepts of the elements of traditional music:* melody, harmony, rhythm/meter, form (i.e., small part-forms). Other important properties and aspects of music can be dealt with most effectively also in this way: melodic contour and direction, nonharmonic tones, expressive and formal relationships between words and melody, rudiments of music (i.e., scales, chords, etc.).

2. Whereas sound compositions were valuable in dealing with general concept-areas, songwriting activities complement those aims by nuturing the *smaller, more detailed aspects that require specific information and readiness*. Songwriting activities aid in listening to smaller forms or the more detailed features of longer works.

3. Since songwriting activities are so useful in teaching the most basic aspects of music "theory," they are particularly useful in *providing a basis for lifelong interest and involvement in music*. From these activities, youngsters can acquire the skills needed to continue their musical involvements far beyond their school years—whether these skills involves playing an instrument by ear, arranging popular songs for an avocational singing group, accompanying songs on the guitar, or composing songs just for the fun of hearing one's own works.

READINESS FOR SONGWRITING

Readiness is the name given to the prior learning (skills, understanding, attitudes, and informal experiences) that students must have to profit from a present activity. Looked at another way, *readiness involves the kind of prior learning that minimizes failure and thus maximizes success.*

It is all too easy to fall into the trap of thinking of the learning process, and hence the readiness of students, as a kind of factual accumulation: adding one bit of information to another. This kind of thinking arises once again from the atomistic tendency of teachers to break things down into their component parts. Each part is "covered" one at a time until all the components have been emphasized. The result, theoretically, is a "knowledge" of the whole. This may be the most successful way for laying bricks or for putting an automobile engine back together, but in musical learning it definitely is counterproductive in several ways.

First, during this time-consuming process of emphasizing one component at a time, students will begin to "forget" whatever they had learned about the components studied earlier. The greater the number of components "covered"—atomists always speak of covering information—the greater will be the incidence of memory failure. Eventually a time will be reached when students are only able to "remember" learnings that occurred in the most recent past (see Fig. 3:1).

It seems pointless to identify any of the eventually forgotten "content" or "subject matter" (more expressions of the atomists' camp) as *learning.* How long must it be remembered to qualify as learning: seconds, minutes, hours, days, weeks, months?

The problem is simplified if learning is considered to be only that knowledge, skill, or attitude which has permanent, long-term benefit for the learner. This approach also avoids the rationalization (cop-out!): "Well, I taught it to them. If they forgot, it's their fault."

Keep in mind that knowledge acquired through action is learned effectively and that we can use what we learn. Then you can see that part of the solution to the problem of readiness is to *use* (i.e., actively involve students with) basic learning in an *increasingly inclusive* manner. This way, by the time one reaches the last stage of instruction, all earlier learnings will have been integrated into the final, total learning process.

The second problem with the atomistic approach to readiness lies in the fact that no two students can profit equally well from the same sequence of studying the component parts. And in general it is true that *no single sequence, no single method is equally appropriate for all students.* Some teachers who realize the dangers just outlined nonetheless fall into the trap posed by this second problem. They argue that *some order* has to be followed; it is, they say, unavoidable! To overcome the liabilities of a merely additive or accumulative

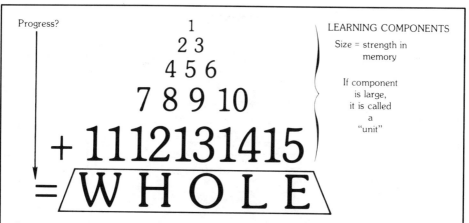

It is presumed that the addition (accumulation) of learning components results in a reconstruction (i.e., understanding) of the "whole." *Unfortunately earlier learning is often forgotten,* or if recalled but not well understood, does not serve later learning well. Also, in this model of learning *all components are considered more or less equal,* although that is seldom the case in real fact. Finally, the *synthesizing of components*—even when adequately remembered long enough—*is left to the student.* The teacher using this rather hit-or-miss "method" feels that *teaching* has been done. So if *learning* is not evidenced by students, the teacher concludes that students' motivation, intelligence, or character must be at fault. Hardly! This is an extremely illogical and unproductive learning format.

Fig. 3:1   The Dilemma and Futility of the Atomist

approach they claim to follow a line of teaching in which each component has an eventual culmination—that is, it is still present, still operative—in the last stage of learning. According to this method, diagrammed in Fig. 3:2, each study of a new component is related (or "tied in," as they would say) to the preceding component.

Notice that each new "unit" that is studied is "tied into" the preceding "unit," and thus—or so it is implied by adherents of this approach—there is no problem with forgetting. Each component is a "means," a preparation for the next component. In effect, then, each component is first a goal in itself and then it becomes the means for reaching the next goal. Thus, for example, unit 3 is at first the goal of which 1 and 2 are the means. Once "covered," unit 3 becomes a means—along with 1 and 2—for achieving unit 4, and so on.

Of course the problem with this process is that such sequential learning always is dependent on the equal functioning of all the links in the sequence. In a sense the chain is only as strong as its weakest link. Students who are taught in this sequential manner find themselves "falling behind" if they miss an assignment, are out sick, transfer to another school district, or do not

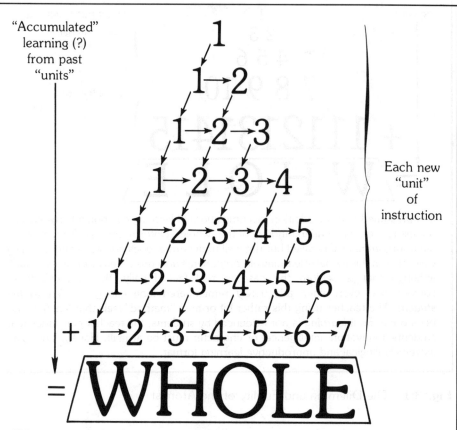

"Accumulated" learning (?) from past "units"

Each new "unit" of instruction

$$1$$
$$1 \rightarrow 2$$
$$1 \rightarrow 2 \rightarrow 3$$
$$1 \rightarrow 2 \rightarrow 3 \rightarrow 4$$
$$1 \rightarrow 2 \rightarrow 3 \rightarrow 4 \rightarrow 5$$
$$1 \rightarrow 2 \rightarrow 3 \rightarrow 4 \rightarrow 5 \rightarrow 6$$
$$+ \, 1 \rightarrow 2 \rightarrow 3 \rightarrow 4 \rightarrow 5 \rightarrow 6 \rightarrow 7$$
$$= \text{WHOLE}$$

This sequential, developmental "refinement" of the atomist still does not take into consideration that *no one sequence will work for everyone,* since each individual's mental functioning is unique. Was the first "unit" offered really the best place to start for *all* students or only for many? Or does the teacher begin with this lesson because this is the way *he* or *she* understands it, or because, *to the teacher,* it seems to be the simplest component? If "units" 1-7 represent a chronological continuum (as in music history), who is to say that it would not be better to proceed in reverse order, starting today with 7 and proceeding backward to 1? But then, this solution would not be suitable for everybody either. Is learning a purely democratic matter of the greatest good for the greatest number and the hell with the rest? Or should we attempt to teach every student?

Fig. 3:2 The "Improved" Atomistic Approach

understand a crucial, early point—just to name a few of the potential problems of this method. Typically a large proportion of students in any class are struggling to "keep up."

Simultaneously, the problem of the slower learners arises. Here the problem is one of dealing remedially with those students who are trying to "catch up" on aspects of past learning crucial to present learning. No matter how it is done, such remedial work is always an additional burden on both teacher and student. Though the student was not able to understand to begin with, he or she is now expected to handle "review" materials or assignments *in addition to* the ongoing study of the newer components in the chain of instruction. Finally, with this approach the more advanced students can frequently be bored and restrained in the rate of their learning.

The last difficulty with this format of teaching is that teachers pay mere lip-service to the question of review by administering doses of large-group review which generally bore everyone, including the teacher. Weak students, already "turned off" by their earlier failure to understand, are unlikely to benefit from such a mass re-infusion of information. Any success with this method simply allows students to "pass" an exam on the "whole" just studied, because the review refreshes their memory and makes past information *temporarily* more retrievable; yet such "learning" is forgotten within minutes, hours or, at best, days of the examination. Then so often—and almost unbelievably, when you consider the absurdity of it all—the next "whole" studied is taught as though everyone had mastered the previous preparatory "whole"!

However, as we all know, teachers using the sequential method assume that not all students will "understand" as thoroughly as the method seems to promise. Such teachers assume that some students will be lazy, dumb, or un-motivated at various points in the sequence and will therefore not learn as much as other more motivated, intelligent, cooperative students. Thus it is assumed that any deficiency in learning must be the student's fault.

The examination grade is used and is regarded by students as a punishment. The teacher imagines that this punishment will "motivate" the student to avoid future punishments in the form of grades—the final stage of which is "failing the course"—and that work will therefore improve and the student eventually catch up on what was "missed" or "learned poorly."

Teachers who blame students' basic intelligence and hence have lesser expectations are making a "self-fulfilling prophecy": students tend to live up to teachers' expectations for them, whether they be very high or very low.[1]

All in all, then, you can see that either form of atomist teaching is laden with a host of problems, many of which plague education today at all levels. In sum, what must be avoided is the progression from what is considered to be the "simplest" component of a "subject" or skill to the next most complicated component, and so on, as though teaching and bricklaying were identical processes.

The atomistic process begins with the simplest component and moves toward trying to construct the whole by a process of adding together all the component parts. Thus *the atomist holds that the whole is determined by the sum of its parts,* and in fact "popular wisdom" often adheres to this old adage.

The opposite approach—the one that is most suitable to the musical art—*begins with the whole* and works toward understanding how the parts influence the whole, interact with one another, and particularly how the whole conditions or influences the nature of its parts (see Fig. 3:3). Thus it is not a question of the whole being the *sum* of its parts. *In the view advocated here, the whole **determines and controls** the nature, quality, and musical function of each of the parts.* Thus music, and its study, is seen as synergic.

Fig. 3:3 The (w)holistic approach to teaching and learning

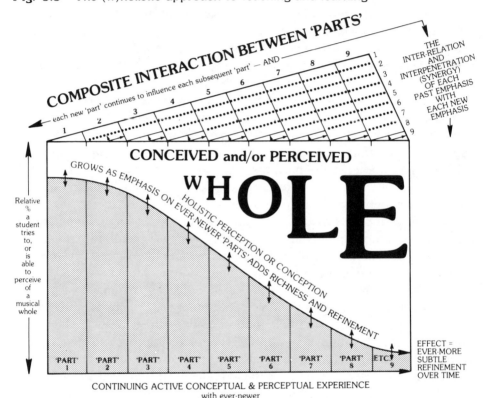

CONTINUING ACTIVE CONCEPTUAL & PERCEPTUAL EXPERIENCE
with ever-newer

'PARTS'

In this approach the "whole" represents an individual lesson or the growing perceptual acuity of a student over time. In the case of an individual lesson the "parts" represent individual emphases within the lesson. Thus each part of the lesson would be related to the whole lesson. Such a lesson, though, always should represent or conclude in some "whole" musical experience; that is, the students should not be left hanging with one or more detached emphases (parts), but rather should have in their minds at the end of the lesson a new concept, a newly enriched concept, or a perception of the whole (namely, the selection listened to or composed) that is richer (more inclusive) and more refined (includes more subtleties).

Fig. 3:3 *continued*

Similarly, when the process illustrated here represents long-term development, then the "parts" represent emphases and experiences provided by past individual lessons (of the kind described in the paragraph above). Here, then, the student's general conceptual or perceptual ability would grow ever richer and more refined over time as each individual lesson (part) makes its new contribution to the continuing interactional effect of past lessons. This increasingly inclusive interaction results in evermore (w)holistic experiences.

Notice that early on, the whole that is perceived on conceived is rather primitive. At such a stage, conscious attention to a part tends to be relatively easier or more natural (e.g., neophytes hear mainly the melody or the "beat"). Over time, one at a time, their attention is directed (and thus enriched) to a variety of parts (and, remember, in the short view a part could be a single emphasis within a given lesson; in the longer view a part represents any single past lesson's effect on the whole of the learner's perceptual or conceptual ability). This attention to the parts increasingly enriches and refines their perception or conception, and any one part becomes increasingly swallowed up by the interactional matrix of all parts creating the whole.

Notice, too, that over time the remaining parts that it is possible to emphasize get smaller and smaller (i.e., increasingly subtle), but that these subtleties, being last and thus freshest in mind, tend to have a correspondingly greater influence than the "larger" emphases (parts) undertaken earlier. But the continuing effect of the earlier, bolder emphases interacts with the more recent effect of the later, subtler parts and results in a more or less equal balance: all the parts still have a general presence in accounting for the whole that is perceived or conceived.

And as this illustration tends to convey, it is not a question of simple accumulation of parts so that the whole becomes the sum of the parts. Rather, in the continuing interpenetration of past and new parts a new dimension is created (shown here as the "matrix") which conditions and significantly influences the whole but is *not the same as the whole* (i.e., the parts by themselves do not create the whole, because some primitive version of the whole was always perceivable even before specific attention was turned to the parts).

Synergy, in R. Buckminster Fuller's words, is "the behavior of whole systems unpredicted by the behavior of their parts taken separately."[2] *Synergy results from the total interdependence of seemingly independent parts.* This not only describes the universe, ecology, and marriage, but is perhaps the most accurate description available of how the various elements work individually and together in an endless web of interdependencies to create that effect we call music.

The only way to maintain this synergy, this wholeness, is to study the parts briefly, *as derived from and related to the expressive or formal whole* that constitutes the musical composition under consideration (no matter how naive or simple such a composition may be, if it is a student's; listening lessons will pursue a similar course with the richer, more mature compositions of acknowledged experts, and will profit immensely from insights acquired in completing student compositions). Once a given activity has been completed around a given focus, a new activity is initiated, with its own new or varied focus, this time with the perspective of past learning as a basis for an enriched knowledge of what the whole entails.

The difference between the "atomist" and the "wholistic" models of learning can be illustrated this way. We do not remember a face by atomistically studying each of its "parts" or features—the nose, mouth, jaw, eyes—individually. When we identify someone, we do not compare one at a time a listing of features we have memorized to the actual face before us. Facial recognition is "wholistic" and instantaneous. We focus on any one facial feature while all other features remain in a subsidiary kind of background (diffuse) awareness. This one feature, perceived in terms of the whole pattern of features with which we have had experience, allows us to identify a person.

Now, music learning is not a simple matter of identifying this or that feature, but it is acquired by focusing on one feature or musical "part" (element, aspect) in terms of the "whole" (which remains in that same kind of subsidiary, background awareness) from which it was derived. Thus in "wholistic" learning the continued presence of a past focus in a subsequent experience is due to the meaningful pattern provided by the presence of a musical "whole" as the basis for the "part" focused on in each experience.

Atomistic learning works toward achieving a "wholistic" understanding only at the *conclusion* of a long series of lessons: The "whole" is literally built up of the parts emphasized. "Wholistic" learning *begins* with some "wholistic" understanding or perception in each lesson—however naive or vague it may be at first—and proceeds gradually to enrich musical responsiveness in general by attending to some smaller part(s) of that experience. After several such lessons, any initial "wholistic" understanding or perception of a new experience will be less naive or vague than at the beginning stages of instruction.

Any atomistic lesson is in itself incomplete. It awaits the future construction of a whole. The more distant that whole, the faster all present preparation slips away in memory or effectiveness. "Wholistic" lessons are in themselves complete and satisfying since they always derive from some meaningful whole. This is an important difference when dealing with adolescents.

It is important to emphasize that a "wholistic" approach does not result in uniform learning on the part of students, nor is it so intended. Given the immense variety of responses, interests, motivations, and needs that characterize the human species, individual students will learn some aspects more thoroughly than others, will be "turned on" by certain things, will be more attentive to certain elements. But all can be expected to evidence *some degree of increased mastery* of all the elements emphasized. It would be a basic misunderstanding of human nature to expect totally uniform results. Such uniformity, in any case, is not characteristic of music or the musical art. If anything, music in particular and arts education in general should be a seedbed for nurturing self-actualization, individuation, and other aspects of human uniqueness.

In covering the "subject matter," atomists expect uniform results. When human nature is *unable* to acquiesce to their demands (and this is especially characteristic of adolescent human nature—the last great period of "natural" or developmental independence from societal norms) such teachers try to "motivate" students extrinsically to learn what the teacher has decided they should learn. "Oughts" and "shoulds," except when self-determined, do not promote the "inner-directedness" characteristic of self-actualization. They promote the "other-directedness" characteristic of conformity and denial of Self. But "someday," the teacher asserts, "you will see the importance of this"; or "someday you will be glad we studied this." Remembering that early adolescents are characteristically eager for immediate results, that they seek relevance for their present existence, you can understand how the atomist teacher can create a variety of disciplinary situations.

In terms of readiness, the method that proceeds from the whole does not postulate some absolute state or degree of prior mastery to be achieved by each student. As long as students are actively involved in the pursuits at hand for each stage—and this is more likely when you start from the whole and hold forth the possibility of present satisfaction—*each profits to a different degree* depending on interest, general intelligence, musical background, and other such variable factors.

On the other hand, *any actions involved in continual use of certain skills or knowledge will be learned almost in spite of a student's background or interest.* This kind of learning also enhances the possibility that students, at some time in the immediate or distant future, *will still be able to use* their knowledge and skill. Once they know this, their attitudes about studying music are enhanced and the likelihood that they will profit from instruction is increased.

Teachers who insist on continuing to perpetuate the atomistic approach will continue to lecture and to demand the total quiet and attentiveness that promotes lecturing. In so doing, they contravene several basic characteristics of adolescents' needs and thereby create for themselves endless discipline problems as they try to "keep the lid on" unruly (i.e., inattentive) students who have no idea where such piecemeal efforts are leading—and after a while they no longer care, for they are busy amusing themselves with mischief.

Teachers who practice perfecting the "wholistic" approach will find that the question of readiness for songwriting boils down to relatively few steps.[3]

1. You will *provide all students with all the musical information necessary to complete a songwriting project.*

2. *This information should be presented by the most efficient means possible.* This is subject to improvement as you perfect your efficiency.

3. *This information should be constantly available to students during the completion of an activity* on a handout of some kind (which is generally preferred) or on the chalkboard or

overhead projector. The idea is that students should be able to refer to the information *as* or *if* they need it.

4. As a background of significant, successful experiences with songwriting projects is built up (and keep in mind that this always involves using the information that is given), *students can be encouraged, but not forced, to rely less and less on the given information.* The student is encouraged to find out how much he or she can accomplish without having to use the handout to refer to the information.

5. Periodically the teacher can determine how much of this information students are able to handle effectively without being given it. This provides you with some indication of how successful these activities have been. However, the information should always be available in some form, even if this means having to "look it up" in sources made available in the classroom or for the student's use at home (e.g., a kind of reference source that collects all the givens of the past in a handy single compilation).

These activities are *not intended to teach musical information for its own sake.* The point is to deal with the *music* itself first and foremost as a whole. Those students who are interested in or motivated by being able to compose their own melodies will learn the relevant information by using it. As long as they have the information available, the others—who are, perhaps, less inspired—can achieve some significant degree of technical accuracy and a whole lot of general musical insight.

Thus the present ability of students to deal with the information will permit them to gain maximum general and long-term conceptual benefits from these activities. And the fact that they never "learn" the information in the sense of "total recall" should not trouble the teacher. It is when students year after year show no or few signs of taking an active personal interest in songwriting that the teacher should be concerned.

MELODIES USING A SCALE AS A "TONE-ROW"

The basic songwriting activity entails the basic unit of traditional music, the eight-note (diatonic) scale. This is by far the easiest activity to implement and the one students can complete most successfully—it is virtually impossible to "fail."

The term "tone row" is derived from composer Arnold Schoenberg's technique of establishing an invariable series or sequence of all twelve (chromatic) tones or pitches. Each pitch of this "row" (or set) was to be used only once before any one could be repeated. This same technique is easily adapted to the needs of adolescents by substituting a row of eight tones—the major or minor scale—for Schoenberg's twelve tones. Thus *the requirement of using a pitch only once restricts the infinite possibilities that would otherwise be confusing* to the student. This restriction provides a necessary minimum guideline for the student to follow. The process can be implemented as described and shown in Mus. Ex. 3:1 and 3:2.

1. Prepare a handout[4] that has two or more musical staves on it. The first staff should show a *C major scale* already notated using the *treble clef sign*.

Mus. Ex. 3.1

C Major Scale (c1 to c8)

Number the scale degrees as shown, and label each pitch with its letter name, *using lowercase letters*. Unless students learn the clef sign by seeing it and using it on many occasions, always provide the name of the line of the staff which the clef sign identifies. In the example above, the *treble* or *G clef* sign is being used, so the little arrow at the left identifies the G line of the staff, which is the second line. Until the students demonstrate this understanding in subsequent songwriting activities, for the time being identify the numbers above the staff as "scale degrees"; also, identify the scale as a "C major scale (c¹ to c⁸)" to lay the preliminary stage for a later understanding that a scale is identified by the name of its first and last scale degree.

Also provide at all times the brackets (⌞__⌟) shown between the third and fourth, and seventh and eighth scale degrees (in major; in minor they are between degrees two and three, and five and six). Do *not* use a curved line (⌣) for this purpose, since it is too easily confused (especially by students who already read music) with a musical *tie* marking. The brackets identify the places in a major scale where *half steps* are found between scale degrees; all the remaining *intervals* between scale degrees are *whole steps*. This information is not immediately useful to you or the class, but the simple fact of its visual presence over the span of many early activities can have a major advantage if scale construction is learned later.

All this visual information—the clef, the scale, and all labeling—should also be placed on the chalkboard or overhead projector. In a pinch, a felt board can be prepared with this information, but it is generally not as easy to use.

2. On the second staff you place only the *treble clef sign* and a meter signature. Meters of two, three, or four main beats per measure are best used at first. Above this staff you have prepared and notated a rhythmic pattern *that will make an interesting eight-note, four-measure melodic phrase.*[5]

Mus. Ex. 3:2

It is on this staff that your students will compose their first melodies. If you plan on doing more than one melody in a class period using the same handout, be sure to have prepared additional staves for that purpose (see Mus.Ex. 3:3).

Mus. Ex. 3:3

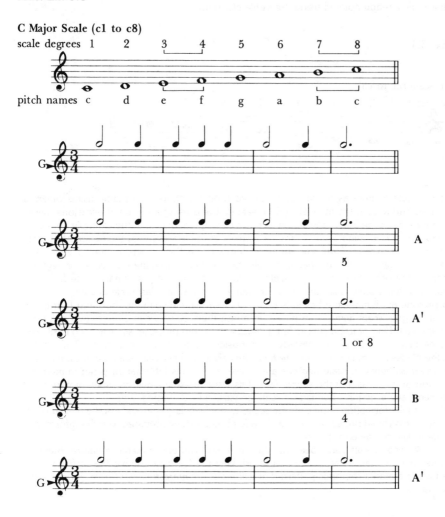

3. After the handouts have been distributed and pencils provided to all those who have none (for which contingency you should always have a collection on hand and already sharpened), direct the students to make a melody by *choosing their pitches from the first staff and placing them on the second staff, using the rhythms of the notes above the staff.* Tell them that they can *use each pitch only once.* As they transfer their chosen pitches from the scale on the first staff to the second staff, direct them to label under the staff the scale degree and letter name of each pitch they use (Mus. Ex. 3:4):

Mus. Ex. 3:4

This is useful, especially when first beginning these songwriting activities, because it (a) helps students avoid using a pitch twice by accident; (b) gradually sensitizes them to thinking in terms of the individual steps of the scale through using the names *and* numbers; and (c) provides the teacher and the class with verbal labels that are useful in discussing the students' melodies but do not have to be known *before* they actually work with melodies.

4. *Voilà!* Your students have written their first melody. As with most of the songwriting activities—especially at first—the melody they write has little importance in and by itself. There is no need to be concerned as yet that little conscious thought or planning by the students has gone into the product. In fact, their melodies will be very "hit or miss" and nowhere nearly as organized as the example given above. Their first melody is much more likely to look something like Mus. Ex. 3:5:

Mus. Ex. 3:5

While some students with experience playing instruments may try to be more thoughtful, you can count on the fact that most children are simply "mixing up the pitches" according to absolutely no particular concept. It is by using this and other early tone-row melodies that you help students establish the first principles by which tones can be chosen in composing a successful melody. In this sense, *the melodies written—especially at first—are never the ends of such activities. They are the means* by which the teacher nurtures an understanding of melody construction. But as *means* they are far more successful than melodies gathered elsewhere, since these are melodies composed by your students.

Thus it is extremely important with these activities that follow-up activities be well thought out by the teacher. *This "second phase" of any songwriting project is crucial to the eventual learning that results.* If your follow-up activities are well planned and successful, your students will begin to be more and more deliberate in how they arrange the tones chosen in subsequent melodies. These choices will be more and more guided by the knowledge that is gained from the follow-up phases of previous songwriting activities.

SUGGESTIONS FOR FOLLOWING THROUGH WITH TONE-ROW MELODIES

Play the four-measure melodies of several volunteers. Discuss whether or not the composer and the class "like" it. What is it that they like or do not like? Establish a routine along the lines of: "What do you think would happen if we changed this?" Experiment with the changes they suggest, or that you nudge out of them by leading questions.

139

Initially, students will have created melodies without much coherence. Most notably these first melodies seldom have a directional thrust; the results are entirely too angular, change direction too often or too radically—all of which results from the arbitrariness of the choices at this stage. There are likely to be too many wide, nervous leaps in these first melodies, or the melodies may be too scalar, i.e., have too many steps. An occasional "wise guy" will simply copy the scale in its original order, but that is usually dispatched with easily by playing it for the class and letting them reflect on whether or not they "like" it.

The purpose of the follow-up analysis and discussion is to discover at least a few guiding principles that the class can agree on concerning the success of these initial products. Such "success" ought to be treated as relative. That is, you should not convey the impression that the efforts are wrong or unsuccessful. Instead, your approach should be one of: "What are some things we could change that might improve these melodies?" You must guide this process of discovery by the leading questions you ask. Also play some of the tunes, ask questions that compare melodies, copy on the chalkboard or with the overhead projector some of the better-liked tunes (thus the savings of time if students originally work on acetate sheets), and compare students' tunes to other samples of melodies you have collected from various sources (e.g., pop tunes from sheet music, songs from song series, folk songs, or songs written by other classes).

Such activities should lead to such potential principles for improvements as these:

1. *Melodic direction and contour:* A melody, especially a short one, usually does not change direction too often. Some possibilities can be actually shown graphically by drawing lines through the noteheads of successful melodies. Generally, the *overall impression* of these lines will be found among these samples:

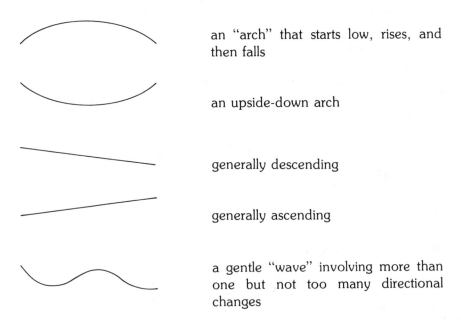

an "arch" that starts low, rises, and then falls

an upside-down arch

generally descending

generally ascending

a gentle "wave" involving more than one but not too many directional changes

one change of direction happening near the beginning

one change of direction happening near the end.

Also, some attention ought to be directed to whether a melody ascends or descends at the end. This is important when two or more four-measure melodies are combined to make a longer melody.

Sometimes the first melodic phrase might end with an upward direction and, for variety, or possibly for a sense of finality, the second melody might end in a descending direction. Reversing those possibilities often results in a melody with a "climactic" appeal at the end.

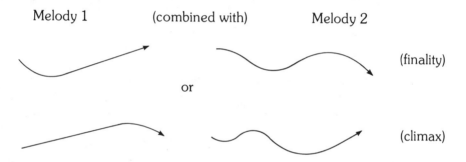

Of course, unlimited combinations of melodic contours can be combined in a variety of ways, depending on the effect sought by the young composer. The important thing is that the student have in mind many possibilities (based upon past experience in class with previous activities stressing melodic direction), and that he or she be able to determine which possibility is presently involved, along with its possible advantages or problems.

2. *Stepwise movement* (in musical terminology, *conjunct movement*) vs. *skips* or *leaps* (*disjunct*): A successful traditional melody does not usually have too many "nervous" skips or leaps, especially ones that involve a change in melodic direction. On the other hand, too many steps results in what is sometimes an overly smooth melody—namely, a scale in its original form, ascending or descending. Some teachers have established, for beginning purposes only, an arbitrary vehicle for students to classify interval relationships:

a. *Step:* any two pitches immediately next to each other, such as 1-2, 2-3, 3-4, and so on.

b. *Skips:* any two pitches on the scale that have one other pitch between and separating them, such as 1-(2)-3, 2-(3)-4, and so on.

c. *Leaps:* any two pitches in a scale that have two or more pitches between

141

and separating them, such as 1-(2-3)-4 or 1-(2-3-4-5-6)-7 and so on. Students can be asked to label the nature of each interval they have used (Mus. Ex. 3:6):

Mus. Ex. 3:6

In this manner, they can become increasingly aware of the choices they are making *as or before they make the choice.* When this analysis is combined with a determination of the melodic contour involved, the specifics of melody

Ex. A. Conjunct

Ex. B. Disjunct

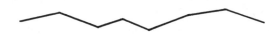

writing become increasingly graphic to students, and subsequent melodies are increasingly refined.

3. *Melodic cadences* (at the very end of a melodic phrase): Traditional melodies do not begin and end on arbitrary pitches. For example, the very last of a group of phrases comprising a complete melody usually ends on the first or last degree of the scale being used, less often on the third or fifth scale degree. Similarly, while the earlier phrases in a full melody may also follow that rule, it does lead to a choppy kind of stringing together of phrases all ending so similarly as to be boringly repetitive.

142

a. Therefore, earlier phrases in a complete melody quite frequently will end on the fifth scale degree, less often on the seventh, second, or fourth scale degrees. The reasons for this will not be entirely apparent to students as long as only the melodic-tone-row activity is being used. Later, when the melody-writing activity with harmonic emphasis is used, the reasons for which one chooses the pitches to end a melodic phrase will become clearer to them (and to any reader whose familiarity with the rudiments of music is presently at the novice level).

b. To establish this principle, it is often useful at some early stage in melodic-tone-row activities to plan a longer lesson involving, for example, the handout illustrated in full in Mus. Ex. 3:3. As you can see there, the last four slaves are already planned to execute a complete, four-phrase melody. After having composed a trial melody on the second staff, the student is directed to revise it (based upon whatever analysis and discussion has followed its composition in class), making sure this time to end it on the fifth degree of the scale[6] (as shown by the 5 at the end of the phrase given in Mus. Ex. 3:3). This phrase is already labeled A on the handout.

The second phrase (labeled A') will have its first three measures the same as A (this is the reason they are both labeled A), but should end on scale degree 1 or 8 (as labeled at the end of A'). Phrase B presents the opportunity for an entirely new melodic phrase (but keeping in mind all learned to date about contour, steps, skips, leaps, etc.), the only requirement being that it end on scale degree 4 (as labeled). For the concluding phrase, the student need only to copy the second phrase (A') over again (see Mus. Ex. 3:7).

With this, your students will have composed their first full melodies. In the process they will have gained invaluable experience and insight about such questions as melodic direction and contour, steps, leaps, skips, and melodic cadences. They also will have acquired Action Learning about musical form, since the example used here results in the very typical small part-form of AA'BA' (sometimes called *rounded binary form*).

Future experiences with other techniques, other forms, and other melodic cadences pre-specified by the teacher will result in increasingly significant melodies composed by your students. And as the other songwriting activities are brought increasingly into play, each new melody will incorporate other insights involving both harmony and rhythm as they pertain to melodies.

Once you have reached such a stage as this the possibilities are limitless. This might be all you do with your class the first few times. But you might have the students save these first efforts, or you can save them for the class to use on a subsequent occasion. What you will do with these phrases and others you will have the class create will depend largely on your instructional intent.

It is recommended, however, that you employ the tone-row activity and related follow-up activities such as the ones suggested above as often as is

Mus. Ex. 3:7

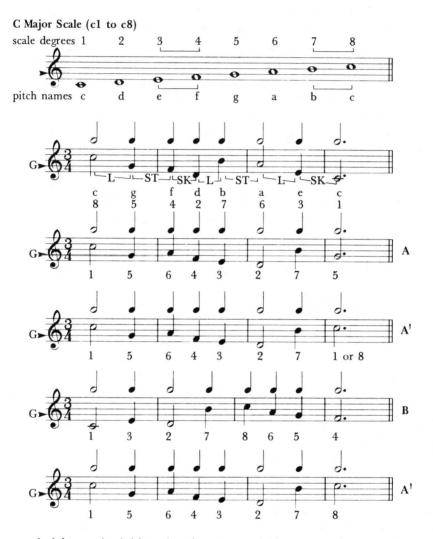

needed for each child in the class to reach the stage of composing a *compe-tent melody* (i.e., technically appropriate) readily and comfortably. There is lit-tle sense in going to more advanced or adventuresome activities until or unless *all* the students are at ease in using the tone-row approach in constructing well-conceived melodies.

It should be noted that it is quite difficult, even for the college music major or the school music teacher, to compose a melody while restricted to using each of the eight tones of the scale only once. It is a truly artificial "gimmick" intended to limit, and thereby structure or control, the possibilities. As usual with the activities recommended here the structure, or teacher's control, still

144

allows significant student latitude. Thus the melodies composed will all be significantly different.

However, even at the beginning stages some students will catch on more readily than others. Often this will involve those youngsters who have richer musical backgrounds; i.e., they probably study or have studied an instrument. It is unfair and unwise to restrict them over many lessons to limitations they already can handle early on, simply in order to give sufficient practice to the remainder of the class. What to do?

Since it is eventually a necessity to remove the restriction of using a pitch only once, the more advanced students may be given this opportunity as soon as they have demonstrated the ability to work within this restriction. And this does not mean after they achieve only their *first* success. After they have composed *several successful melodies* within the "Use each pitch only once" restriction, then and only then can they be allowed to use any pitch twice. After a while, allow them to use a pitch three times. After that they may be allowed free scope in how often they repeat a pitch. They will need some help in seeing that pitches can be repeated immediately (Mus. Ex. 3:8).

Mus. Ex. 3:8

or at various points in a melody (Mus. Ex. 3:9)

Mus. Ex. 3:9

in order for them to be fully aware of the potential this new set of circumstances allows.

Eventually you should aim for extending this option to all students as and if they demonstrate the ability to handle the earlier restrictions. In this way it is entirely possible to keep track of a class of twenty to thirty students, each of whom is working with restrictions geared to present ability. The teacher carefully monitors everyone's work in order to know when an individual's achievement warrants additional opportunities of free choice.

When all students have been extended the opportunity of using repeated pitches, these new alternatives should be added to those listed above on page 141 under section 2. Thus five possibilities will exist: stepwise movement, skips, leaps, and tones immediately repeated or tones repeated at various points in a melody—all aids in allowing the composer full control over melodic direction and contour, and over the nature and effect of melodic cadences.

SUMMARY OF TONE-ROW ACTIVITIES

1. Prepare a handout on which a C major scale is notated and labeled, with the clef sign and scale degrees clearly indicated (see Mus. Ex. 3:1).

2. Prepare a second staff with the same clef sign and four empty measures, above which is notated a rhythm pattern containing eight notes (see Mus. Ex. 3:2).

3. Students are directed to compose their melody by choosing their pitches from the first staff, using each pitch only once, and transferring the pitches to the second staff using the rhythms prepared by the teacher above the staff. Have them label each pitch with its letter name and scale degree (Mus. Ex. 3:4-5).

4. Many of these tunes should be heard and analyzed, leading to the increasing ability to deal successfully with melodic direction and contour; steps, skips, leaps, and repeated tones; melodic cadences; and eventually the combination of all these aspects into eight-, sixteen-, and thirty-two-measure melodies made by stringing together the appropriate number and kind of four-, eight-, and sixteen-measure phrases (see Mus. Ex. 3:6).

5. As students demonstrate their competence at handling the limitation of using a pitch only once, they should be extended the opportunity to use a pitch twice.

6. Do not move on to the other kinds of songwriting activities until everyone in the class has demonstrated sufficient competence in writing tone-row melodies easily and successfully.

7. Keep in mind that the melodies written are *means* for the teacher to have students analyze and learn the principles of melody construction. They are not *ends* in themselves. This does not prevent them from being regarded *by the students* as ends. This is a problem only when some youngsters are too easily satisfied with their first efforts and prefer, if left free choice, *not* to improve upon them (and thereby gain additional insight and expertise). Otherwise, the fact that students consider them as ends is a sign of your success, since in effect they are indicating that some *thing* (an end) has been achieved, accomplished. This is a relatively rare thing for them in most of their classes, and certainly a rare thing for many whose only experience in music class has been singing.

8. Finally you are reminded that songwriting—any of the varieties—is not intended as a "unit" to be done once, and to which you never return (see about units in Appendix A). Similarly, too many consecutive classes of songwriting activities—the tone-row variety or any variety—will become boring and hence progressively ineffective. These activities should be intermingled with sound-composition activities and listening lessons. While the outer form of the lessons (i.e., the activity employed) may be different, the "content" (what is to be learned) can be the same, similar, or related. For example, at the time you are first expanding songwriting into AABA form, sound compositions can be composed in that form, and listening lessons devised for compositions featuring that form. Thus there can be a unity of focus (in this instance the emphasis might be on "AABA-ness") while maintaining the benefits of a diversity of methods (i.e., songwriting, sound compositions, and listening lessons intermixed for maximum impact). This has the added advantage of involving your students over several classes in all three types of musical behavior: composing, performing, and listening. They *compose* melodies and sound compositions; they *perform* sound compositions; they *listen* to recordings in formal listening lessons, but also to their own creations when doing songwriting or sound compositions. This is teaching efficiency and effectiveness at its best.

146

SUGGESTIONS FOR "ADVANCED" (8TH GRADE AND e.g., HIGH SCHOOL) TONE-ROW ACTIVITIES

1. Have the class create a phrase that *ends* on scale degree 5, 7, or 2. Have them complete another that *begins* on 5, 7, or 2, but *not the same pitch the previous phrase ended on.* Make sure the second phrase ends on 1. Put the two phrases together and a *binary* (AB) melody will have been created. A reminder from you of past lessons, and many of these melodies will be more coherent than you might expect.

It is *not* necessary to identify these forms by name as so-called parallel or contrasting phrases or periods. Just use letters to label phrase relations (AB; ABA; AABA; ABACA; ABBA, etc.) and you can have the class create melodies in a variety of part-forms without being technical in your terminology (which they will forget anyway if you try to teach them the technical labels).

If you accompany their singing of these melodies (have them sing on "la" or make up words to the rhythmic figure you gave) on the piano, guitar, or autoharp, you should attempt to make students increasingly aware of the sound and "feel" of the harmonies that accompany what up to now have been only melodic cadential considerations. The main difference between the A sections will be whether or not the first phrase ends with a so-called half cadence (i.e., on one of the tones of a V chord).

If students can begin to hear or "feel" the difference between the melodic and harmonic interactions of a cadence on the V chord and a cadence on the I chord, they will be even better prepared for the "harmonic emphasis" songwriting activities that will follow.

2. If some of the students are old enough and studying transposing instruments, *they can transpose their melodies and play their instrument along with the class.* All that needs to be done is to tell them what scale to use in relation to C major (N.B.: using C major a lot, at first, simplifies many things). Then all they have to do is find each step in the new scale that corresponds to their pitches in C major. The instrumental teachers can also help them to learn which scales to use in this regard.

3. *Add words to the melodies* created by this method. Or have the students make up their own words. Word activities combined with songwriting activities often can be jointly approached with the language-arts class or specialist.

4. *Rework some of the better songs* on your own, making slight changes that in your judgment improve the melodies, and retain these songs for future singing activities. You will see a sparkle in students' eyes when they sing songs composed by classmates.

5. *Use other major scales,* especially those with up to three or four flats or sharps. *Use minor scales* once the class has become accustomed to using major. Eventually, even *modes* other than major or minor can be used. *Modulations can be planned.* For example, once students can make independently, say, an AABA form, have them compose the first A phrase in C major and end on scale step 5. Let the B phrase be in G major, beginning and ending on step 1 of G major. Then repeat phrase A, but have it end on scale step 1 (c).

6. *Students can learn to construct scales from a given pitch by using sharps or flats, and the pattern of half steps for major and minor.* This can be done best by high school theory and general music (or "appreciation" class) students. In middle and junior high, those students capable of and interested in such learning can be assisted individually. Constructing scales from a given pitch is probably *not a realistic goal for students at any level who have or see no use for such a skill.* If and when they do see relevance in such knowledge, then independent or individualized study can be made available for them too.

7. *Arrange some of the better student-composed songs for chorus performance (or have this as an assignment for high school theory or general-music class).* At the least, perform them for a few weeks or a few times in the chorus rehearsal at that level. If you do not conduct a chorus, convince the teacher who does to use these compositions for sight-reading practice. In middle and junior high you can also produce an entire assembly or PTA program featuring the class(es) involved singing student compositions, even if only as unison songs. By all means, include any especially satisfying songs as part of a concert program, and be sure to introduce the young composer(s) to the audience. This approach will do wonders for your "public relations" image, and this means the potential of greater recognition and support from your principal, PTA, and administration.

147

8. *Encourage students to compose songs at home on their own.* Issue a standing invitation to accept and hear any melodies composed by individuals or groups outside of class time, or outside of school. This is so important in emphasizing (not only to the students but also to their parents and the school administration) that what is learned in music class is not simply a school pursuit. It is a lifelong pursuit, and hopefully one that eventually will have permanent significance in the out-of-school life of each student, even as an adult.

9. *Coordinate your songwriting efforts with the instrumental music teacher's program.* The aim is to encourage transfer of learning between general music and instrumental music instruction. The simplest way is to identify for the instrumental music teacher which instrumental students are working with what aspects of melody construction, notation, harmony, and rhythm, etc., at the present time. A cooperative instrumental teacher can devise appropriately related activities of special importance to the budding instrumentalist: e.g., the transposition activities suggested in item 2 above; scale construction (rather than memorizing key signatures); using student-composed melodies as at least a partial basis for solo-literature study (student melodies are no worse and often better than those contained in many instrumental teaching books—and in any case, students are more motivated to play and practice melodies of their own).

10. *Use student songs as at least a partial basis for singing and music reading in your program.* For the reasons cited immediately above, students are invariably more motivated to perform and study melodies of their own or their classmates than most others (with the possible exception of current pop hits).

SONGWRITING WITH HARMONIC EMPHASIS

The initial stages of this type of activity, like most songwriting activities, will be similar. You provide the class as efficiently as possible the musical information necessary to the completion of a composition. They, in turn, will learn this information over a period of time simply by using it, and by the kinds of emphases you provide on this information in your well-planned follow-up activities to the composition of a melody.

1. In this instance, provide a scale, just as you did before (Mus. Ex. 3:3), but this time *have chords already constructed on the scale,* as shown below (Mus. Ex. 3:10). Make sure you *build only those chords that will be used for the present activity.* Once the students have "discovered" (with your guidance) that the I chord is built on the first scale degree and the IV chord on the fourth degree, and so on, you can have them build the chords themselves (i.e., piling up the notes on the next two lines or spaces above the given note of the chord—the *root* of the chord). So take a moment to discuss the visual appearance of chords—i.e., that they involve the two lines or two spaces immediately above the scale pitch.

Mus. Ex. 3:10

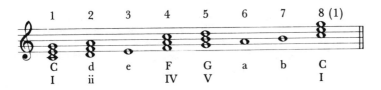

Notice that here when you label the pitch names of the scale degrees you *use uppercase and lowercase letters and roman numerals to represent major and minor triads.*[7] Capital letters and uppercase roman numerals represent major triads; lowercase letters and roman numerals (i.e., roman numerals without the horizontal line across the top) represent minor triads. If you have no intention of teaching the construction or use of major and minor chords in the future, you may leave this step out. Then use capital letters and uppercase roman numerals to represent all chords.

This has value in two ways: (1) the roman numerals show functional harmonic relationships, i.e., that chords are based on scale degrees and that a chord's function is related in importance to the scale degree of its *root*; (2) the capital letters have a natural transfer value for those students who play piano, guitar, accordion, or chord organs from sheet music having chords symbolized. The kind of "fake book" symbols used in most such sources is consistent with the approach taken here in using capital letters to represent a chord's spelling (i.e., the pitches it contains—thus in such music when a chord is specified "G," it indicates a g-b-d triad, however arranged from lowest pitch to highest).

Some teachers find it useful to darken the notes of the scale, while leaving open the chord tones added above the scale tone (Mus. Ex. 3:11). This enables beginners, or those having difficulty understanding, to visualize the scale easily and to see more clearly the tones added above it. In effect, *this interpenetration of the horizontal scale or melody and the vertical chords is the essence of what is to be learned from songwriting activities with a harmonic emphasis:* that melodies are derived from scales; that harmonies are derived from scales; and that melodies are "supported" by chords in the same way a bridge over a river is supported by pillars.

Mus. Ex. 3:11

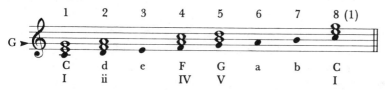

2. As with the tone-row activity, empty working staves should be already set up with a clef sign, measure lines, and rhythms notated above. *For the harmonic-emphasis activities you also provide chord symbols (both roman numerals and letters) under each working staff* (Mus. Ex. 3:12).

Mus. Ex. 3:12

3. As with the tone rows, you direct the students to create a melody. This time using the given rhythms, the students are directed to compose their melody by *using in a particular measure any tone from the chords indicated for that measure (Mus. Ex. 3:13 below). Have students refer to the staff which has the chords built over the scale (Mus. Ex. 3:10 or 3:11) to find out which tones are contained in the chord notated for that measure.*

Mus. Ex. 3:13

4. Depending on how extensively you worked with melodic direction and contour, steps, skips, leaps and repeated tones, melodic cadences, and other such factors during earlier tone-row activities, you may or may not want your students to keep track of the pitches they used (or did not use) and how often; labeling the intervals is also an option (see no. 2, page 141).

You should consider, however, any such problems and principles in the melodies that students compose during the activities with harmonic emphasis. Remember that the melody is a *means* for extending their knowledge, and *not an end* in itself. *All the principles of melody construction cited previously with regard to tone rows should be again and equally emphasized here* with suitable follow-up questioning, analysis, and derived activities. Of special importance here, however, are those aspects which have the most direct bearing on, or relationship to, harmony.

CADENCES, HARMONIC RHYTHM, AND CHORD PROGRESSIONS

a. *Cadences.* Students should come to understand that *the melodic cadences they choose are in reality based on the underlying harmonies;* i.e., that the pitches ending melodic phrases have a direct and necessary relationship to the harmonies chosen to support the melody at that point. Thus the question of melodic cadences is a bit simplified by the presence of underlying chords, since now the student has only to choose from among the pitches contained in that chord. And, for now at least, the teacher is choosing the chords.[8]

b. *Harmonic rhythm.* Harmonies have an aspect related to rhythm in that chords occur in a certain sequential order. And just as there are strong and weak beats in rhythms, so there are strong and weak chords. You are advised to begin by using strong chords (the primary chords—I, IV, and V chords) in important places in a melodic phrase and weaker chords (the secondary triads—ii and VI chords) for the remaining portions. Although the chord built on the seventh scale degree is a secondary chord, it should be avoided by all but high school theory or other advanced students who learn how to use its special attributes correctly.

Here are some possibilities in diagram form for you to consider:

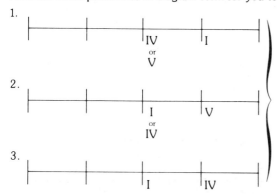

All would be followed by a phrase ending on the I chord.

When you provide a chord pattern from which to work, you can indicate whether the phrases should be the same, similar, or contrasting; or indicate whether this choice is left up to the student (as it should often be). The results should be discussed. In the majority of cases where the choice is left up to the student, simply ask each student to identify the kind of relationship among phrases (same, similar, contrasting) that has been achieved. Consider using the following technique to facilitate identification:

(1) Have the student diagram each phrase in the melody, using this symbol to represent the phrase:

(2) Above the symbol the student uses letters to represent the relationship between phrases. Two phrases labeled A and A are the same; A and A ′ are similar; A and B are contrasting. When more than two phrases are involved, teach the class to use additional letters as needed.

(3) Under and at the end of each symbol the student indicates the actual chords used for the *cadence* of his or her melody:

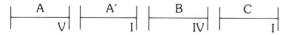

A brief and easily done diagram such as this can be assigned by the teacher as a criterion, or it can be added by the student to a project with very little fuss. It clearly shows the teacher whether or not the student was aware of what he or she was attempting. In and by itself the diagram is a much more useful teaching aid than a verbal label, since the diagram is not only almost as efficient but embodies or graphically represents what it symbolizes or what it refers to. Therefore each time the diagram reference is used it is a reminder or reinforcement of the learning.

c. Finally, among the factors stressed in songwriting with harmonic emphasis is *chord progression* (see Fig. 3:4, page 152). The term refers to the "movement" of one chord to another. This is one of the hazier areas of music, since, above all other criteria, the ear makes the final judgment of suitability. However, since neophyte composers in the middle school do not as yet have a very selectively developed ear, they may accept too readily any chord change as satisfactory.

151

In one sense, this can be desirable. Many fresh, new progressions have been invented (or at least dusted off) in the course of the history of folk music, and in recent years in the popular-music field, especially in rock music. However, students also should learn the "standard" or "academically accepted" progressions as the basis for whatever harmonic exploration they may be able to do on their own instruments at home or in school. Since most children do not and will not play an instrument, and will seldom develop an effective ear for anything except whether they like what someone else has done or not, it is wise to proceed from the more standard progressions. Accept those other progressions that students have in fact *discovered aurally* (as opposed to abstractly at their desks without an aural reference) when the student is genuinely captivated by the discovery.

There are no real "rules" for these progressions, but some principles can be developed with students:

(1) Typically the I chord can be followed by any chord.

(2) Typically the I chord is preceded by a V or IV chord.

(3) Chords seldom move effectively to the adjacent lower chord: e.g., ii→I, iii→ii, IV→iii. The one exception is the V→IV progression found in a specific location in the classical twelve-bar blues progression.[9]

(4) Typically a chord can move strongly to the chord built on the scale degree four steps higher or five steps lower (which in any case is the same pitch): e.g., I→IV, ii→V, iii→vi, V→I. Exception: do not use IV→vii.

(5) Typically a chord progression moving down to the chord built on the scale degree three steps down, and arranged as a pattern of chords progressing in sequence, is generally effective: e.g., I→vi→IV. Less effective, and less often used is V→iii→I. In any case the I→vi→IV progression is very often followed by V→I, as in the old "Heart and Soul" piano accompaniment people have enjoyed playing for years without knowing what it was.

(6) Chords can often move to the next higher, adjacent chord. Two in a row is maximum, however. Thus, IV→V, or V→vi, but not IV→V→vi. The progression vi→vii is very weak and should be avoided; ii→iii is also regarded as weak.

(7) All these suggestions are illustrated as though used for a melody in a major key. The chord degrees would remain the same and equally applicable *most* of the time in minor, but the pitches making up the chords would change, of course, because the scale serving as the basis for the chords would have different pitches in major than in minor.

The table in Fig. 3:4 below is useful but not one hundred percent accurate for all instances, so use your ear to verify progressions derived from it.

Fig. 3:4

Major Key	Can be followed by:	Can be preceded by:
I	any chord except vii	V, IV, sometimes vi
ii	V	I, vi
iii	IV, vi	I, vi, V
IV	I, V, ii	I, ii, iii, V
V	I, vi, IV, iii	I, IV, vi
vi	IV, V, iii, ii	I, iii, V, IV

I, IV, V = primary chords: use on strong or weak beats, (e.g., $\underset{>}{1}$ 2 3).

ii, iii, vi = secondary chords: use on weaker beats (e.g., 1 2 <u>3</u>).

ii can be substituted for IV where IV would be used on a weak beat and when greater variety is desired.

vi, less often iii, can be substituted for ı (usually not at cadence points) when greater variety is desired.

Minor Key	Can be followed by:	Can be preceded by:
i	any chord except VII	V, iv, VI
ii° (dim.)	V	i, VI
III	iv, VI	i, VI, V
iv	I, V	i, V, III
V	i, VI, iv, III	i, iv, VI
VI	iv, V, I, III	i, III, V, vi

The same rules for primary and second chords apply here. Substitutions are trickier in minor; do not encourage their use. Notice that each mode has three major chords (the V being major in both). Major has three minor chords, but minor has only two minor chords. This may account for the difficulty neophytes sometimes experience in identifying the minor mode by ear.

SUMMARY OF SONGWRITING WITH HARMONIC EMPHASIS

1. As with the tone-row activity, here you also prepare a handout with a clef sign and a scale. This time you construct on the scale those chords you intend to have your students use to compose their song (Mus. Ex. 3:10). Remember, show only those chords that will be used for the day's activity. Showing any others is just likely to confuse. Label the scale degrees and chords as shown in Mus. Ex. 3:10 and 3:11. It is useful if you can lead your students to discover that the chord number and name is the same as the scale degree and name and that the chord consists of only two pitches added on the next two lines or spaces above the scale pitch.

2. As with the tone-row activity, your handout should contain additional staves showing clef signs, measure lines, and rhythms notated above (Mus. Ex. 3:12). Here you need not restrict

students to only eight tones, since any pitches may be used as long as they are indicated by the chords (which you also indicate underneath this staff).

3. The students create their melody by choosing their melody tones from among those contained in the chords indicated for each measure (see Mus. Ex. 3:13).

4. Once the melody is composed, as before, you should play the efforts of many students, analyze them for strong and weak points, and re-emphasize the principles of melody writing first learned during tone-row activities. Here, also, you should follow up the melody-writing phases with emphasis on cadences, harmonic rhythm, the principles of chord progression (Fig. 3:4), and the manner in which melodic cadences, melodic similarity or contrast, and harmonic cadences work together to create small part-forms.

SUGGESTIONS FOR "ADVANCED" SONGWRITING ACTIVITIES WITH HARMONIC EMPHASIS

1. *Melodic phrases can be combined and recombined* into various eight- and sixteen-measure melodies. *Words can be added* and the class can sing these longer melodies with accompaniment by students on the autoharp, guitar, or piano (assign one student per chord—they play their "block chord" at the appropriate time) or tone bells (one student per chord, or one student per pitch—for the latter, students must be savvy in order to know when the required chord includes their pitch).

2. *The structure of melodies composed can be studied* in terms of melodic direction, contour, steps, skips, leaps, and repeated tones, and appropriate improvements or revisions made.

3. *Revised melodies can be made by changing a chord here and there* and by studying the effect by aural and visual analysis. Is it better or worse, or just different? Have students "improve" their melodies by using the substitute chords indicated earlier in Fig. 3:4.

4. *Reverse the chords in measures 3 and 4* of melodic phrases and study the effect made on the feeling of cadencing. Is the cadence stronger or weaker? How, in general, does the feeling of the cadence change?

5. Make sure students have *experience with the wide variety of typical kinds of small part-forms* which result from various combinations of melodic relationships (i.e., motivic relationships between phrases) and harmonic cadences. To give such experience, provide students with the diagrams described earlier in the discussion of harmonic rhythm. Vary the melodic relationships by the kinds of letter you use to label phrases; and vary the harmonic cadences by providing different chord combinations at the cadence points.

6. Over the course of time, make sure you *provide the class with as many typical chord progressions as possible.* Aside from simply using a wide variety, you can also assign them to find interesting progressions from the sheet music they have access to at home, in a media center, or in the library (where you can make such music available). Compose new melodies to these "found" progressions. Determine whether or to what degree these chord progressions agree with the general principles given earlier. Try to discover special qualifications for those rules when "unusual" progressions seem to sound good.

7. *Prepare staves for melody writing that give a choice of progressions.* For these assignments, under the staves provide a choice of chords—at first for one or two measures, later for all measures (Mus. Ex. 3:14):

Mus. Ex. 3:14

Ex. A

C–I   F–IV   C–I   d–ii
                                   F–IV
                                   G–V

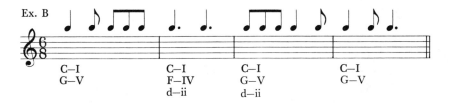

Ex. B

C–I	C–I	C–I	C–I
G–V	F–IV	G–V	G–V
	d–ii	d–ii	

In example A, it would be hoped that previous songwriting activities with harmonic emphasis would lead students to avoid choosing the ii chord for the cadence point. This is a secondary triad, and thus a weak chord ill-suited for the strength required at a cadence. While the IV chord would be correct, some students may consider that since a IV has already been used earlier in the example it would provide more variety and be stronger to use a V chord for the cadence.

Example B would be an activity for a more refined stage of development—perhaps for high school or any time after students have had considerable experience with chords and progressions. Here students plan their own progression from among the chords given. Many possibilities exist, and the task would be to put together a strong progression. For example, if a student chooses to begin on a V chord, the I chord would be most appropriate for the next measure, since a movement from V to IV or ii, according to the general principles, would be weak. If a I were chosen to begin, any of the chords in the second measure would be technically correct, though to repeat the I might seem boring. If the ii is chosen for measure 2, the V ought to be chosen for measure 3, since ii→I is very weak, ii→IV is somewhat weak (they have two tones in common), and ii→ii is a nonprogression and thus boring. The chord chosen for measure 3 should logically determine the chord to be used for the cadence in measure 4.

Activities such as this provide increased choice, and therefore provide an increasingly stronger indication of student understanding and mastery of the principles of chord progressions. Do not, however, let the students get so carried away with chords that they ignore all that was learned about melodic construction during the tone-row activities.

8. Provide a song or songs written by students in other classes, by students in this class sometime in the near past, or from popular music or song series sources. *Have students go through, measure by measure, and determine by analyzing the melody tones present in each measure, which chords would be suitable for accompaniment.* This is important for those students for whom this learning will be the first step toward figuring out accompaniments for songs that they sing while themselves playing the guitar, piano, accordion, or chord organ. This would satisfy the most basic aims of Action Learning since it teaches students how to harmonize melodies for recreational playing and singing.

9. Eventually, after students have shown considerable ability in successfully handling melody writing based on chords, you may *extend to them the opportunity to use certain nonharmonic tones.* This allows a much greater potential for creating an interesting, singable melody.

At first, they should be limited to two basic kinds of nonharmonic tones: neighboring tones (Mus. Ex. 3:15) and passing tones (Mus. Ex. 3:16).

Mus. Ex.   3:15

upper neighboring tone   lower neighboring tone

Neighboring tones "embellish" what otherwise would be two repeated tones. They can be combined one after another to "dress up" a sequence of three repeated tones.

155

Mus. Ex. 3:16

Passing tones are used to connect, in a stepwise movement, two pitches that otherwise would be a *skip* (i.e., one scale degree separating the two pitches).

At first students should be directed to identify all such nonharmonic tones in their melody by circling the pitch and also by labeling it as shown above. This way *you* know if *they* know what they are doing. Later they may use these tones as their ear dictates, and even utilize the possibility of having the passing tones happening *on* the beat. The ear is the best judge of the success of this approach (Mus. Ex. 3:17).

Mus. Ex. 3:17

10. Finally, after the class, or the more gifted or interested students, have had much experience with chords and melody writing, you should *entertain all possibilities of chord progressions and melodic writing using nonharmonic tones*—just as long as (a) the student can explain what he or she has done, and why; and (b) the result is justified by the judgment of the ear. Somewhere along the line, too, *the V⁷ chord can be added* (with no special fuss necessary) simply by showing it in this manner (Mus. Ex. 3:18):

Mus. Ex. 3:18

Sevenths can be added to ii or II chords as well (but make sure these are followed by V or V⁷ chords). This additional choice of V⁷ and ii⁷ or II⁷ chords adds "spice" by means of the mild dissonance of the added seventh. The melody tones now additionally available increase the potential for an expressive melody, as well.

So once again the possibilities are fruitful for your instructional purposes. Once again the idea is to get a product as quickly and efficiently as possible. It is not important that the students "understand" anything in particular *at first*. You are providing them with all the information that they assemble like building blocks or erector sets. Just as they do not understand structural or mechanical engineering when involved with such divertissements of childhood, but soon learn some of the guiding principles through action or use, so they can use the musical information you provide and learn much just by using it.

Revising, refining, working out other alternatives becomes the highly productive phase of such songwriting activities. And youngsters are more than eager to do such things because they are using and working with *their own compositions!* That makes a considerable difference at the present time, and it will enhance the likelihood of action transfer to in-life situations.

SONGWRITING WITH RHYTHMIC EMPHASIS

These activities can be particularly productive when it is possible to combine or relate them with language-arts activities. But even when done for strictly musical purposes, they are useful in many ways. *These activities always begin with a set of words.* Generally a very short poem of two to four lines in a regular poetic meter is most satisfactory. It is especially important that the words be relevant and interesting to the group, be within the capabilities of the group as far as the meter and rhythmic complexities go, and be *short.* The younger the group, the shorter the poem should be.

First experiences with fourth or fifth graders probably should use a poem or segment of a poem around two lines long. Sixth, seventh, and eighth graders and beginning-level high schoolers can handle a four-line poem for the first experience. Length of the poems used can increase as students demonstrate their increasing competence in analyzing them and setting them to rhythmic notation. Ultimately it is useful to allow students to bring in their own words, write their own words (preferably as part of language-arts activities, and not taking time away from music classes), or at the very least choose from among listings of poems provided by you (this allows you control and the students some freedom).

The process of rhythmic emphasis is quite straightforward and invariable, at least at first.

1. *Have the poem provided on a handout, syllabized.*

2. *Begin by reading the poem to the class.* Then have them read it with you in unison, striving for *a uniform rhythm.*

3. If the children have studied scansion, and *can all do it well(!),* scan the poem. If not—and that is usually the case—direct them to read the poem again or listen as you read it, and *identify which syllables receive a stress, an accent, a pulse,* i.e., which syllables are slightly louder. Have them *underline these syllables* on their papers.

4. *Now have them put a vertical measure-line before each underlined syllable:*

/Mu-sic,/mu-sic,/fast or/slow,/   ← Always use measure lines at end of lines.

/Tells me,/all I/need to/know.//   ← Always use double lines at very end.

5. *Read it to them again, asking them to decide whether the poem "moves · in twos or threes."* If your class has never done this before with poetry or music, now is the time to begin. Explain and demonstrate that the poem or music can be arranged into two or three sounds per group (i.e., per measure). Let them determine which this is.

6. When they have agreed on the appropriate beats per measure, *have them each place its number at the beginning of the poem.* Then, under the text, have them number the *counts:* in this case, two per measure.

meter **2** <u>Mu</u>-sic, <u>mu</u>-sic, <u>fast</u> or <u>slow</u>, ←counts per measure
1   2   1   2   1   2   1   2

<u>Tells</u> me <u>all</u> I <u>need</u> to <u>know</u>.
1   2   1   2   1   2   1   2

When one syllable gets two counts (or more), as with the last word of each line here, connect them with a dash (1—2) or a tie (1_____2). A tie has greater transfer value to rhythmic notation and is recommended over the dash.

7. After *you* have determined how many different kinds of rhythmic symbols are required, *provide a chart on the chalkboard like this* (Mus. Ex. 3:19):

Mus. Ex. 3:19

♩ = 1 count

𝅗𝅥 = ♩ ♩ = 2 counts
      1   2
   (1 + 1)

You could, of course, assign any note value per beat, depending on what the students may already know or what you want them to learn (Mus. Ex. 3:20):

Mus. Ex. 3:20

♪ = 1 count

♩ = ♪ ♪ or ♫ = 2 counts
    1 2   1 2
  (1 + 1) (1 + 1)

8. Have the children refer to the chart and *notate the rhythm of the poem* by placing the appropriate notational symbol *over the counts* that are already under the syllables of the poem (Mus. Ex. 3:21):

Mus. Ex. 3:21

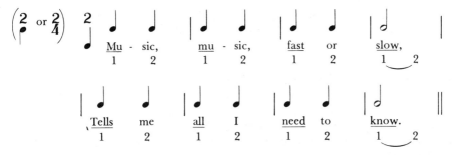

For now, use the *meter signature* as shown above. As the class comes to understand that it means—in this case two quarter notes or the equivalent per measure—you can begin to use *standard meter signature* with arabic numbers for note values, or with the note stem heading down (as in the parentheses above).

As you may have noticed, *"songwriting" activities having rhythmic emphasis do not result in melodies—at least, not at first.* But they are a preparation for eventually writing melodies for which the student also conceives of his or her own rhythm, and a preparation for providing a metric/rhythmic setting of lyrics before a melody can be composed. This group of activities in the early stages is also the only one in which it is expected, *but only at first,* that all final products will be uniform. That is, when working with a given poem, there exists a correct setting according to the meter decided upon and the rhythm chart (see point 7 above) provided by the teacher. For this reason, it is possible to do this activity as a large-group activity for the sake of efficiency. This allows a greater variety of follow-up activities to be attempted in conjunction with matters of rhythm/meter.

SUMMARY OF SONGWRITING WITH RHYTHMIC EMPHASIS

1. *Prepare a poem on a handout.* Be sure to provide enough space above and below the words for the notes and counts to be added above and below each line, respectively. It is helpful, at first, if you prepare the handout with the words already syllabified. Later students can syllabify on their own.

2. *Read the poem* to the class; *then have them read it,* more than once, until they have the "feel" of the meter you have chosen.

3. Students then *decide which words or syllables receive a stress,* an accent. *These are underlined* on the handout (or scansion symbols are used if students are very good at scansion). *Add a vertical measure line* before each underlined syllable.

4. *Read the poem again,* deciding whether the poem moves in "twos or threes," i.e., whether it has two or three main beats per measure. Place the number decided on at the beginning of the poem.

5. *Provide a rhythmic notation chart* for the class showing the note value that will receive one count and all other derived note values (i.e., longer or shorter) necessary to notating this particular poem.

6. *Have the class notate the rhythm of the poem* by referring to the chart, using the measure lines and counts already marked in on the handout.

SUGGESTIONS FOR "ADVANCED" SONGWRITING ACTIVITIES WITH RHYTHMIC EMPHASIS

1. Students can—as a group or individually—*learn to conduct the metric pattern of the poem*. It assists in establishing the correct meter if they conduct while reciting the poem until they find the conducting pattern which fits the poetic meter. See Fig. 3:5.

2. When they return to class the next time, *the teacher can have composed a little tune to accompany their poem*. Therefore it is useful to use a different poem with each group within a class. This also dispels your own boredom as the day progresses. Due to the prior rhythm work, it is likely that the class will have little or no trouble performing the rhythm of the new song to be sung. Thus emphasis can be on its melodic construction. Any or all of the factors emphasized in conjunction with tone-row and harmonic-emphasis songwriting activities can be studied before the piece is sung. This kind of analysis *before singing* adds immeasurably to students' music-reading ability. In fact, all the songwriting activities combine to vastly improve the music-reading ability of all ages. If singing is combined with all phases of these activities, your program of music reading will advance by leaps and bounds.

3. The rhythm patterns derived from this kind of activity can be divorced entirely from the words and used for *a purely rhythmic performance activity, involving, perhaps, rhythm-band performances* and questions of timbre, etc. Later the rhythm band can be used to accompany a singing of the song by the class.

4. Rhythm patterns created and learned in this way can be combined with those created and learned in earlier lessons into more adventurous rhythm-band or rhythmic activities. *The rhythms can form the basis of a notated sound composition* in which timbre or rhythmic variety are the main contributors to the structural coherence (unity and variety). This is merely one way songwriting using standard notation can be combined with sound-composition activities.

5. Once a poem is completed, the rhythmic/metric notation can be changed. In the example illustrated earlier, it would be very interesting and profitable to notate the poem with another

Fig. 3:5   Rather than counting out loud for the beat numbers, have beginners at first say the directional words (shown in quotation marks above).

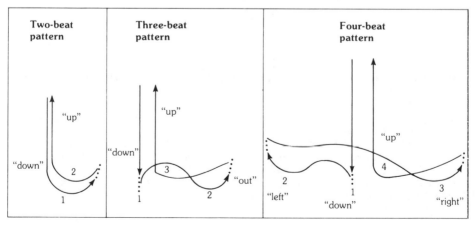

note value as the basis (see step 7, page 158). The more of this you do, the more the class will be inductively prepared to understand the subtleties of rhythmic notation and gain experience in working with various metric values.

6. Many poems are susceptible to readings in more than one meter. The example used here, for instance (Mus. Ex. 3:21), can be read almost as easily in a triple meter. Once the students have completed the poem in duple meter, and repeat this process in the new triple meter (Mus. Ex. 3:22).

Mus. Ex.   3:22

In either meter, you can *experiment with having the students use all possible notational arrangements.* In the present example, half notes could be shown as two quarters tied, etc., with dotted halves shown in two or three possible arrangements.

7. Each rhythmic activity ought to consider how, whether, or in what way(s) the rhythms used in a song contribute to the form (unity and variety) or interest of the work in question. For example, suppose a song has these rhythms for each of its phrases (Mus. Ex. 3:23):

Mus. Ex. 3:23

As you can see, the rhythms *alone* contribute to the form, which in this case is AA'BA'. So once students become familiar with rhythmic notation by means of these activities, any song composed or sung can be subjected to a formal analysis not only for factors pertaining to pitch (i.e., melodic contour, direction, steps, skips, repeated tones, and leaps) but also for rhythmic unity and variety.

8. Most poems in meters having two, three, or four beats per measure can be re-notated and performed as *two-part polymetric choral readings,* with each half of the class reading the poem in a different meter (see Mus. Ex. 3:24).

It is useful to notate the parts, at first, for the class. After they can perform a piece such as this, and have had experience notating a variety of rhythms and meters, then they can notate a given song-rhythm in two-part polymeters.

Notice that in example A, two measures of $\frac{3}{4}$ coincides with three measures of $\frac{2}{4}$. Thus every so often, the two meters coincide and start *simultaneously* on the first beat of their respective measures. This is shown here (and you should do it too, as should your students) by connecting their respective measure lines. Example B featured the same principle, but is more difficult since the second part comes in late. Timing that entrance and immediately "feeling" the second meter is tricky—but profitable. This is one of the few areas in which students can experience directly

Mus. Ex. 3:24-A

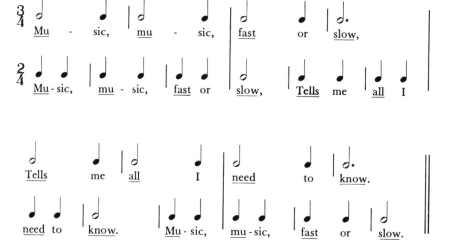

Mus. Ex. 3:24-B

through composing and performing some of the rhythmic complexities featured in contemporary music today—including, not incidentally, rock music.

9. As a preparation for the above activity, or as a follow-up, *metric chants* are easy, and usually fun to do if used sparingly (see Mus. Ex. 3:25).

Mus. Ex. 3:25

Metric Chanting

Main beats per measure	Chant: primary accent underlined like this ____ ; secondary, underlined like this: _ _
2	1 2 Base - ball (also used for 6 at fast tempo)
3	1 2 3 Bas - ket - ball (slowly: Bas - ket - ball)
4	1 2 3 4 Foot - ball play - er
5 (2+3)	1 2 3(1) 4(2) 5(3) Ten - nis ⋮ tour - na - ment
(3+2)	1 2 3 4(1) 5(2) Tour - na - ment ⋮ play - er
6	1 2 3 4 5 6 Bas - ket - ball tour - na - ment
7 (3+4)	1 2 3 4(1) 5(2) 6(3) 7(4) Soc - cer and ⋮ foot - ball play - er
(3+4)	1 2 3 4(1) 5(2) 6(3) 7(4) Soc - cer is ⋮ En - glish foot - ball
(4+3)	1 2 3 4 5(1) 6(2) 7(3) En - ter ten - nis ⋮ tour - na - ment

These may be recited one after another, keeping the value of the basic beat constant. This results in the feeling (experience) of *changing meters*. When any or all of these are recited simultaneously with the basic value the same for all meters, students will be able to perform polymeters with little trouble (see Mus. Ex. 3:26).

Mus. Ex. 3:26

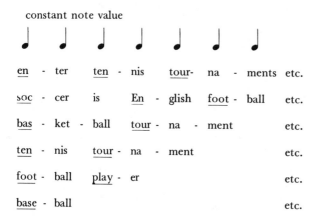

constant note value

| en | - | ter | | ten | - | nis | | tour- | na | - | ments | etc. |

soc - cer   is   En - glish   foot - ball   etc.

bas - ket - ball   tour - na - ment   etc.

ten - nis   tour - na - ment   etc.

foot - ball   play - er   etc.

base - ball   etc.

This is not difficult to do when the tempo is slow. But as the tempo is gradually increased and the underlined syllables are given a vocal stress (accent) it becomes increasingly tricky, and increasingly a realistic polymetric experience. If you mix together a meter based on a *duple* feeling (2 or 4 beats per measure), one based on a *triple* feeling (3 or 6 beats per measure—but remember, when a meter of 6 gets going fast, it lapses into a feeling of 2 main beats divided into 3 counts each), and one or more of the *complex meters* (the asymmetrical ones containing a mixture of 3 and 4 beats within a measure; e.g., 5 and 7 beats per measure), it is a real challenge, and yet attainable by many groups, especially in high school.

10. *Have students invent and notate their own metric chants*, using not only words but rhythmic values as well. The same can be done with class *members'* names as the basis, or using other words and word combinations (e.g., rivers or cities, such as Mis-sis-sip-pi; Min-ne-ap-o-lis, St. Paul). Use such rhythms/meters for rhythm band or sound composition activities as strictly rhythmic compositions.

11. Have students *notate a word canon or round*. Later on, they can notate their own word fugue. A word canon or round is a relatively easy process. Choose a one- or two-sentence prose or poem segment. For some reason these seem to be most appreciated when the words chosen are amusing to the class. Derive rhythmic notation for all the words chosen. Now set up the words and the notation in canonic form, with one part beginning, then another beginning one or two measures later, and so on up to four parts.

12. As shown in Mus. Ex. 3:27, give students on the chalkboard, overhead projector, or handout a one-measure rhythm such as:

Mus. Ex. 3:27

$\frac{4}{4}$ or C

Their challenge is to *rearrange the note values in as many different combinations as they can imagine.*

164

even

Now have them take all of these variations and compose a rhythm piece. You can specify certain forms (as exemplified in item 7 above), or otherwise specify that they be able to identify the unity and variety in the composition. Another challenge is: "Compose a rhythm composition you think you can perform, and be ready to perform it without practice." Sometimes, when the competitive spirit is high: "Compose a piece that has unity and variety, which will be attempted in performance by the girls. They in turn will do the same thing, and try to trick you boys too."

13. Another variation is a *"name that tune"* or *"name that student"* contest. You yourself begin by notating the rhythm of a song all students should know (try patriotic, Christmas, and folk songs first, then branch into pop tunes, etc.). The students try to determine the name of the song from "mentally" performing the rhythms. The same activity is amusing when the rhythms of names of persons in the class (or teachers in the school) are notated and the class must determine whose name goes with which rhythm. The sequel to such activities eventually is to have the class notate the rhythms of familiar songs, one another's names, etc., in an attempt to "stump" one another. Activities such as these are made easily and profitably into games, as long as the emphasis is not too heavily on the extrinsic competitive motivations (as opposed to the intrinsic desire to succeed because of interest).

14. To add further to rhythmic-performance skills, take rhythm phrases and perform them from beginning to end. Then, immediately, *perform them backward*, starting with the last note (retrograde motion). This is a useful procedure to employ with any song, particularly familiar ones such as patriotic songs. Among other things, the idea of rhythmic retrograde motion is introduced for potential use in sound compositions.

15. Finally, it is effective and useful to re-notate both student-composed and established familiar songs. For example, have students notate "The Star-Spangled Banner" in 4/4 meter so that it still makes musical sense. This, too, can be made into a game: a familiar song which everyone knows is subjected to a new rhythmic treatment using changing and complex meters. The idea is that the composers (arrangers) should be able to perform anything they notate. In order to encourage them to be adventuresome enough to challenge themselves, the game becomes one of seeing if another group or individual can be tricked while trying to perform the new version correctly. Let the class, or the composers (arrangers), analyze whether someone else's performance of their score was correct. This aids their diagnostic skills and ability to produce "mental images" of rhythms.

Rhythmic activities similar to these can enhance all the previous songwriting activities. As students become more and more capable of handling rhythmic and metric factors, they soon can begin to notate rhythms without any recourse to words. Those who can and do make use of this potential can get on to the business of composing not only with "academic competence" (i.e., technically correctly) but creatively (in the artistic sense) as well. And remember, form should be an inherent part of every compositional activity. Among the activities suggested so far, only those carried out in a "gamelike" atmosphere might be excused from having a discernable form (i.e., unity and variety).

How successful your efforts with the three varieties of songwriting activities have been will be noted when you attempt to have your class write their first full song (described below). Remember, up until this point, these activities have constituted emphases on single specific aspects of traditional music and its composition. (1) *Tone rows* emphasize the principles of successful melody construction. (2) *Harmonic-emphasis* activities illustrate the interpenetration of vertical elements (chords, harmonies) and horizontal elements (tonal succession, melody). (3) *Rhythmic activities* develop skills of rhythmic/metric performance and notation, and generally help nurture a fruitful concept of rhythm/meter.

When done in this order—first tone rows, then harmonic-emphasis, and finally rhythmic activities—each activity involves Action Learnings that contribute to refining students' understanding of elements and techniques encountered in the earlier variety. So once you leave tone rows to first attempt harmonic activities, you do not ignore all that was accomplished with the tone rows. For example, do some tone rows after students have become more acquainted with the harmonic bases of cadences as a result of their experiences with harmonic activities. Similarly, work with rhythm activities contributes to an understanding of the rhythmic/metric bases of harmonic rhythm which is featured as a part of harmonic-emphasis activities.

Thus, though it is necessary to attempt at first one of these types of activities before another (and the sequence followed here often works well), this linear sequence is not to be confused with the atomist's approach, in which once a "unit" has been "covered" it is not returned to or reemphasized (see pages 129-131). Transfer of learning will occur only when the teacher attempts to have students relate the different emphases derived from each of these three activities by *returning to each periodically after the initial sequence of three is first encountered.* Only when this has been accomplished, can "full songwriting" (see below) be attempted with a significant chance for success. And full songwriting is not only the overall goal of these three preparatory activity-types, it is the goal of all music instruction: to work as synergically as possible, when students are in a position to knowingly act upon or with as many musical elements at a time as is possible.

FULL SONGWRITING: TOWARD SYNERGIC ACTION LEARNING

The entire process of unifying, or synergizing, the separate concepts that will arise from each of these three separate activities is enhanced and *transfer* is facilitated if the activities are used in *alternation*—regular or irregular—*and combined* at various times in different ways. All such activities and their combination in various forms provide the experience that develops the readiness for more ambitious creative undertakings.

Each opportunity with a tone-row, harmonic, or rhythmic songwriting activity should expand and refine the experiential base upon which concepts arise. Each small combination of activities provides for transfer and helps insure that concepts acquired separately will be synthesized (overlapping) to some degree. And again it is necessary to emphasize that *virtually everything the nonprofessional musician needs to know about music can be taught by these methods.* It is only when various subtleties and refinements are undertaken that advanced approaches such as those of a high school theory class become necessary. But even then, the inductive foundation established by these means provides the possibility that more complex instructional patterns can succeed.

The more transfer and synthesis that arise from the interaction of these activities, the more useful and long-lasting will be the results for the children. For this reason, and for the sheer satisfaction of a more specific creativity, all the prior activities covered so far reach their ultimate culmination in full-song-writing activities done for their own sake.

As long as readiness has been developed by means of ample individual work with the three foregoing activities, writing a complete song the first time is relatively uncomplicated. The entire process will be described first; but you must keep in mind that *you can stop at any stage for review, clarification, or emphasis.* Seldom does any songwriting activity proceed at first without a hitch from beginning to end. This is to be expected and therefore is normal. You should be flexible enough to seize upon certain occasions during an activity to deal with problems as they arise. When many students experience the same problem it is a sure sign that one or more of the three preparatory activities were not given enough treatment. No matter; use the present situation to begin to make repairs.

The three songwriting activities described thus far are really not truly independent activities. Rather, *they are emphases derived from the larger activity of writing a full song.* In other words, the process of writing a song involves, to one degree or another, the conjunction of the three smaller activities already described. Thus it is possible to dwell on one stage if considerable confusion still exists.

1. *The first phase of writing a song involves taking a set of words and subjecting them to exactly the kind of treatment described as part of rhythmic activities.* Thus, after reading the poem and determining its meter, underlining accented syllables, and putting in bar lines, counts, and note values, the students can begin musical treatment of the poem.

2. Before this can take place, however, an intervening step is necessary. *You could have the students copy all that was accomplished in step 1 on music-staff paper.* But this can be time-consuming busywork. So *whenever possible you should have done this in advance on handouts.* This will also insure that no errors in copying complicate things, and will permit *your* nota-

tional neatness to help middle school youngsters *visually organize their songs.* Your handout should look something like Mus. Ex. 3:28.

Mus. Ex.   3:28

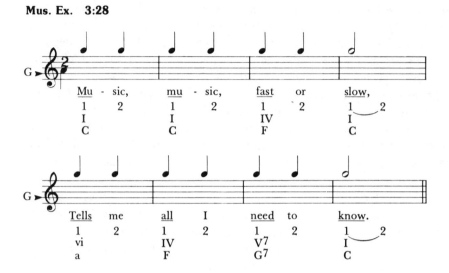

As you can see, *this involves the combination of the rhythmic and harmonic songwriting techniques.* The rhythm and meter of the words are set above an empty staff; the chords are provided below, as is the scale from which they are drawn. All of this should be neatly presented.

3. *The remainder of the full-songwriting activity involves completing the song in the same way as the many times the class has done harmonic activities.* Now, however, the music has words. Students' ability to compose an interesting melody will have profited by the learnings that resulted from tone-row activities. You may wish to specify a form or a special type of phrase/cadence structure at first. Later, once students are accustomed to the process, this is one more decision that can be left to them.

4. *Once the product is completed it should be subject to the same processes as the previous, less comprehensive activities.* Many songs should be listened to, and performed if possible. The examples ought to be analyzed for structural conditions, accuracy, and other matters of interest. Comparisons among songs can be drawn, and revisions and alterations can be carried out. The result often can be a particularly satisfying song for teacher and students alike. And the look of accomplishment and satisfaction they can manifest is reward enough for the teacher who has steadfastly prepared for this moment.

The first times any of these activities are done, it is wise to proceed with the entire class doing the same project at one time. As individuals begin to acquire the learnings—and at different rates, as is inevitable—then the whole group may be divided into smaller and smaller groups, culminating sometimes in individual work.[10] At first, therefore, the teacher plays a leading part in the creative process.

As the groups become smaller and smaller, the teacher's role becomes more and more one of the "driver education teacher," i.e., guiding and putting on the brakes, but not steering. You move quickly from group to group giving whatever help you can in the form increasingly of questions designed to assist the learner's in discovering for themselves the solutions to the problems at hand. Then you reestablish control when all projects are completed. You must hear *many* of the works and establish the analytic climate necessary for the class to profit richly from the experience. You guide any subsequent analyses and discussions as efficiently and profitably as you can. You go where the class leads you if it is productive. When the class does not appear to be going anywhere in particular, then you can lead.

While songwriting activities have dealt mainly with composing melodies efficiently, other learnings can be introduced at any time in the process as benefits the needs and interests of the students.

SUGGESTIONS FOR "ADVANCED" FULL SONGWRITING ACTIVITIES

1. *Motives:* in an analysis of a particularly good song, you will eventually find *motivic development* (i.e., a rhythmic/melodic unit of a few notes serving as the basis for much of the melody). Or you may plan this analysis by writing a melody of your own or by using one already known to the class. *The idea of establishing certain motivic relationships within a melody begins the process that often culminates in effective melodies.*

2. *Nonharmonic tones:* without getting into the specifics and terminology of music theory, *it is possible to demonstrate how non-chord tones can be added in between chord tones when a smoother melodic line is desired.* Usually this process goes no farther than dealing with unaccented nonharmonic tones that immediately resolve to chord tones, and this can be included thereafter as a possibility—one that will always be subject to verification by the ear (see point 9, page 155-156).

3. *Text and music:* from the beginning but increasingly thereafter *the teacher should stress the relationship (if any is necessary or important) between text and melody.* Does the melody reinforce or heighten the words? Or do the words add tangibility to the music? Or do the two merely coexist uncomfortably (sad words, happy melody)? What contribution do the harmonies and rhythms make? In other words, be concerned increasingly with bringing up *questions of musical expression in relation to the words.* All musical elements should be considered eventually.

4. *Modulation: modulation becomes possible when students have worked with chords well enough to be familiar with the strongest, most basic patterns.* Then the so-called *common chord modulation* can be used (i.e., one achieved by a chord that is common, and often strong, in both the old and the new key: the V chord in C major is the I chord in G major). The melody begins and ends in the same key, but somewhere in the middle it leaves the original key, only to return before the end.

5. *Scale and chord construction:* at a fruitful time the question of *constructing major and minor scales, and deriving chords from them, can be undertaken.* The appropriate time will be when everyone has had ample opportunity to work with the "given" material that is usually a part of songwriting activities. Then, with this readiness, the premises of steps and half steps can be studied. An eventual goal could be to have students construct scales independently and derive chords from them accurately.

6. *Similarly, another sign of musical independence is the individual's ability to choose and arrange his or her own chord progressions.* This will require, first, much experience with melodies that have one chord change per measure. Then much experience with two chords per measure at regular and predictable intervals is needed. Finally, some experience with less regular *harmonic rhythm* can be provided. And even then, not everyone should be expected to achieve complete independence. By this time you will know who is likely to succeed and who is

169

not, and your groups can be assembled and assigned as the circumstances or their readiness permits.

While items 1, 2, and 3 could be studied to some degree by everyone, 4, 5, and 6 likely will be most fruitful for the more advanced, particularly those who may be studying musical instruments—or reserve these activities for high school classes.

It may be apparent that all such melodies as result from the activities described here will be derived from harmony as "given" by the teacher or figured out by the student. Some readers may feel that this is artificial and unnatural. It is—there is little doubt of that. But it is efficient and effective in facilitating teacher control over learning. It is almost impossible to deal *pedagogically* with songs if the melody is conceived "by ear" first, then harmonies added—there is nothing uniform to which you and all the children in a group can relate.

If children are ever to grow into young adults capable of composing a melody with harmonies already in mind or implied, and one that fits a given set of words well, then the *systematic approach* described here will have to have been experienced for several years. These activities will provide the conceptual readiness that nurtures the greater potential for creativity of certain youngsters. They cannot create from "nothing." The activities described here provide a "something" from which creation can arise, be compared and analyzed, on a singular basis. As youngsters benefit increasingly from these activities they can (and will) become more and more independent of such structures (or strictures) and better able to carry on a more natural creative act by themselves.

Remember, too, that each songwriting activity—be it one of the three less comprehensive varieties or writing a full song—provides the opportunity for emphasizing certain learnings. If on a certain occasion the class seems stumped by some facet of the problem or is really "turned on" by a musical technique, make good use of the opportunity. Do not "put it off" because you did not include it in today's lesson plans: leave your plans for a few minutes and *deal with the immediate, immediately!* Then return to your plans when you can. You also can make a mental note to build a subsequent activity entirely around the thing that caused the immediate preoccupation, in order to give emphasis.

Finally, remember that everyone will profit to different degrees and in different ways from these activities. Do not expect results to be uniform and consistent. As students' abilities and interests diverge increasingly, you become more and more responsible for groupings that take these differences into consideration.

A program of songwriting, begun in the earliest years of school and continued through the elementary years, promotes valuable and long-lasting musical learning. When these techniques are combined with those of the sound compositions, and with the other aspects of a total music program, a teacher can go amazingly far in stimulating the musical independence necessary to effective Action Learning and to the enhanced attitudes and responses that make a music education worthwhile.

TEN REASONS FOR USING SONGWRITING ACTIVITIES

1. To teach all aspects of music "theory" that any non-musician would ever have to know.

2. To involve students from a creative, manipulative, inductive point of view in those aspects of standard musical notation that can be of use to them in life.

3. To generate melodies, melody segments, and songs that are susceptible to promoting further learning through performance, analysis, and revision. Middle schoolers in particular are often much more eager to do these activities with their own songs rather than songs from the song series.

4. To produce tangible sound products that serve as evidence to parents, administrators, and students of classroom learning, and also serve the teacher in evaluating the success of his or her teaching.

5. To provide skills in musical creation that can be applied out of school or after graduation from school. Students, especially the musically talented ones, often will compose songs of their own without being asked. This is a sure sign of the success of Action Learning.

6. To personalize, individualize, and humanize music instruction. Students create compositions that are theirs alone (no matter how much help they may have received from peers or the teacher!). If words are chosen by students or well chosen by the teacher, their songs can have a very personal meaning for them.

7. To produce materials for singing and other performance that otherwise might not be available to the teacher for financial or practical reasons.

8. To provide the opportunity for youngsters studying instruments to play their own tunes, and learn such skills as transposition for their instruments. When these songs are performed by the "composers" on their instruments for the class, a uniquely "live" listening experience is provided.

9. To provide the opportunity for student pianists, guitarists, and accordionists to accompany songs written by the class, or their own songs, with an accompaniment already worked out at home or by the teacher.

10. To use in singing activities. Most singing activities can be applied to songs written by the children. Especially useful are the kinds of singing activities that deal with the analysis of the melodies sung. Ideally, much analysis of the songs will have taken place during composition. Therefore if the students have been assigned to compose, say, an AABA melody and have analyzed the fruits of their labors aurally and visually, these cognitions assist them in learning their scores: they know, for example, that the three A phrases are very similar in melodic content. This simplifies the performance. Here cognition precedes performance. So often the reverse is done: analysis follows performance. This effectively limits transfer of learning in future music-reading situations. Much of such analysis after the fact is forgotten, since it is not immediately used. When students perform their own songs, this is not true. They can directly transfer the cognitions gained during the composition and analysis process to singing their songs.

SPECIAL HINTS FOR IMPROVING SONGWRITING ACTIVITIES

1. Some teachers find that it is desirable to begin instruction with songwriting and then move to sound compositions. In certain classes or certain communities—especially when sound-composition techniques are used for the first time with students who are not used to the "open-ness" of these activities—students are so "turned on" by the adventure and excitement of sound compositions that they are reluctant to move to the more restricted structure of songwriting activities. Their teachers find it best to begin with songwriting. This, they feel, introduces classes slowly and under control to the arena of musical composition, and slowly prepares students for the more far-flung possibilities inherent in sound compositions.

On the other hand, this approach has the disadvantage of beginning classes with "readiness"-oriented materials. Activities that depend for their success on the prior readiness of students—in this instance on preliminary experience with the rudiments of traditional music—have a greater opportunity for consequences that students can label or at least feel amount to *failure*. Songwriting activities proceed according to strict rules. And for the sloppy, careless, or initially unmotivated student there are ample opportunities for clear failure. When a student uses too many or too few tones in tone-row activities, or cannot improve a tone row according to principles uncovered by the class; when a student chooses melody tones inap-propriately based upon given chords; when a student has difficulty with the arithmetic involved in rhythmic notation—all these provide ample occasions for a feeling of failure to arise.

Thus, when songwriting activities are introduced first, and without the classroom ambiance of experimentation, of "we learn as much from our mistakes as from our successes," the chances are that students will not participate as fully as they might have if sound compositions (in which the opportunities for failure are truly minimal) were introduced first. At the very least, if you feel it is necessary or desirable to begin with songwriting, please take much care to en-courage an open attitude among your students. Whatever you do, *do not grade students or single them out for any kind of criticism or negativism* that can be read by the individual or class as "failure."

Otherwise, it is recommended that you initiate creative activities with the sound composi-tions. Many of the concepts developed there, such as those pertaining to form, will simplify your job when you eventually move on to songwriting. All that is learned by means of the sound-composition vehicle can more easily be transferred to the songwriting activities. Thus ABA form can be a constant, regardless of the activity; students gain the advantage of seeing the principle work both in a traditional and nontraditional format.

2. Some teachers have markedly enhanced the effectiveness of songwriting activities and have introduced other learning factors by purchasing for use with songwriting the small electric push-button chord organs usually found at reasonable cost in novelty, variety, and discount stores (see Fig. 3:6).

These can be placed around the room at strategic locations (or in interest centers, media cor-ners, etc.) where students can go to "check" (i.e., confirm aurally) their songs. Even more useful in some ways are the tiny electronic organs that have a stylus which is used to touch (rather than press) the appropriate keys (see Fig. 3:7).[11]

Students can pass these around and stay in their seats. Students also can take these home to compose songs or to practice playing them, or can use them in media corners or other approved places in the school.

The more of these or other melody instruments you can acquire for student use, the more often they have the opportunity to go to one to try out their melody and check it by ear. The more their "inner ear" can become a contributing factor, the greater the chance that eventually they will use it to give them some aural idea of what they are composing *as they compose* it. They will also be learning to *read music* better!

This is ultimately most desirable. Without this element the situation will remain rather abstract and academic, although considerable gain still can be achieved. But with melody instruments, the possibility is greater for achieving the more natural state of composition in which the "inner ear" hears and tries to execute a melody in notation. For this reason, too, the little electronic

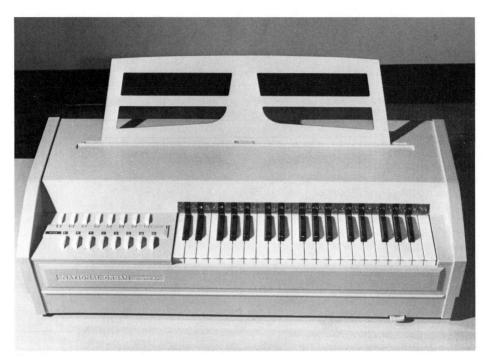

Fig. 3:6

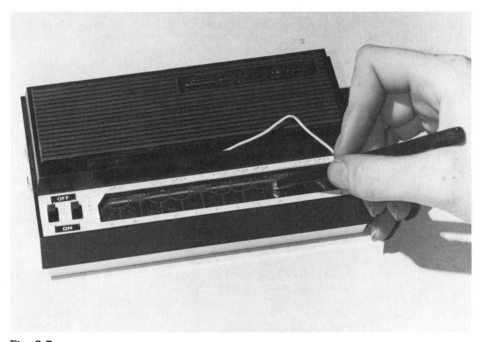

Fig. 3:7

chord organs are to be preferred to Orff instruments, melody bells, tone bells, and the mini-electronic organs, etc., simply because they have the capacity for playing chords and melody simultaneously. On these the student can either play his or her melody alone or by simply pushing the appropriately labeled button can also play the accompanying harmonies. While some of the more advanced and interested students will do this in any case on their pianos, accordions, guitars, and chord organs at home, it is impossible to expect or encourage this with most students if you do not have the means of achieving it in school. In middle school, two students can do this together: one plays the melody while the other plays the chords—then switch.

Thus you are encouraged to consider gradually purchasing many of these inexpensive musical teaching aids over a long period of time. You will not find them at reasonable prices in the catalogues of those companies which specialize in sales of musical materials to schools. The best buys will be in local variety stores, often around or just after Christmas, or sometimes in the national mail order catalogues (e.g., Sears, Spiegel, J.C. Penney).

3. You will do yourself, your students, and your school a great favor if you *make some of the better songs of your students public in some way!* It is extremely impressive to parents and administrators when such evidence of creative activity, so often found verbally in curriculum plans, actually is shown to be a fact. Public visibility can only enhance your standing, and in return often leads to greater availability of budget funds, which in turn can improve your program (e.g., by making possible the purchase of chord organs for classroom use).

4. All aspects of songwriting activities are enhanced in effectiveness and efficiency if they are done on *clear acetate sheets for viewing by means of an overhead projector.* This allows performance, analysis, and discussion of each student work considered. It puts a premium on clarity and correctness of notation that students, especially in seventh and eighth grade, otherwise do not usually care very much about. Strangely, over a period of time, it is really cheaper this way than preparing individual handouts time and time again, each of which, for all practical purposes, is used up.

If an overhead projector is not available (though it should be mentioned that many teachers buy one themselves because it makes their lives so much easier) or if funds are not available for thirty to sixty acetate sheets prepared with staff lines (using either permanent felt-tip pens or the Thermofax® process), an *opaque projector* can be used. This machine must be used with the lights off (or very dim), but it will effectively project on a large screen an image of a student's work from his or her paper. It usually has a built-in pointer system that allows you to point to specific aspects of the score for the class's attention.

If neither aid is available, you will have to go the paper-and-pencil route. But please do everything you can to achieve the following conditions:

    a. Efficiency in using time.

    b. Hearing as many melodies as you can, during and outside of class time.

    c. Using the chalkboard for analysis by the class of some student-produced melodies.

    d. Avoiding too much "copying over" by students: this takes time and contributes many unnecessary errors of copying.

5. It is important to *stick with an activity* (emphasis) *long enough to insure some skill and understanding* on the part of everyone. Similarly, mix up the three preparatory activities once all three have been encountered sufficiently. Once you begin writing complete songs, it does not mean you refrain from doing the tone-row, harmonic, or rhythmic activities. Just the opposite. You periodically return to them, at even higher levels of accomplishment and challenge, to review, reinforce, and extend understanding and skills relevant to those activities. This is especially so if, for example, you notice that students' ability with chords is behind their ability in other aspects of songwriting. Then it is fruitful to reemphasize chords by a few activities so that students can make better use of harmony in their songs. Thus, alternate between the full songwriting activity, which promotes synthesis and creativity, with the three activities that focus on one musical "part"—melody, harmony, or rhythm.

Along the same lines, alternate songwriting activities with sound compositions. The occasion should never or seldom arise that students walk into your class and say (or think), "What? Songwriting (or sound compositions) again?@#$%¢&*!" We are about to delve into listening lessons, and you will be able to add these to the two basic activities covered so far: sound compositions and songwriting. You should *never consider these three basic activities as "units" done once* and not returned to in any way. They should be constant, intermixed, ongoing, alternating.

What *is* varied along with the shifting back and forth among these activities is the *content* of the activities: *that which is to be learned*. Virtually everything in music (except useless information) can be learned *by means of* these three activities if they are effectively alternated, and if the content they deal with is varied, relevant, and attainable.

If students do come in complaining about doing songwriting again, or are acting as though they wished they could complain, something is wrong! What? Somehow you are impressing the class that the activity is the *end*, instead of the *means*. *If they complain about the activities*, then they still see the activities as the *sole end of music classes* instead of as the means by which they can reach interesting and relevant musical goals. If, on the other hand, you can reorient your own thinking and successfully rekindle student interest, your students will be engrossed in the pursuit of Action Learning in the form of composition, of learning more of the "innards" of the musical art, of increasingly mastering and understanding how music is put together. This is the state of affairs toward which you should aim. Action Learning goals—ones students can find to be interesting, useful or personally applicable, and challenging—are the key. Unless you set such goals, and *unless students generally accept them as their own*, no significant progress can occur, but discipline problems will!

Thus you are cautioned not to make a panacea of the method—of the activities themselves. Nor should you think that the activities automatically work by themselves. They are useless if you are not able to "fill them with content" (learning) appropriate to the needs, interests, sense of relevance, and in-life (not to mention lifelong) musical behavior of your students. A Sufi saying reminds people that "every quality is in need of a vehicle—speed is a virtue only in a horse." Similarly, the activities recommended so far are only the vehicle. You must "fill them" with the musical qualities that will be regarded as vital by your students. No one can teach you how to do that, or what that content should be. For this you must attempt to "get inside your students' heads," put yourself in their position, and empathetically select the experiences that will result in a quality music education for your charges. It is unfortunate that this prime quality cannot be directly taught to teachers. But now, at least, you are advised of the problem and some very useful approaches to a solution.

SUMMARY: ADVANTAGES OF SOUND COMPOSITIONS AND SONGWRITING ACTIVITIES

Working with student-created sound and song products has several advantages over the same activities completed using commercially available or teacher-designed materials.

1. Since the materials are the students' own creations, the chances are far greater that these materials are suitable to their individual *levels of readiness*.

2. Student *motivation* can be much greater. This is especially obvious with youngsters whose previous participation in activities was either negligible or negative.

3. The teacher has an *endless source of materials* to use, thus saving the time of constantly looking for appropriate materials. Money can be spent on other things.

4. To parents, the music program becomes far more tangible than an occasional concert. Children talk at home about their creations, and often bring them home, just like their art projects.

5. Because students created the works in question, chances are that they already understand its basic facets and thus can begin more quickly to work on the "advanced" activities without prior review or analysis. This permits an unbroken use of song and sound composition activities from middle through high school (see Appendix A for a sample curriculum).

6. The Action Learning involved in having students produce these materials all the more prepares and inclines them to *use* such learning in activities out of school and in later life. When you learn by Action Learning, by use and involvement in realistic ways, you are able to incorporate such learning into your life pursuits. *Action Learning promotes musically active people.*

NOTES: CHAPTER 3

1. See Robert Rosenthal, "Self-Fulfilling Prophecy," *Psychology Today*, Sept. 1968, and "The Pygmalion Effect Lives," ibid., Sept. 1973.

2. See *Synergetics*. (New York: Macmillan Co., 1975).

3. Keep in mind that sound compositions require little if any readiness to initiate; and each successful project provides built-in readiness for other or subsequent projects. Given the nature of the multiple results possible, the readiness promoted *by* sound compositions *for* subsequent activities of all kinds is equally variable, and students will continue to work at the individual levels of ability and interest.

4. It is a major advantage if this can be in the form of acetate overhead projection sheets processed by a Thermofax® machine. This makes possible a tremendous saving in time; and with proper planning, these sheets can be reused for many years. A black crayon or special felt-tip pen for writing on acetate must be provided, but these materials easly wipe off the acetate for reuse, even during the same class.

5. With this or any other aspect of the songwriting activities, teachers who feel unsure of their ability to create rhythmic patterns or harmonic progressions, etc., can "borrow" them from the song series or other available music. This technique is even recommended on some occasions as a special activity, since then students can compare their "tune" with the original from which the chords were "borrowed."

6. When a pitch is prespecified in this way by the teacher, students are allowed to use it twice: once as specified by the teacher, and once wherever they may otherwise decide to use it.

7. Or some other comparable device: e.g., $\underset{M}{|}\ \underset{m}{|}$ where M = major and m = minor.

8. Once again you are reminded that if you feel inadequate in this regard, simply borrow chord progressions from other sources, such as from songs in the song series.

9. A V chord preceding a IV chord is considered technically incorrect or weak, even though such an example is found in the "classical" twelve-bar blues progression:

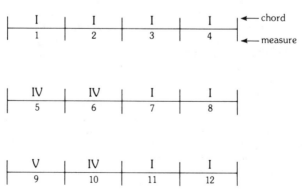

10. This may take the form of homework, or independent study; in the form of goal cards or learning contracts.
11. Sources: R. and M. Merchandisers Co., 5901 North Cicero Avenue, Chicago, Illinois   60646; Wallace Brown, Dept. M, Baltic, Connecticut   06329.

4

Listening and Musical Synergy

Listening is the culmination, the synthesizing agent, of a successful Action Learning program for general music education. Because it involves so very many intangible factors and influences, listening is by far the most difficult of activities to use. Listening, especially, has the potential for misbehavior problems. Generally any negative emotions or attitudes that may result from listening lessons can undo and negate whatever success the teacher may have forged with the preceding activities. For these reasons, listening activities, more than any other, must be undertaken with great caution.

As a group, listening activities are the least subject to prescriptions for a step-by-step structuring. As a group, they require the most of teachers' musical and pedagogical insight and flexibility, and especially the skills of "thinking on your feet." For these reasons, it will be necessary to review and survey major factors that are involved in listening lessons, with the hope of developing a successful enough general understanding to minimize problems and to maximize the main benefits of listening. Only with an awareness and understanding of these factors on the part of the teacher can listening lessons assume their crucial role in an Action Learning program of general music education.

SUMMARY OF FACTORS RELEVANT TO A SUCCESSFUL LISTENING PROGRAM

Generally speaking, a distinction should be made in your mind between the *musical score* as an *art work* and the *audited performance* as an *art (musical) experience*. The musical *art work* (score) is only a musical experience in latent form. Under certain conditions it may be studied and thereby profit the musical experience. But *the essence of music is its perception as an aural phenomenon in the mind of each listener*. Without this, for all practical purposes, music does not exist.

TRADITIONAL ROLES OF THE COMPOSER AND THE PERFORMER

1. The composer is responsible for the creation of the art work, the musical score, by means of which the musical experience is embodied in latent form, awaiting birth.
2. The performer has the responsibility of bringing to birth—into being—the musical experience latent in the score. To this end, performers study and practice those skills that allow the most accurate rendering of the composer's intention.
3. A musical performance includes the notated intention of the composer, mixed, inevitably, with some of the humanness of the performer which comes through in the live performance. Too much of the performer can result in excessive virtuosity, or virtuosity for its own sake, and can diminish the import of the composer's intent.

NEWER ROLES FOR THE COMPOSER AND THE PERFORMER

1. In electronic music the composer's intentions are realized directly in recorded sound without the intermediary of a performer or live performance. This allows the composer com-

180

plete control of the product without fear of misinterpretation by performers, and insures that the product is invariable.

2. Electronic synthesizers allow the introduction of electronic sounds—original ones and manipulated sounds—into the "real time" of live performances. This allows the incorporation of an expanded vocabulary of sounds as potential for musical expression, yet retains the advantages of live performance.

3. Recordings, whether produced in a studio or "live," have the inherent disadvantage of fixing in one version a performance that would otherwise be somewhat varied and fresh from one occasion to another in a really live performance. Recordings engineered in the recording studio permit ultimate creative control, but they also allow a certain unnatural "perfection" through electronic manipulation that is not characteristic of a live musical performance.

4. Composition itself has undergone significant changes in three directions.

a. *Improvisation* is the musical creation through performance according to certain structural conditions and controls. It does not result in a notated or stable (i.e., repeatable) musical product.

b. *Indeterminant music* (aleatory and stochastic)[1] leaves many of the specifics of performance up to the performers. The composer creates the conditions of performance, suggests or even notates the "musical events" to be used, but these are realized according to chance factors in performance. Thus the musical product is not stable (in terms of a fixed form), and varies greatly from performance to performance.

c. *Composition as "working it out by ear"* (for example, in the recording studio) results in a product that is unnotated and worked out by trial and error. The ear confirms the result, and the mind remembers the result long enough for it to be recorded. These works promote results not possible or as likely in notated music.

IMPLICATIONS FOR LISTENING

1. Each of the above types of music requires the listener to adopt the attitude appropriate to its specific nature.

2. Because a type of music need not be notated, because it can exist in a purely aural tradition passed on by ear, this should not mean that it is less important, less music. In many ways, such music permits advantages not possible in music which must restrict itself to what can be notated. The history of music, and comparison of Western to Oriental music, points out that each approach has its advantages and disadvantages and that each should be considered in listening. Do not expect from unnotated music what can be expected from notated music.

3. Certain advantages with unnotated music involve the emphasis it puts for performers on the music itself, instead of merely "playing notes." Unnotated music can change gradually over time, as errors in transmission become the accepted version. All the above factors must be considered by the teacher if the success of listening lessons is to be insured.

THE RESPONSIBILITIES OF THE TEACHER

Too many people equate *listening* and *hearing*. Adolescents in general are perhaps the prime offenders in perpetuating this mistaken view of perception. While hearing can be understood in terms of being in the path of and aware of sound waves, listening involves listening *to* or *for* something in an active, intentional manner.

It is often very difficult to convince middle school and high school adolescents that listening is preferable to mere hearing. Among other things, *listening requires effort, whereas hearing is passive.* Listening requires an intention to aurally discriminate, whereas hearing requires no such prior intent. Adolescents tend only to *hear* much of their popular music, though they may sometimes tend to *listen to the words* (in those compositions, at least, where the words are audible or intelligible).

Generally, neither adults nor adolescents pay attention to things they do not perceive. We do not perceive these things because we are not aware of their existence. When we are interested in something, perhaps as a hobby or because of our vocation, we tend to be much more aware of its existence. We also tend to notice more of its qualities, more of its nuances, more of the smaller refinements that most other people tend to ignore.

The key elements, therefore, in learning to listen are *awareness* (of the existence of the thing) and *interest* (in the qualities of the thing). These two factors are among the most important that the teacher must nurture in any program of music education.

Awareness must be specific. Awareness of music in general is, of course, basic. But it is required that this awareness be further sharpened. The ability to respond to refinements must be developed. This is where interest becomes important. *It is interest that provides the intention of seeking to become aware of refinements.* When a student is interested in, for example, responding to nuances of melodic construction or musical form, that student will actively attempt (intend) to direct his or her attention to these aspects. But once again, if the student is not aware of the existence of these factors, it is difficult to *make* him or her aware or interested.

In the program of music education outlined so far, students will become increasingly aware of such individual musical elements (or "parts") and will have a knowledge of their existence and operation that arises from *using* these elements in an Action Learning program of musical creation. Furthermore, sound composition and songwriting activities also involve some degree of listening to the sound products thus created. Therefore, if these parts of the program are operating as recommended in Chapters 1 and 2, there should be little problem with developing students' *awareness* of the main elements of the musical art. This leaves *interest* as a problem. How do you, or can you, stimulate interest?

It is not possible usually to *directly* stimulate or *motivate interest.* Many men have found this to be true as they have attempted to *make* their wives or girl friends interested in football on Sunday afternoons. And teachers fail all the time in similar ways when they try to *make* students interested in various things *before the fact.* Before the fact? What is the fact?

It is the point at which several conditions come together in order to make interest in something a possibility. What are these conditions? The first is generally that *the person has to have had significant prior experience* in a variety of situations with the thing towards which interest might be shown. The second is that *these past experiences need to have had some pleasurable consequences* or to have stimulated the person's responses to some degree. Finally, there needs to be something that enables *the person to predict that contacts with the thing in question will result in enjoyment, productive involvement, or challenge.*

So often these conditions are not fulfilled, or are not fulfilled sufficiently. A child so often decides to study a musical instrument on the basis of the flimsiest contact with the instrument, with music, or with the study of music. It is not unusual, then, that students' initial *curiosity*[2] never pans out. They are totally unaware of the factors involved, such as practicing. If the lessons are in themselves interesting—as opposed to fear-producing, boring, or unrewarding—the student will *not* gradually lose interest. If the music and practicing assigned are mechanical, dull, and unproductive—as the student sees it—then interest *will* be lost. If, most importantly, the student does not feel that he or she is *improving* to the point of being able to predict more enjoyment from the higher level of performance opportunities made possible by studying and practicing— if these factors are not working positively, the student will gradually but surely lose interest.

Music also must cope with the increasing number and variety of competing interests that arise in the lifetime of most youngsters, and precisely most significantly with the onset of puberty. If the interest *and intrinsic rewards* of musical involvement are not firmly established prior to or no later than adolescence, it is unlikely that significant musical interests can survive. This is precisely why all music instruction up to and at the time of middle school is so crucial: it is for most people the last real opportunity to develop an interest and continuing skill in some aspect of musical involvement. It is almost a law of human nature that *interest is determined almost entirely by some sort of potential benefit perceived by the individual.*

While *extrinsic* rewards, such as notoriety, winning prizes or contests, wearing band uniforms, and going on trips, manage to maintain some kind of tentative interest through the end of the formal public school years, such rewards almost never stimulate interest in music as a lifelong pursuit. As soon as the opportunity for such extrinsic rewards is withdrawn upon leaving the school setting, the interest ceases. Grades in general-music classes can have the same results. In general, extrinsic motivation has been found to be less effective than intrinsic motivation, and in some regards is considered counterproductive.[3]

Intrinsic benefits—the self-evident joy of music, the magic of its world, its self-actualizing and humanizing effects—these are the kinds of rewards that sustain an in-life involvement. These can result only from continued productive interactions with music whereby the student "feels good," feels fuller or richer (and we can never pin it down any further) as a result. This is simply one more major reason why musical instruction should not become atomistic or reductionistic, and why it should always deal with a musical whole. It is only from the effect of the "whole" that such significant rewards can be perceived from the student's point of view.

Thus, once again, it will be difficult for you to *directly* interest your students in music: extrinsic rewards and motivations (these include, not incidentally, the fear of failure or punishment, which are overly and stupidly employed by unthinking teachers) will not help. The only avenue open to you is fortunately a fruitful one. You involve your students at their level of ability in the very same kinds of musical actions that all musically involved people follow: composing, performing, and listening.

Such an Action Learning program of general music education is one oriented to integrating learning as part of the in-life functioning of each and every student. Here "in-life" refers not only to adult life but also—and this is important—to the out-of-school pursuits of students *now*. Remember: adolescents are notorious for expecting quick results! They are interested in *now* and not necessarily in their musical accomplishments as adults.

A student cannot be "structured" for listening lessons in the same way or to the same degree as in the other two types of activity described so far. Structure is present, and it must be—you cannot just say, "Listen!" But you cannot directly "steer" students' responses in this area the way you can in the other areas. First of all it is more difficult. The listening response is by its very nature one hundred percent less tangible than composing or performing, each of which results in an overt, observable product.

We should pick up the hint from rock concerts, however, and *attempt to make listening experiences more tangible*, more overt, at least for purposes of in-school instruction. This, among other results, enables adolescents to feel that some "thing" has been accomplished. It is a relatively tangible goal that suits their desire for immediate results.

The second reason for not controlling students' responses in listening is that it is not an ethical thing to do. We must not impose our values directly on students. They are having enough difficulty coming to grips with, or rebelling against the other values interposed by society, their parents, their church, and government. When we attempt to interpose our values, we run smack into the same nonacceptance, the same rebellion, the same discipline problems as do authority figures in these other arenas of life.

Indirectly we do impress one value by the very fact of teaching music in school: that music is worth learning! We must not impose, however, our specific values on these young people. If we think seriously enough about it, our belief in music's efficacy in life is generally predicated upon its humanizing and self-actualizing capacities, its ability to reach noncognitive, "feeling" aspects of people. For this reason music's meaning is lost if students' own "feeling" values are ignored.

Music instruction in particular, and arts education in gneral, may be a last major source of "affective education" left in the majority of public schools. The music class should be somewhat subversive of the entire school mentality by emphasizing "feeling," subjective, freely individualizing responses. We should not allow ourselves to be influenced any more than can be avoided by the mentality prevailing in other parts of the school: pursuit of knowledge for its own sake, of facts and information to pass tests, earn high grades, get a good job, etc. Instead we must emphasize the total person, not only as a "knowing" but as a "feeling" being.

Education, generally, has recognized this need and we read much about "affective" or "confluent" education today in professional sources. Music, however, is already an established fact in most schools. It has behind it thousands of years of precedent in performing at least part of this role of humanizing humanity. The middle school is a particularly important stage for music to work its magic (if allowed), since it is at this stage that most damage or good can be done to the student's psyche. It is an apt time for music to resume the humanizing function lost in those settings where skills, facts, and information have been taught as ends in themselves. It is, in any case, the last time formal music education is likely to make a lasting impact.

This does not diminish a "music for its own sake" point of view at all. Music is a medium. A medium, according to Marshall McLuhan, is any "extension of man," any manner whereby a person spreads his or her influence, qualities, abilities. Since the "content of any medium is always another medium," we can see that the "content" of music is humanity. Music is humanity-for-its-own-sake glorified—in this instance, through the medium of music. And an apt medium it is, if only allowed to function as it was intended. This is a great responsibility, indeed. Ultimately the greatest responsibility of the teacher is to nurture the student's own sense of responsibility.

SUMMARY: THE TEACHER'S RESPONSIBILITIES

1. Distinguish between *listening*, which is active, and *hearing*, which is passive.

2. Understand that listening is entirely dependent for its success on (a) *awareness* (of the existence of a musical aspect), (b) *interest* (desire, intent), and (c) *prediction of pleasure* of some kind that results from awareness.

3. Since it is not possible to *directly motivate* interest, the teacher must *indirectly interest* students through successfully engaging them in musical activities that develop awareness and prove to be predictably pleasurable.

4. *Extrinsic* rewards are not long-lasting and are essentially futile and false. Only *intrinsic* benefits stimulate true interest with the possibility of long-lasting results.

5. Do not impose your own values on students. Adolescents typically resist imposed values. Besides, music's special quality is its ability to generate personal, human values in listeners. To introduce your values is to deprive students of this important quality possessed by music. Help them, instead, to develop their own values—values independent of their peers and commercially inspired fads in popular music genres.

THE ROLE AND RESPONSIBILITIES
OF THE LISTENER

Along with composing and performing, *listening is essentially a creative act.* A musical response while listening is not simply a reaction, a conditioned response. Each listener mentally *creates* his or her own response at a given moment. This is why listening is active (as compared to hearing, which is passive).

But a creation usually involves a creation of some "thing" out of component "things." What are all these things? They are those experiences that make up the unique humanness of each person. The building blocks of the musical response created by each listener are influenced by and constructed out of all our prior experiences—musical and otherwise—including the more immediate experiences we have before and during listening.

We "are" all our experiences: those we have actively chosen and sought, and those that have simply "happened" to us. These past experiences, those we are aware of and many more that we are not aware of, are sifted (abstracted) by our mind in search of common or related elements. Those factors we can find to be related or similar remain with us in the form of concepts. *Concepts are the means by which we actively give form or structure to and thus "understand' or "make sense of" OUR experience.*

Thus, all of our responses are active and creative as we seek to connect each new experience to past ones. New experiences allow our understanding to grow and enrich itself. People who do not appreciate this fact of human functioning are considered "thoughtless," or "mindless." They often complain that their lives are controlled by fate, or other such malign forces. They fail to realize the degree of control we have over our own responses. There is evidence indicating that the "old brain" (which we inherited from and share with our fellow animals) is complemented by the "new brain," the cerebral hemispheres possessed only by human beings. Among other things, the new brain allows people to speak, to deal abstractly with time and space, and to control their emotions.[4]

THE NEW AND THE OLD BRAIN

The old brain seems to be the source or cause of many of our "programmed" responses such as the need to procreate and certain basic emotions such as fear. The new brain, however, has two hemispheres. For most people the *left hemisphere* is dominant because, among other things, it controls the speech and reading functions highly prized by our culture (and, thus, our schools). *It can respond to stimuli only one at a time.* This, in comparison to the functioning of other areas of the brain, is a slow process. Thus "thinking"

186

(subvocal speech) and other forms of rational, intellectual activity take some time to unfold.

The *right hemisphere* in most people deals with the more generalized abilities involving time and space, and most notably, also involves certain "feeling" responses. These are distinguished from the "emotions" of the old brain. The former are much more primitive and powerful than the latter. The right hemisphere, because of its unique makeup, is able to perform many tasks simultaneously. That is, it *is able to pay attention to, to be aware of, more than one thing at a time.* Obviously this is of great importance for listening to music. In consequence, the responses of this hemisphere seem more "intuitive," since it appears to operate instantly as opposed to the more time-consuming "thinking" of the left side.

Normally the left and right hemispheres cooperate in functioning. In fact, each can often perform the functions of the other if necessary (as in the instance of brain damage) and each can complement the deficiencies of the other. Thus both used together assist us in "creating" our responses to life, our environment, and in the present instance, to music.

Much of the daily educational process is directed toward the left hemisphere: to the verbal, logical, linear functions. Music, by its very nature, involves the right hemisphere to a much greater degree. Basic perception of pitch, melody, chords, and timbre, and a host of other basic musical responses, have been shown time and again to be under the control of the right hemisphere even though the whole brain is always involved. Thus even though the left hemisphere assists this process in a variety of ways (e.g., by directing attention, by labeling percepts for future reference), a musical response occurs as a "feeling" response, a spontaneous "flash" of significance or insight from the right hemisphere. It might even be said that this response is an almost "pure" one, at least in comparison to the verbal impurities the left hemisphere adds to experience.[5]

The old brain seems to cooperate in the musical endeavor by responding directly in certain more "primitive" ways to such factors as rhythm, amplitude, and intensity (volume). But it also is influenced by the new brain. The net result of the activity of the old brain being acted upon by the new is physiological and automatic changes in the body (which, except by biofeedback control, we cannot influence directly) such as increased heart rate and an increased level of electrical activity on the surface of the skin (a result, in part, of the increased moisture level and thus electrical conducting ability that results from glandular activation).

All in all, then, our experiences—past and present—are stored by the mind[6] with a potential for recall and use in creating our responses. But we must be willing to expend the effort in this direction by intentionally mustering the *mental actions* necessary to this result.

CREATING RESPONSES

Whether or not this is done, of course, once again depends on *interest*, on whether or not we are interested in achieving this aim. It helps greatly with adolescents if they can discover that the responses they create for and within themselves are essentially *individuating*. That is, these responses are, by their very nature, unique to each individual, and thus can affirm—if we choose to allow them to—the uniqueness of the individual who so responds.

This is important at precisely the time in life—the onset of adolescence—when everyone must grapple with such problems as "Who am I?" and "How am I different from everyone else?"[7] At the time of adolescence the individual student is trying to sort out the problems of becoming integrated into society—one of the goals of schooling—with the corresponding uniformity and conformity of behavior believed minimally necessary to the operation and continuation of our society. But the adolescent also suffers the inevitable pangs of concern for how personal uniqueness can be retained while acquiescing to the demands of society for conformity. Much adolescent conflict—both internal conflict and its undesirable external manifestations—results from this intensely difficult situation. It plagues many people for the remainder of their lives, especially those who are not assisted during the formative years. In this vein, music education can be viewed as music therapy done early!

The musical response, particularly the listening response, by its very nature serves this need for perceiving one's uniqueness and individuality. It also proves that an individual's created response can still be socially validated by others who often have very similar but not identical responses:

> Language and even nonverbal communication, in gestures and bodily attitudes, cannot possibly give full expression to the felt emotional experience. Our action systems are crude instruments when it comes to describing the fine distinctions among emotions that we can inspect in consciousness. This does not deny that, because of the essential identity of mental structures (but not their content) from individual to individual, much of private experience is made of the same stuff across individuals, but it does suggest that similarities are due to similarities in language and action systems that are, after all, to a very large extent influenced and molded by the social community.[8]

Once this individuating capacity of music is realized by the student, *interest* in music can be revived or intensified. Truly, this indirect motivation is the only one available to any teacher. We cannot motivate by fiat or pronouncement; we must motivate by experience. We must provide successful examples in personal experience of listening activities that have been interesting and vital. The more such examples we can provide, the more success we can enjoy in working with increasingly interested students.

This long introduction to the questions of the various roles of composer, performer, listener, and teacher is necessary because *no listening program has any chance of success unless one has duly considered and provided for all these factors.* To do anything less will be to "go through the motions" of teaching without significant interest or learning occurring. What will occur is one kind of "discipline problem" or another, because listening, above all, is the least physically active of all the activities described here and the one, therefore, most vulnerable to problem behavior.

The notion of "active listening" is not one susceptible to direct teaching: you cannot inform students that now their minds will be active and that therefore they should be as actively interested as they might have been in sound compositions and songwriting, which involved both minds and bodies. You can only establish the conditions—namely, successful lessons that consider all the aforementioned factors, and that result in this understanding by students and their consequent interest (willingness to participate fully in this species of activity with its unique advantages).

SUMMARY: THE LISTENER'S ROLE

1. To create one's own musical response.
2. To seek full use of the mental potential possessed by all people—one involving the "old" and "new" brains—in realizing the uniqueness of one's own response to music.
3. To attempt to actualize one's humanness by means of the uniquely created listening response.
4. To seek to discover interest (meaning, relevance) by comparing present experiences to past ones, or by evoking new experiences with the intention of human growth.
5. To work toward the kind of response that affirms one's own identity while confirming one's role in the larger society.

PSYCHOLOGICAL BASES OF AURAL PERCEPTION

It is of fundamental importance to understand how we perceive and respond to music. Only with such knowledge is the teacher able to devise and carry out successful listening lessons.

Listening, as opposed to hearing, *is directed.* It is *aural attention intentionally directed toward specific factors.* In the final accounting this should be self-directed attention. For purposes of music education in the schools, however, the direction is provided at first by the teacher until the student is aware of what music involves that one can direct one's attention toward. Without such teacher direction, music is so complex that students literally do not hear certain musical elements. What they are not aware of, they do not direct their attention toward, and therefore do not perceive.

AN OUTLINE FOR THE TEACHER

In this regard, the process of directed listening has four requirements.

1. *You must provide the prior experiences, the readiness for listening experiences* by means of other activities so that students can be aware of certain musical elements in order to perceive them while listening. Sound compositions and songwriting activities are intended to provide just this function. Generally *do not expect students to be able to adequately perceive any musical factor that is not given substantial treatment beforehand by means of these activities.*

2. For listening lessons *you must select compositions that contain appropriate attensive qualities.* The term "attensive" is derived in part from the word "*atten*tion" and implies qualities that trigger attention, that reach out and demand attentiveness. The term also is derived in part from the word "*intensive.*" This implies that attensive qualities should not only grab at students' attention but should be those qualities that do so most intensively. Therefore attensive qualities are those factors in a composition that you select for a listening lesson because they are most striking, the most notable, the most clearly perceived, the most attention-grabbing. They are those qualities which stand the greatest chance of being adequately perceived by novice listeners.

Selecting recordings for purposes of listening activities is mainly a problem of selecting those compositions that possess attensive qualities appropriate to the interests, readiness, and perceptual abilities of a given group of students. For this reason—especially the readiness factor, which will vary greatly from class to class and school to school—*it is impossible to rely on prepackaged listening lessons, or compositions that have "worked" for another teacher.* You must use your judgment in all cases of selecting recordings in order to determine for each class whether the attensive qualities of the recording are appropriate in terms of the readiness of that group.

The presence of *too few attensive qualities can be as confusing to the beginner as too many.* If a piece has too many, none stand out as more important, and thus none are really very attensive. Too few attensive qualities prevent a composition from sufficiently engaging the attention of a student throughout its duration. And when adolescent minds wander it does not take them long to invent new sources of interest and amusement—discipline problems!

3. Your next responsibility is *to direct students' attention,* by the devices suggested later in this chapter, *to those attensive qualities you have chosen to emphasize.* You do this by means of questions and various other kinds of directions given to the students *before* the listening lesson begins. *You do not talk* (direct attention) *DURING the playing of the recording.* That is not directing attention, it is doing the students' work for them.

4. Your final responsibility is *to determine by some means whether or not,*

or to what degree, students have adequately perceived those attensive qualities, i.e., to what degree they have been able to follow the directions successfully. Remember, first of all, that the listening response is typically *covert.* This means that generally we keep our responses, our feelings, *within ourselves* as we listen. There may be some vague outward expression of our inner feelings such as a smile or a wrinkled brow, but generally we do not respond overtly to music (unless we are dancing to it) except by tapping the foot or by doing a little conducting with the hand or fingers. You must devise means by which some kind of overt, observable action is elicited which stands a good chance of representing fairly accurately the nature or degree of each student's more natural covert perceptions and responses.

Each of the listening-lesson techniques outlined in this chapter will suggest a great variety of means for doing this. However, in short, the overt responses are usually elicited by the directions you give for listening. Students are directed to listen for the attensive qualities, and by some overt means to indicate perception of these qualities as they happen. After the listening these responses are shared, discussed, and analyzed by the class. The teacher observes and guides this interaction, and if necessary supplements it by collecting (if the lesson involves tangible products) the record of these observable responses.

It is a ghastly mistake to grade these responses. This diminishes their sincerity, freedom, and authenticity; inhibits students in subsequent efforts; and maximizes extrinsic reward (or punishment) for what should be an inherently intrinsic reward situation: listening to the music for its pleasures.

A MODEL OF AURAL PERCEPTION

To understand the discussion of this process, refer to the model of aural perception in Fig. 4:1.

1. Consciousness is made aware of the need to perceive certain musical elements by means of the *teacher's directions* as to what to listen for in the music. In a well-conceived lesson, the student is directed to listen to the attensive qualities present in the piece of music chosen for that purpose. Thus the "directions" of directed listening can be compared to a spotlight illuminating or focusing attention on only a small part of a larger or more complex reality.

2. Any composition, from an aural viewpoint, consists of a multitude of *percepts.* Percepts are the mental products of perception. In order to simplify students' efforts in making sense of the bewildering number of possible percepts, even in the simplest music, the teacher has selected this composition for the attensiveness of its perceptual qualities. Furthermore, the teacher has provided students with directions that focus their attention (hopefully) on *one*

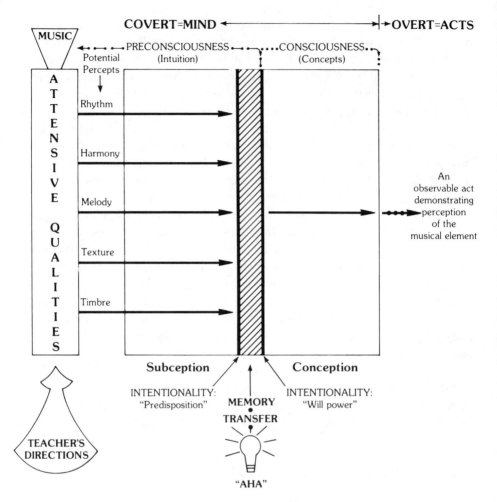

Fig. 4:1

percept at a time, in accordance with the traits of the left ("dominant") hemisphere of the brain discussed earlier.

Let us assume for this discussion that some aspect of *melody* was selected for the moment diagrammed in the model and that the teacher has directed the student's attention to this possibility. When the student is able to fix his aural attention on the melodic factor in question, that attensive quality becomes a percept in that student's mind. At this moment the preconscious mind is aware that the quality has been perceived (whether appropriately or not, it does not know yet), and it can become a conscious perception.

3. Whether or not this result is achieved depends ordinarily on several intervening factors: first, on the student's *intentionality* (the desire to perceive the attensive qualities in question); second, on the student's *memory,* i.e.,

whether or not the student has "in mind" a concept of melody. Assuming that intentionality and memory operate effectively, the final factor is the student's ability to *transfer learning* from all past experiences with melody (i.e., to transfer his or her concept of melody) to the new present percept. *When the student can relate (transfer) this present (attensive) perception to past experiences stored in memory in the form of concepts, the "aha" (or "lightbulb") effect is experienced. Thus, understanding occurs when a "fit" is achieved between the past (i.e., the concept in memory) and the present perception.* Usually the new perception is assimilated into or accommodated by the existing concept. By such means existing concepts are either strengthened or broadened.

4. Since the teacher has prepared directions that call for an overt response, the student externalizes this heretofore covert response (the "aha" of the right ["minor"] hemisphere at the fitting of the present percept with the concept in memory) as an overt act. This may be a physical gesture such as raising the hand, or a written response on paper, or some other indication.

5. Meanwhile, the remaining parts of a musical stimulus, the other attensive qualities it possesses at that moment (if any), are unattended to. They are noticed only peripherally as the "context" or diffuse background against which the perceived stimulus is contrasted. Thus these background qualities remain preconscious, at least for the moment.

Musical perception is conscious and concept-oriented to the degree that we can perceive only what we are aware of and looking for in the music. Such conscious concepts result in what may be called *selective attention:* the attention is selectively directed to the attensive quality represented in the teacher's direction for this moment of the music. However, selective attention can result in what might be called "tunnel vision." This would be an overly selective attending to some aspect of a composition to the exclusion of all other aspects. This is counterproductive since it diminishes the perception of music as "a whole," as a synergistic system. Therefore, the model must be expanded (see Fig. 4:2).

6. Depending on the wealth of prior experiences with such focused, directed, intentional listening, any *percept is "conditioned" through the process of subception*[9] *by all the other background percepts at that moment* (Fig. 4:2). Each of these "conditioning" (though less strongly sensed) percepts have been *strengthened in their contribution to the "wholistic" effect* by being the individual focus of past experiences. Thus, any percept occurs in and through a total musical context, a musical "whole," and is not heard in isolation. Even though a percept (for example, melody, as shown above) is the major aural goal at this moment, it is heard in terms of and is determined and controlled or conditioned by many or all of the other musical events (percepts) that occur simultaneously with it as its background.

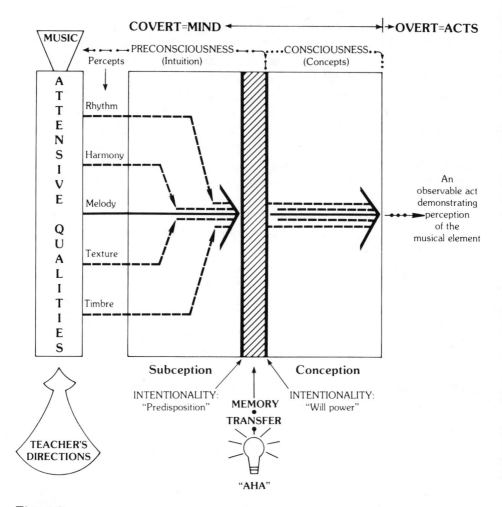

Fig. 4:2

This function has been called *subception*. For some reason it has not been given adequate recognition in music education. It is that capacity, referred to earlier, by which *the mind is able to perceive, record, and use sensory data without direct or total consciousness of it.* It is sometimes referred to as "subliminal," "subconsciousness," or "nonattentional" consciousness (i.e., perceptual responding without direct awareness). It is pivotal in the musical response and deserves more emphasis.

Subception is seen in daily life when, for example, we recognize a friend. We are not consciously aware of all the aspects of our friend's face, nor do we compare such features to a mental list we have in mind of all the characteristics of all the people we know. We just instantly "know." By similar means we can identify the voices and the sound of footsteps of people we "know" well.

194

These instant and seemingly "intuitive" judgments we make all the time. In fact much more of our daily existence involves this kind of right-hemisphere functioning than consciously thought out, deliberate, left-hemisphere modes of functioning. One writer calls this ability *tacit knowledge*.[10] Tacit understanding is implied or implicit understanding without conscious deliberation. It is "knowing" without being able to *say*, to make explicit, *how* you know. Tacit knowing arises when a perceptual focus (percept) is acquired against, or in terms of a background awareness. This results in a "wholistic" response that is due to an integrating action (intentionality) of the perceiver that seems spontaneous.

The conscious operations of mind are largely modes of the left hemisphere of the brain. Remember, it is this hemisphere that controls speech and logic, and any conscious attempt at detailed thinking also stems from this source. Also, recall that this hemisphere takes time to effect its function. This accounts for the time involved in such thinking.

Subception and tacit knowing seem to be controlled largely by the right hemisphere, which is more generalized in its functions than the dominant hemisphere. They also seem to draw on the more primitive emotions of the old brain. This is seen in the fact that a musical response seems to be almost an instant arousal. It seems intuitive since results come with virtually no conscious thought or control. The conscious thought occurs during the left-hemispheric process of directing the attention to the relevant qualities in the music. But *the "wholistic" musical response is due to the capacity of the right hemisphere instantaneously to process individual bits of sensory data simultaneously* rather than one at a time as the left hemisphere is limited to doing.

We must also recognize that it is difficult—virtually impossible, it seems—for us to divide our conscious (left hemisphere) attention equally among two or more sources of interest. It is not possible to read, watch television, and listen to a record with simultaneous and equal attention directed to all three. Yet, we all recognize the fact that in music not only are there a multitude of aural events happening simultaneously, but these simultaneous events all condition one another in a total kind of way. Therefore melody, harmony, rhythm, and tone color—while each an element capable of separate focus, separate identification—all interact to create an effect that is greater than the sum of their individual parts (see Fig. 4:2).

This kind of mental functioning that allows a focus on one element, while at the same time this element is conditioned by the context of all remaining elements, is a result of *subception* and of right-hemispheric processes of the brain. This also explains why it is so difficult, virtually impossible, to verbalize or rationalize a musical response to a "total" piece of music. Our basic response to that "whole" has not been conscious, nor has it happened in the

195

speech-controlling left hemisphere. It has happened under the control of the minor hemisphere, which is basically nonverbal. But it has happened in conjunction with the guidance and direction (selective attention) of the major hemisphere, and the emotional reinforcement (arousal) of the old brain.

Thus *cognition*, as such, *is not the goal of listening.* Cognition is the (left-hemispheric) *means* that permits the listener to orient attention toward certain factors in the music that are recognizable from past experience. Cognition is not the faculty of mind that appreciates as such; it is only the *means* by which our capacities for subception have been heightened. This can be called *cognitive strengthening.*

Cognitive strengthening is important only as a means of developing concepts. These concepts help to focus aural attention productively on the music. *All past conceptual emphases* (conceptual strengthening) *make the percepts thus noticed stronger in their effect when operating in the synthesis of subception.* Thus a cognitively strengthened percept has a greater role in subception and contributes more profoundly to a "wholistic" response.

Listening "appreciation" is therefore the result of subception. Subception's faculties are sharpened or heightened by past cognitive "exercises" or emphases on *separate percepts.* Ideally all major musical elements ("parts") should receive due and *equal* emphasis through cognitive (or conceptual) strengthening. *Unequal* strength results in "preferences"; the preferred element (i.e., the one the person is most easily able to perceive; the one he or she has had the greatest prior experience with; the one which is most naturally attensive) is the most clear and influential.

Thus individuals tend to prefer (i.e., seek) only percepts that the subceptual mind can handle. We find adolescents "tuned in" to rhythm and meter, while older untrained listeners often prefer clear and pretty "tunes." Either type of listener is befuddled by music that has other attensive qualities. Each would have to "work" at perceiving and understanding it. Each claims, therefore, not to like the music or not to understand it because such a listener prefers to listen passively rather than actively.

In subception, all elements function together in a total or mutual thrust or impact as illustrated in Fig. 4:2. At any one time one quality may stand out, only to retire to that continuous background of percepts which conditions each attensive quality one at a time. Like a revolving door, one major quality—one major focus at a time—moves into consciousness, then back into its unity with the other elements in the realm of subception.

Attention can also alternate very rapidly in successive microseconds between two separate qualities. In counterpoint, the impression of the two separate melodic strands may appear to the perceiver as two simultaneous qualities. In reality, though, subception fills in the "missing gaps" in each sequence of alternating attention (Fig. 4:3).

196

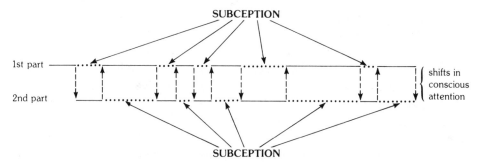

Fig. 4:3

A good listener, therefore, has adequately prepared his or her subceptual mind by means of the cognitive strengthening of many past conscious experiences with isolated qualities. All such cognitive emphasis heightens the probability that the percept will be strengthened and thereby play a correspondingly more profound role in the "appreciation" of music by subception.

In music, as in daily life, subception—among other of its attributes—is the ability or capacity (based on past experience) to respond to an emotion-provoking, feeling-laden stimulus that is not consciously perceived or cognitively labeled; i.e., it is not intellectualized as an identifiable, conscious concept. Subception is clearly central to the unified and "wholistic" perception that characterizes a rich musical response, because it is the result of particulars we cannot itemize, focus on individually, or verbalize. "Meaning" (relevance, value, appreciation) arises in this way. It is not explicitly stated or recognized, but is instead "tacitly felt" as meaningful, as valuable.

For this reason the results of this process have been called "qualitative intellect" or "qualitative intelligence."[11] This is an apt term for use in arts education, since it implies perceiving and "knowing tacitly" in terms of qualities and their relationships and mutual interactions.

Applied to music education, qualitative intelligence is the "halo" of feeling (sense of value or relevance) surrounding the results of our perceptions. It is not some ephemeral, pretty, extra something so often attributed to music and the arts. It is intelligence, just as much as the abilities of the left hemisphere are. But it is the mode of intelligence characteristic of the right hemisphere: a "wholistic" sensing or intuition of value that is tacit because it cannot be itemized or verbalized except in the most general of ways. Qualitative intellect, in comparison to the left hemisphere's clearly conscious functioning, seems diffuse and preconscious. We seem to be aware only of its results rather than the step-by-step processing that characterizes left-hemisphere thinking. As a result, qualitative intellect seems instantaneous in comparison to the plodding logic of the left hemisphere.

The prejudice against this kind of mental functioning is first seen in the distinction society has made between these two modes of functioning, calling the left hemisphere's mode "major" and the qualitative intellect of the right hemisphere "minor."[12] This is a battle to be fought, too, in school, since music addresses itself most fruitfully to subception's qualitative intellect. It is useful, then, that we now refer to musical responding as due to qualitative intellect, thus somewhat restoring such right-hemispheric functions to the status of intelligence—something denied to it by those who have regarded its intuition, its "feeling response" as anti-intellectual at worst and nonintellectual at best.[13] Now it can be seen that we have two forms of intellect: the conceptual kind and the subceptual kind. The former results in conscious concepts, and the latter in seemingly subconscious or preconscious qualitative intellect.

Before leaving this complex topic, one further note can be added. The qualities just described are just as true for other aspects of teaching-learning situations as they are specifically for listening activities. Concepts not only direct our attention but also arise in consciousness along with their complementary feeling-tones through subception and qualitative intellect. Thus what learners perceive is influenced by their qualitative intellect's verdict of what is worth learning, what is interesting, valuable, relevant, etc.[14] Similarly, the learning process is influenced through subception by the feeling-tone qualities associated with the methods used. Thus while a student might very much enjoy music, his qualitative intellect may respond negatively to authoritarian or mechanically boring or repetitive methods of instruction. This will not enable him to maintain interest (i.e., a positive feeling-tone) enough to learn.

Keep this in your own conscious mind as much as you can, and you can thereby train your subception to attend to it at moments when your attention is diverted by other concerns. It is perhaps the most important factor in teaching: what a student *feels about what he learns,* and *as he learns,* is more important than *what he learns.* Without the feeling component properly in place, no matter what you think you are teaching, learning will not be effective. Much negative learning occurs instead. This is especially so with adolescents because of the very strong emotional life that is characteristic of this age group.

PSYCHOLOGY OF AURAL PERCEPTION SUMMARIZED

1. Conscious concepts direct the attention of the learner toward the relevant attensive qualities in the music by means of the directions given by the teacher and as based on the past experience of the learner (i.e., conceptual readiness).

2. The object of such aural attention becomes a percept in the mind of the student. This is ordinarily covert. The teacher must try to make it outwardly observable (overt).

3. Such individual percepts are qualitatively influenced by other percepts that are not the major focus of attention at the moment. This process is known as *subception*. It is the ability to respond to a variety of percepts simultaneously without direct awareness or cognitive labeling. From particulars we cannot itemize subception produces a unified and wholistic "felt" knowledge. It involves what we commonly call "meaning" or the sense of "relevance." It results in qualitative intellect.

4. The capacity for subception is influenced by *cognitively strengthening* the perception of musical elements; but such *conceptual learning is not the goal of aesthetic education!* Concepts help focus attention. They also strengthen the percepts (cognitive strengthening) which mutually interact through subception. Thus concepts are but a *means* of music education and *not its self-sufficient end*. The end is the "wholistic" response resulting from subception's ability to deal simultaneously with a great variety of percepts, most of which we are not consciously aware at any given moment. They are preconscious and form a background for cognitively strengthened percepts.

5. Therefore the teacher must (a) provide the cognitive readiness for listening lessons; (b) select compositions for listening lessons that contain appropriate kinds and quantities of attensive qualities; (c) provide directions that steer the learner's attention to those attensive qualities; and for purposes of indicating whether perception was accurately or adequate, (d) attempt to make overt the student's otherwise covert responses.

6. The teacher must always continue to maximize the potential of subception, of the feeling response, by emphasizing this response as the end of instruction. Cognitive lessons prepare the student for a feeling response, but the feeling response is the goal of instruction, and therefore listening lessons should feature this response of the qualitative intellect more heavily than cognitive responses.

TYPES OF FORMAL DIRECTED-LISTENING LESSONS

There are *two basic types of directed-listening lesson* you can devise: *formal* and *informal*. This section will deal with the formal kind, by far the most useful in establishing a structured and controlled listening program.

Formal directed-listening lessons are characterized by a rather formal set of written-out directions. These directions serve two basic purposes. First, as described earlier, they should focus students' aural perception on certain attensive qualities. Secondly, they should elicit an overt, observable response on the part of students.

THE BASIC QUESTION-TYPE FORMAT

The most basic listening-lesson format is the *question-type directed-listening sheet*. It has a long history of trial and error by many teachers and has earned a well-deserved reputation. Therefore it is recommended that you investigate its potential fully before moving on to other varieties.

The sample to be discussed here is illustrated in Fig. 4:4.

Fig. 4:4

Listening Sheet # _____ .   Name _____

The composition you will hear begins with an *Introduction,* which sets the mood; this is followed by a *March,* which continues this mood.

The composition has only one melody (theme). I will play this melody on the piano. You circle whichever of the two examples below that I play.

Now that you have learned to recognize the *melody,* read the following ten questions carefully so that you will understand them quickly as the composition is played. Ask any questions you may have before we begin.

Wherever there is a choice, circle the answer you think is correct. Otherwise, answer the questions as directed.

1.	Which design do you think describes the opening of the Introduction? What are your reasons?	1. a. [arrows] b. [wavy arrows]
2.	Which line has the same feeling for you as the music that follows the Introduction? Why do you think so?	2. a. ———— b. ～～～ c. ／\／\／\
3.	Pick a color which you think might go with the music now. Can you think why you chose it?	3. a. bright red b. yellow c. light blue d. _____
4.	Raise your hand when you feel the March begin.	4. Raise your hand! Don't look around at your friends.
5.	Along with the drums, which other instrument plays the beat of the March?	5. a. clarinet b. trumpet c. tuba d. flute
6.	Which family of instruments plays the March melody?	6. reeds? brasses? strings?
7.	Do you think the marchers move closer or farther away? How can you tell?	7. closer? farther? _____
8.	Does the March get more relaxed or more tense for you as it moves along? How can you tell?	8. more relaxed? more tense? ____
9.	Do you think the March ends up in the air (seems incomplete) or do you have the feeling of a final ending? What influenced your choice?	9. incomplete? final ending?
10.	For which event do you think this March could be a good accompaniment? Can you think of your reasons?	10. a. wedding b. protest c. funeral d. parade

IDEAS?

It consists, in this instance, of "top matter" of relevance to the lesson that follows, directions for its use,[15] and a series of questions enclosed in boxes, with corresponding answer choices in parallel boxes. This particular listening-sheet example does not identify the title of the composition, since the title would provide a verbal hint to some of the answers. This would make some of the responses "educated guesses" based on the information suggested by the title, rather than responses based on aural perception.

Such listening sheets may or may not identify the title and composer. If the listening sheet does not provide this information, you may give it at the conclusion of the lesson. In the event that you would care to listen to the composition on which this sheet is based, and to use the sheet yourself, the composition is "Protest" from "Spirituals for Orchestra," by Morton Gould (Mercury [Wing], SRW-18034).

Principles for Developing Question-type Directed-Listening Sheets

1. *Always use the visual format shown* in Fig. 4:4—two columns of rectangles, with the left column containing the questions and the right column containing the answer choices or spaces.
   a. This format has been proven over many years to be the most effective. It is:
   (1) less visually confusing to slow readers.
   (2) most efficient in terms of the quickness with which a student is able to respond.
   b. Simply prepare questions and answers in these two columns, then add lines with a ruler to make the rectangles.
   c. Always type it. Don't be lazy! If you cannot type it well yourself, prepare it enough in advance to have a secretary type it for you. A typed sheet:
   (1) minimizes reading and word-recognition problems among slow or poor readers.
   (2) elicits greater "respect" from the class as to the seriousness of the project (i.e., it doesn't look as if it were thrown together at the last moment).
   (3) therefore there are fewer problems of all kinds in the carrying out of the activity.
   d. Underline or type in capital letters any key words, musical terms, or the like, for *visual emphasis.*
   e. Underline words in the question that will be used also in the answer or as answer choices. See questions 7-9 of the sample listening lesson.
2. *Make all questions as short, as clear, and as direct as possible.*
   a. Choose vocabulary commensurate with the reading abilities of the group. This may mean more than one version of a listening lesson if you have normal and good reading groups and also groups of slow (or bilingual) readers.
   b. The intent is to enable your students to read and understand the question as quickly as possible.
3. Do not *end* questions with a fill-in-the-blank, or the word "What?"—e.g., "The instrument playing now is what?" This is merely a substitute for a blank. Avoid ending questions with a preposition—e.g., "Which event would this March be a good accompaniment for?" End all questions with a question mark and all directive statements with a period.
4. *Do not imply in your questions that music "makes" one do (i.e., feel, think of, visualize, etc.) anything*—e.g., "How does the music *make* you feel at this moment?" should be rewritten as "Which word describes how you feel during this section?" or "Choose a color that goes with your mood now," or some equivalent expression.
   a. Music "makes" us feel, think, or do nothing!
   b. If you insist upon using that expression you open yourself up to the conclusion on the

201

part of students that if the music "makes" them feel nothing (or nothing good), it is either the composer's fault (i.e., bad music) or your fault for choosing this composition.

5. Use the word "which" when a choice from multiple answers is given or possible. Do not use the word "what" except when one answer involving no *given* choice is involved.

a. *Which* family of instruments plays the theme?	brass strings woodwinds	
b. *What* instrument is playing the melody?	_____	

6. For questions eliciting affective (i.e., feeling, mood), imaginative, subjective responses, include the expression "do you think" (or its equivalent) in the sentence in some way. See questions 1-3, 7-10, in Fig. 4:4. Other examples are:

a. "Which color *do you think* goes with the music now?"

b. *Do you think* the people for whom this music was composed were *aristocrats* or *common people?*"

c. "Which words describe *how you feel* during this section?"

d. "Choose a color that goes with *your mood* now." This technique insures that the student is clearly advised that you are seeking a personal response in these questions.

7. Totally *avoid the expression "best" in subjective questions.* It smacks of the technique used in objective tests, and causes students to be inhibited on questions to which you want a personal response, i.e., questions that have no wrong answer let alone a "best" one.

8. Immediately after subjective questions there should be in the question box *a follow-up question* that encourages students to think about their reasons for choosing or providing the answer they did. From the teacher's point of view this response is really more important than their answer, since, when it is discussed following the listening session, it informs you of what they heard in the music or thought about that was responsible for their response (i.e., it makes certain covert mental acts into overt verbal behaviors). Follow-up questions may include such short expressions as:

a. "Why do you think so?"

b. "How could you tell?"

c. "Can you think of your reasons?"

d. "In what way?"

Seldom is the lone word "Why?" appropriate. See questions 1-3, 7-10, in Fig. 4:4.

9. Objective (cognitive) questions having only one specific, unarguable answer should have no such follow-up (and should be relatively rare in number!). See questions 4-6 in Fig. 4:4.

10. "Problem solving" questions (such as those in which the student has to determine the overall form of the piece) should have some kind of follow-up that will serve as the basis for an explanation of the elements the student perceived which led to the conclusion. For example:

a. "Which factors provided unity, and which provided variety?"

b. "What was the major characteristic of each section?"

11. All listening lessons of this type should be at least 60 to 70 percent affective, subjective, and imaginative. (See questions 1-3, 7-10, in Fig. 4:4—they represent 70 percent of this lesson.) Such questions:

a. maximize the feeling-response, subception, and the synergy of qualitative intellect.

b. minimize the feeling of failure, vs. objective (cognitive) questions, which are either correct or incorrect.

c. deemphasize any test-related apprehensions on the part of students. If they feel it is a test, no matter what you disclaim, they will be inhibited.

12. *Never grade directed-listening sheets.*

a. You can collect them for your perusal, in order to determine the nature and range of each student's response.

b. You can write comments on papers you collect, but do so as suggestions for further thought, and not as direct criticism or as "corrections."

13. At the early stages of directed listening, *provide choices for all answers.*

a. As classes become less inhibited and gain in "readiness," you can provide more freedom.

(1) Provide a space for "other," in addition to choices given (see question 3 in Fig. 4:4).

(2) Provide no given choices for certain questions.

(3) But still retain some given choices for the majority of questions, if only for students who are less sure. Strong students will always choose their own answers no matter what you give them.

(4) Sometimes provide lines for a written response to a "Why" follow-up (see question 9 in Fig. 4:4). Such opportunities as these should be located where students will have time to write a response before the next question is due for their attention.

14. Put *at the very beginning* all questions that require directed attention *throughout* the composition. They need not be labeled as question 1.

a. "Listen throughout the entire piece and identify its form."

b. At the end of the piece, you remind the class to go back and answer the question.

c. It is usually wise to provide choices for such questions, especially with form, since many compositions are subject to a wide variety of form labels depending on how one hears them. Therefore, giving choices simplifies or clarifies the task realistically.

15. Deal only with questions of perception for which students have been adequately prepared through previous activities (i.e., questions for which they exhibit readiness).

16. Each listening sheet should always contain at the beginning the expression, "Ask any questions you may have before we begin." You do not want interruptions during the lesson or cop-outs afterward, e.g., "I didn't know what you were after!"

17. "Top matter," or any other introductory material, is optional. Provide it only if it has direct relevance in improving the readiness of students or in some way enhances their listening efforts. Do not provide musical information for its own sake here: it will only be ignored.

It should be made very clear that successful directed-listening sheets using this format require much practice and patience to perfect. Do not expect your first efforts to succeed immediately. After you have developed and used a few, you will gain experience in aspects of presenting questions and answers that will dictate the kinds of changes you will make in subsequent lessons. You are especially warned that *this format does not itself guarantee success.*

The success of the lesson depends much more on the suitability of the recording you choose in terms of its interest for a given group, the attensive qualities it features, and their relationship to the cognitive readiness of your class. How you run the subsequent discussion is also very important. This listening format is merely a means for presenting directions for aural perception in an organized, tried-and-true manner. Rules can, of course, be bent when the exceptions to them prove to be successful in actual use.

The Process of Preparing a Question-type Directed-Listening Sheet

1. Choose a recording that is appropriate for the interests and cognitive readiness of the class and that has significant *attensive qualities.*

a. These qualities should be very striking and should "jump out" at students.

b. These qualities should be the focal points of your lesson, i.e., the musical "parts" you intend to strengthen cognitively. Many, if not most or all, of the questions should refer to these "parts."

    c. As students progress in skill, greater refinement in the questions can elicit subtler nuances in the answers.

    d. The attensive qualities should be chosen not simply because they exist in a given piece, but because they relate to your curriculum (i.e., your instructional goals at the present time).

2. Choose a recording two or three minutes long for grades 4–6, and three or four minutes long for grades 6–8. Seldom is anything longer than five minutes appropriate for even a high school theory or music appreciation class. Students are not used to the intensity of effort required by listening so attentively over such a long period of time.

    a. If a piece of the appropriate length does not exist that meets your instructional needs, choose *logical sections* of longer pieces: e.g., the Shaker Theme section of "Appalachian Spring," by Aaron Copland, can be exerpted for a listening lesson.

    b. Entire musical theater pieces are not appropriately used with directed-listening sheets, although separate sections can be used this way as long as they fall within the time parameters recommended.

3. Listen to the record several times yourself *without the score*. If *you* have to use a score to make up the questions, it is unlikely that students will succeed with your questions without the same advantage.

    a. In rough wording, and *in order of their chronology in the composition*, create as many appropriate questions as you can.

    b. *These questions should serve*, in part at least, *as a "road map" that sequentially guides students through the composition.* Therefore, seize upon "aural landmarks" having attensive qualities that help the students locate themselves in the piece: e.g., "After the cymbal crash, what are your feelings?"

    c. From the list of all your questions select:

        (1) A variety of affective and cognitive questions (but the affective questions should outnumber the cognitive ones).

        (2) Enough questions to occupy students' attention for the duration of the composition.

        (3) But not so many questions that students have little time to read and think about their answers, and to respond in writing.

    d. Any questions not used for this lesson should be retained for a follow-up lesson at some later date (either formal or informal).

    e. Usually a total of seven to twelve questions turns out to be appropriate; but more or fewer are certainly permissible under certain conditions.

    f. Cast the questions you have chosen for the present lesson in an appropriate form, using the seventeen principles in the preceding section as guidelines.

4. Type the questions and directions on some form of master for a handout. Make every attempt to be very clear and neat in your visual presentation. It surely helps if you have an overhead transparency made (by the Thermofax® process) to which all children will respond. Be careful that the type size and other elements of the visual presentation are such that all students can read it adequately, even from the back rows. Have available paper for the class to use to write their responses, and have some clear arrangement in mind for how they will do this: for example, must they number from 1 to 10?

It is a useful idea in any case to have an overhead transparency made for you to use during the discussion that will follow listening to the record.

Using a Question-type Directed-Listening Sheet Effectively

1. *Before listening:*

    a. If there is introductory or top-matter material, go over it. In the case of themes or rhythms related to the listening lesson (i.e., to be identified during listening), perform them for or with the class.

b. Preview all the questions on the listening sheet, constantly asking if everyone understands the intent of the questions. Be sure to emphasize those questions for which you want personal, subjective (affective) responses.

c. Make sure everyone has a writing implement for responding.

d. *Have the music pretaped* wherever possible. This crucial step avoids any "drop-the-needle" or "hunt-to-find-the-proper-band" annoyances and saves wear and tear on your records. It also prevents any straying of attention from the activity that is about to begin.

2. *During listening:*

a. Begin the recording playback.

(1) No talking is allowed during the playback of the record, and *this includes the teacher.*

(2) If the questions you have devised do not provide self-sufficient guidelines so that students know when each question ought to be answered, indicate when to answer the next question. You can:

(a) Use wood block, etc., as an aural signal for each new question to be answered.

(b) Put numbers on the chalkboard or overhead projector in accordance with the total number of questions and point to the appropriate question number at the appropriate moment.

(c) Simply say out loud the number of each new question as it arises—this is the maximum talking allowed during listening!

(3) If you have a question such as number 4 in Fig. 4:4 that requires raising hands, conducting with the music, or any other such physical response to be initiated *by students* at a certain time, *do not look up expectantly* at the class just before you assume you will see the response. This functions as a visual clue, and the class will respond to your expectant look rather than to the musical stimuli. These questions are of limited use in any case, since they permit students to "copy" from one another. But that is sometimes useful as a learning experience for some students.

b. At the conclusion of listening, allow only one minute (not more!) for students to finish any responses, particularly the kind that require directed attention throughout a composition. Allowing longer results in the use of *tonal memory;* but you are more interested at this stage in *direct aural perception.*

(1) Exception: imaginative responses calling for the creation of a story or any other such question calling for an extensive response.

3. *After listening:*

a. *Conduct an extensive discussion of students' responses. This is the major phase of this activity.* Without such a discussion, students do not have the opportunity to observe and note one another's responses, and therefore to compare them. They learn, by this means, that their responses are often very similar to those of their classmates and yet are personally unique. Similarly, the discussion allows you to use their overt responses to determine, by inference, what they perceived. Thus you must use this occasion to elicit the reasons for answers to subjective questions that concluded with "Why did you think so?"

(1) Take each question in order. Elicit responses from a variety of individuals, perhaps by taking a row at a time or by asking "How many people chose (a) for this question?" *Do not settle for one or two volunteered responses!* You must predictably get around to *each student* several times during the discussion. If students can predict you will not get to them if they don't volunteer, many will be less inclined to respond at all during subsequent lessons.

(2) Try as much as you can to *be genuinely accepting of all answers to subjective questions.* Doing otherwise will inhibit students in the future. Excessive enthusiasm on your part for one or two responses has the same effect.

(3) On so-called objective questions dealing with such cognitive information as instrument identification, try to *stimulate controversy,* especially when a large number of students have arrived at the same answer. Be forewarned: if a "good" or likely answer arises early during a discussion before some class members have given their answers, they will often agree with this "good" answer, even if they had another answer originally. You can respond, "Are you really sure that this was ABA form? Were all you guys listening

carefully when you compared the first and third sections? I don't know; maybe you should check this answer when we listen again. . . " All this said with a straight face, since in effect you are challenging them to stick by their answer and prove that they are sure of it. Middle school students like this kind of "gamesmanship." Sometimes it is not a game, because students climb on an inappropriate bandwagon.

(4) When appropriate, the teacher—as a member of the group—can also contribute points of view as long as such options do not predispose or prejudice the class to favor the teacher's answer. Be clear that your remarks are only your opinion, and are no more correct than those of the class (except where truly objective answers are involved—which should be relatively infrequent).

b. **Play the recording again.** This step must *always* be followed! It implements the sequence: the **whole** to the **parts** (the verbal analysis of the questions and their responses), back to the **whole.** If the lesson has been successful to this point, the students will be listening this second time with "newly informed ears" that result from the cognitive strengthening of the previous listening and discussion.

(1) They will be listening in terms of their previous answers, but also in terms of responses gleaned from classmates during the discussion session. Many will have their "feeling repertory" enhanced or expanded by sharing expressions of feeling-responses with the class in this way. They are not generally reluctant to switch their responses on the second hearing when they hear a response or rationale by peers that they feel is more appropriate.

(2) If you have been successfully clever in steering the discussion of objective questions, they will listen attentively in order to confirm or change their original answers to these questions or your "gamesmanship" (See [3] above).

(3) In any event, a recording is not sufficiently "studied" in one hearing. The second hearing, in addition to the above factors, allows a more "natural" listening attitude—one that permits or even encourages an enriched responsiveness.

c. Briefly review any changed answer students may have. You may also inquire whether they understood the composition any better the second time. This helps them realize that the second hearing is important, since they usually respond in the affirmative, assuming that they found the piece at all interesting.

d. Stay away from "like-dislike" kinds of dichotomies. Always deal with class preferences in terms of "interesting-not interesting," since it is possible to not "like" a piece but still to find it "interesting." Help the class learn that distinction.

e. During the discussion phases of question-type directed listening, note any of your questions that were confusing and other such inadequacies of the lesson you have prepared. Change these before you use the lesson again. It is also very important that you maintain an atmosphere of open inquiry with the class. Above all, do not treat such lessons as though they were tests. This will happen in any case if more than half of the questions are objective and therefore have correct or incorrect answers.

Through the "feeling response" questions in these lessons you are trying to encourage the use of the right hemisphere of the brain, the "feeling-response" center. But in most instances you are using verbal directions, requiring a verbal response in writing, followed by a verbal explanation or rationale for the answer. Because the left hemisphere is mainly responsible for verbal operations, do not be surprised if middle school students' answers do not meet your expectations or vocabulary. They do not have as rich an "emotional" vocabulary as do adults or even adolescents of high school age; or when they do, such language will not be understood by adults (e.g., "in-group" slang) or cannot be uttered in front of an adult.

For similar reasons, younger adolescents are not always able to "explain their feelings" adequately to themselves, or to you. None of us can, usually.

Feelings are seldom adequately accessible to speech. In these listening lessons the verbal response is utilized solely as an opportunity for an overt personal expression of some kind, with the hope that some degree of successful expression occurs at least between peers. The very occasion of a teacher encouraging, let alone allowing, such personal expression is notable in itself to most adolescents. This is why you must evoke such an openly expressive atmosphere. It is so very important that students' open attitude toward expressing feelings be a result of such lessons.

Verbalizations give a tangible guide to the teacher of what students perceived as they listened. In explaining their responses to question 1 in Fig. 4:4, students may say "I chose (a) because the music swept up, then crashed down to the drum" or "I chose (b) because there was a weaker-feeling section followed by the strong 'boom' by the drum." Either kind of answer informs you as to *what they heard* and that the answer was not just chosen at random, by luck, or simply to have an answer to satisfy the teacher.

Question 2 in Fig. 4:4 can be reused on many occasions. Students often choose (a) when they feel a continuous tension, as in a stretched string. Those choosing (b) often are responding to melodic contour, or to undulating waves of tension (i.e., more and less tension, in alteration). Students who choose (c) react to the line in terms of its dynamic graphic qualities and use it usually to respond to tension, although they may use it to refer to melodic contour if that was very jagged.

Color responses as elicited in question 3, Fig. 4:4 are often just as useful in determining what they heard. In this piece, bright red often evokes images of blood and violence, because they perceive the music as growing increasingly violent. Yellow is often associated with such ideas as the sun setting or a bright dramatic sunrise, an association they sometimes make with the suggestive movement of this composition. Light blue often is chosen as being a "nightmare" color, an overall haze in which nothing is clear because everything is always changing, always in motion. As you could see if you listened to this composition, all of these responses to some degree indicate aural perceptions easily validated by your own ear. You may not have thought about these responses, but when they are articulated by students, you can understand them because—upon reflection—you not only "see" what they are responding to in the music, you can understand their response to be richly accurate.

In making up subjective questions for this kind of directed listening you will often have in your own mind choices that *seem* more likely than others. This leads to the danger of thinking that one answer is preferable to others, that one answer shows a more adequate understanding or feeling-response than another. This is always a mistake and you must avoid having such preconceptions.

In another listening lesson when students were asked to associate a very powerful, dramatic, and tense composition with color reproductions clipped from magazines, one student chose a photograph of a chick hatching from an egg because the music seemed appropriate for the struggle she imagined to be involved for such a birth. Another chose a picture of a fisherman on a calm, serene lake in his boat. You might think this an unlikely choice unless you heard the youngster's full response: he had concocted an engaging and imaginative tale of a monsoon about to engulf the unsuspecting fisherman. This story fully conveyed the student's perception of the nature of the music; his response was simply more complex. The majority of the class chose the reproduction of a grotesque German expressionist painting (Charles Munch's *The Scream*). This latter choice might have seemed the most appropriate, but the verbal explanations of students' responses to it often were quite conventional and not particularly sensitive to specific qualities in the music.

On another occasion when a color response was at stake, a funeral-like dirge was the object of listening. One girl chose yellow. This seems a very unlikely choice, since this is not a color we ordinarily associate with sadness and grief. But her reasons were more than adequate: her canary had recently died! This very literal response more than adequately conveyed a clear impression of what she had heard in the music. So you are once again cautioned against holding preconceptions about the choices you present for subjective questions. Successful lessons will often result in a variety of very imaginative, deeply felt responses to many if not all the choices you provide.

Some teachers are skeptical of the "programmatic" nature of many of these responses. In answer, it can be said that responses of the kind recommended here should be distinguished from truly programmatic ones evoked by the teacher's insistence that the music involves a specific picture, story, or idea. The figurative answers of Action Listening are simply ones intended to make responses somewhat more tangible and relevant to the age group. They are not meant to suggest that such mental images or tales are *the programmatic intention of the composer*, and teachers should avoid such impressions. If anything, they are merely *metaphors, similes, or analogies* used as a *means* for the adolescent to express figuratively his or her right-hemisphere responses to music.

In ordinary daily life, metaphor, simile, or analogy are often the only kinds of expression we have for conveying emotions and feeling responses. For example, when explaining the intensity of a headache people are liable to say "It feels *as though* my head is in a vise" or "It feels *as though* my head is going to explode." Students' responses to music, similarly, may often be metaphors, analogies, or similes. In effect, they are saying that the music "feels like" such-and-such a story, such-and-such an image or color, such-and-such a physical fact. Figurative language of this kind is useful in "poetically" communicating feeling-states more vividly. If anything, this kind of listening lesson adds to or helps refine the repertory of such responses available to adolescents. It also gives them the opportunity for such expression—something often entirely missing in other classes in school.

The color response, in particular, is considered valid since many people are known to experience *synesthesia*. This is the tendency or capacity for a response to stimulation of one sensory mode by means of another sensory mode. In the case of hearing music, the response may be visual and given in terms of visual imagery, or especially color. It is not accidental that the descriptive term "blues" is given to that kind of music, or that a trumpet is often described as having a "brilliant" or "fiery" sound. For some people these are apt metaphors; for others, and their number is not insignificant in the general population, the response is actually a color response to sound.[16]

Program music, metaphor, and similar issues are discussed in greater depth later in this chapter.

Hints for Long-Term Use of Question-type Directed-Listening Lessons

1. Put the leftover questions not used for the first listening sheet on a second listening sheet. This will constitute a third and fourth hearing, in the near future, of the same composition that was heard twice in the first lesson.

a. These questions can be somewhat more refined, or predicated on the experience of the first two hearings that took place in the first lesson.

b. Form identification or responses requiring *tonal memory* (i.e., attention to the entire piece, and the ability to synthesize an overall response in a few seconds at the end of the piece) are often most appropriate during the second activity.

2. Keep the master for each listening lesson on file. Keep a file-card index of each listening sheet. Catalogue lessons as to forms, instruments, and other aspects for which each lesson is particularly suited. When, at some future date, you need a listening lesson that features certain musical aspects for cognitive strengthening, thumb through your card file until you find something appropriate. Run off the required number of copies. Have secretaries make you new masters as you exhaust old ones.

3. *No listening lesson of this type works perfectly the first time!* Invariably questions have to be rewritten for greater clarity, or to avoid certain problems. Sometimes questions have to be added (i.e., the present number did not hold students' attention sufficiently). Sometimes there were too many questions (i.e., they didn't have enough time to think, listen, and respond). Sometimes, in addition to questions you found the first time around, you conjure up new ones you feel should not be left out the next time.

Therefore, before you file and store your listening lessons, make all necessary revisions, and "retest" (your listening sheet, not the class) until you arrive at a workable version. File and store *this* version, and not preliminary versions.

4. Pretape all recordings. This is not as much a matter of preserving the records as it is of the smoothness of the lesson; you don't have to play find-the-band-and-drop-the-needle for each hearing. For each tape (and on your file cards) note the footage numbers for the beginning and end of each selection, and for specific points within the selection that you might want to isolate on occasion (e.g., the "development section" of a sonata, the "stretto" of a fugue). A cassette tape deck (one of decent quality—not the small, portable kind) can be more than adequate for listening lessons such as this and those to follow, *if it can be played through quality speakers*. Therefore, if it has the capacity for patching into a speaker system, use cassette recordings. They are by far the easiest to use, and the most convenient to store and locate.

5. Some directed-listening lessons are appropriate for independent work in media centers, media corners, or at home (where media are available). In these instances, consider the following items.

a. Pretape the selection, usually on cassette. Because of the equipment on which these tapes are likely to be played, responses for which high fidelity or stereo are required (i.e., subtle instrumental timbre distinctions) are best avoided.

b. Provide, in a separate source, a *discussion* of answers against which the student can compare his or her responses.

(1) Alternatively, if most or all of the class will be doing this as an assignment "outside" of class, answers need not be provided. A class discussion, as usual, can be conducted. Immediate reinforcement in this case is not terribly strong, so it is customary to hear the piece once in class before such a discussion. In this instance the second hearing in class *may* be eliminated, but if time permits it is still most desirable.

(2) For subjective questions have the students prepare in writing explanations of their responses, just as they might do orally in class.

c. Provide detailed instructions. Where relevant, for example, provide directions for turning on and using the tape recorder.

THE TIMBRE-CHECKLIST FORM

This is a listening-lesson format used mainly in practicing the identification of instrumental timbres by name (see Fig. 4:5). Down the left side of the form you will note that the common instruments of the orchestra are listed according to families. Notice, especially, that *the French horn is shown adjacent to both the wind and brass groups*, visually identifying it as capable of functioning with either or both. Also notice that some blank spaces are provided for other instruments to be added in the percussion group, and at the bottom of the form.

Fig. 4:5

FORM	Verses or Sections of the Composition					
	I heard:					
	violin					
	viola					
	'cello					
	bass					
	flute					
	clarinet					
	oboe					
	bassoon					
	saxophone					
	french horn					
	trumpet					
	trombone					
	tuba					
	tympani					
	snare drum					
	bass drum					
	bongo					
	tom-tom					
	cymbal					
	gong					
	triangle					
	chimes					
	glockenspiel					
	xylophone					
	marimba					
	piano					
	organ					
	soprano					
	alto					
	tenor					
	bass					
	electronic					

(Vertical labels at left: strings, winds, brass, percussion, voice)

Turn paper over when the composition is finished and *write your ideas* on how the instruments (timbres) in this composition contributed to the FORM (unity and variety) and EXPRESSION (your feelings) of the composition.

If you reproduce this form exactly as it appears here, you will find it very useful and will not have to make any special effort to produce a new format for each lesson of this kind. You will, of course, still have to prepare the lesson by selecting a composition having appropriate instrumental timbres as attensive qualities. But the form is reusable any time you have such a recording or purpose in mind. It can be used over and over by simply replenishing the supply you have on hand.

This is a convenience, but it is also an unfortunate inducement to overuse this particular kind of lesson. There are many stumbling blocks to be wary of with listening lessons based on instrument recognition. While it is useful to conduct such lessons, they do not have the value that so many teachers seem to find. For one thing, instrumental timbres are imperfectly reproduced on all but the most expensive and sophisticated sound systems. This kind of lesson is all but useless if the quality of your recording (tape or record) and your sound system is not appropriate.

Secondly, knowing the *name* of an instrument is not that useful in itself. It is useful that students know that the oboe exists, and have some experience in hearing and identifying it. This way they are made *aware* of its existence and thereby are more likely to hear its presence. But its presence is often not as important as the music it is playing.

For this reason, listening lessons dealing with instrumental timbres are most fruitful when used mainly to emphasize timbre, usually in regard to sound compositions. It is the question of timbre as a musical element that is at stake, not an exercise in instrument identification. For that reason, any lesson dealing with timbre, but especially listening lessons, ought to discuss as its major or final consideration *how the timbres used contribute to the expressive or formal aspects of the composition.*

Were certain formal sections characterized by one or more families of instruments? Was the theme of a rondo (ABACADA) always played by the same instrument, or the same family? How did the instrumentation (orchestration) used contribute to the expressive results? What would have happened if the composer had chosen winds instead of brasses for the climactic section of this composition? How might the effect have been different? Do you think it was appropriate this way?

The form shown in Fig. 4:5 is rather simply used. The large blank boxes at the top are to be filled in by students at your direction. Usually letters identifying each section of the form (e.g., ABACA) of the composition to be heard will be placed there. Verse numbers for popular music or music in strophic form can also be placed there. As the students listen, you usually identify for them which section (vertical column) they should be using at a given moment. That is, depending on which section of the composition or which verse is playing, the students use that vertical column by placing a check mark or an "x" on the line across from each instrument they hear in that section, and each *separate time* it is heard.

The directions at the bottom of the page are quite self-explanatory. That they are at the bottom does not mean that they are an afterthought. As indicated just earlier, this amounts to the major focus of the lesson. You often will have to have two hearings for students to complete their checklists. Therefore choose a piece of appropriate length so these two hearings can be supplemented by one more following the discussion. All of this should take place during one class.

211

A listening format such as this has several advantages over the kind of listening lesson that specifies only "Make a list of all the instruments you heard." First of all, with the Fig. 4:5 lesson you are able to tell whether students heard the instruments at the proper places in time. Otherwise when they say that they heard a bassoon, you will not know when they *thought* they heard it, and therefore whether their response is accurate. Secondly, with the vague assignment to make "a list," virtually any list of instruments will give students a good chance of hitting a few correctly. With Fig. 4:5, however, they must locate their identification at a specific time, and must be able to discuss the overall formal or expressive effect of the instruments used.

For a composition having more than five sections or verses, simply have students divide each column into two narrower columns by drawing a vertical line down through the center of each (or as many as are needed). This form is relatively simple for you to produce and for students to use. You are reminded, though, that the follow-up discussion is the *goal* of the activity. Using the form is only the *means:* (a) of having students record their perceptions; (b) of having you check the accuracy of these perceptions; and (c) of making them available for reference in the discussion that follows. Thus, as usual, your skill in conducting the discussion is most crucial. This skill depends on your understanding of the music in question, and the interests and characteristics of your students. Always keep these three things in mind. Beginning teachers are advised to prepare pivotal questions in advance!

THE MUSICAL-ELEMENTS-CHECKLIST FORM

As you can see in Fig. 4:6, this is the logical extension of exactly the same principle employed in the timbre-checklist form. Actually, timbre is just as important as the other elements listed on this form. But it is so extensive an area in itself that it is worthy of singular emphasis if only for the practical value of dealing with its many variables at one time.

You need not use all categories on this sheet at once. It is entirely possible to listen only for texture, or for melody, etc. *Do not use any category until students are already familiar with the terminology involved through prior experiences with sound compositions, songwriting, and other listening lessons.* Do not use this form by first explaining the meaning of the terms, then listening to a recording and having students use their notes on this information. Students must already have a well-developed concept of whichever terms or group of terms will be used.

The music selected for use with this form should feature the attensive qualities that appear on the form. If these terms, these particular qualities, do not suit your needs, feel free to use the form with whatever labels you wish. Keep them simple, though: usually one or two words. Ideally, you should aim at the possibility that allows students to consider all five elements at one time. This is usually reasonable only in high school or with advanced younger students. Certainly by that time, but even at earlier stages, it is usually necessary to play the recording *at least twice* for students to make their judgments. For very inexperienced students even more time is recommended. Therefore, the selection should be quite short. This way you can play it at least once more after the discussion time and have all this activity take place within one class period.

As with the previous activity, the directions at the bottom apply to the follow-up discussion which is the *real focus* of the lesson. Every attempt should be made to prepare and conduct this phase successfully.

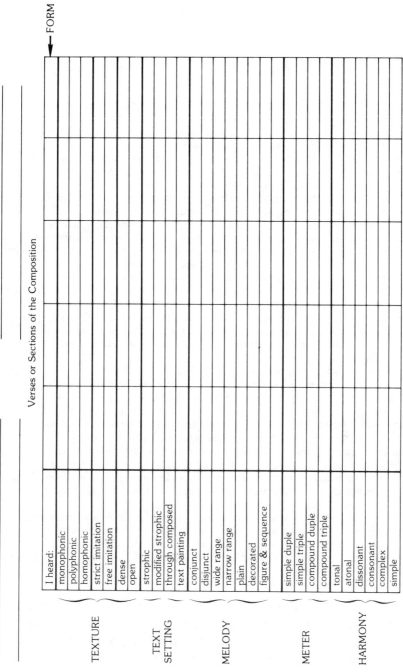

Fig. 4:6

THE OPEN MUSICAL ELEMENT FORM—
RHYTHM/METER FORM

This form (see Figs. 4:7A-D) is very similar to the preceding checklist. Its differences:

1. Here the letters indicating the form or the numbers for verses are indicated along the left-hand and righthand sides, for each horizontal column (see Fig. 4:7B, which illustrates a lesson featuring a hypothetical theme-and-variations form).

2. Across the top are indicated the musical elements for which the class would listen, but no checklist of individual factors is provided. The student is expected to recall these, or to use only those that are featured in this composition (see Fig. 4:7B).

3. You are not restricted to the set of elements suggested in Fig. 4:7A, although you should notice that mode, mood, timbre, and text considerations are provided here. Thus students can indicate whether a section is in the major or minor mode, their feeling-response to the mood of the section, the instruments featured, and—if text is used—what the relationship is between music and text (e.g., is the same music used for places where the text has different sentiments expressed? Does the music fit the sentiments of the text as the text changes?).

4. If you look at the form upside-down (see Fig. 4:7C) it serves an entirely different purpose. You still list the sections or verses along the left and right margins, but across the top you fill in a variety of rhythms (with their given meters: e.g., ♩ ♩ ♫ ♩ ;♩ ♩ ♪♫) or meters. Obviously, the meters or meters and rhythms you provide should be derived from the composition chosen. Even if you provide some meters or rhythms that are not in the composition (in hope that students will not identify them as having been heard) they should be reasonably close to what is featured in the composition.

As the students listen, they mark the places where they hear a given rhythm or rhythm and meter. Thus you would do well to choose a piece in which the sections or verses have rhythmic variety. A final product might look like Fig. 4:7D. The piece in question here would have had the rhythms/meters shown in columns 1, 4, 5, 6 for its A section, the rhythmic figure shown in columns 2 and 7 for its B section, and the one shown in column 3 for its C section.

You need not, however, use all the vertical columns. Use only as many as you need for the composition in question and in order to provide a realistic challenge for your class.

6. Although neither of the two-forms-in-one specifies further directions to determine how the elements contributed to the formal and expressive factors of the composition, this follow-up must be made just as in the earlier instances. It is eliminated here simply in order for the form to be used with either side up.

7. The two-way function of this form makes it especially flexible and efficient for your purposes. This form will work best with students of any age who have had a year or more of experience with aural-perception practice along these lines, and who have demonstrated some significant success in aural perception. Younger students will generally perceive less and thus will provide fewer responses.

Note that the lessons shown in Figs. 4:7A-D, are mainly cognitive. That is, most of the responses will be objective and therefore correct or incorrect. This means that you should use these lessons sparingly, and only at times when you have good reason to expect that students will experience minimal difficulty. Even then, be careful to minimize a test-like atmosphere or any potential feelings of dissatisfaction arising from a not too successful record of responses made by individual students.

Fig. 4:7A

MELODY	HARMONY	MODE	MOOD	TIMBRE	TEXTURE	TEXT

Rhythms/Meters

Fig. 4:7B

	MELODY	HARMONY	MODE	MOOD	TIMBRE	TEXTURE	TEXT		Rhythms/Meters
Theme	aba smooth	consonant – supportive but not a major interest	major	romantic	piano	homophonic	N/A		
Var. 1	aba	counterpoint	major	flowing	"	polyphony	"		
Var. 2	ababa	more dissonant	minor	somber	"	trick homophony			
Var. 3	aba but jumpy	simple – few chord changes	major	light happy dance-like	"	homophonic			

Fig. 4:7C

Rhythms/Meters

Section	$\frac{3}{4}$	$\frac{3}{4}$	$\frac{6}{8}$	$\frac{3}{4}$	$\frac{3}{4}$	$\frac{3}{4}$	$\frac{3}{4}$	
A								A
B								B
A								A
C								C
B								B
A								A
	TEXT	TEXTURE	TIMBRE	MOOD	MODE	HARMONY	MELODY	

Fig. 4:7D

Rhythms/Meters

Section	MELODY	HARMONY	MODE	MOOD	TIMBRE	TEXTURE	TEXT
A	✓	✓	✓	✓		✓	✓
B	✓					✓	
A		✓	✓	✓			✓
C					✓		
B	✓					✓	
A		✓	✓	✓			✓

THE FEELINGS/INSTRUMENTS FORM

This is another dual-purpose form (Figs. 4:8A–D). Whichever direction is used, the required response involves drawing lines according to the categories suggested (and feel free to change these to suit your purposes). When the form is used for instruments (Fig. 4:8A), students draw a line in the appropriate prelabeled vertical column (again according to sections of the form, or verses) as they hear a family of instruments or an instrument from a family. One space is provided for other instruments. Electronic synthesizers, etc., may be entered here if used in the piece.

The result is a line-diagram of instrumental usage (Fig. 4:8B).

The intent of this format is not so much one of simply identifying the instruments heard. It is most useful in identifying those that are judged to be of *major importance* to the form or expression. Thus, the response in Fig. 4:8B indicates that the strings and percussion were both important throughout section A, while the winds were important at the beginning only, and the brasses at the end only. In section B the percussion continues in importance, while—in order—the woodwinds, brasses, and strings are featured in importance; the brasses assume importance again at the end of the section. Section A repeated is similar to its first occurrence (as would be expected), except for the woodwinds, which are now important throughout.

This form and this technique allow students to make value judgments about what they perceive. In comparison to the timbre-checklist form (Fig. 4:5), it is not now simply a question of which instruments are heard (although that may arise if students think a section is important even when a particular family does not play at all in that part or at all in the piece). More important is the issue of which instruments are considered to have aural importance in the formal or expressive sense. The value judgments shown in Fig. 4:8B are related mainly to formal concerns; but the follow-up discussion can and should emphasize the impact of the instruments used for the expressive effectiveness of the composition.

Figure 4:8C shows a feeling-intensity graph. Provide the form or verse indicators across the top. While listening the students draw a *continuous line* that records changes in their feeling-tone intensity. As you can see in Fig. 4:8D, it is not necessary to stick strictly to the categories' levels; the in-between spaces can be used and a line can be shown to be midway between relaxed and sleepy, or closer to one or the other. The follow-up ought to bring out a large variety of students' responses with a discussion of specific musical elements they can attribute as the sources of their feelings: "Why do you think the music began relaxed and sleepily for you?" "What happened in the music that 'turned you on' toward the end of the second verse?" Devise questions similar to these to reveal *what students heard in the music.*

This is important and should never be overlooked. Otherwise, you run the risk of the "Take it or leave it," "I only know what I like, not why I like it" kind of response some youngsters are all too ready to advance. This is how they already listen to popular music, and our task is to improve their perception and also, hopefully, their capacity for a significant musical response. Perception will not improve, and thus response capacity will stagnate, if this kind of questioning approach is not used.

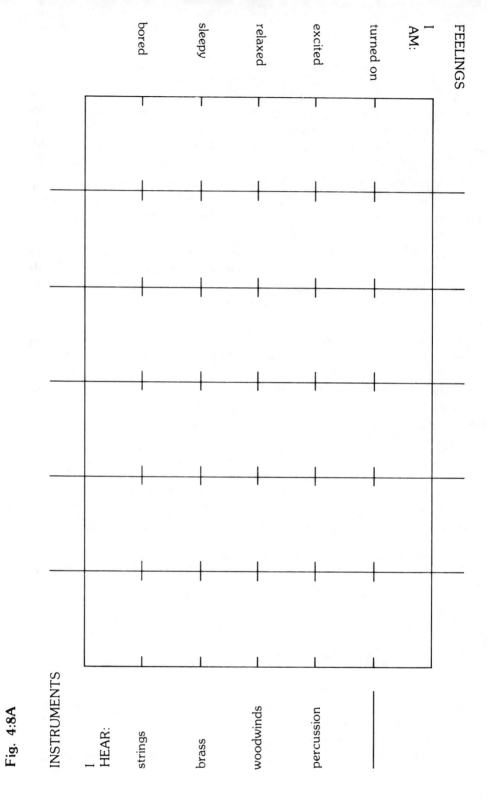

Fig. 4:8A

Fig. 4:8B

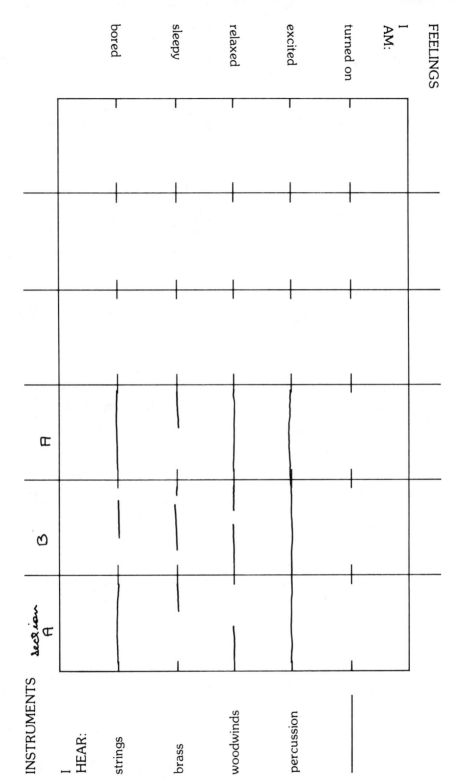

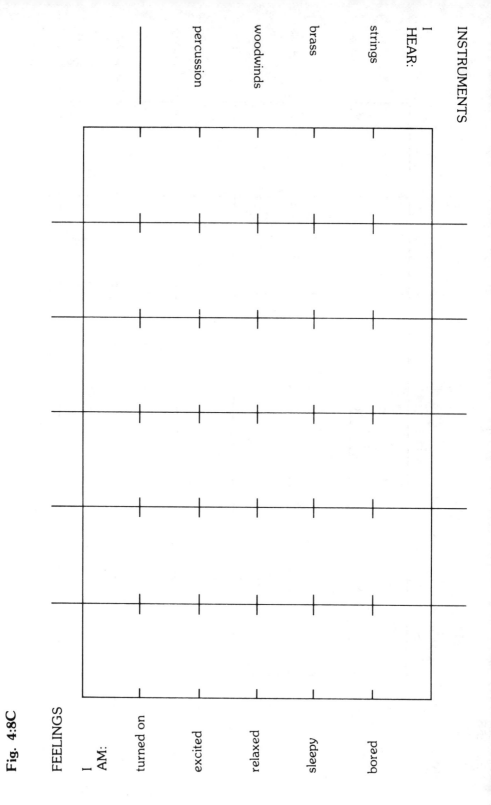

Fig. 4:8C

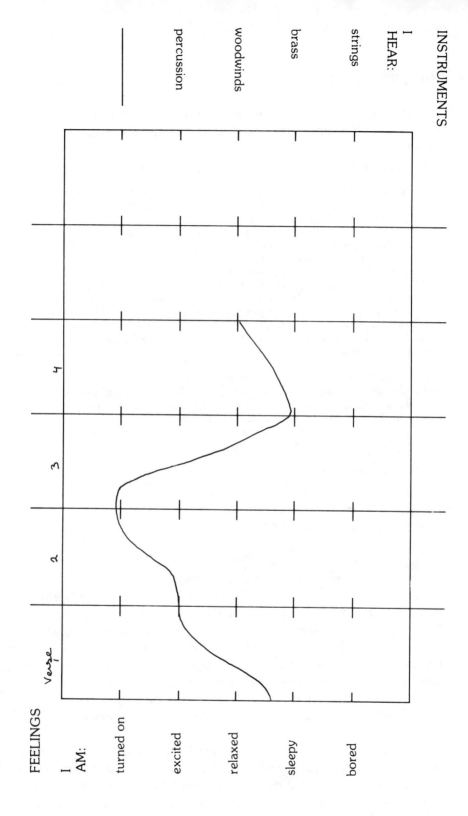

Fig. 4:8D

THE LINE-INTERPRETATION FORM

Here is another format that facilitates emphasis on the feeling-response (Figs. 4:9A-B). It can also be used to represent graphically value judgments of a cognitive nature.

1. Along the thin left-edge column, indicate verses or sections of the composition to be heard.

2. Across the top, indicate the factors to be listened for and diagrammed. These could be chosen from among, but not necessarily limited to, these possibilities:

    a. Highness or lowness of pitches, of melodic contour.
    b. Loudness or softness as a relative factor within the piece.
    c. Tension or relaxation levels.
    d. Thinness or thickness of texture.
    e. Mood evoked (e.g., happiness or sadness).

3. The form can *rate only one pair of these factors at a time*, so choose a composition that features considerable variety in whichever factor you choose for emphasis.

4. The meaning of the arrows should be discussed briefly. To use the example shown in Fig. 4:9B, where the level of tension is being rated, a line drawn *high in the box* would represent the student's feeling of *high tension*. A low line would represent *relaxation*. And the passage of the line between the two extremes would represent the student's impression of changing levels of tension.

In rating volume, the top of the box would be used for loud passages, the bottom for soft. For pitches or melodic contour, high in the box would indicate higher pitches, and the opposite for low pitches. The texture, similarly, could use the upper limits to designate a thick texture (more), the lower limits to indicate thinness of texture (less).

5. The students draw the line as they listen. Usually, therefore, you *have the class listen once without drawing* in order to familiarize them with the sections, and especially the length of each section. The second time they draw their lines *as they listen*. After a discussion of the variety of feeling-levels experienced, the third listening provides an opportunity for "pure" listening.

THE SOUND-BLOCKS FORM

This form (see Fig. 4:10) is rather easy to use. The sections or verses of the composition to be heard are indicated along the lefthand side. As they listen, students jot down as best they can what they hear (instruments, themes, texture, etc.—whatever they find most attensive) and how they feel about it. In other words, after noting what strikes them most, they indicate what feelings are engendered by what they heard. It is possible to use the "early, middle, and late" designations along the right side to refer to early, middle, and late parts of the section or verse. Therefore *a preliminary hearing is recommended so that the class can simply listen.* They can respond on the second listening. Once again, after discussion, a third ("pure") listening experience should be provided.

It is quite important that this listening technique be used in some form, if not in the exact format shown in Fig. 4:10. It is an important goal of any listening program *to have the mind think about what it hears.* Similarly, it is important to encourage students' minds to have *feelings* about what they hear, or *to*

Fig. 4:9A

Line Interpretation: Free or Given

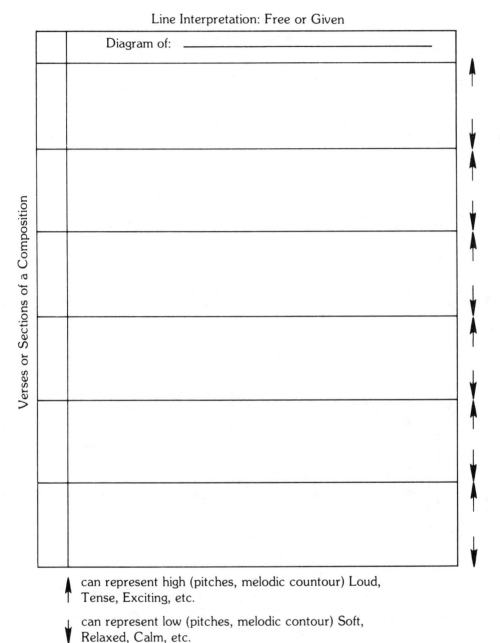

Diagram of: _____

(vertical axis label:) Verses or Sections of a Composition

↑ can represent high (pitches, melodic countour) Loud,
  Tense, Exciting, etc.

↓ can represent low (pitches, melodic contour) Soft,
  Relaxed, Calm, etc.

(N.B.: Sometimes divide class into groups where each group "designs" a specific factor of the composition. Compare responses to "discover" whether any factors seem related; e.g., are the designs for loud, tense and exciting similar between groups.)

Fig. 4:9B

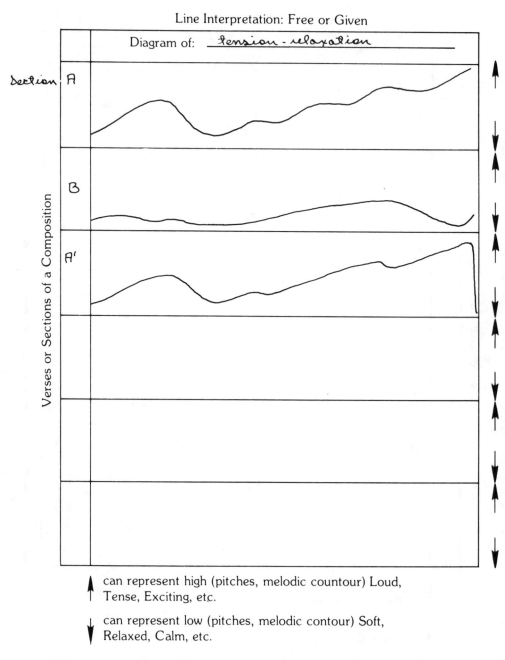

Line Interpretation: Free or Given

Diagram of: _tension - relaxation_

Section | A

B

A′

Verses or Sections of a Composition

↑ can represent high (pitches, melodic countour) Loud,
Tense, Exciting, etc.

↓ can represent low (pitches, melodic contour) Soft,
Relaxed, Calm, etc.

(N.B.: Sometimes divide class into groups where each group "designs" a specific factor of the composition. Compare responses to "discover" whether any factors seem related; e.g., are the designs for loud, tense and exciting similar between groups.)

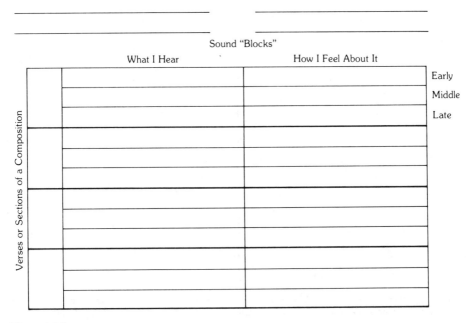

Fig. 4:10

think about the feelings they experience. Increased aural perception, therefore, should be complemented with increasing efforts on the teacher's part to enable students to put their new perceptual powers to work in creating their own enriched feeling-responses.

THE COMPARISON-RATINGS GRAPH

This graph (Fig. 4:11) is similar to the feeling-intensity graph (Fig. 4:8C) in that it tangibly represents students' value judgments (cognitive) or feeling-responses (affective). In Fig. 4:11 there are five rating scales, each of which is used for separate sections or verses of a composition; you can add more if needed. At the top of each scale, the factor to be rated is filled in. Factors could include:

1. *The amount of pleasure experienced.* How much interest did the student have in a section or verse?
2. *The intensity of a specific emotional state.* For example, in a scherzo movement in ABA form, which sections were rated as having the most musical humor? Specify the emotional state and choose music with the corresponding attensive qualities.
3. *The successful wedding of words and music.* In which verses are the textual sentiments and musical expression the closest?
4. *Use of a specified compositional technique.* Which section uses more imitative counterpoint (vs. nonimitative or free counterpoint) or conjunct melody (vs. disjunct melody)?

227

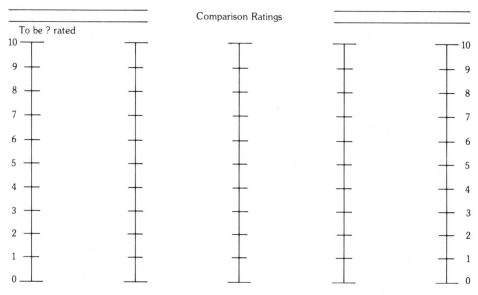

Comparison Ratings

To be ? rated

Turn the page over and explain your ideas for your rating decisions. Give your major reasons for each of your rating decisions. Can you explain or describe how some people might have a widely different rating?

Fig. 4:11

Once the single factor to be rated in *all* sections or verses is discussed and entered on the line next to number 10 on the form, identify the sections or verses by labeling each under each rating column. Then, as students listen, they each rate the factor under consideration by placing a check or "x" somewhere on the rating scale: "0" represents no presence of the factor; "10" represents a large amount or the continuous presence of the factor.

The directions at the bottom of the form are once again very important. Besides simply insuring that students have some musical perceptions in mind standing behind their judgments or feelings, the discussion for this phase of the lesson will once again serve to illustrate to students the wide variety of responses possible; each person may have perceptions that are valid for him. Sometimes ask students *to relate their perceptions to the way in which someone else might respond*. This encourages them to manipulate their perceptions creatively in search of nonhabitual responses; it opens the possibility for continuous growth in their responses, and minimizes a response—for example, always associating minor modes with sadness—that is set or fixed.

This form can also be used to directly compare more than one composition or arrangement: e.g., a Bach fugue played on the piano, on a harpsichord, on an electronic synthesizer, or by an orchestra; or the first verse of the same composition as arranged and performed by different popular performing groups. Use one rating scale for each selection. Identify the variable to be rated: for the Bach fugue it might be which timbre is preferred; for the popular song arrangements it might be which group does greatest justice to the meaning of the words. Here, too, the follow-up assignment and discussion predicated in the directions at the bottom is very important.

THE COLOR-RESPONSE FORM

This form (see Figs. 4:12A–B) is usually suited to feeling-responses associated metaphorically with color responses. In the center of the form there is a horizontal row of boxes labeled "music." Here you indicate the sections of the composition or the number of verses it contains. As the students listen, they respond by drawing a line to the appropriate box from the color they "hear" (if they have synesthetic tendencies) or the color that reflects their perception of the "mood" of the music for that section. Their line should pass through the "bright-dark" continuum on either side of the sections/verses indication. If no color seems suitable, you should suggest their use of white (all colors; neutral in a positive sense) or black (absence of color; neutral in a negative sense). Fig. 4:12B illustrates what a final response might resemble.

Fig. 4:12A

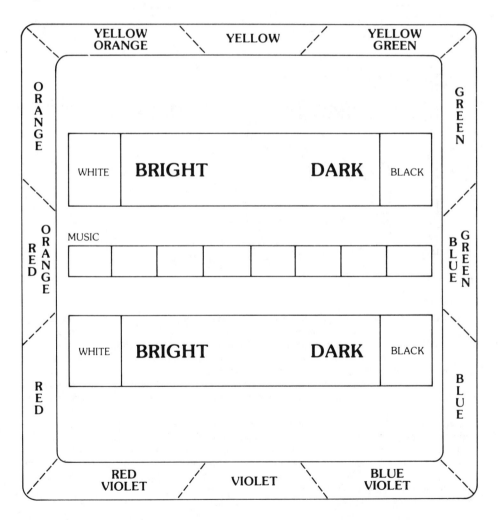

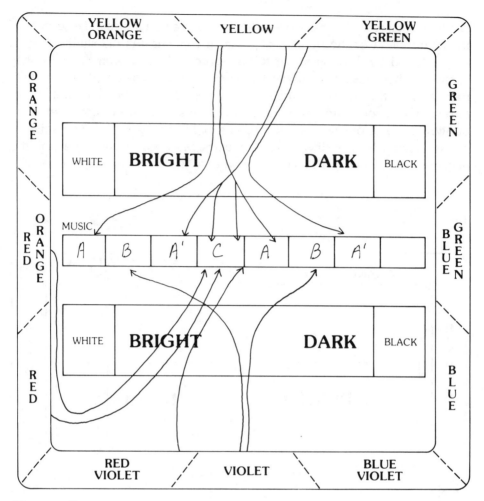

Fig. 4:12B

Notice that it is possible to choose more than one color if the student perceives changes within a lengthy section or verse. The example illustrated is a sonata rondo form (ABA'CABA') in which the C section would amount to a development section: a section that "works out" material from the previous sections to explore its expressive musical potential. Thus one might expect some variety of mood response in such an active or dynamic section. Note, too, that lines from the colors in the center on the left and right sides also should pass through the bright-dark continuum, even though the route is circuitous. It is inevitable that lines will cross.

If you consider this rectangle to be a squared-off circle, other interesting observations can be made and brought to students' attention: namely, that directly acrosss from each color is its complement, its opposite or contrasting hue according to color theory. The color chosen to represent changing musical moods may represent, in the same way, *subtle changes* (as between the color recorded in Fig. 4:12B for the two A' sections) or *striking contrasts* (as between any of the A sections and the B sections).

Much more can be made of this is an early experience with this response form and appropriate music is used in conjunction with the investigation of a reproduction of an "op art" painting based on color contrasts (see Fig. 4:13). Any standard art history text should contain a good example. In such paintings, the optical effects (visual vibration, after-images, etc.) are created by using complementary (contrasting) colors which play all sorts of tricks with visual perception. Such a visual experience will greatly assist subsequent use of this form in musical circumstances.

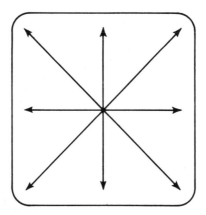

Fig. 4:13

Contrasting Colors

As with all of the formats suggested for listening thus far, this one too should be followed by a discussion that considers such factors as:

1. The varying color selections of students.
2. The musical perceptions that stand behind their color judgments.
3. Subtle differences in their choices (e.g., when some students choose yellow orange and others yellow green, but most choose yellow "something").
4. Significant differences in their choices (e.g., Why do some choose red orange and others blue green, which are visual opposites? What are these students relating to in the music?).

You are reminded to avoid the impression that some choices are good or correct, whereas others are poor or wrong. The important thing is for you to explore students' reactions publicly and note what perceptions stand behind their responses. In this way the students profit by sharing their responses and rationales.

THE ADJECTIVE-CIRCLE FORM

This form (see Fig. 4:14) is intended mainly for feeling responses. It is based on an original by psychologist Kate Hevner that uses a more extensive vocabulary, and was originally used to statistically quantify subjects' responses to music in order to discover certain patterns of response to a given piece. It has, therefore, a significant history as a device for externalizing musical responses in a way that permits observation.

231

A
serious
sacred

H
majestic
broad
military

B
sad
gloomy
dark

G
dramatic
exciting
restless

YOU

C
dreamy
tender
sentimental

F
happy
bright
cheerful

D
quiet
soothing
calm

E
playful
light
humorous

COMMENTS:

Fig. 4:14

In the school setting, the words chosen should be well within the vocabulary of the class or age group. Language Arts and English teachers can assist you in preparing an initial version, but after use you will discover which words do not mean much to students and will be able to add words that arise from the group. This is why the blank lines should be provided.

The form is arranged in a kind of circle. As with the previous color responses, each group of adjectives is directly across from its opposite group in terms of feeling-tone: A vs. E; H vs. D; G vs. C; F vs. B. But, as with the colors, each group is also adjacent to feeling-tone adjectives having a more subtle distinction. Thus A-H represents a continuum, a full circle of moods from deadly serious through dreamy to playful and happy and dramatic and majestic, back to serious once again.

The form permits great flexibility in its use. You may direct students to choose one or two words which characterize their feelings about an entire piece, in which case the piece should probably be relatively short and unvarying in mood. Or you could use the five columns of blank spaces at the bottom to represent the sections or verses of the composition (label them a, b, c, etc., or 1, 2, 3, etc., on the little line above each column). Students can then be directed to choose a specified number of words or can be given a free choice of number; they write the words they choose on the spaces for the sections to which the choices are related. Music for such a use of the form should have sections or verses with distinct moods, or should have contrasting moods within sections or verses.

In the follow-up use of this form, it is often useful to have a show of hands: "How many people chose words from group A for the first verse?" From among those who raise their hands, ask for an identification of which specific adjectives they chose, and any reasons they have in mind for their choice. Go around the adjective circle in this manner. As you do, note the frequency of responses for each adjective group. Keep a tally. Discuss the final result with the class.

Especially fruitful are those occasions when a class-wide pattern of some kind emerges— when, for example, virtually everyone chooses adjectives from two or three adjacent groups for a given section. This, among other things, illustrates that responses can be similar (i.e., coming from adjacent groups) yet unique (i.e., a variety of adjectives is chosen from these adjacent groups according to each person's perception of the music and "interpretation" of what the adjective chosen "means" for him).

If no pattern emerges, if there are significant numbers of adjectives chosen from contrasting groups, the reasons for this phenomenon ought to be explored by the class. Certain "vague" kinds of music will have this result. Such music will not have clear "attensive qualities," at least for novices. Thus much impressionistic music will have this result since its rhythms, melodies, forms, harmonies, timbres, and other elements are handled in very subtle ways. To the experienced listener it is often precisely this subtlety that is attensive. For this reason, this kind of music often is not suitable at the early stages of a listening program and should always be included judiciously.

THE MELODIC-PERCEPTION FORM

Finally, the melodic-perception format (Fig. 4:15) is an entirely different kind of listening format. It is not a form in the sense that the early examples have been. *Its purpose is to place aural emphasis on melodic contour, pitch relationships, and intervals.* It is an exercise, or practice, in perceptual acuity. It will have major impact on your students' ability to perceive certain melodic qualities aurally, and thus to improve their own melodies done during songwriting. It also will have great relevance for your singing and music-reading program, but as you shall see, *no direct attempt to relate it to musical notation should be made.*

It works like this. Begin with the visual setup shown in section 1, Fig. 4:15.

1		1	2	3	4	5	6	7	8	9	0	1	2	3	4	5
		•	•	•	•	•	•	•	•	•	•	•	•	•	•	•
		•	•	•	•	•	•	•	•	•	•	•	•	•	•	•
		•	•	•	•	•	•	•	•	•	•	•	•	•	•	•

Fig. 4:15

Melodic "Dictation" for the Beginner: An Exercise in Applied Perception

The horizontal numbers represent each individual pitch in the sequence you will play at the piano. The dots represent *one diatonic scale degree*. Begin these exercises using only three scale degrees: the first, second, and third. Thus you might play this example at the piano:

C Major

Students should respond in this manner (Fig. 4:16):

Fig. 4:16

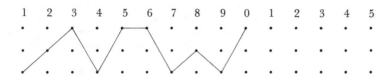

Play the example two or three times. Class responses can be checked in several ways. It is most helpful if you have an overhead transparency prepared with the numbers and dots (in this case, three rows of dots). Students volunteer who think that they have it correct (or choose a student by moving progressively in order up and down rows) and come up to the projector and quickly copy their result for total class consideration. The result is then discussed and any errors noted by class members, until a correct version is reached.

If an overhead projector is not available, it is possible to have several students quickly record their responses on the chalkboard. It is also possible to verbalize the results. The example given could be verbalized in this manner:

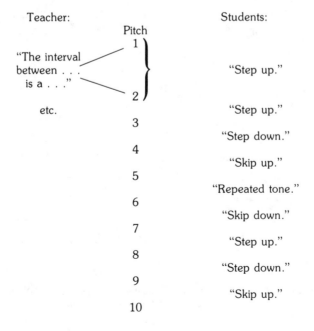

235

The same system of listing the pitch numbers vertically can be used for quickly noting students' results on the chalkboard rather than copying rows of dots, etc.

It is important that a full inventory of students' responses is taken and noted by you. Therefore, more than occasionally, collect their papers and note (do not grade!) the success of their efforts. Do this after and in addition to the discussion. If a student has a specific difficulty, such as with identifying a skip, plan some individual assistance. Where possible, give individual practice using cassettes in activity centers, media corners, etc.

As illustrated in Fig. 4:16, when students can demonstrate their ability to handle three pitches *competently* and *consistently* you may add a fourth row of dots, thus adding the fourth scale degree to the possibilities. Here, verbalizations for "leaps" should indicate "Leap up two" (i.e., from the first to the fourth scale degree—*two* pitches are leaped over) or "Leap down two" (i.e., from the fourth scale degree to the first—again leaping over two pitches). Eventually, five rows of dots can be added, then six, and so on, up to a total of eight. This possibility is well within the capacities of students who have been doing this often for a year or two in a continuous, though not incessant, program. Seventh graders are usually excellent at this if started at it in fifth grade.

With older or more advanced groups (mainly advanced middle schoolers and most high school students) the possibility illustrated in section 4, Fig. 4:15, can be used. Here the movement from *a dot or dash* to the next highest or lowest *dot or dash* represents a *whole step*; from *a dot* to the next higher or lower *dash* (or vice versa) represents a *half step*. Use only the total number of dots and dashes shown in Fig. 4:17. Diatonic examples (no "accidentals") that simply feature the steps and half steps of the *lower or upper tetrachord*[17] of a major scale, or melodic fragments up to the range of a perfect fifth are all that should be used.

The examples shown would be indicated as in Fig. 4:17:

Fig. 4:17

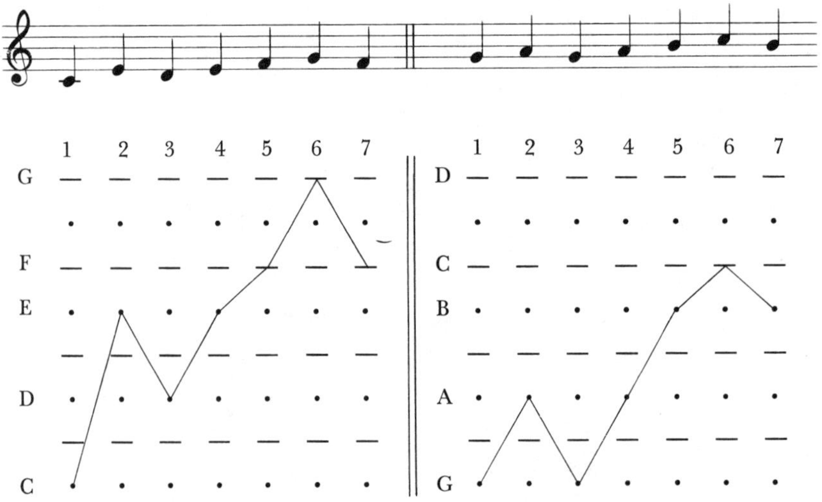

Later, you might expand to using more chromatic examples (with accidentals) or examples that mix pitches from major and minor together in the same example.

236

WARNING: **Do not expand** this whole-step, half-step exercise with more rows of dots or dashes. It won't work! With any of these melodic-perception exercises, **do not attempt to transfer the dots or the dots and dashes directly to, or compare them with, musical notation.** The purpose of this listening activity is to sharpen aural skills for listening and not for musical performance (music reading). **Any attempt at applying this activity to standard notation will result in confusion** between two entirely different visual (notational) systems.

In the systems of dots, whole-step and half-step relationships are shown as visually equal, i.e., having the same amount of visual space. The dots and dashes in the advanced version are subject to being confused as lines (the dashes) and spaces (i.e., where the dots are in between the lines). Neither of these factors will transfer to music reading. In fact, it is more difficult for people (students or teacher) who already read music to use this form than to simply use a staff. Nonetheless, for beginners it discriminates between half- and whole-steps in a way a five-line staff does not.

However, melodic aural skills—the increasing ability to aurally perceive steps, skips, leaps, melodic direction, repeated tones, etc.—provide the perceptual (aural) readiness, the "inner ear" training, that should greatly improve students' music-reading skills whether using voice or instruments. Just keep the two skills—aural perception using dots and dashes, and music reading—entirely separate in your own mind, and your students will improve rapidly on those occasions (such as in chorus) when music reading is the sole occupation.

SUMMARY OF COMMON PRINCIPLES FOR DIRECTED LISTENING

1. Preview each form or format for the students' benefit each time you do a listening lesson. This insures that they understand what is required.

2. For all but the question-type form (Fig. 4:4) you usually supply the form of the composition by using letters or the verses by numbering. Students copy this information quickly in the places provided on the form.

3. Some forms require two hearings (one for orientation, one to actively respond) before the discussion.

4. Every activity *must be* followed with a comprehensive discussion. Observe the perceptions reflected in the students' responses. Be sure to solicit responses from many, most, or all students regularly.

5. Each discussion should be followed by one more hearing, thus permitting a "pure" listening response. Encourage students to regard this hearing as a "concert situation," and you should encourage "concert decorum."

6. Use the lines provided at the top of each form for such information as the student's name, the date, the class or section, and the name of the composition.

7. Periodically collect listening lessons after discussion, and study them. *Do not grade them!* Grading listening lessons is the surest way to destroy a listening program.

INFORMAL LISTENING LESSONS

This category of listening lessons is referred to as informal simply because *a printed set of questions or a prepared form is not employed.* "Informal" should not be equated by you or your students with "less important," "off the cuff," or similar expressions of laxity. Above all, you should not employ informal listening lessons because you are too lazy to prepare formal ones. Both formal and informal lessons have a specific purpose, and each should be in a coherent listening program.

WHEN TO USE INFORMAL LESSONS

Informal lessons are useful in the following situations:

1. To listen to a composition again that was first studied in a formal listening lesson fairly recently.
2. For very short or uncomplicated music, e.g., much popular music, individual songs from musical shows.
3. For listening lessons prepared by students for the class as an assignment or project.

Informality is possible in a repeated hearing of a work studied earlier because of the more formally focused earlier experience, and the familiarity that results from such earlier lessons. With some music, especially in the popular vein, the level of complexity or the number or nature of attensive qualities is such that it is difficult or impossible to invent sufficient questions of a formal variety to sustain attention throughout the entire piece. The same is true of very short pieces. In these instances, informal listening lessons are ideal, and in the case of popular music they are better suited to the informal character of students' listening habits. Finally, encourage students to share a favorite recording with the class by preparing, voluntarily and outside of class, a listening lesson. The informal variety is preferred for such occasions.

HOW TO USE INFORMAL LESSONS

Informal listening lessons are usually based on the same kinds of ideas for directions illustrated in the first ten examples suggested for formal listening lessons. They may involve one or two questions, of the kind found in question-type formal listening lessons, and one or two other challenges (e.g., color responses, instrumental identification, mood or adjective responses).

For example, these directions could be given verbally to the class: "There are four verses in this piece. Make a list of the instruments featured in each verse. Rate each verse as to how successfully you can understand the words, and how closely related the words and music are. Raise your hand when you think you hear an instrumental improvisation."

Write these directions in "shorthand" on the chalkboard or with the overhead projector:

4 verses.

List major instruments.

Are words understandable?

Words and music related?

Raise hand for improvisation.

Paper and pencil should be available if written responses are required (as they usually are). Play the recording; hold your discussion; play the recording again. Finis!

238

VISUAL AIDS

Other kinds of informal directed listening can feature various visual aids for students to relate to or choose from. Some of the following are suggested as examples, but you should always be inventing others, or variations on these, yourself.

1. Begin to make a collection of *large* and interesting photographs, painting reproductions, etc., from magazines. Photography magazines discarded by the library (or a local photo enthusiast) are perfect, as are various nature and ecology publications (put out by the Audubon Society, the Wilderness Society, etc.). Choose several contrasting examples for a composition you have in mind. Mount pictures on gray construction paper (use clear plastic tape, not glue, cellophane tape, or rubber cement; these would eventually ruin the picture). Hang the pictures where they are easily seen by the class (e.g., taped to the back of the piano facing the class, on a bulletin board). Play the recording. Direct students to choose the visual example that evokes or represents the same mood or feelings as they experience in the music. Discuss the variety of choices, the students' feelings, and especially the musical perceptions behind their responses.

2. Over a period of time, collect from local paint stores the card samples of multiple color-chips for a brand of paint. Have enough copies for each student, or one for every two students. Play the music and have them make their color response to the moods experienced by referring to actual colors by name. The more colors and shadings available on the sample, the more interesting and valuable is the experience.

3. Collect samples of wallpaper having a variety of designs, colors, and textures. Conduct activities similar to (1) and (2).

4. Diagram the form of buildings in the local community (as in Fig. 4:18). Use either geometric forms similar to the building or—eventually—letters. Thus the local church,

Fig. 4:18

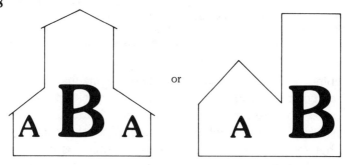

the school itself,

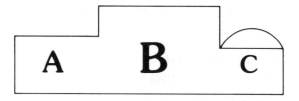

and other structures generally known to the class can serve as the basis for identifying the forms of compositions played. This, among other things, enriches students' understanding of "form" and tends to enable them to experience form in many ways outside of school.

5. Have students "diagram," by free or given means, a piece they hear for a lesson. That is,

direct them to visually represent what they hear, either by freely creative means or by using diagrammatic forms given by you (e.g., geometric shapes only or lines only).

Thus, for example, an ABA form containing different themes within each section might be diagrammed using geometric shapes as in Fig. 4:19:

Fig. 4:19

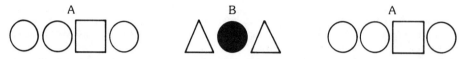

Younger students, or less inhibited classses, can freely interpret music by drawing using crayons or other coloring media as they listen. Here it is often useful to listen to two or three contrasting, short compositions (or logical sections) and compare the visual responses created by the class.

One teacher played a portion of a Mozart "Divertimento," part of Debussy's "En Bateau" (programmatically based upon water, waves, and boats), and a Sousa march. The interpretations for the Mozart (almost without exception) used light pastel colors—but reds, blues, and yellows—in lines that were quite varied in character. Students used the entire page, but didn't crowd lines too tightly. For the Debussy, the results were a general use of pastel pinks, yellows, and light blues, with wavy lines and very few lines on the page. For the Sousa March, bright primary colors, jagged, exciting lines, and a dense visual texture were characteristic.

These responses are very useful, especially if you take care to minimize "copying" and thus the spreading of one student's interpretation up and down the rows.

6. Another idea is to use colored slips of paper to identify certain musical perceptions. Play an example and direct students to hold up a certain color—on cue—to identify such perceptions as major or minor mode, a certain form, or the use of a certain technique. The virtue of this approach is that students must make up their minds and on cue quickly hold up the paper. This minimizes "copying" responses that can happen when such factors are merely discussed, or when hands are raised (leaving only two options, since we have only two hands). The teacher can also see at a glance the overall response of the class (i.e., whether most students have an appropriate color in their hand) and individual responses (i.e., which students have an inappropriate color).

Most listening responses involve providing the means or opportunity for some kind of concrete response to music. This serves two advantages: it makes responses overt and thus observable to both students and teachers; and it makes musical listening somewhat *more tangible* for students. They have the impression that some "thing" has been accomplished, as opposed to simply sitting there and listening. However, the final hearing in a listening lesson—the "pure" response—should also notify them that music is essentially a purely interior and private event involving personal responses.

DIRECTED LISTENING IN SOUND COMPOSITIONS AND SONGWRITING

In chapters 2 and 3 frequent mention was made of the need to perform and *listen* to sound compositions and songs created by the class. This is an important ingredient of these individual activities since *creation without aural results is merely an abstract exercise* and has little role to play in a program designed to enhance students' ability to respond to music more fruitfully. These listening occasions are also considered as important in your "total" listening program. They should not be conducted in a slapdash manner, nor casually. In every regard they should adhere to the same basic principles of aural perception as were outlined at some length earlier.

1. The teacher must *provide directions as to what the students should listen for* (directions for attensive qualities).

    a. In sound compositions the listening assignment is directed toward those members of the class who are not involved in performance. For this reason it is useful not to involve the entire class in a performance. At most, have half of the class perform while the other half listens.

        (1) Since you know what the composers have been attempting—because you gave them the assignment and criteria—this usually provides the basis for the directions you give to the class for listening. For example, "This will be a programmatic piece. See if you can figure out what the subject of the composer's program was, or what a suitable subject might have been to go with this music"; "This composition is supposed to have a specific form: listen and see whether you can tell what it is"; "This composition is supposed to be a rondo (ABACA); as you listen, see if you think it is or in what way it is."

        (2) On those occasions when unusual things happen—when, for instance, students accidentally "discover" a standard musical device—you can play the tape you have made of the live performance; or if possible have the performers repeat the composition or the relevant portion of the composition. Direct the listeners to try to focus their attention on whatever is at stake, and to be prepared to describe how it worked. Some kind of tangible response on their part is desirable (rather than you just saying "Listen to how they achieved retrograde motion"). Without some response, you will never know who heard what, if anything.

    b. In songwriting, you play the samples of student-created melodies.

        (1) Direct attention to whichever relevant considerations—e.g., skips, leaps, steps, contour, direction—you are currently cognitively strengthening.

        (2) Call for responses—judgments of suitability—from several students. Note the accuracy of their responses.

2. *Provide for some kind of overt response* to such verbal directions given orally.

    a. As with other kinds of directed listening it is absolutely necessary to elicit some kind of observable response from a *large number* of students. It is only in this way that you are able to note the general sufficiency of the class' perceptions, and to thereby improve perception where it is inadequate.

    b. There is seldom a need to announce that a student's response is "dead wrong." In fact, if you call upon enough students, the cumulative effect of responses—assuming that the majority are appropriate—will have the intended corrective effect. At worst, students are left to assess the inadequacy of their own response by comparing their answer to the cumulative impression received from the other responses.

3. *Relate sound compositions, songwriting assignments, and formal or informal directed-listening lessons by cognitively strengthening similar or identical musical aspects for each.* If you are emphasizing form in a sound-composition activity, then follow this with a similar focus when next doing songwriting; and devise one or more listening lessons around the same form(s).

    a. Make suitable emphasis on the aural *attensive qualities* of the form(s) under consideration in the creative activities. Sometimes in these activities, "form" is perceived by students only in visual terms.

    b. Make suitable *reminders* of such previous experiences with the form(s) under consideration before and as you conduct the related listening lesson.

This does not mean that as a general rule each new element or "content" factor you cognitively strengthen should be treated in sound compositions, songwriting, and directed listening in an invariable sequence of three-way emphasis. This would be too repetitive, too artificial, and above all too predictable. It does mean, though, that you should use every available opportunity to establish such relationships *naturally*. This facilitates transfer of learning between the activities, and the different skills and learnings each emphasizes.

Always keep in mind, too, that listening is the raison d'être of music, and thus is in effect the minimum goal of Action Learning. It is the benefit that everyone can derive from music education, and the one musical involvement most available to all people in their lives after and outside of school. Therefore, emphasis on listening responses should be as much a part of all activities as is possible.

LISTENING PROJECTS

To whatever degree it is possible in a given teaching situation, it is a desirable ingredient of Action Learning to involve students in listening activities outside of school or outside of music class. It is necessary to stress the availability of perceptive listening (as opposed to hearing) in their daily lives: active listening is not something they should come to believe can be done only in the music class under the teacher's direction.

While it has become increasingly rare for music teachers to expect work of students outside of class, there is no reason why this trend should continue. Among other things, outside work earns a certain kind of respect from adolescents (and often from taxpayers!). However extrinsic this advantage may be, the intrinsic advantages involve *the need to expand musical functioning beyond the classroom* and beyond the time limits during which the teacher has contact with students. Furthermore, *music learning must be used if it is to be retained.* And if it is relevant and interesting to students, what is used in this way will more incline them to its continued use outside of school. This is the major premise of Action Learning.

Listening projects, however, need not be treated strictly as homework: that is, *they need not be assigned* as being due within very specific guidelines on very specific days. They can be more open-ended, as can some of the choices or approaches to listening used. Listening projects of this kind involve two basic approaches: either the teacher prepares both music and directions for listening and responding or the teacher prepares general listening instructions or criteria but leaves at least some degree of listening selection to the student.

With the first kind, the teacher prepares several copies of listening lesson selections on cassette tapes (or, at great risk, makes available the record) for student use at home, in a library, or in a media center where playback equipment is available. Small, portable, inexpensive cassette recorders are found in more and more homes. Another alternative in many situations is to sign out school-owned, small cassette players for student use. The teacher should also prepare and provide the formal directed listening form for use with the prepared recordings.

With the second kind of project the teacher prepares the formal listening lessons, or provides general criteria for a variety of listening projects, and the students are free to some degree to choose *what* they will listen to in fulfilling the assignment.

In either case the teacher may prepare more projects than are required, thus allowing the students to choose those that interest them the most (or, at worst, those they dislike least). Following are some suggestions for listening projects. You should add to the list as you learn or think of other kinds, for the greatest variety will present the greatest interest and learning benefit.

TEN SUGGESTIONS FOR OUTSIDE-LISTENING PROJECTS

1. Students can prepare their own informal listening lessons for class use. The teacher should preview and "adapt" these before using them.

2. Have students assemble "song cycles" of popular music by collecting recordings with related texts, arranging them in suitable order, and explaining the overall expressive result of such a collection of related songs.

3. Similarly, students can assemble a kind of "cantata" by putting together a variety of songs that present a progression of ideas represented in the texts and enhanced by the music. In this and the previous example, students might use school facilities to pretape their assemblages for playback and discussion during class time.

4. Students can be given the option of choosing a certain number of recordings, perhaps specifying a variety of types (rock, folk music, jazz, musical theater, classical, etc.), and writing analytic reports *that evidence detailed perception and responses* along guidelines given by the teacher.

5. Students may write detailed critical reviews of performances, record albums, etc., *as though for a newspaper* (perhaps these could actually be published in a school or local paper). The teacher should provide examples of successful music criticism, from sources such as *Time, Newsweek,* or *High Fidelity.*

6. Students may write critiques of music criticism located in such weekly newsmagazines or audio magazines, based upon their own listening to the recordings reviewed and their own value judgments.

7. Students can prepare their own detailed listening projects along guidelines you should prepare for them. For listening purposes, however, make sure these materials are based on or related to actual listening experiences. You should retain the best of these for your own use in other classes.

8. By all means, have students review performances by local school or community band, chorus, and orchestra, according to some prepared format. When possible, take a general-music class in to rehearsals as observer-auditors, and let them prepare their reports in this way, or use this as preparation for their attendance at assembly programs or concerts. Don't forget to incorporate local "concert series" of visiting artists in your listening program.

9. Students can complete formal directed-listening lessons outside of class. This is best done by allowing them to choose a specified number to do from a longer list.

10. Students can program a hypothetical concert (of any kind or mixture of musical styles you may specify) by choosing the compositions (freely or from a given list) and preparing written program notes based on their listening. Show them as a sample some well-written program notes of the kind that assist a person in listening to a composition for the first time.

With all of these activities, and any others you may invent, be sure to provide specific and clear criteria as guidelines for students' efforts and for evaluation. You are especially encouraged to use a mixture of the suggested activities, rather than only one kind.

Make sure that all outside-listening projects clearly emphasize aural perception. It does absolutely no good if these projects amount to pure book research in the library of no conceivable derivation from or relation to listening. The point of these projects is to involve students in considerable and intense listening outside of the music class. Only this will result in Action Learning.

THE TOTAL LISTENING PROGRAM

All listening efforts should result from and have a specific place in an organized listening program. The various factors that should go into consideration for establishing such a program are all of equal importance.

FREQUENCY OF HEARING VS. TOTAL
NUMBER OF SELECTIONS HEARD

Research has suggested that familiarity bred by repeated hearings of musical selections is an important factor in listening among adolescents.[18] When recordings were heard on a weekly basis an optimum response level was reached during the sixth to eighth hearing.

After that the adolescent listeners were still able to perceive new features, but not at a rate, perhaps, that justifies more hearings. The most significant rise in the number of responses (i.e., the musical features perceived) was noted at the second and third hearings. Negative reactions were attributed most frequently to hearings that were too close together.

The implications of such research, borne out by the experiences of teachers with successful programs, would seem to be that *listening to a given composition several times is not only warranted but is required if the student is to derive full benefit of the percepts available in a typical piece.* Maximum gains in responses are noted around a second or third hearing. This tends to justify the recommendations made to *hear a composition at least twice in one lesson, and plan for a third and fourth hearing at a later date.*

On the other hand, hearing the same recording too soon can be harmful. Thus the trick is to time repeated hearings at appropriate distances from each other, but so that the third and fourth hearings are related to other relevant undertakings that are still fresh enough in mind. This is not an unwarranted conclusion even if we use our own experience as a basis for a judgment.

Any composition worth hearing, is worth hearing more than once. A well-chosen piece will provide a wealth of perceptual opportunities. To listen to it only once or twice neither makes use of the aural stimuli available nor familiarizes the student with it enough to "understand" or "appreciate" it. We seldom can react with full appreciation on one or two hearings, especially when the music in question is rich in aural complexity. With music already quite familiar to students (or short, or not complex), two hearings may suffice. This has been the recommendation here for informal listening, especially to popular music.

The research cited and classroom experience, then, indicate that a teacher is on solid ground in planning a total of at least *four* hearings of a given composition in a course of studies. Some benefit can be gained from six to eight hearings, but practical considerations seem to indicate the total of four as a realistic use of limited time. This allows you to increase the total listening contact students have with a variety of musical styles while still retaining the time for repeated hearings. So rather than hearing, say, one hundred recordings once or twice—and not gaining maximum benefit from each—you are able to listen to fifty on three or four occasions and to derive realistic benefit from each. You still will have considerable variety in your listening offering. This seems to be a realistic compromise in solving a long-standing dilemma. However, most informal listening lessons involving popular or other "lighter" styles seldom profit from more than two or three hearings.

STYLISTIC VARIETY

It is quite important, of course, that your listening program provide a rich variety of musical styles and types from different eras. Some teachers are intimidated by adolescents in listening situations and capitulate by providing them with a steady diet of popular and rock music. Other teachers insist on a steady diet of classical music because they feel that students otherwise encounter so little of it. Some teachers group listening lessons around a topic such as American music or folk music. However, these usually turn out to be listening lessons that exemplify certain facts and information *about* the music considered rather than lessons which cognitively strengthen certain musical qualities.

Ideally, a program should involve recordings within the perceptual abilities of students and of interest to them. Most teachers are unable to succeed with any kind of classical music for listening simply because the students have neither the cognitive readiness (prior concepts) nor perceptual readiness (perceptual skills) to respond fruitfully. However, in a program of sound compositions and songwriting where students encounter and employ the variety of musical elements, techniques, and devices described so far, they have a better conceptual and perceptual readiness.

Students with this kind of learning preparation are also less resistant to labels of "classical" vs. "popular" and can sometimes be more tolerant or open than are many trained musicians. When they learn factors through listening lessons that improve the success of their own compositional efforts and enhance their pleasure in these efforts, they will listen more readily to music regardless of style or type. And when creative activities contribute to the success of their perceptual efforts in listening lessons, the sense of accomplishment is its own motivation (regardless, again, of musical style or type).

So the question is not so much one of whether or not students will tolerate certain styles or types. It is a question of which styles they feel best prepared to respond to, which they experience predictable feelings of success from, and which they feel are most profitable to them in tangible ways. Listening lessons by a music teacher who is a rock aficionado can be so complicated, so involved, so laborious that students are "turned off" or feel "put down" by the teacher's expertise. Lessons based on other styles or types which are more straightforward can be more satisfying to them. So with these caveats in mind, consider the following suggestions for variety in your program.

Suggestions for a Varied Listening Program

1. Include sufficient experience with a variety of major instrumental media (orchestras, bands, and small ensembles such as quartets, trios, and quintets).

2. Be sure to include not just vocal media but choral media. The latter are typically ignored by most music teachers, and most record collections designed for public school listening generally ignore them as well. Music for mixed chorus, men's chorus, women's chorus, children's chorus, and boys' chorus should be included in a well-rounded program.

3. Some "classics" chosen from each of the following styles are recommended: popular, rock, musical theater, jazz, authentic folk music (i.e., *real* folk songs performed by *real* "folk"), urban folk music (i.e., composed folk songs or folk-like songs such as Bob Dylan's "Blowin' in the Wind"), and classical music. Whether or not you include country-and-western music is your decision, based upon local conditions and preferences. Ethnic music should be included, as well, for each such group in the community.

4. Sufficient experiences with all of the above types of music—with the basic duality of "romantic" (i.e., *emphasizing expression* but not ignoring formal factors) and "classical" (i.e., *emphasizing formal factors* but not ignoring expressive elements)—are recommended. Each of these two basic musical mentalities can be applied to a variety of musical styles such as jazz and rock as well as to the traditional repertory of music history.

5. If any stress on the so-called historical styles in Western music (i.e., Renaissance, baroque, classical, romantic, impressionist, modern) is thought wise, it should be strictly an aural one. Students should not be forced to memorize long lists of stylistic characteristics that they cannot perceive in the music. Of far more impact, in any case, is their ability to perceive and respond to the musical techniques and forms most characteristic of each era. Some are suggested:

    a. *Renaissance*: polyphony, especially counterpoint; chorus as an expressive performance medium; polyrhythms; indistinct phrases or hidden "seams" in the music.

    b. *Baroque*: imitative counterpoint; opera, oratorio, and cantata devices (e.g., da capo aria, recitative); the concerto grosso principle of a large vs. a smaller group in a kind of "musical combat"; small multi-movement forms.

    c. *Classical*: the sonata principle, including the solo concerto and sonata rondo forms; larger multi-movement forms such as the symphony; homophonic emphasis.

    d. *Romantic*: orchestration; enlargement and expansion of classical forms and ensembles; harmonic enrichment with increasing dissonance; solo piano music; virtuoso performance; small "character" pieces for the piano.

    e. *Modern*: increased rhythmic/metric complexity; new sound sources; "harmonies" based on intervals other than thirds, and super-dissonant tonal combinations; serialism (Schoenberg's tone-row compositions); electronic music.

Most of these elements can be incorporated in the listening program either before or after treating them by means of sound compositions or songwriting activities—and many more as well. It all depends on how many years you have your students, how often during the year, and how many times a week.

Keep in mind that *historical information* (characteristics, etc.) *will almost invariably be forgotten*. Broad concepts and perceptual abilities (i.e., the ability to respond to imitative counterpoint, polymeters, etc.) are applicable when listening to any style of music now or in the future. It is therefore strongly recommended that you concentrate on such widely applicable concepts and percepts, and not attempt a boiled-down music history course.

If, in listening to a piece for its major attensive qualities, a certain stylistic characteristic is outstanding, it can be dealt with in that context. In this way the baroque-like counterpoint of dixieland jazz can be observed. A straight historical survey inevitably results in skimming the surface of information that most adolescents find to be entirely irrelevant. It is certain to result in resistance in most teaching situations; and even if resistance is not overt, little covert progress is made in long-term learning. Names of composers, their dates, and the titles of their major compositions have been pounded into the heads of generations of public school and university students to no good effect, no lasting benefit, either to the students or the status of such music in their minds. If anything, their attitude has become increasingly negative under such conditions.

In sum, if you insist on categorizing music in front of your students (e.g., "Today we are going to hear a current pop hit" or "This composition is a famous symphonic work of the romantic period in music") you will inevitably condition your own students into such categorizing. If, on the other hand, you sincerely try to choose from a variety of styles good music that has appropriate attensive qualities and make no special "deal" of its category or label, you will find your students more ready to participate fruitfully almost without regard for style. Sure, they will have their preferences, but so do we all. But they will realize that aural perception is the goal, rather than entertainment; and that this aural perception works for them regardless of what style they may be listening to.

They should also be able to take an increasing pride in their growing perceptual powers. This in itself is its own inducement for productive involvement. Finally, and especially important, is the need to establish an open, responsive atmosphere by emphasizing the feeling-response (as based on verified perception) rather than cognitive or objective responses of the identification or recall kind. Cognition is of course necessary to feeling; therefore when feeling-responses are elicited both are in evidence. But cognition without significant feelings proves very little.

Cognitive or objective lessons for their own sake are self-defeating. Lessons where objective perceptions are enlisted in enhancing feeling-responses are most desirable. Feeling-responses without some tangible perceptual basis are no more useful than asking people whether or not they like a food they have never eaten!

THE PROBLEM OF PROGRAM MUSIC

Program music is *inspired by* a nonmusical idea such as a picture or other visual imagery, or a story or story-like ideas. The nonmusical idea on which a programmatic piece is based is often indicated in the title of the composition, and by explanatory notes often used as the "program notes" to guide listeners. While this kind of composition has a long history, it is often most associated with nineteenth-century romanticism. With a typical romantic fervor, many composers based compositions on their travels, children's stories, abstract philosophical ideas, musical "interpretations" of visual images, and the like.

Segments of the public became so endeared to this practice that music editors often added a program when one was not intended by the composer. Chopin was constantly at odds with his editor over this practice.

However, there is little evidence that composers intended or truly imagined that music *by itself* could adequately "tell" a story or "paint" a picture. *The extramusical idea was a source of inspiration to them* and was meant to have little or no measure-by-measure storytelling capacity. In other words, *music is and always was abstract and incapable of direct representations of the world.*[19] Imitation of nature was a strength of such other art forms as painting, photography, sculpture, and literature. Programmatic music has usually been judged by serious musicians for its musical merits regardless of whether it was based on programmatic sources.

Many music teachers have realized the usefulness of making listening lessons and responses more tangible. Thus they have seized heavily on program music as the main or sole source for their listening lessons. Such compositions as "The Sorcerer's Apprentice," "Peter and the Wolf," "The Carnival of the Animals," and "Pictures at an Exhibition" have bombarded young ears and minds with strong implications of music's literal storytelling or picture-painting ability.

While some useful purposes may have been served with younger, primary-school-aged children, often irreparable harm was done in greater measure, especially beginning in the late elementary and junior high years. This harm came from conditioning children to believe that music always, or usually, tells a story or paints a picture; that music is a literal representation of the real world using sound; that music—just as their literature teachers implied for poetry—always has a tangible meaning, message, or moral; and that music is virtually a parable in sound.

This impression on the part of students simply must be avoided. For one thing, it is most assuredly not true, and thus misrepresents music's potential and strengths. For another, it causes practical difficulties. Children, just as most adults, usually cannot "find" the story or picture in most music, especially without the title. When they cannot, they are understandably confused. In some cases they blame themselves, which later results in such adult attitudes as "Well, I like music, but I don't *understand* it." In other cases they blame the composers for creating incomprehensible art works. Thus they avoid any involvement with such music and restrict their music intake to popular or semiclassical entertainments. In still other instances they blame the teacher for having selected a composition that does not "work" for them. The result here is either unresponsiveness or misbehavior.

Among the first twenty-five or so popular programmatic compositions that a person might list "off the top of his head," very few represent a quality of music worthy of students' listening efforts. In any case, most people would agree that there are far better selections available that are potentially more beneficial from the point of view of increasing students' aural perception.

If for no other reason than that the length of most programmatic compositions exceeds learners' limited attention spans, it is recommended that they not play any significant part in a listening program. Truly attentive perception is rare even among trained listeners, whose attention varies and wanders during longer compositions. It is even less likely with prepubescent and early adolescents, who can seldom exceed *two or three minutes* of such intensive listening efforts (and even then, attention is not constant or total); or with adolescents, whose ability for concentrated attention seldom exceeds *three or four minutes.*

However, it is still possible to use certain extramusical associations or responses in making students' responses more tangible and thus overtly observable to the teacher, who must be able to observe accurately students' growing perceptual acuity. Therefore the following are suggested, along with some rationale, as some means by which listening may be made less abstract.

SUGGESTIONS FOR CONCRETIZING LISTENING RESPONSES WITHOUT PROGRAMMATIC ASSOCIATIONS

Use *figurative responses* to assist in the communication of abstractly experienced emotions and percepts. Emotions, feelings, moods, etc., are often clearly present in the minds of young people yet often are not accessible to verbal communication. Similarly with adults these same feeling-states resist adequate conveyance in direct verbal expression. We resort to indirect expressions. Art itself is considered to be such an expressive metaphor of the nondiscursive, inexpressible realities of existence.

a. Color responses, adjective associations, concrete designs, textures, and graphic designs (lines, shapes) all can serve well as such metaphoric expression.

b. Responses in which an aural experience is compared to or associated with a visual or other tangible experience fulfill a similar purpose. Associating a piece of music with a picture selected from among a number of choices is successful when the *emphasis is on the similarity of feeling-content involved in each separate work,* and not on any presumption that the music directly "pictures" the meaning or story of the visual.

c. Physical responses involving interpretive or coordinated movement to music (as in dance) directly signify the music response in a gestural (physical) metaphor. Unfortunately some learners, especially boys and middle and later adolescents, often have deep-seated inhibitions about such movement, except when popular dances are involved—perhaps because of some "sex stereotype" whereby boys learn to believe that this is not something a *man* does.

d. Direct creative responses are suitable if used to create imaginative stories that *could go* (not *must go*) with the music, or if responses from the visual arts (drawing, designing, etc., to music as it plays) are used. Here it is expected that the results are a direct *transformation* of what the students heard and what their feelings were, and not an attempt to realize the "correct" interpretation.

e. Indirect creative responses are also suitable as long as clear attempts are made to insure that results are related to aural perception. Suitable student projects include those described earlier as outside-listening projects. Also useful are other projects such as selecting

249

music (through listening) that would serve well to accompany a drama (use of the "melodrama principle") or the reading of a poem. All of these can reflect, or express metaphorically, what the student heard and how he or she feels about what was heard.

In the case of all these figurative uses, the effect is one of "What I heard sounds *as if . . .*" Recently reported research indicates that *concepts are at first nonverbal* in their origin. We "know" or sense these "neuronal messages" without words. Should we have the need or desire, we may *try* to find words to convey their messages.

But even pre-verbally we are "aware" of them as "felt" or "sensed," and ultimately *we may or may not have words available* to overtly express or communicate them or even to understand them by "thinking" (inner speech). Thus, the "patterned neuronal message" sent by the brain "to the nonverbal concept-mechanism" may never become speech (as in aphasia—the inability to speak—or with generalized feeling-states for which no concrete verbal association suffices). Then we may resort to one kind or another of gesture or metaphor.[20]

It is interesting to consider that music itself performs a very similar function. Viewed from this perspective, musical concepts are neuronal messages that need not and cannot be verbalized. They are intrapsychical, purely mental, purely covert. *Music*—composed, performed, or listened to—*functions as a sound metaphor*[21] that "expresses" these patterned neuronal messages without recourse to words. That is its special magic.

The meaning of such musical concepts is perceived in the stream of consciousness, and is felt or sensed as neuronal pattern, not as words: " . . . the contents of consciousness are not simply reproducible by some one-to-one mapping into verbal report."[22] However, concrete associations, such as color responses or the other types of response suggested earlier, do permit *some degree* of externalization of response. But such responses are only figurative and try to express or capture, in some analogous terms, the neuronal state that is otherwise felt or sensed in nonconcrete terms. "The private consciousness, once expressed in words, gestures, or in any way externalized, is necessarily a transformation of the private experience."[23]

The musical response so encouraged remains "pure" in the responder's mind, although the teacher still uses whatever expressive means seem to suffice for enabling such a response to be shared. One could even contend that if some *thing* could be directly communicated in music, it would render music mundane and trivial, and no more significant than the communication involved in using a mail-order catalogue.

You are warned against trivializing the musical responsiveness of your students by reliance on program music, or reliance on *direct* programmatic responses. Music can be dealt with in its purity without denigrating its special status to mere storytelling. It is its "specialness" in human affairs that insures its continuation as a prime vehicle for expressing and sharing the indefinable experience of humanness.

THE TOTAL SYNTHESIS OF SYNERGY

You should recall that synergy is found where the operation of the individual parts constituting a system does not predict or explain the total operation of that system. The human brain and body is such a system, as is music. It is, therefore, the most desirable goal of a music-education program to seek to fully reintegrate all the various components of music as have been singled out over time for emphasis (cognitive strengthening). Such emphasis makes possible a heightened awareness in the form of the nonverbal concepts or neuronal messages that constitute the tonal musical response.

Every learned-reaction that becomes automatic was first carried out within the light of conscious attention and in accordance with the understanding of the mind. Each skill, acquired in the light of conscious attention, soon becomes automatic and runs itself even more skillfully that the individual could carry it out by conscious direction.[24]

Throughout a program of sound compositions, songwriting, and directed listening the overreaching goal is to bring musical principles, techniques, and devices "within the light of conscious attention" of our students. Without this cognitive strengthening, which is a result of left hemisphere emphasis on the "parts" of music, students cannot possibly be aware of the many aspects that are responsible for the special power of music. But, on the other hand, we must do this by always relating such emphases to the total musical context from which they stem, and also to the total musical context in which they will work. Just as we should relate to the "whole person" of our students and not to their momentary behavior, their manner of dress, or their physical appearance, the musical response is not to melody, or harmony, or rhythm. It is to the "whole piece" (see Fig. 4:20) and thus takes place in terms of the right hemisphere's predeliction for integration and pattern-making.

Of the activities treated so far, each has its special virtue in the process of working from a vaguely perceived whole, to an emphasized part, which is then reintegrated in its cognitively strengthened effect as part of a richer musical whole. Sound compositions and directed listening, in particular, have the greatest potential for this kind of musical synergy. Sound compositions involve all three musical behaviors: composition, performance, and listening. Emphasis of musical elements is done from three varied points of view, and the "stream of consciousness" is therefore benefitted in establishing those nonverbal neuronal messages that stand behind human responsiveness. Similarly, because all three behaviors are present to some degree, there is a greater insurance of musical "wholeness"; a greater likelihood that responses will be from and toward an expressive musical whole, no matter how naive.

Directed listening, for its part, begins with an entire piece of music perceived aurally. In the process of listening, the teacher directs students' attention to certain attensive qualities. After discussion of classs responses and perceptions, the entire piece is heard again, thus allowing any newly strengthened perceptions to take their place in working toward an enriched responsiveness on the part of students.

The emphases characteristic of songwriting are smaller, and more specific. But they have their use in bringing to "the light of conscious attention" certain techniques, refinements, and percepts that are best approached through this means. However, they do not begin and seldom end with what could be considered an expressive musical whole. To the degree that you can bring your students to the stage of truly composing interesting songs that involve all aspects of melody, harmony, rhythm, and form (and text, where appropri-

251

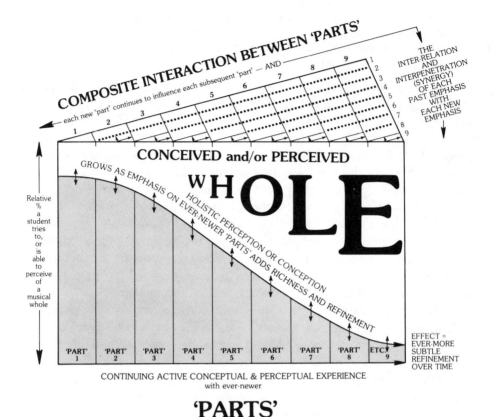

Fig. 4:20 The (w)holistic approach to teaching and learning

ate), this synergy can be served better. But even if this is not always or usually possible for all students, benefits gained in these activities can contribute to the success of sound-composition and directed-listening activities.

CONCLUSION

A program leading toward a synergetic responsiveness will be predicated mainly on listening, the most realistic and universally applicable of Action Learning goals. Composition and performance (including music reading, singing, and playing instruments) will have their role as well, especially in the process called cognitive strengthening. Composition will be added in greater proportion than is characteristic of much general-music instruction today because of its effectiveness in promoting perceptual and conceptual gains. As a result of such cognitive strengthening, and its effect in subception, listening will be restored to its original, prime status as the major vehicle and reason for musical involvement. To do less is to contradict and contravene the very nature of the musical art. This will not only do irreparable harm, but worse, will do irreparable damage to the attitudes, values, and responsiveness of students who otherwise love and seek music but who are "turned off" by the irrelevance of music class.

Skill in listening, increasing perceptual acuity, is Action Learning at its best. A program oriented in this manner, and using the activities recommended so far over a period from middle school (at the latest) through high school, cannot fail to influence the learner in the direction of increased contact with music and increased responsiveness to whatever music is thus heard.

NOTES: CHAPTER 4

1. Aletory (or aleatoric) music, it will be recalled, is music in which free chance is employed in the compositional process, in performance, or in both. Stochastic music might be considered a subspecies of aleatory music, since it involves the use of the "laws of chance" or "probability" as its basis. Both are often referred to as music of indeterminancy, or indeterminant music.

2. As used here, *curiosity* is the important first step leading to lasting *interest*, but it will not grow into that more durable quality without proper nurture and sustenance.

3. See, for example, James Garbarino, "The Impact of Anticipated Reward upon Cross-Age Tutoring," *Journal of Personality and Social Psychology*, vol. 32, no. 3 (Sept 1975), pp. 421-28.

4. William B. Gevarter, "Humans: Their Brain and Their Freedom," *Journal of Humanistic Psychology*, vol. 15, no. 4 (Fall 1975), p. 79.

5. See Thomas A. Regelski, *Brain Research and Arts Education* (Reston, Va., and Washington, D.C.: MENC/Arts Education Alliance, 1978); also Robert Ornstein, *The Psychology of Consciousness* (New York: Viking Press, 1972); *Essentiasheet No. 3* (Evergreen State College, Olympia, Wash. 95505); *New-ways*, vol. 1, nos. 2 and 5 (Jan.-Feb. 1975 and Sept.-Oct. 1975) (Educational Arts Association and Advisory for Open Education, 90 Sherman St., Cambridge, Mass. 02140); and *Brain/Mind Bulletin*, ed. Marilyn Ferguson (P.O. Box 42492, Los Angeles, Calif. 90042).

6. And there is clear evidence that this storage is total, with our mind functioning dually like a tape recorder and a moving picture camera, to record virtually all sensory data that enter the stream of consciousness. See Chester A. Lawson, *Brain Mechanisms and Human Learning* (Boston: Houghton Mifflin Co., 1967), p. 5; and Thomas A. Harris, *I'm OK—You're OK* (New York: Avon Books, 1973), p. 25, both of which report the same research by Wilder Penfield in his *Speech and Brain Mechanisms* (Princeton, N.J.: Princeton University Press,

1959), pp. 14, 49, and 53, and his "Memory Mechanism," *A.M.A. Archives of Neurology and Psychiatry*, vol. 67 (1952), pp. 178-98. For a general and up-to-date summary of this research done just before his death, see Wilder Penfield, *The Mystery of the Mind* (Princeton University Press, 1975), *passim*. The reader should be aware that not all scientists equate mind and brain.

7. "If decisions as to the target of conscious attention are made by the mind, then it is the mind that directs the programming of all the mechanisms within the brain. A man's mind, one might say, is the person."—Penfield, *The Mystery of the Mind*, p. 61. Thus the "I" is the controlling *subject;* "me" is the *object* of the attention of "I." Together they make the "Self," the mind referred to as my-Self.

8. George Mandler, *Mind and Emotion* (New York: John Wiley & Sons, 1975), p. 80.

9. See Richard S. Lazarus and Robert A. McCleary, "Autonomic Discrimination Without Awareness: A Study of Subception," *Psychological Review,* (vol. 58 (1951), pp. 113-22.

10. See Michael Polanyi, *The Tacit Dimension* (Garden City, N.Y.: Doubleday & Co., Anchor Books, 1967). See also, Sam Reese, "Polanyi's Tacit Knowing and Music Education," *The Journal of Aesthetic Education,* vol. 14, No. 1 (Jan. 1980), p. 75.

11. See Elliot W. Eisner, "The Intelligence of Feeling," in *Facts and Feelings in the Classroom*, ed. Louis J. Rubin (New York: Viking Press, 1973), pp. 201-8.

12. The Orient, with its emphasis on various kinds of meditation and thus on favoring subception over conception, has been guilty of going too far in the other direction. The growth of interest in meditation among people in this country testifies to a new awakening to the importance of right-hemispheric subception.

13. It should come as no surprise to most music teachers that there is even a strong prejudice among musicians to regard musical thinking, whether in performing, composing, or listening, as a type of left hemisphere, "intellectualized," logical, and strictly explicit (as opposed to tacit) process. At the college level most of what passes for music theory, fundamentals of music, musicianship skills, style and form analysis, and music history is taught in this mistaken belief. As a result such studies are clearly atomistic: music is constantly fragmented (analyzed) into its "parts" and simply is never put back together again. That synthesis is usually left to each student to achieve. Because this kind of instruction has formed the preponderance of the teacher's own *training* (as opposed to education), it is important to be on guard lest this practice be perpetuated with middle school and high school youngsters who have even less reason or use for such piecemeal training. All the teacher has to do, if the folly of the atomistic method is doubted at all, is to try and remember most of the terms, dates, labels, rules, and other individual items of knowledge that constituted his or her musical training. There is simply no doubt about the results: the individual teacher will remember only an incredibly small fraction of this fragmented information. It is likely that what is remembered will either be the kind of information that musicians tend to use daily, such as key signatures and performance terms, or the kind of things the teacher, for better or worse, tends to teach. In either case, only that which has

been used has been remembered. And no reasonable person would conclude that the individual who remembers the most fragmented information therefore has the richest "wholistic" musical response. Therefore teachers convinced of the need for a "wholistic" rather than an "atomistic" approach to music *education* (rather than training), should not be surprised to find individual educators and researchers defending the traditional left-hemisphere approach to music learning, or denying the validity of the more "wholistic" right-hemisphere approach.

14. This is called "cognitive appraisal," and is pivotal in attitudes and other feeling responses; see Mandler, *Mind and Emotion*, pp. 54, 55, 60, 67-69, 70, 72, 76-77 ,106, 118, 151, but especially pp. 30 and 205.

15. Although they always should be present, these directions have less importance after students have had sufficient experience with the formal directed listening format and procedures to fully understand their use.

16. See, for example, Lawrence E. Marks, "Synesthesia: The Lucky People with Mixed-Up Sense," *Psychology Today*, vol. 9 (June 1975), p. 48. While there are several types of synesthesia (such as an aural response to vision), these are not at stake in the present context. It should be emphasized that synesthesia is not some kind of illness or condition requiring correction. It is simply the manner in which the sensory systems of some people function. There is evidence that Chopin heard music when looking at painting, and that his friend Delacroix saw colors and visual images when listening to music. The innovative results of their unique perceptions advanced the arts of music and painting respectively.

17. A tetrachord is a four-tone scale segment.

18. Pennsylvania Department of Education, *Journal of Research in Music Education,* vol. 14, no. 3 (Fall 1966), pp. 190-91.

19. With the very occasional exception of birdcalls and a few other real-world imitations.

20. "A dog appears in the stream of consciousness, whereupon the highest brain-mechanism carries a patterned neuronal message to the non-verbal concept-mechanism. The past record is scanned and a similar appearance recalled. . . . The mind compares the two images that have thus appeared in the stream of consciousness, and sees similarity. There is a sense of familiarity or recognition. While all this is still in the stream of consciousness, another patterned neuronal message notice that this is a second, separate message, distinct from the previous "sense" concept is formed, made up of the remembered concept modified by the present experience. This message is sent to the speech mechanism and the word 'dog' flashes up into consciousness."—Penfield, *The Mystery of the Mind*, pp. 58-59. See also pp. 57 and 51-54 for fascinating insights of significant value to all teachers. Speaking about deactivation of the speech mechanism during a surgical experiment, Dr. Penfield relates: "It is clear that while the speech mechanism was temporarily blocked the patient could

perceive the meaning of the picture of a butterfly. He made a conscious effort to 'get' the corresponding word. Then not understanding why he could not do so, he turned back for a second time to the interpretive mechanism . . . and found a second concept that he considered the closest thing to a butterfly. He must then have presented that to the speech mechanism, only to draw another blank" (p. 52).

21. See Donald N. Ferguson, *Music as Metaphor* (Minneapolis: University of Minnesota Press, 1960).

22. Mandler, *Mind and Emotion*, p. 52.

23. Ibid., p. 51.

24. Penfield, *The Mystery of the Mind*, pp. 59, 61.

5

The Challenge of General Music

☐ Principles and Problems of Teacher Planning

    Creativity and Spontaneity in Teaching
    Advantages of an Eclectic Approach
    Fluidity vs. Rigidity
    Permissipline: Creative Tension

☐ A Music Curriculum

    Implementing a Curriculum
    Planning and Behavioral Objectives
    Format for Writing Behavioral Objectives
    Covert Musical Behaviors
    Overt Musical Behaviors
    Samples of Objectives
    Venture Planning Forms: Specific Plans for Implementation

☐ Controlling Aspects of Creative Activities

    Degrees of Control: Free, Given, or Mixed
    Aspects Controlled: Materials, Procedures, Product
    Samples of Teacher Controls over the Three Aspects of Creative Activities
    General Guidelines

☐ Grouping: Patterns and Principles for Use with Creative Activities

    Five Principles of Group Work
    Fifteen Suggestions for Choosing groupings

☐ Timing Creative Activities

    Creative Activities as Homework

☐ General Application of Creative Activities to Three Readiness Levels

    Using Readiness Levels

        Level I: General
        Level I: Specific Examples
        Level II: General
        Level II: Specific Examples
        Level III: General
        Level III: Specific Examples

☐ Ten Practical Suggestions for Planning Creative Activities

STRETCHING MUSICAL ALTERNATIVES

The human condition in part stems from our need to make decisions and choices between given or free alternatives. Where there are no or very few alternatives, human choice is necessarily limited. Where human choice is limited, the affirmation of our humanness is limited as well. It is in this sense that music education is a stretching of alternatives. It operates in the belief that there are many kinds of music, and that any one person can find different significance from various kinds of music at various times. *Music education is the process by which such musical alternatives can become better known to children* and thus afford them a real choice of alternatives as they grow older.

The home environment, the community, the mass media are all likely to have had a significant and long-lasting impact on the musical tastes and preferences of all but the very young. By the time most children approach nine or ten years of age their musical tastes begin to bear a striking resemblance to those of parents, older students, or brothers and sisters. It is an unwarranted imposition of your values to presume in any way to change their tastes *except by extension*—by stretching their alternatives to include types of music not ordinarily encountered in their informal learning environments. In fact, it is usually a good idea to build your music program on the musical concepts (readiness) students have learned from the formative environment outside of school. From this base you can enrich, refine, and extend their understanding and ability to "feel" music more deeply.

THE PROGRESS OF MUSICAL LEARNING

Building upon this base of readiness does not involve a lockstep sequence of learning. It is not a necessity to understand concept A before understanding concept B. This would be the lockstep curriculum of the reductionist outlined earlier. Concepts are very interrelated at various points, and any simple arrangement into priorities that must precede others is usually artificial and arbitrary. (See Fig. 5:1)

At one time, music educators tried to parallel a sequence of musical concepts with what had been assumed to be well-defined developmental stages in the growth of children. It was this same belief in stages that caused age to be used to group children in "grade" levels. Now this belief and the resulting teaching formats have given way to understanding that *people do not learn at the same rate of speed in each area of instruction, nor is age a good basis for grouping.* Similarly in musical instruction, *it is unwarranted to assume that all learners in a given age group can profit equally well from the same kind of instruction or the same kind of instructional content.*

There are only a relatively few basic concept-areas in music. There are only a few ways in which children can experience music. Therefore *what is varied in musical instruction is the nature of the "content," the nature of the cognitive strengthening sought, the nature of the results.* To achieve these different levels of insight, different activities and strategies are employed. It is quite possible to involve learners of mixed ages in a single activity involving identical materials and have multiple results of benefit to each. Each will take from the activity in accordance with the individual readiness, needs, or interests brought to the activity. Uniform progress and results are not expected merely because students happen to be grouped together on some basis for the administrative convenience of the school.

Understood in this sense, *concepts are individual and unique.* Each person's biological perceptual apparatus and hence perceptual abilities vary qualitatively and quantitatively. In the same stimuli different people will notice

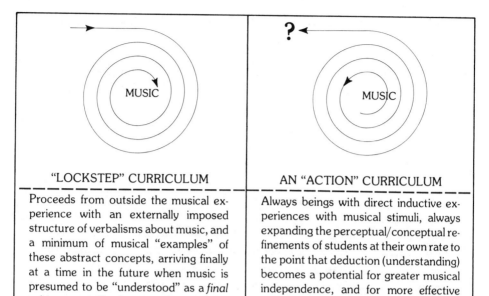

Fig. 5:1 Antithetical Curricular Styles in Music Education

"LOCKSTEP" CURRICULUM	AN "ACTION" CURRICULUM
Proceeds from outside the musical experience with an externally imposed structure of verbalisms about music, and a minimum of musical "examples" of these abstract concepts, arriving finally at a time in the future when music is presumed to be "understood" as a *final* achievement. Further growth potential is not envisaged beyond completion of the prearranged sequence for which a particular teacher is responsible. College courses are often clear examples of this process at work.	Always beings with direct inductive experiences with musical stimuli, always expanding the perceptual/conceptual refinements of students at their own rate to the point that deduction (understanding) becomes a potential for greater musical independence, and for more effective problem solving and decision making. Total or eventual growth potential is never artificially postulated and remains an open question depending on the interest and abilities of the student. Learning is not regarded as *final* or "covered."

more or fewer features, and they will respond to the features they perceive to different degrees. It is the perceptual apparatus guided by intelligence that provides the experiencing of stimuli which results in concepts. Therefore *it is not possible for any two children to have the same concepts of anything.* Their percepts have been different, their prior musical experiences in any case have been different, and various nonmusical attributes such as self-confidence are all different for each person. This is not to say that concepts held by people cannot be similar. Often they are. It is only when they are similar that we can meaningfully use a word to refer to the concept. Thus, even though people perceptually experience colors with qualitative differences, they often agree in identifying certain colors by name.

READINESS FOR MUSICAL INSTRUCTION

When all of these variables are taken into account—conceptual and perceptual differences, learning styles, and different teaching formats—it is obvious that music education requires considerable flexibility in order to be successful.

This flexibility can be controlled only by the teacher who has worked with and thus understands the *readiness* of individuals for certain musical learning, and the variety of readiness that any group will have. Here, three levels or conditions of readiness will be considered, keeping in mind that there are various shadings of readiness between and within these arbitrary groupings.

THREE READINESS LEVELS

Level I

The most *basic* or *preparatory level* will apply to those students, regardless of their age or accomplishments in other school activities, whose readiness in music is least developed. Such students will have had the least opportunity to develop informally those concepts that can make formal study most profitable, or they will have profited little from prior formal or informal experience. They are not behind! They have not failed anything! They need not be considered dumb or untalented! Their readiness for musical instruction is simply least developed.

Level II

This *intermediate level* will apply to those students whose readiness for formal musical instruction is realistically positive. By virtue of certain informal advantages they may have had at home, they are able to undertake instruction of a higher order than Level I youngsters. Their conceptual framework is established partially and requires increasing refinement and particularity. By whatever means, they come to you sufficiently well prepared to profit from musical instruction.

Level III

Students at this *high readiness level* are exceptionally prepared for formal instruction. They may have profited well from earlier experiences, or they may possess that elusive quality called talent. Therefore, they may be studying an instrument already or taking dance lessons, or may be otherwise involved in experiences that are conducive to their conceptual growth in music. They require a somewhat unique approach that varies from the norm represented by Level II and the preparatory stage represented by Level I.

These levels may be accommodated in two ways, depending on the circumstances. In more "open" teaching formats, which allow for various kinds of individualized instruction, these readiness levels can be used as they may apply in the teacher's judgment to certain groups of students. Therefore, just as students of different ages can be brought together to work on reading, arithmetic, or science, so they can find themselves regularly grouped according to their relative readiness for musical instruction. In less "open" circumstances the teacher can attempt to take these traits into consideration informally by planning lessons that are oriented to the level at which the majority of students in a class are found, and by making special provision for the others.

TEACHER GUIDELINES FOR RECOGNIZING MUSICAL READINESS LEVELS

Level I

Students cannot consistently match pitch easily. While they may be able to move to music, they have difficulty in successfully reflecting an understanding of meter. This also is detected in their difficulty strumming an autoharp or guitar with a constant or accurate pulse. Stories they make up to music they hear, moods or colors they suggest, often do not seem tangibly related to the music: they seem more like free flights of imagination rather than directly reflecting a perception of qualities heard in the music. They are not easily engaged and their minds wander: their attention may not be easily directed for more than very short periods of time to music or musical activities.

Level II

Students generally can match pitch without undue effort, although they may not yet be entirely consistent. More often than not they can determine that the music has a basic pulse of two or three, and they can move or strum with a constant pulse. They are usually able to verbalize stories and suggest adjectives, colors, or pictures that seem to clearly reflect elements perceived in the music they hear. While their attention is not necessarily engaged easily, they do not have much difficulty in tending to musical matters they find relevant; once their perceptions have been directed by the teacher, they are able to engage themselves for moderate periods of time in the attensive qualities of the musical stimuli or activity.

Level III

These students easily match pitch and learn songs quickly. Their rhythmic/metric movements are well coordinated and clearly reflect the pulse of the music. Their verbal responses to music are clear indications of the fact that they perceive the desired elements in the musical stimuli or activities that confront them. They are easily engaged by the attensive stimuli or activities at hand, and show genuine interest and enthusiasm for most of these musical contacts. They often study an instrument or dancing, or have avocational access to an instrument at home (e.g., piano, electronic organ, guitar).

All activities presented by the teacher should be conceived of and assigned in terms of these three increasingly refined levels of readiness. The teacher may use any level for a group of students depending on the judgment made of their readiness. One group might be generally able to handle Level II activities, while another might be better off working at Level I for a while. Also, within a grade or age group, some students may be working on activities from each of the three levels according to their readiness. Some students may be less ready in rhythmic/metric areas, depending perhaps on their conceptual understanding of arithmetic or their reading ability. They might profit more from Level I rhythmic activities for a while. But with other concepts—say, melody—they are more ready and thus can be working on Level II activities.

PRECAUTIONS

It would be a terrible mistake to envisage these levels as representing a hierarchy of success or failure. No such success or failure is implied, nor should such an impression be conveyed by the teacher. The arrangement into levels is intended to recognize the simple fact that people are different and at various times require tasks that correspond as closely as possible to their present needs and problems. Since there is no absolute or ultimate stage of attainment proposed, there can be no "falling behind" or failure.

Similarly, these levels should not be regarded as separate, self-contained entities that are mutually exclusive. The sensitive teacher will have no difficulty in arriving at "mutations" in the form of activities that "bridge" levels by achieving an overlapping degree of refinement. One basic activity can be so rearranged or altered by slight deletions or accretions that students with varying degrees of readiness can all be served by it. While it is likely that some students may eventually settle in either Level II or III, it is more likely that they will alternate between two levels, and on occasion fluctuate across three levels according to the variation of their readiness in different concept-areas of music.

MEETING STUDENTS' NEEDS

A prime benefit of the three-level approach is its use in facilitating those arrangements where students teach students and thus learn, reinforce, or ex-

tend what they already know. Level III students from time to time can be put with Level II students, one per group. No specific attempts or arrangements need be made to formalize this experience. Obviously the same opportunity exists for putting Level II students to work in Level I groups.

In this kind of teaching based on three levels of readiness, *flexibility and structure need not be antithetical.* In fact, in a successful program the two go hand in hand. *Flexibility* is provided by having access to ability groupings within a class. But each ability group can be *structured* according to its differing needs. This need not involve wholesale differences in the way the groups are assigned activities, in the various limitations given each group; the refinement expected of their products can vary according to the readiness level of the group.

This kind of planning is much simpler than trying to permanently arrange the components into an arbitrary or artificial hierarchy. *It is only necessary to persistently implement experiences within the same rather small number of concept-areas.* The transfer or connections students may make in their own minds can be aided by certain kinds of activity, by certain kinds of teacher questioning or guidance. But in the end, these connections will be just as unique to each individual as are the concepts that are so connected.

A BRIEF OUTLINE OF THE MAJOR CONCEPT-AREAS OF MUSIC

1. *Sound:* the sounds and sound qualities a composer chooses are a raw material that directly influence how we respond to music.
2. *Time:* music creates the impression of the passage of time that is different than real, clock-time.
3. *Sounds in succession:* because music occurs in time, tones follow one another.
   a. *Melody,* or linear succession of higher or lower sounds.
   b. *Meter,* or the division of musical succession into units of organization based on the number of pulsations in each unit.
   c. *Rhythm,* or the relative length or shortness of sounds within the units of organization established by meter.
   d. *Tempo,* or the impression of speed or slowness created by the composer's use of meter and rhythm.
4. *Sounds in combination:* tones also occur at the same time (i.e., simultaneously).
   a. *Timbre,* or the "tone color" created by the composer's combination of different sounds (instruments).
   b. *Texture,* or "density," due to the number and kinds of sounds used.
   c. *Simultaneity of sounds,* the pleasantness or resolution of harmonic combinations; or the clashing, active quality of nonharmonic combinations.
   d. *Dynamics,* or the relative loudness or softness within a composition resulting from the numbers of sounds used and how performers are directed to play.
5. *Unity and variety:* organizes successive and combined sounds into *logical* and *characteristic* musical forms.

    a. *Logical form,* a unique form that is self-sufficient in creating the appearance or organization.

    b. *Characteristic form,* general organizational formats that aid in aural organization through their familiarity, but which themselves are unique from piece to piece.

    c. *Unity,* which results from musical features that are repeated, or are recognized as similar or related.

    d. *Variety,* which results from the contrasting of musical features in order to maintain aural interest (e.g., an impression of newness or surprise).

    6. *Unity in variety:* results when musical elements are retained recognizably enough to unify, while being varied enough to create extra interest.

    7. *"Expression":* in one way or another, music "sounds as feelings feel" and embodies "felt life."

These concept-areas do *not* represent "the" concepts students are to learn. Each student can learn only "a" concept appropriate to his or her total readiness. As outlined here, these are broad, general *areas* of learning within which each student can manifest increasing growth of his or her *unique concept.* Thus concepts can have considerable similarity from person to person, but by their very nature they are qualitatively and quantitatively unique for each person. In this sense, a concept just "is" whatever it is: it is neither right nor wrong. It may be workable or not, appropriate in musical decision making or not. But it just "is." Teaching should facilitate the growth of workable concepts.

MUSICAL ACTIVITIES

The most consistently successful approach for insuring that all relevant concept-areas are encountered in relation to one another, and at the level of readiness of each student, is through actions that include large creative problem-solving or decision-making facets. *Musical learning is most concrete, complete, and successful when students manipulate, organize, and arrange or rearrange pitches, sounds, and silences into various kinds of expressive entities.* This kind of learning activity provides the most comprehensive basis of experience for learning, since more elements, more concept-areas are involved than in merely singing or playing, and they are related and working together. *From this creative center of action all other activities can be spun off.* Students can listen, sing, and play, and move to their own sound products. The study of already-composed music becomes seen by them as a vehicle for improving their own compositions.

This approach is most susceptible to varying kinds of instructional format. Students can work in large, moderate, or small groups, or can work independently. *It is difficult for a student to "fail" with this teaching format.* While accomplishment varies, the absence of absolutes in such manipulation of music allows every effort to result in some honest achievement that is conducive to feelings of success, or at least conducive to preventing feelings of failure.

MULTIPLE RESULTS

When the Action Learning approach is used within the various levels of readiness, each student can take away from the situation considerably different things. Yet each can progress along the same general lines, gradually refining concepts in his or her own way. No predetermined or arbitrarily imposed hierarchies are necessary.

Multiple results from various students or groups can fulfill the conditions or criteria of an activity equally. Nonetheless these results can also be unique to each individual in terms of refinement, sophistication, and creativity. Thus when some students or groups are still wrestling with the problem of achieving sufficient unity *and* variety in their works, others may already be striving to embody unity *in* variety in their works. Both kinds of results can satisfy the general intent of the instructional goals, yet each group or individual is allowed to manifest those differences that make music a useful vehicle for humanistic education.

MUSICAL INDEPENDENCE

It is important to realize that *only those students who find successful and practical (relevant) actualization of their needs and interests in music class will continue to seek musical learning and musical contacts.* All others—those who have been bored, failed, or frustrated—will "take it or leave it" outside of school activities. Action Learning *holds forth the most potential for inducing a lifelong desire for musical contact.* In fact, that is its premise! Activities involving music tend to impress on the student the "things" they can do with and through music and the "things" they can feel and "appreciate" in music. This is Action Learning at its best.

The kinds of musical activities recommended here put a premium on student involvement. *Students should not become dependent on the teacher for all learning.* The teacher facilitates musical learning by establishing activities through which students acquire it. If such musical learning is secure, it can and often will be continued and expanded. Then the Action Learning of a student grown into an adult becomes Continuing Education.

In lockstep curricula, students are dependent on the teacher for information, examples, and structure. When they leave the confines of the music class, they are lost. With the direct experience of an Action Learning format,

267

students can continue to grow and mature musically. As with the hobbyist, we tend to learn what we use and use what we learn. Such *musical independence is the ultimate goal of Action Learning* in general-music education. It is *not a finite goal, but an infinitely continuing search* on the part of successfully taught students for increased musical understanding and increased musical rewards. Nothing could be more rewarding than the realization that you have guided a student to such a condition of musical independence. Tests will never prove this:

> No real teacher will proceed on the basis of an examination that merely asks for answers. He will find a way to bring the independence of his student into play. He will devise a problem which in all probability the student has never seen before. In this way he will come to know not only the measure of acquired knowledge the student possesses but also the degree to which he understands how to use it.[1]

THE TEACHER'S RESPONSIBILITY TO EDUCATE, NOT TRAIN

A teacher's own educational experience provides a profound model upon which his or her attitudes, points of view, and life-orientation are based. These influences are often unconscious because teachers have not been led to analyze their own values and assumptions about education systematically. Often any challenge to a teacher's pet assumptions will result in rationalizations that serve to justify the continuation of what the teacher finds most comfortable to do. This is often determined by what teaching approach the individual had to use to survive student teaching. Having been successful in that situation, the approach is carried over unthinkingly into the teacher's first professional position.

CHANGE IN THE TEACHER'S ATTITUDES

Research of attitude development suggests very strongly that *any challenge to the consistency of our present belief-structure is strongly resisted.* Furthermore, "taking the path of least resistance" accurately characterizes the normal tendency to retain our present attitudes; we follow the least effortful path (even, often, in the face of failure—for to change would force the self-admission that we were wrong). Thus we persist in our old attitudes. *Only when we can clearly see a potential for less effort are we likely to change our attitudes.*[2]

Education, like any other "living" endeavor, must—or in any case does—keep changing in order to grow. Thus teachers whose attitudes were formed in another educational milieu, especially the latter years of college (and especially in schools or departments of music, which tend to be resistant to change), are likely to be always at least one step out of synchronization with recent advances.

Fortunately there are always those teachers—usually educational leaders and innovators, but always superior teachers—who manage to outgrow their own educational heritage and to thus transcend its limitations. The remaining vast majority of teachers have no difficulty articulating a litany of problems they experienced as students. But upon reaching the place in society where they could do something about these problems, they too often thoughtlessly allow themselves to become part of the continuing problem rather than of the solution.

NARROW TRAINING

When this happens in music education it is perhaps all the sadder, since many of the operations in the rest of the school are not usually conducive to the best interests of the musical art or its students (unless one happens to be in an enlightened, advanced school system). In the school, training in "tool skills" generally regarded as indispensable to the "practical" life of a fully functioning individual in society (reading, 'riting, 'rithmetic, rote, restraint, and regurgitation) is involved. This has been the major intent of all so-called "back to basics" movements and of new regulations in many states for "minimum competencies" as criteria for graduation.

This kind of *training,* however, should be considered as something quite different from the *education* that is involved in facilitating an understanding and appreciation of the fine arts. Training involves the acquisition—by force-feeding if necessary—of skills, facts, information, objective data, and the like, acquired by rote or by memorization. The focus of application for such learning is very narrow, usually the pursuit of a job or some other such specific survival value.

TRUE MUSIC EDUCATION

Education involves the broader and ultimately more important *freedom of mind* that allows us to ourselves seek and use (or sometimes decide not to use) certain training. If only training is featured, much that is learned is simply forgotten when the specific focus for which it was learned doesn't materialize or doesn't end up necessitating the learning. What do remain after such training is forgotten are the attitudes, values, and beliefs based upon such variables as how we were treated by our teachers in the pursuit of such training, how school socialized us without our knowing that it did so (the "hidden cur-riculum"), and above all, the typical teaching approaches based on the lecture-demonstration and other traditional forms of large-group instruction in which the teacher is regarded as an *authority figure*. This *social role*, you should note, is not necessarily the same as being an authority, as being *authoritative*. It more often results in *authoritarian* teaching. What is the dif-ference?

When a learner freely acknowledges the *authoritativeness* of a teacher, then that learner affirms *the need or desire for help* and the recognition that the teacher is a source of that help. If the teacher is unable to help or if the learner no longer wants or needs help, there no longer is the free acceptance of authoritative help that constitutes an *educational* transaction. Rightly or wrongly on the part of the student, educating is no longer possible, only train-ing that is force-fed. Thus the nature of educating is determined by what might be called the freely realized "help-requiringness" of the potential learner.

Training *can* fit into the design of a true education when a learner's help-requiringness takes the form of acknowledging a recommendation by the authoritative teacher that such training is needed. Thus, as long as such train-ing itself meets the criterion of help-requiringness, it can be justified without reservation.

The word "education" stems in part from the Latin *educere*, meaning "to draw out." In this sense "discipline" is best understood in terms of its root word (Latin *discipulus*, meaning "learner" or "pupil"), which refers to the fact of being a *disciple* to an *authoritative* teacher whom the learner freely acknowledges for the purpose of eliciting help. In such a setting, help-requiringness is the initiative, the motivation for personal discipline on the part of the learner; such discipline is not the result of arbitrary standards or force. Authoritarian teachers adopt the abstract authority of their *position* (role and title). The authority vested in the position is used in forcing students to submit to the *teacher's requirements*. Authoritative teachers are recognized by learners as authorities who can meet to some significant degree the *students' requirements*, i.e., their help-requiringness, their expressed goals. The au-thoritative teacher needs only to "draw out" that natural student interest or need, not "put upon" the student a host of teacher's demands or needs.

In the case of music and the arts, this need not even be a process of "draw-ing out." It need be only a "leading out" of the values and interests that naturally attract young people to music, and a "seeking out" of the standards, needs, and requirements that are natural to the musical art. Thus educating is distinguished by the existence of noncoercive, nonthreatening conditions of learning. If the learner does not enter the learning transaction *willingly* and in-stead only submits *unwillingly* to the authoritarianism of the teacher, there is no educating. Learning of some kind may result, but properly regarded it is schooling or training and not educating. And it is predictably very short-term, for once the authoritarian presence of the teacher is removed the student ceases to "toe the line."

As you can see, then, the main purpose of a public school program of Action Learning in general music is *not* to *train* specific musical skills and knowledge. That, like so much of the training involved in all subjects throughout our own schooling, would inevitably be forgotten if only through lack of use. What Action Learning in general music seeks instead is the kind of education that can never be forgotten because it will or can be, consciously or naturally, *used* by the learner in daily life now and as an adult.

Felix Greene, an educational commentator, has assessed the main tasks of education and has provided many significant ideas which can be interpreted as they might apply to an education in music.[3]

1. The acquiring of technical skills, however useful, is not a true education. Education, in part, may be acquired through using such skills, but it is *not the same* as acquiring them. Albert Einstein warned, "Education is what remains after we have forgotten everything we were taught." Such forgotten learning is the result of training and not of education.

2. The acquisition of so-called culture is not true education. When our so-called historical heritage is taught technically—that is, with emphasis on facts, on information—it is lost as soon as the technical details are forgotten. A true education leads a student to understand and appreciate a culture. This would be a broad, internalized result—not a narrow, factual one. It would bring the past to life in the "now."

3. Intellectual cleverness in the sense of well-honed intellectual skill for its own sake is not true education. True education uses intellect to freely determine the course of one's life. It leads to the freedom to live a fully rewarding, self-actualized life.

4. True education has, as its major and constant concern, individual freedom: the freedom to be unique. True education, in a sense, liberates the individual to perceive things as they really are, not as he or she is trained unthinkingly or unknowingly to *accept* them.

5. The acquiring of knowledge *for its own sake* is not true education. Therefore, grades, credits, examinations, and diplomas are all irrelevant to the concerns of an enduring education. An education, in whatever area of human endeavor, results in habits, dispositions, and abilities that influence the quality of one's life. Too much of *schooling* amounts to the kind of training that is not educating because it is so easily forgotten no matter what final examination was passed, no matter what grade was "earned," no matter whether or not a diploma was awarded.

6. Education is not harmful in any way, nor does it increase a student's fears, misapprehensions, or negative self-image. These all destroy the opportunity for independent thinking which is the major benefit of an education: the ability to arrive at freely chosen paths knowingly and without the fear of being different, and the freedom to be conventional without the fear of being a conformist. Musical choices involve just such decisions daily.

7. The personal, human problems experienced by people—especially young people—are not solved by technical know-how or intellectual cleverness. In fact these may be the source of some of these problems. Instead, "wisdom" based upon broad and freely chosen experiences of real and lasting effect is the potential cure for human problems. Wisdom is the result of individual freedom. No amount of facts, information, or technical training can provide the kind of wisdom fruitful to people in forging for themselves a rich, musically involved life. Educating in terms of increasing students' experiences nurtures young people "wise" beyond their years.

8. Much of conventional education emphasizes knowledge for its own sake—most of which is forgotten. This emphasis leads to an *unreal* kind of thinking perhaps best represented by the stereotypical "intellectual" who is "out of touch with reality" or so high in his "ivory tower" that reality is but a distant annoyance that gets in the way of the fun of mental games. Such unreal thinking by teachers is the root cause of the vast majority of misbehavior that arises in music classes. Young people crave the kind of personal relevance that Action Learning provides in assisting them to establish self-identity.

9. Forcing young people to acquire knowledge that is abstract and irrelevant to them, or to any reality they can predict, results in their resenting it. This leads to their disinclination to *think*, when it is precisely this process—thinking in its broadest sense (rather than simply remembering information)—that is at the basis of a significant education. Though musical responses of the kind that constitute a general education are not the result of thinking in the sense of logical, cognitive thought, they are the result of thinking in the sense of applying the mind to aurally perceiving music and being aware of its effect. This capacity for conscious self-reflective thought arises during preadolescence. To willfully or benignly ignore it insures that your efforts at a musical education will fail, especially in the long-term Action Learning sense.

10. Much of the most valuable or harmful learning of a child's life occurs before he reaches school age, i.e., in the home. Among the most valuable things a school can do is to allow the youngster the freedom of his or her own feelings and thinking. The most harmful role is to even further delimit this freedom of feeling and thinking. Since music involves both feeling (affects) and thinking (cognitions), education in music has everything to gain from putting thinking at the service of an enriched capacity to feel. And with this should come an increased individuation enabling the person to recognize his or her *uniqueness* in counterpoint to the emphasis much of the rest of schooling gives to *sameness*.

11. Even though a major part of a child's learning occurs at home before school age, what the child experiences and learns in school will be a significant factor in his life then and later as an adult. If he comes to hate music *class*, it is not unlikely that he will consider himself to be unmusical or to hate *music*, regardless of home influence. Similarly, regardless of the paucity of positive musical influence in the home, an education in music in school can have a lasting positive influence on musical choices in adult life.

12. An education seeks to preserve and encourage a student's individual freedom, and to remove or avoid fears. A truly educated student, as an adult, will be free to live a full life within the positive framework of continuing personal growth. Where education in music pursues this course we can expect that some form of significant musical involvement will be one of the factors that contribute to such a more fully actualized life.

ATTITUDES AS THE GOAL OF AN EDUCATION IN MUSIC

The essential goals of an education in music involve far less the kinds of facts, information, skills, and technical training so often involved—for better or worse—in other sectors of public schools. Such things are useful to some degree; but they are not useful in, by, and for themselves. They are useful only to the degree that they enhance and facilitate the individual's ability to respond fully to music.

As a result of an over-emphasis on singing in music classes, many adults are led to rationalize, "I enjoy music, but I can't carry a tune in a paper bag," as if enjoying music and being able to sing were the same thing. Other adults, whose music classes have emphasized facts and information in the abstract pursuit of "understanding," are led to remark, "I enjoy music, but I don't understand it," as though music were something similar to a technical manual, to be understood before it can be meaningful or enjoyable.

Music is more like a sunset: even when its physical or technical bases are understood, they really do not lead to a greater *apprehending* of its *beauty*. In fact, we can appreciate its beauty *as though we did not understand* its bases in the same way as we can love someone without truly understanding that person. It may be precisely because we do not totally understand the person—we cannot predict the person's every move—that we find a certain mystery, a certain aura, an uncertainty and resulting excitement, and thus are able to sustain interest and love.

Therefore, what remains of a public school education in music will be attitudinal. In psychological terms, an *attitude* is "the *set* of 'predispositions to respond in a particular way toward some particular class of stimuli' " (in our case, musical stimuli); attitudes are "predispositions to respond in a particular way toward a specified class of objects"[4] (i.e., the musical "objects" of music education). Thus music education must concern itself most assuredly with instruction that results in some degree of positive or favorable "predispositions to respond in a particular way" to music.

The "predispositions to respond in a particular way" does not here mean that you set out to condition such responses. It means nurturing a favorable outlook on music, to seek involvement with it and personal enrichment from it. Therefore, attitude education in music involves facilitating the *likelihood* that students will now and in their adult lives have a positive attitude toward music and thereby seek musical contacts. This, in sum, is what Action Learning is all about.

NURTURING POSITIVE ATTITUDES IN THE GENERAL MUSIC CLASS

A program of education *with* (not merely about) music, one that is designed with attitudinal development foremost in mind, has an excellent chance of effecting some permanent change. At the very least, the goal of such a program should be to enhance the freedom of students to choose music as an avocational pursuit to some degree or another. No amount of facts, information, or technical training will accomplish this alone.

In fact, such technical information and training for its own sake is guaranteed to breed apathy and disinterest at best, resentment and resistance or rebellion at worst. Only those technical aspects of music that enhance musical perception should be the focus of an Action Learning program since aural perception is the most available application of musical learning to life. Beyond that, individual students who are gratified by some skilled aspect of music, such as singing or playing instruments, should be encouraged and assisted in that pursuit. While all students should not be expected to have such interests or talents as an outlet for *their* musical involvement, they *can be* expected to become more perceptive listeners.

At the very least, then, Action Learning in general music seeks to nurture the predisposition for listening to music, and it works at increasingly refining the accuracy and scope of students' perceptions of music. But being predispositions, attitudes "are not directly observable or measurable. Instead they are inferred from the way we react to particular stimuli."[5] Therefore it is not enough to believe or hope that your teaching activities have automatically resulted in the intended changes of attitude you sought. You must be more certain. You must create many opportunities to observe students' attitudes through the way they react to your activities. This, too, is the basis of Action Learning: the more and wider the scope of musical experiences, the greater the breadth of students' responses in the future.

Attitudes fall broadly into three categories of somewhat different types: cognitive, affective, and behavioral. These arbitrary distinctions help distinguish between attitudes and the conditions that create them.

Attitudes based on *cognitions* "include perceptions, concepts, and beliefs about the attitude object"[6] that might be referred to loosely as *opinions*. They rest on information, misinformation, or misinterpreted information and predispose a person to respond in a certain way.

The *affective component* of attitudes deals more with "feelings," usually perceived in a very diffuse, general way. *These are not easily changed by means of direct explanation or coercion.* They are unconscious or preconscious to some degree. Because they seem to be mediated by the right hemisphere the individual is not explicitly aware of the nature or degree of the feelings that are significantly influencing his or her attitudes. Early adolescents, moving to or through the most feeling-laden time of their lives, are certainly not immune from the effect of such affects. Indeed, this condition is probably the major basis for the attitude problems that arise in music classes! There is no explicit cognition involved in their negative or resisting attitude. It is simply their *feelings* which disincline them from a more positive attitude toward music class. Obviously the feelings behind such negative attitudes are the result, in large part, of past music classes.

The *behavioral component* of attitudes involves overt actions that usually result from holding a certain attitude under certain conditions. These actions are not of major importance, except perhaps if they constitute certain kinds of misbehavior in school or home situations. Some of the overt misbehavior (e.g., unruliness, "standing up" to the teacher) may stem from certain deeply seated attitudes held toward authority figures. However, since it is the interrelation of the various kinds of attitude components that determines the basic attitudinal problem, it seems likely that such overt behavior stems mainly from cognitive or affective factors.

Thus we look mainly to cognitive and affective components of attitudes for insight in solving the challenge of nurturing positive attitudes in or as a result of music classes. *Positive feelings nurture, the growth of positive attitudes* and open the door to other possibilities, namely, the increasing ability or willingness to master those cognitions which in turn make possible even more, or more powerful, positive feelings. *Positive feelings arise when students' musical or personal goals are satisfied,* or when they are equally accepting of the teacher's goals for them.

Negative feelings lead to no learning or negative learning. If the teacher can by whatever means—luck, exorcism, prayer, or determined effort—devise and carry out activities that effectively generate positive feelings, the door is open. At first these feelings may not be directly related to students' musical goals. Personal interest or challenge, the opportunity to suceed at something, or other growth-typical needs often need to be addressed before authentic musical goals arise in students' minds. Whatever the "foot in the door" may be, it is the only real opportunity the teacher has to make a start along the road to positive attitudes.

Be clear on one fact. Adolescents—early or late ones—do not enter your classes attitude-free. They most definitely come to you with well-developed attitudes toward music and music classes. In addition they have a host of attitudes unrelated to music—attitudes toward teachers in general, music teachers, authority figures, and so on. You must deal with these attitudes, neutralizing the negative or nonproductive ones as best you can, and enhancing, extending, or refining the positive or productive ones.

If this means "catering to" students to some degree, then that is what you must do *at first.* Somehow the idea of catering to students has gotten a bad press, although it seems that catering is exactly what the process of education should involve: meeting as many individual needs, interests, learning styles, and readiness patterns as is possible. The teacher's musical interests should be subordinate to the growth needs of students, and it is axiomatic that you must "begin where they are."

But too many teachers never go much farther; and as it turns out too often, potentially favorable attitudes are never sustained unless profitable, new, interesting, and challenging things are continually introduced into the picture. Then the student can feel that something relevant has happened that he or she would not otherwise have been able to know, do, or feel.

One other element is required, and this is the simple fact that positive attitudes arise and are dependent to some degree or another upon the student's feeling of *success. Failure motivates only the student who already has both a positive attitude and goals that urge him on in the face of what he considers to be only a temporary setback.* To such a frequently successful student, certain periodic failures to reach his goals are foreseeable and acceptable.

But for the student whose initial attitude is negative, doubting, or at best neutral, *feelings of success are especially important in inspiring the positive feelings that motivate positive attitudes.* However, success has little potency unless certain conditions are fulfilled. First, the activity must be regarded by students as *sufficiently important or relevant to warrant their desire to succeed.* Otherwise, an "I could care less" attitude will dull any potential good side-effects of success. Remember, at first this need not especially be a *musical success.* But as soon as possible the rewards of success should become increasingly musical.

A second condition of success is that *the activity must be sufficiently challenging.* No matter how relevant the activity is, success achieved too easily—without any effort, without some degree of "risk" involved—will not be regarded very highly, especially by students ten to eighteen years of age who are "turned on" particularly by realistic challenges to their newly developing mental powers. Potential *excitement* is involved in a challenge. Dangle the carrot just far enough and they will perceive the challenge as interesting and realistic. Dangle it too far and the challenge becomes a threat, which inhibits any serious response at all.

Much pre- and early teenage behavior—including misbehavior—is motivated by the excitement or daring of just such challenge in the face of certain risks such as punishment or other forms of teacher disapproval. Even when a teacher is willing to "up the ante" by increasing the risk (i.e., inviting misbehavior by authoritarian coercion), some student will call the teacher's bluff. If it was a bluff, students quickly learn that the teacher will not hold good on such threats. If the threat was not a bluff, a confrontation ensues. The teacher, operating from the lofty position of *abstract* authority (i.e., authority granted by higher-ups rather than *earned* in the eyes of students) usually thinks that he or she has "won" such a confrontation. But this is *never* the case!

The teacher, and inevitably the study of music, will *always* be the loser. Attitudes are not enhanced by such battles won through the exercise of abstractly granted *power! Students must respect a teacher as a person* (or as an authoritative source of help) rather than the *power* granted with the *role* of "teacher" (i.e., authoritarian control). The power you should seek is the power of music. Employ it to attract, develop, and sustain increasingly positive attitudes. Otherwise, regardless of which side "wins," *confrontation always results in a heightening of general antagonism and in the worsening of attitudes.*

It is precisely circumstances such as these that harden certain students' negative attitudes toward teachers, adults in general (e.g., parents), and authority or power figures. It is precisely confrontations like these that equally harden the attitudes of those teachers who increasingly come to regard all but a few students—especially in the early years of adolescence—as "animals," basically evil, out to get teachers, or at least as unmotivated and unwilling to cooperate.

Among all factors, perhaps none is so pervasive as this increasing hardening of the "self-fulfilling prophecy" concerning pre- and early adolescents. Many preservice teachers tremble at the specter of teaching this age group. Some inservice teachers react as if they were banished to Siberia if they are reassigned to teach junior high or middle school. Official "school disciplinarians" often handle discipline problems with the mentality of prison wardens. Yet daily hundreds of teachers, of their own free will, choose to teach this age group especially because of the energy, the spontaneity, the expressiveness, the enthusiasm of which these young people are capable *when taught by teachers who understand and accept their growth-typical characteristics.*

Until *you* understand, accept, and appreciate this age group for what it is, you have little chance of engendering positive attitudes in those toward whom you harbor (however unconsciously) negative, suspicious, or fearful attitudes and expectancies. Thus any *preexisting prejudice by teachers against students inevitably promotes instructional failure!* Further, it promotes exactly the unhappy kinds of teachers who hate what they are doing and often end up unconsciously hating themselves.

All this said, we can now turn to a consideration of planning for musical growth; to suggestions for efficiently and effectively implementing such plans; and to discussion of what to do when things go wrong—the inevitable occurrence of misbehavior.

PRINCIPLES AND PROBLEMS OF TEACHER PLANNING

Some commentators have lamented the growing standardization of teaching procedures, and have shown even more alarm at the standardization of attitudes among teachers themselves. Teachers, too, are hemmed in by rules and regulations enforced coercively by the leadership structure of schools (including, not incidentally, unions).

> So long as the teachers themselves are not independent from societal pressures exerted on them, it will be extremely difficult to convert the schools into oases of truthfulness in a desert of erroneous ideas and false values. And right now the schools themselves are shining beacons for conformity![7]

To the degree that teachers may in fact be losing their sense of autonomy, self-direction, and self-confidence, such tendencies toward teacher conformity are unfortunate: "Good teaching, which to be good must be creative and largely spontaneous, cannot long survive in an atmosphere in which conformity to regulations and to set patterns plays so dominant a part."[8]

CREATIVITY AND SPONTANEITY IN TEACHING

Much is said and written about teaching being creative, but so often the emphasis is placed on the wrong aspect of teaching. There are two major aspects to teaching: (1) the act of planning instruction and (2) the act(s) of executing those plans. Creativity in teaching is often attributed only to the invention of creative lessons or activities. While such creativity is surely necessary and will not be disputed, it does not amount to creative teaching. The best-made plans will fail miserably unless the teacher is able to translate the abstract plans into the concrete experiences and learning of the actual lesson itself. Creativity in teaching is fully actualized in the *execution* of lessons just as musical perform-ance is creative in the execution of a score.

In order for the execution phase of teaching to be creative, *it must be to a large degree spontaneous.* "Spontaneous" as used here should not be con-fused with "playing it be ear" or "winging it." No indeed, this is not the case! This, in fact, is the great failure evidenced by so many so-called natural teachers, who appear to be gifted with a certain intuitive ability to improvise *successful-looking* lessons. Their problem stems from the fact that while a lesson may *appear* on the surface to be truly creative, seldom do any two or more lessons have much direct relationship to one another. What learning may occur in a single successful lesson is hit-or-miss. Any relationships that arise between such separate successful lessons are also left largely up to chance.

Teaching can and should be spontaneous if it is regarded as a kind of *im-provisation around a given, preplanned format.* This format is the behavioral objectives that serve as the bases for the class. A behavioral objective applies only to one lesson or activity, has a clearly specified overt outcome that can be observed as an indication of success, and has equally well specified conditions from which the overt responses should arise.

The daily behavioral objective is drawn from or related to the long-term, more structured curriculum that gives direction and meaning by establishing clear relationships between otherwise separate activities or lessons. Such a hypothetical curriculum, specified also in behavioral terms and with suggested means of organization and record keeping, is provided in Appendix A to serve as a model for you. Even the tremendously gifted teacher profits much from the overall organization, structure, thrust, and transfer of learning made possi-ble by a curriculum of this kind.

Such a curriculum allows the teacher to implement any given activity drawn from it in a creative, spontaneous, and improvisatory manner. Thus a given class may look quite informal, but in the teacher's mind it has its very in-dividual and specific niche in the overall scheme of things. Sticking too closely to a daily lesson plan when you should be flexible, planning too far in ad-vance, or being generally too structured in following the steps or procedures you originally had in mind are all *faults of being too plan-bound.*

A teacher, therefore, should *not* standardize his or her own teaching pro-cedure, should *not* fit such teaching into a preexisting recommended or recognized standardized teaching *mold.* What is needed to organize daily teaching efforts is a general curriculum specified in terms of overtly observable behavior. Then, with this as background and support, the teacher should thoughtfully experiment with and evolve a basic kind of teaching format that allows teaching strengths to be most successfully employed in a spontaneous and improvisatory style. This basic format is not a fixed, inflexible, inalterable one. It is simply a basic "style" that is unique to the teacher's personality, teaching strengths, situation (classroom, nature of students, etc.), and goals. Over time, this style or teaching personality will evolve to take into consideration ever-new teaching ideas, new goals, the changing nature of students, and new "content" of musical instruction.

ADVANTAGES OF AN ECLECTIC APPROACH

Proponents of the single-minded methods that employ truly *standardized teaching formulas* are fond of criticizing so-called eclectic teaching as though being eclectic and being sloppy or disorganized were synonymous. As truly humanistic teachers know,[9] this is patent falsehood! Truly humanistic teachers,

> will be open to the experience of each new class encountered and will let the situation and all that is in it, including themselves and their students, influence the choice of teaching techniques, rather than slavishly adhering to some predetermined mode of instruction.[10]

The kind of humanistically eclectic teaching recommended here involves the original meaning of the word "eclectic," namely, collecting or selecting the best from diverse sources (from the Greek, *eklektikos*). It also is realistic in several ways that "cookbook" methods are not. (1) It takes the unique characteristics of the teacher—his or her personality, teaching strengths and weaknesses, and life-situation (e.g., time available for planning outside of school)—and makes possible a teaching style based upon *a real human being.*[11] (2) It similarly takes into consideration the unique aspects of the teaching-learning situation (e.g., the school's physical environment, the nature of the students, their readiness, and the socioeconomic climate of the community). These are real considerations. (3) Such an approach is not predicated on the possession of special teaching equipment, or upon long intensive training in the application of a single "method" devised by someone else. From the best of all teaching "methods" *the individual teacher evolves a "method" of his or her own*—one that is understood very well, because the teacher is the creator of it. (4) Finally, this eclectic approach not only provides a structure that is often ignored by critics, but it provides a *better structure* than mono-methods. Its structure is flexible, able to truly bend as required by the unique characteristics of the student clientele served. With the inflexible mono-method, heaven help the student who misses several weeks of school, or who transfers into the school after several years in a school using a different method.

Planning for Action Learning should allow the teacher to draw fully upon accumulated musical insight, almost unconsciously, for use almost as an inspired creation or at an inspired moment. Nothing is left out because the lesson plan was not approached as a research project of finding and organizing information (e.g., "units") or because a crucial item was mistakenly not included in the lesson plan. But teaching for Action Learning is not really intuitive either. It is intended to draw spontaneously upon deeply ingrained resources, while using the cognitive framework or skeleton of the curriculum, daily lesson plan, and behavioral objective as the basis around which the improvisation is organized.

This kind of teaching is no more unstructured than jazz; and those who accuse either of involving mere "fooling around," of being "expression without discipline," are not only foolishly misinformed but do a grave disservice to both activities. Both, in their own ways, are an art, both are a performance.

FLUIDITY VS. RIGIDITY

This eclectic style is especially recommended for pre- and early adolescents because it is adventuresome, exciting, and "real." It encourages serendipity as a genuine teaching resource. An absolute axiom for working with young adolescents is: *Thou shalt not be predictable!* Eclectic teaching not only is not predictable (except in the broad dimensions of its major outcomes), it is downright *fluid*. Fluidity is the highest quality you can seek, for it is most characteristic of the course of real life.

What is fluid, of course, flows; and fluidity in teaching is characterized by the flowing together of otherwise diverse elements in a natural way. Flux is, similarly, characterized by a melting together or fusing of previously separate elements. This kind of flexibility or flux is often symbolized in the Orient by the willow branch, which bends under weight; it "gives" under pressure but is able to flex back to its original position once normal conditions are reached. The branches of stiff, inflexible trees, on the other hand, try to rigidly support, or bear up under, weight or pressure. If the pressure is great, they snap! Water is a prime symbol, too, since it flows over, around, and sometimes through things, slowly wearing away resistances and shaping them gradually through its natural energy.

These are useful metaphors or models for teaching. A teacher should not be committed before the fact to a hard-and-fast structure that, unlike the willow, cannot bend under pressure. Whether this pressure is some abstract desire to stick to a plan or formula, or whether it arises from the nature of students' responses at the moment, the teacher—and the structure—can bend *without breaking, without snapping.* Losing one's temper or becoming frustrated or impatient are all signs of an overly rigid approach.

Similarly, teaching should be a manifestation of a psychological energy similar to the physical energy of water. The course of learning should flow around resistances, gradually wearing them away and shaping them gradually according to the nature of the resistance (i.e., each teaching problem, each student misbehavior problem) and the nature of the energy itself (i.e., the teacher's uniqueness). No activity, method, or approach will be instantly successful, and teachers must sustain their goals and ideals until, like water, they slowly wear down student resistance and break through student apathy!

Even though schooling is formal (in distinction to the "informal" education a student receives in out-of-school experiences) a teaching-learning structure need not be rigid or inflexible. Where learning seems "natural," what is learned can be used in life more "naturally." *This sense of naturalism or realism must be at the very heart of Action Learning.* Thus the challenge is to set up enough structure (teacher control, preliminary organization, etc.) to maintain the direction of the formal educational plan (the curriculum) while at the same time permitting the fluidity most characteristic of daily life.

PERMISSIPLINE: CREATIVE TENSION

A teacher has another option beyond either enforcing strict *discipline or being permissive.* Imposed discipline puts the teacher too much in control,

Fig. 5:2

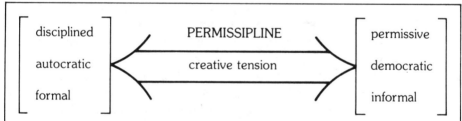

A once-and-for-all balance is neither sought nor expected. At times the creative tension will feel a stronger pull from one direction, then another. A *permanent* "compromise" or balance is impossible; and even if it were possible, it would result in complacency and predictability, neither of which is a desired state of mind in teaching-learning.

This is not a description of a battle scene or a power relationship. It describes the quite-natural way we deal with polarities every day of our lives. Freedom vs. control, individual vs. society, Self vs. not-Self, husband vs. wife, adult vs. child—all of these are subject to such a give-and-take relationship. In each case, a hard-and-fast rigidly upheld prior position will often lead to a break: a psychological one (breakdown) or an external one (breakup). This is not a description of something "ideal." It describes the "reality" which anyone can confirm by introspection and thought.

281

while permissiveness allows students more control than they can often handle. The best teaching involves some measure of both discipline and permissiveness in an ever-shifting balance or even creative tension (see Fig. 5:2). The term *permissipline* has been coined to describe this condition, the condition that rejects an "either/or" posture.[12]

A MUSIC CURRICULUM

The arrangement and total effect of musical activities or experiences that you provide for your students constitutes your curriculum. It is *not* some abstract "subject matter" or "content" you "cover." You do not *directly teach* a curriculum. You teach *with* your curriculum. Your curriculum is what you have your students *do* in actively experiencing music. Its effect is the synergic total of these experiences on students' abilities to respond as fully to music as their assets will allow. The effect of a curriculum is seen in what *students* are able *to do* as a result of instruction.

Because people vary so greatly in their musical potential and in most other ways, *a curriculum is not established in separate stages or levels.* This would infer that certain concepts should be "taught" or "learned" at a given time, in a certain order, once and for all. If they are not, the student has "fallen behind," has "failed" to progress the predetermined amount in the time period set. *Rather, the curriculum should be somewhat open-ended and spiraling.*

Create broad conceptual and perceptual goals (see Appendix A) that you know all students are likely to be able to achieve in some measure. Your efforts for the first years will be only "educated guesses." Each year they will need to be improved in light of your experiences—i.e., by considering how well students managed the existing version. Such a curriculum will give direction to instruction because all students work toward the same general goals. But it is more *open in terms of the degree of quality or quantity of results you expect.* As long as each child continues to grow, the curriculum is spiral. It returns again and again to the same few concept-areas and thereby gradually expands and refines students' concept-growth in each area. The teacher attempts to maximize quantity and quality to whatever degree is reasonable with given students or classes, without expecting uniform, lockstep results from each student (see Fig. 5:3).

IMPLEMENTING A CURRICULUM

1. The teacher creates the structure of a learning situation, and an environment that together have the anticipated result of musical growth toward a goal selected from among those prespecified in the curriculum.

LOCKSTEP CURRICULUM

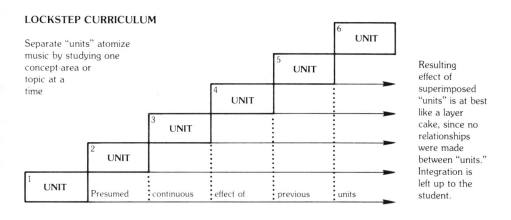

Separate "units" atomize music by studying one concept-area or topic at a time

Resulting effect of superimposed "units" is at best like a layer cake, since no relationships were made between "units." Integration is left up to the student.

SPIRAL CURRICULUM

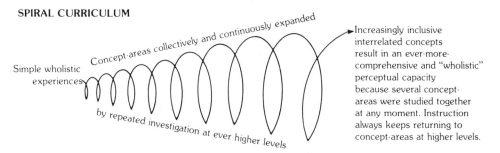

Simple wholistic experiences

Concept-areas collectively and continuously expanded by repeated investigation at ever higher levels

Increasingly inclusive interrelated concepts result in an ever-more-comprehensive and "wholistic" perceptual capacity because several concept-areas were studied together at any moment. Instruction always keeps returning to concept-areas at higher levels.

Fig. 5:3

2. The teacher also must set a problem or challenge in terms of the students' participation in an Action Learning experience designed to enhance musical growth in the desired direction.

3. Once fluidly set in motion, the activity largely moves under its own energy as fueled by student interest and involvement with music and by the teacher's guidance.

4. The teacher intervenes only to guide, observe, redirect attention; to calm things down when enthusiasm bubbles over.

5. The teacher encourages self-evaluation, and in turn evaluates both achievement and students' self-evaluation of their achievement.

6. On these bases, new experiences are planned at ever higher or more complex levels of refinement so that each student can rise up to *his or her own level* of attainment.

PLANNING AND BEHAVIORAL OBJECTIVES

Curricula are implemented by means of behavioral objectives. *Such objectives state the intended results of instruction in terms of changes in the frequency of the behaviors specified.* Further, Action Learning objectives will result in musical behaviors that are as close as possible to ways in which music can be used in daily life, or that clearly are an inducement to such continuing use.

The benefits of this approach are great.

The students:
1. See directly the fruits of their work, and are increasingly inclined to work when something realistically rewarding and concrete seems to have been accomplished.
2. Are provided with a kind of feedback that makes increased learning more likely and leads to increased musical independence.

The teacher profits:
1. By observing how successfully the students have used their cognitions and skills, and how their feeling-responses are becoming more refined.
2. By being able to plan accordingly on the basis of these overt indications of progress and student growth.

Overt behavior in and by itself, especially on a one-time basis, is not a reliable indicator of musical learning. Unless some special effort is made to encourage certain mental processes (*covert* musical behaviors), overt responses can be misleading. For this reason behavioral objectives for music classes seek to isolate and *cognitively strengthen the covert musical behaviors* that are being emphasized in a certain lesson. These, in turn, are evaluated by having such mental processes result in some overt musical behavior. *Overt results provide evidence from which covert (mental) processes are inferred.*

The purpose of a lesson is the *covert musical behavior* that is elicited. Except in performance classes, then, the mental process represents the *goal* of instruction. The *overt or observable musical response* is the *means* by which the inner mental activity is demonstrated.

FORMAT FOR WRITING BEHAVIORAL OBJECTIVES

Behavioral objectives specify the factors "given" in the learning environment, and the criteria or proficiency that you, the teacher, and your students should accept as concrete evidence of learning. Therefore, behavioral objectives, in order to be most useful, should specify the following information:

1. *Given* factors: materials, time limitations, and other such *factors that you wish to control.* This can sometimes be left open, or student freedom can be mixed with teacher control when this suits your instructional goals.
2. *Who* will be influenced by instruction: the entire class as a large group; all the individuals in the class; smaller groups (specify the number when possible).
3. *Covert musical behaviors* you wish to elicit. The whole range of covert behaviors (divided into three categories) is listed on page 285. Simply choose from this list of cognitive, affective, and psychomotor behaviors the *one* you intend to elicit.
4. *What content or concept-area* is at stake: form, timbre, melody, a mood response, a feeling-response, etc. This aspect of an objective specifies *what is to be learned as a covert musical behavior.* You can choose this from the section on concept-areas earlier in this chapter (page 265–266).
5. *By what overt means* accomplishment will be judged. The word "by" in an objective usually insures that the student will demonstrate his or her mastery of the content as an inner, covert musical behavior *by doing something.* This objective involves your choosing from the three categories of overt behaviors listed on page 285 (verbal; making or doing; performance) the one most suitable to the content at hand.

6. *Criteria of proficiency:*list those requirements by which the success of the products, or overt behaviors, that result from the activity can be judged. The more advanced the activity is, the more specific the criteria can be. *Activities intended mainly to elicit feeling-responses should have no criteria other than the implied one that a response should occur.*

7. *Other:* Certain other requirements or conditions may be added at the end of an objective. These usually involve subsequent use of the product through performance, discussion, etc. If these additional aspects are substantial enough in themselves, a separate behavioral objective may be in order.

Covert Musical Behaviors

Cognitive	Affective	Psychomotor
perceiving	responding intuitively	hearing inwardly (with
analyzing	interpreting freely	the inner ear)
comprehending (under-	preferring	attending to cues
standing)	enjoying	monitoring oneself
remembering	characterizing in terms of	following instructions
identifying	feelings	fixating in practice;
comparing	creating in subjective	refining
differentiating	terms	coordinating acts and
evaluating	choosing on the basis of	cues
judging	feelings	acquiring speed
synthesizing		lessening time
(combining)		perfecting (normalizing)

Cognitive behaviors involve those basically left-hemisphere mental activities associated with consciousness and concept development; *affective* behaviors involve inner feeling-responses, subjective responses; *psychomotor* behaviors involve those mental steps involved in a musical performance or movement skill. Covert behaviors are, therefore, *mental actions* or processes. A more complete description of each of these, and their importance, can be found in the next chapter. For a fuller description, along with exercises to aid you in understanding these behaviors, see Regelski, *Principles and Problems of Music Education,* chapters 7 and 8 (cited fully in note 12).

Overt Musical Behaviors

Verbal	Making or Doing	Performance
speaking	composing	playing instruments
writing	creating	singing (use of voice)
	arranging	conducting
	organizing into some-	moving to music
	thing new	dancing
	notating	

These *observable actions* are used to indicate to some degree the appropriateness of a student's inner *mental actions,* his or her *covert responses.* In and by themselves overt acts are not the goal of instruction: they are the proof that covert learning has occurred. They show what a student *can do* as a result of instruction. They involve the *use* of learning: students who learn by using are more likely to use what they learn. A fuller description of these overt behaviors and their importance can be found in the next chapter. For a complete description, along with exercises to aid you in understanding these behaviors, see Regelski, *Principles and Problems of Music Education,* chapters 7 and 8.

285

Behavioral objectives can be specified in outline form using the format given earlier. This is most suitable, especially when you are beginning to design and use behavioral objectives, since it insures that you will not leave out one of the crucial parts. The example that follows demonstrates how each provision of the outline is used to arrive at an objective that is completely stated—even though sometimes in a complex or inelegant manner:

[1. *Given*] "Given a choice of either wooden or metallic sounds and fifteen minutes of preparation

[2. *Who*] each group of three students prearranged as a learning group

[3. *Covert*] will *differentiate* [covert behavior chosen from the cognitive list]

[4. *What*] between A, B, and C sections according to factors other than timbre [this is the "content" of the lesson—what is being learned by use]

[5.] *by* composing [chosen from the overt-behavior list; a "making" action] a planned improvisation sound composition

[6. *Criteria of proficiency*] at least one and a half minutes long, in ABACA form, with each contrasting section made clear by varying pitch, rhythm/meter, volume, and texture or density,

[7. *Other*] and by performing for and discussing with the class how they achieved the contrasting sections."

You will notice that the above formulation results in a sentence if read from top to bottom. As you become more proficient in writing behavioral objectives, you may want to write them directly as a sentence, and only use the outline to check the result to make sure that each of the seven provisions has been considered. Provisions 1 and 7 could be left out if not relevant to the activity, as when these are the students' free choice; *item 6 must be left out if the covert provision* (3) *is affective.* Thus objectives with affective emphases have no specific criteria.

Each section of a behavioral-objectives outline is indicated in parentheses in the example that follows:

(1) Given two cards of different colors—one marked *major*, the other marked *minor*—and a hearing of ten familiar songs, (2) each sixth-grade student will (3) *identify* (4) the mode of each melody as major or minor (5) by holding up at the teacher's signal (6) the card which properly identifies the mode with an accuracy of six out of ten correct (7) and discuss, when called on, how he or she made the decision. The activity will be repeated immediately with ten new examples, and each child shall improve his or her performance by at least two more correct responses.

You would benefit yourself greatly if at this point you would turn to Appendix A and study the objectives of the sample curriculum provided there. Try to discover how and where the two specific behavioral examples given here are derived from provisions of that curriculum.

Behavioral objectives such as these should be presented in some means directly to students, usually paraphrased in simple language that they can understand. It is usually effective to place these paraphrased objectives on a 3" × 5" card and to hand these directly to the student(s) involved (see Fig. 5:4).

Fig. 5:4

II

Planned Improvisation on a Specific Form

1. Using only your choice of either wooden or metallic sounds

2. Compose a planned improvisation in ABACA form.

3. Make sure the A, B, and C sections are distinctly contrasted by varying such things as pitch, rhythm/meter, volume, texture, density, etc.

4. You have 15 minutes to prepare this composition.

5. Perform for class; be prepared to discuss.

It is useful to keep these cards and use them again, assuming that they were successful; otherwise, improve them and retain the new version. They can be kept and catalogued according to the nature of the assignment which is summarized in the title at the top of the card. Create as many categories as you will be using, or create them as you work your way into ever-newer categories. Because such cards are reused, usually you will specify neither the group size, nor the names of students who will do the product. You will have organized students into groups as a separate operation. Even when an activity is made up for a specific group, it is still a good idea to leave off the names. In this way, you can still reuse the card in the future.

You also may categorize your activity-card files according to the levels suggested earlier. Thus, under the category "Planned Improvisation on a Specific Form" you might have a selection of Level I, II, and III activities from which to choose according to the needs of the groups you have assembled. It is necessary to identify the card by levels in order that you can recall which cards are suitable for which levels. This can be done on the front (as shown in the upper right corner of the card in Fig. 5:4) or on the back. In either case, it is not useful to inform the students as to the meaning of the numbers.

VENTURE PLANNING FORMS: SPECIFIC
PLANS FOR IMPLEMENTATION

In addition to the behavioral objective, your lesson plans should also include specific plans for implementation. This information is provided in the lower portion of the venture planning form shown in Fig. 5:5A.

Fig. 5:5A

Class _____

A. DOMAIN: cognitive   affective   psychomotor   (circle)

B. OBJECTIVE (itemize or freely):

☐ Given (+ short time)

☐ Who

☐ Covert

☐ Content

☐ Overt

☐ Proficiency

☐ Other

C. ACTIVITIES: singing; playing; creating; listening; discussing; _____ .

D. READINESS:

E. PROCESS:
(Implementation)

VENTURE
ACTIVITY
RESULTS
EVALUATION

F. FUTURE PLANS:

288

Indicate in the margin to the left of the "venture" box any book or music page numbers, titles, and bands of records you plan to use, or any other such reminders for ensuring the efficient *implementation* of the activity. Within the venture box, you should outline the various stages entailed in the conduct of the lesson. This is the *structure* of the lesson. You will use this to "improvise" or "create" your lesson.

Venture: this term is related to ad*venture* or being *venturous.* It is the beginning stage where the teacher sets the challenge or problem represented by the activity that will follow. A well-planned venture might involve leading questions, or a review of past activities. In every case the teacher should seek to incite the imagination, curiosity, and commitment to action of the students, to arouse students' self-motivation.

Activity: here a brief sketch is included describing the steps to be followed in the activity. This helps the teacher remember what you intend to occur first, second, third, and so on. In the activity illustrated in Fig. 5:5B (page 290) the entire class is involved. Therefore, no cards are passed out. Rather, the information is copied from a card in the file onto an overhead transparency.

Results: here the nature of the expected results is indicated. Will the results be a composition, a verbal action, a performance, or some combination of these? Will students need paper and pencil, or other materials (such as the flash cards required for the objective given earlier)?

Evaluation: as the lesson or activity is concluded, the teacher notes whether or to what degree the lesson succeeded in developing the musical behaviors that were specified above in the objective.

In the space remaining at the bottom, or perhaps continuing on the back of the form, the teacher should note *plans for the future.* These are based on the relative strengths or weaknesses of the evaluated results. Such a memo might remind the teacher to repeat the activity again soon to reinforce the present learnings, or it might be a reminder that this lesson did not succeed well and should be repeated or should be preceded in the future by more readiness.

These forms should be kept in some kind of filing system. Punching holes for a ring-binder is best, since it allows the teacher to thumb quickly through all of the past lessons to review quickly what has happened, how well, and what still remains to be accomplished. The top part of the form is especially important in this regard, since it quickly identifies the prime orientation of lessons as being cognitive, affective, or psychomotor. *Some balance between these three conditions is most desirable.* If one or two are featured more often than another, your program is out of kilter. Some teachers find it useful to keep three separate sections in their filing system for the three possible instructional emphases. This way, it is relatively easy to keep count of how many of each you have taught. Others prefer to keep their planning forms in chronological order in order to keep track of their sequence.

Either way, or others you might invent, the point is to keep your planning forms in some kind of system that allows you to periodically review what you have done, what the students have learned, and what remains to be redone, reviewed, or refined. Your future planning always depends on having this information at your easy disposal. Simply duplicate a large number of these blank forms and use them as you plan. (More specifics on planning are found in Appendix A.)

With experience your plans will become somewhat less specific as you establish your "style" of certain habits and routines for certain kinds of activities. As your students become more experienced with the formats of various activities, they too will need fewer step-by-step directions. However, keep three things in mind.

Fig. 5:5B

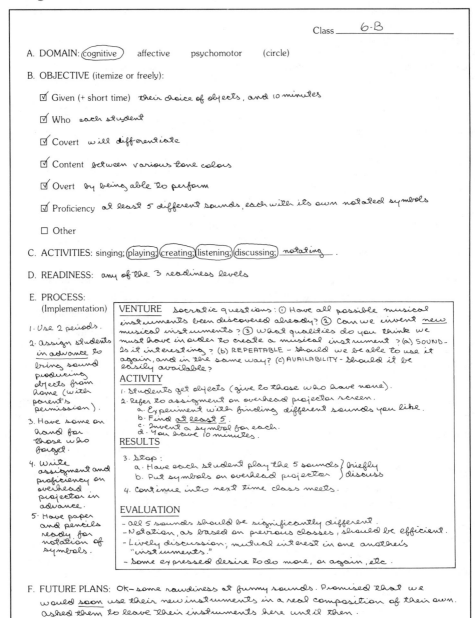

Class _____ 6·B _____

A. DOMAIN: (cognitive) affective psychomotor (circle)

B. OBJECTIVE (itemize or freely):

☑ Given (+ short time) *their choice of objects, and 10 minutes*

☑ Who *each student*

☑ Covert *will differentiate*

☑ Content *between various tone colors*

☑ Overt *by being able to perform*

☑ Proficiency *at least 5 different sounds, each with its own notated symbols*

☐ Other

C. ACTIVITIES: singing; (playing;) (creating;) (listening;) (discussing;) *notating* .

D. READINESS: *any of the 3 readiness levels*

E. PROCESS:
(Implementation)

1. *Use 2 periods.*

2. *Assign students in advance to bring sound producing objects from home (with parent's permission).*

3. *Have some on hand for those who forgot.*

4. *Write assignment and proficiency on overhead projector in advance.*

5. *Have paper and pencils ready for notation of symbols.*

VENTURE *socratic questions: ① Have all possible musical instruments been discovered already? ② Can we invent new musical instruments? ③ What qualities do you think we must have in order to create a musical instrument? (a) SOUND— Is it interesting? (b) REPEATABLE — Should we be able to use it again, and in the same way? (c) AVAILABILITY — Should it be easily available?*

ACTIVITY
*1. Students get objects (give to those who have none).
2. Refer to assignment on overhead projector screen.
   a. Experiment with finding different sounds you like.
   b. Find at least 5.
   c. Invent a symbol for each.
   d. You have 10 minutes.*

RESULTS
*3. Stop:
   a. Have each student play the 5 sounds } briefly
   b. Put symbols on overhead projector } discuss
4. Continue into next time class meets.*

EVALUATION
*– All 5 sounds should be significantly different.
– Notation, as based on previous classes, should be efficient.
– Lively discussion; mutual interest in one another's "instruments."
– Some expressed desire to do more, or again, etc.*

F. FUTURE PLANS: *Ok— some rowdiness at funny sounds. Promised that we would soon use their new instruments in a real composition of their own. Asked them to leave their instruments here until then.*

1. Do not establish routines that become so predictable that the classes begin to feel that they are in a rut.

2. Your plans should be virtually complete enough for a substitute teacher to use if your school or district uses substitutes for music class (and if they don't, what must be the administrative attitude toward your classes?).

3. Your plans must be descriptive enough for you to review your teaching efforts periodically in order to understand in toto what you have already accomplished with your instruction.

One other factor can be suggested also: apprise your administrator(s) from the very beginning as to how you intend to plan and evaluate your music program if the system recommended here deviates in any significant ways from the format usually used in your school. Most principals will be more than happy to acknowledge and approve such a systematic approach to instruction if they are assured that you are at home with a system that is more in keeping with the nature of music education than would be those planning formats designed for other aspects of the school's instructional program.

Above all, do not become lazy and cease to make written plans. Even if you do not think that you require them, because you can make them up rapidly in your head, two important purposes are served by actually writing these plans:

1. You insure that you cover all of the bases, and do not accidentally leave out an important component of instruction, or fail to have arranged to have all of the required materials, etc.

2. With no written plan, there is no satisfactory alternative for keeping records of class and individual accomplishment, and thus no systematic way of planning and executing a viable curriculum. (Such a system is suggested in Appendix A.)

In other words, failure to make written plans often leads to seat-of-the-pants, hit-or-miss teaching, in which each class may seem to be successful but classes have very little if any relation to one another or to long-range curricular goals. Thus, one of the prime *roles* for the teacher is that of *quartermaster:* planning for individual needs and keeping a record of accomplishments.

CONTROLLING ASPECTS OF CREATIVE ACTIVITIES

There are three different *aspects* involved in any creative activity over which the teacher has three general *degrees* of control.

DEGREES OF CONTROL: FREE, GIVEN, OR MIXED

1. *Free,* or open-ended: students are allowed to choose for themselves.

2. *Given:* the teacher imposes specific limitations on the students.

3. *Mixed, or hybrid:* some limitation by the teacher is coupled with some student choice.

These two sets of three variables interact in various ways, depending on the situation and the teacher's instructional goals (See Fig. 5:6).

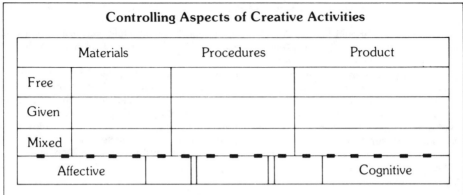

Controlling Aspects of Creative Activities

	Materials	Procedures	Product
Free			
Given			
Mixed			

Affective   Cognitive

A form similar to this can be used, at least initially, to help you choose the kind and degree of control you wish to exert over particular activities. This choice is determined by the nature of your teaching goals. Place an "x" in the appropriate boxes and you will have a graphic reference to the nature of your lesson. On the bottom line, check (✓) whether the lesson will emphasize affective goals (feelings), cognitive goals (understanding), or some confluence of these two types (use the center area between the two sets of double lines).

Fig. 5:6

ASPECTS CONTROLLED: MATERIALS PROCEDURES, PRODUCT

Aspect 1: Materials

1. May be *given* by the teacher, as with the materials you prepare for songwriting activities, or when you specify the sounds used in a sound composition.
2. May be *freely chosen* by the students, as in sound compositions when they are allowed to choose their own sounds.
3. May be *mixed,* as when you limit students to wooden and metallic sounds but let them choose freely within those groups.

Aspect 2: Procedures

How your students will go about completing an activity:
1. Can be *given* by the teacher, as in the step-by-step procedures of beginning experiences in songwriting, or when limiting the amount of working time.
2. Can be *freely chosen,* as when students are left alone to decide whether or not they will notate a sound composition.
3. Can be *mixed,* as when (within certain restrictions) students have some choice as to how to proceed, or have a choice from among ones prepared by the teacher.

Aspect 3: Product

What the final product will be:
1. Can be *given* or determined by the teacher, as in certain rhythmic songwriting activities of which all products will be identical.

2. Can be *freely chosen,* as when groups choose their own titles for a sound composition and execute it; each product will be entirely different.

3. Can be *mixed,* as when all students may be assigned to compose an ABA song or sound composition, each of which will be somewhat different, yet comparable to the others.

In any of these instances your intention for the lesson will dictate the amount of control you exert; but the physical setting of your room and adjacent rooms, the size of your class, and other such factors may influence your choice of both materials and procedures. Remember, too, that your control over procedure also involves whether or not you choose to delimit the amount of time available for the completion of the project.

SAMPLES OF TEACHER CONTROLS OVER THE THREE ASPECTS OF CREATIVE ACTIVITIES

1. Given a free choice of sounds, each group of three students will demonstrate its understanding of ABA form by composing a sound composition in that form, notating it in original graphic notation and performing it with or without conductor.

Materials: Free. Choice of sounds.

Procedures: Given. Class is limited to ABA form and a notated score; groups of three.

Product: Mixed. Each product should be in ABA form, notated, and performed. But each one will be somewhat different; a variety of notational systems will result; and some will be performed with conductor, others will not.

Note that all three kinds of control are represented here. This is very useful in controlling an activity while still allowing for individual needs, interests, inclinations, and choices.

2. Given their own choice of self-generated body sounds and a choice of those forms listed on the chalkboard (AB; ABA; AABA), each group of four will compose and perform a composition of no more than one minute, achieved mainly by the use of timbre.

Materials: Mixed. The students have their own choice within the category of self-generated body sounds.

Procedures: Mixed. Groups of four are specified, but they are free to choose whether they will do a free improvisation, a planned improvisation, or a notated score; they also have a choice of forms, and of length of time to work.

Product: Mixed. Must involve timbre and be under one minute in length, but given the variables in materials and procedures, the final products will vary.

Here all of the variables are *mixed.* This is common, since it allows considerable teacher control while permitting considerable student choice. This is the only instance when a straight, horizontal line of "x's" would appear across your chart.

3. Given the title "City" and the duration of the period to work, students in groups of three will compose a work that musically interprets their feelings about or impressions of the title; the composition may be worked on outside of class but will be limited to two minutes of performance time, and will be heard at the next class meeting.

Materials: Free. Class members may choose sounds or other materials.

Procedures: Mixed. A title is given as a limitation (control device), but considerable free choice is permitted in interpreting it; time for work and time of performance are limited, but in each case the time could be shorter than that given; the specified performance at the next class confers a limitation, but students are free to work outside of class or school.

Product: Free. The teacher has little control over what the final nature of each composition will be.

293

When a feeling-response (here, "Musically interpret your feelings about or impressions of the title") *is at stake, allow much freedom.*

As you can see in these examples, the possibilities for controlling activities of this kind are infinite. A few general ideas may help guide you in the kinds of decisions you are called on to make.

GENERAL GUIDELINES

1. *Seldom are activities free in all three regards.* This would amount to directing students to "compose a piece." Most adolescents feel more comfortable with some minimal guidance, if only as an aid to spurring their imaginations into action.

2. *Feeling-responses* (i.e., affective domain, appreciation, interpretation, valuing) *are encouraged by having at least one, and sometimes two, free aspects.* the freer students are in completing an activity, the more their own feelings, choices, and values are brought into play. Therefore, if you indicate on your planning chart that the activity is to be affective rather than cognitive, you ought to have a pattern of "x's" that permits much freedom.

3. *Cognitive activities* (understanding, analyzing, perceiving, etc.) *will usually involve one or two given or mixed elements.* The more that you control (i.e., give) the more cognitive the activity is, and the less *directly* it is *intended* for involving the feelings (although some feelings will be present).

4. Therefore, *seldom should activities involve given determinants for all three aspects.* No situation ought to be devoid of an affective emphasis. At least one free or mixed aspect ensures that some feeling-response is emphasized.

5. *Activities that feature largely mixed control, or that have one of each kind of control, encourage the confluence of cognition and feeling.* In other words, considerable scope is allowed within certain given cognitive frameworks. In terms of percentage, you should probably have somewhat more of this kind of activity than any other. This kind of activity maximizes the benefits of *permissipline.*

6. *Psychomotor behaviors* (i.e., performance) *are specified as a condition of the procedures.* Since most creative activities should be performed, this is in a sense an implied given or mixed factor; however, the specific nature of a performance may be left up to the teacher or at least partly to the teacher. Since creative activities are seldom devised primarily for the sake of performance, the eventual *performance is the means, not the end.* Therefore, creative activities are invariably oriented toward either affective or cognitive behaviors, or the confluence of both. *Before you begin to plan activities, you should have in mind which of these choices you intend to emphasize.* If you choose to emphasize either feeling or cognition, place a check in the box closest to your choice. If your activity is to be balanced in order to emphasize the confluence of feeling and cognition, check the central box between the two sets of double lines.

When you are through completing the upper part of the form, check and see whether your choices lean largely to *free* (affective) or *given* (cognitive), or whether they seem to favor the *mixed* (balanced, confluent) control characteristic of permissipline. In this way you are able to maintain control over yourself and the direction of your instruction. Among other things, you ought to make it a regular habit to look back over your plans and see what kind of balance you are striking. In terms of percentage of frequency, are you emphasizing cognition to the detriment of feeling, or feeling to the detriment of cognition? Or, as is most desirable, are you striking a balance between these two conditions and achieving a state of synergistic music education in which feeling and cognition are always interdependent?

Balance is desirable not only for philosophical reasons, but also for practical reasons. If too much free choice is allowed, over the long run students can quickly become lost, waste time or lose interest for lack of guidance (i.e., permissiveness). This is especially true the first few times you do an activity format such as sound compositions. *Until students are familiar with the nature and operations of a basic activity, greatly limit their choices.* Aside from increasing efficiency, too much free choice runs the risk of an extreme form of hit-or-miss instruction.

GROUPING: PATTERNS AND PRINCIPLES, FOR USE WITH CREATIVE ACTIVITIES

The kind of student groupings you choose for creative activities will be determined by your teaching circumstances and by what is best for the students.

Grouping is intended to facilitate the implementation and benefits of creative activities. There are only five grouping patterns available to the teacher: (1) individual work; (2) small group; (3) a moderate group; (4) a large group; (5) a mixxture. *No one kind of grouping is satisfactory as the sole basis for instruction.* This is particularly true of large-group instruction.

FIVE PRINCIPLES OF GROUP WORK

Large-group instruction has been most characteristic of music instruction in the traditional middle and junior high schools because most general-music programs have been biased toward singing and music reading. The newly evolving middle school philosophy makes this inappropriate as the only format for instruction, especially where creative, individualized instruction is sought. Due to the collegiate model, high school courses, such as theory or "appreciation" classes, have also featured the traditional large group format in which the teacher is the center of attention. In both middle and high school settings, attention must shift to the students if Action Learning is to become a reality.

1. *When creative activities are new to students, large-group work is most effective and efficient in introducing classes to their goals and procedures.* Once students have become accustomed to the basic activities (e.g., songwriting), move to moderate-sized groups, and then to smaller groups as the class can handle the increased self-direction. As the groups become smaller, increasing freedom of choices concerning creative controls can be allowed.

2. *Moderate-sized groups* (i.e., dividing the class into thirds and quarters) *are almost always a realistic alternative to large-group instruction.* They also serve as an intermediate stage between introductory large group work and the small-group work that gives freer vent to individual progress.

3. *Small-group work* (i.e., groups of three to five students) *is the most desirable format.* It permits a great deal of individual effort and progress while still using time economically. Small groups generate a great number and variety of products and thus enrich the total learning environment.

295

4. *Individual work is desirable for advanced or talented students, or as independent study.* Otherwise, it is inefficient use of time in most instances to hear the compositions of each member of the class.

5. *Mixtures of group sizes* are employed when very heterogeneous abilities or interests are present, or when the daily teaching format does not permit assembling students for the single purposes of music instruction. Mixed group sizes can also result when the teacher's plans include a variety of activities requiring work in small groups, other work in moderate-sized groups, and also some individual work.

FIFTEEN SUGGESTIONS FOR CHOOSING GROUPINGS

Where possible, the size and makeup of the group ought to facilitate instructional purposes. Therefore, the questions of how large the groups are and which students should be in which group are determined largely by your instructional intent.

1. As students demonstrate increased ability with certain activities, groups should generally become smaller and controls somewhat freer.

2. Students of similar ability can be placed in the same groups in order to facilitate assigning activities at their level of readiness.

3. More-advanced students can be included in groups whose other members are at a different level of readiness. This is the planned situation in which students (peer tutors) teach students.

4. Individual work for the entire class is best undertaken as homework or independent study, except in the case of songwriting activities when individuals work on their own song but the entire large group is really engaged in the same activity.

5. Have your grouping worked out in advance of the lesson and publicly announced on the chalkboard (or in some other manner); use names and cite locations in the room or elsewhere where the group will work.

6. Be aware of personality clashes and other difficulties that may arise (i.e., "unproductive" combinations) and avoid these in future grouping patterns.

7. Do not be unduly bothered by talking within small or moderate-sized groups that are otherwise busily engaged in productive work. When such behavior becomes unproductive or disturbs other groups, then step in and redirect the group's efforts. Several groups working in this fashion may generate an overall hubbub, but most adolescents are easily able to work within their groups effectively under these natural conditions, much as office workers do. Talking usually bothers the teacher more than the students.

8. An activity may involve more than one grouping pattern. For instance, when a small group composes a composition, the remainder of the class or a moderate-sized group may be required to perform it.

9. Occasionally, students may be allowed to choose their own groups. This is especially useful for preadolescents or adolescents for whom peer groups and cliques are important. Make sure that the activity is suited to such random grouping, and be on guard in the event that work becomes unproductive or groups evolve that are unwieldy and require subdivision.

10. With individual or small group work, and often with moderate-sized grops, the teacher should walk around checking progress over shoulders, assisting where possible, redirecting unproductive work where required.

11. If physical conditions permit, chairs or desks should be moved around to physically separate groups as much as possible. This helps discourage to some degree nonproductive contacts between groups.

12. Setting and maintaining *firm time limits* usually encourages productive work by groups. They feel that they do not have time to fool around.

13. Recalcitrant students who *seemingly* prefer not to participate should be isolated (i.e., left alone). Allow them only to watch from the "sidelines" without any other divertissement. They will usually, under these conditions, opt to join a group either by overtly changing their minds or by covertly edging their chair toward a group until they are part of that group—if not today, then soon!

14. Explain to administrators from the first what the nature of your program of creative activities will be and what physical format it will adopt. This way, when they look in on your class, they understand immediately the nature and cause of the physical and oral activity that they see.

15. In moderate-sized and small groups, make sure that most or all of the work is not completed by only a few individuals. While walking around, ensure and encourage productive participation by *everyone in the group.* If need be, when you know that certain individuals always seem to dominate, appoint other individuals as "chairperson" or put all of the dominant types in groups of their own.

Remember that musical independence is an ultimate goal. Each class member should be able to make an independent and important contribution to each group. So even in those formats that are larger than individual or independent work, you must encourage productive participation by each individual. Similarly, students' independence is not enhanced if you are too domineering in monitoring their progress—making corrections or suggestions that are too "bossy." Rely instead on the time-tested leading questions of the Socratic method.

TIMING CREATIVE ACTIVITIES

There is little doubt that creative activities take a considerable amount of time to complete: the time it takes to get the activity started; the time it takes for the students to complete the product; the time necessary to perform and discuss the product.

1. Getting an activity started should be the smallest problem. You must have all materials and groupings ready to go. It also helps if you have prepared how you will give verbal directions for the "given" aspects of the lesson (i.e., procedures, materials, and nature of the final product). These are best indicated on the 3″ × 5″ card that you hand out.

2. Sometimes you may wish to allow as much time as may be necessary in order to give full scope to classs efforts, or in realization of the fact that people work at different rates of speed.

Usually you should delimit the amount of time available for completing the activity. At first, this is just an educated guess on your part. As you gain experience, you will be able to estimate a realistic amount of time with greater accuracy.

3. Most usually, you must attempt to have performed as many projects as is feasible. Students whose works are not heard today should be kept in mind for tomorrow. Ideally, *students must frequently hear the aural results of their efforts for those efforts to improve over time.*

Projects can be heard outside of class: during lulls in the day, after school, or immediately after lunch (or during it, if students eat in the room). Notated or electronic compositions can be handed in for teacher evaluation. In the case of songs, the teacher can perform many more than the entire class could perform.

Often the first two phases of an activity will take place during one class period. The third phase (the performance) occurs during the next class or is distributed—along with other activities—over several subsequent classes. Because of the time lapse between composition and performance in such instances, you should review the intent of the activity and reestablish the ambiance of the earlier class.

In general, timing is less and less of a problem when the teacher can derive additional activities from the products of any given activity. Songs that have been composed by your students become material for singing; sound compositions serve as performing and listening experiences. Some activities need no immediately performed product—they can be combined with a second activity immediately, and the second activity would result in a performed product. The lesson shown in Fig. 5:5B is suitable in this regard (see section F, "Future Plans").

CREATIVE ACTIVITIES AS HOMEWORK

Teachers often seem reluctant to assign students homework for music class. Some teachers seem to believe that the work done in school is self-sufficient. On the contrary, you should attempt to integrate musical instruction more fully in the lives of your students, and one way of doing this is to give them certain responsibilities and (musical) things to think about outside of school. Many of these assignments are small and easily accomplished.

Homework *can* influence your use of time in class, but *do not use it solely to increase efficiency.* In general, assignments should be simple, and should emphasize that the concerns of music and music class can be and often are applicable outside of class. Much time is wasted when students learn bad habits or do the asssignments incorrectly outside of class. Homework facilitates Action Learning to the degree that assignments involve the kinds of musical activities most related to how people can use music to enrich their lives, namely, in listening, playing the guitar, and other hobby-like pursuits.

GENERAL APPLICATION OF CREATIVE ACTIVITIES TO THREE READINESS LEVELS

Creative activities are easily adaptable to the three levels of readiness outlined at the beginning of this chapter. This is especially true where you have all three levels in your class. But even when the class works as a large group, creative activities tend to act as a "leveling factor" for the following reasons: (1) Regardless of prior readiness, most students are initially unfamiliar with these activities and cognitions. (2) Few specific prior learnings are required for most students to be productive and successful. (3) Most of the basic concepts of music arise inductively from these activities and serve as readiness for subsequent activities. (4) Students at higher levels can work unimpeded; thus the teacher avoids merely "teaching to the norm" and can devote more time to those who require help. (5) Similarly, less able students can receive added attention while at the same time experiencing a significant feeling of accomplishment. (6) Even when children who have learning disabilities are "mainstreamed" in a "normal" class, creative activities hold forth many opportunities for satisfying participation; often these children are the least inhibited initially. Because of recent changes in the law, even more such children will be mainstreamed, and many of the activities suggested so far—especially sound compositions—will be an effective way of integrating them productively. Classes emphasizing notetaking, quizzes, and competition for grades are sure to create problems for them.

USING READINESS LEVELS

Level I: General

At this level are included learning-disabled and physically handicapped children who are being mainstreamed, and those other students whose readiness for music learning is minimal in a given concept-area or areas. For these reasons all of the activities described thus far—sound compositions, listening, and songwriting—should be (1) simplified, (2) shortened, and (3) guided.

(1) *Simplification involves emphasizing only one or two salient features or criteria at a time.* For obvious reasons, these should be the most important, the broadest cognitions. They should be as tangible, as nonabstract as possible. *The "rules" or procedures should also be simplified.* (2) These students will be relatively impatient and require rather *quick results.* If small-group work makes the short length of some projects too apparent in comparison to Levels II and III, the fruits of two or three groups can be combined into a multi-sectional work of more comparable length. (3) The *guided aspect* (see pages 291–295) involves *more teacher participation* in activities and/or *peer tutoring* by a more advanced student as part of the group (a possibility most fruitful in the late middle school and high school). People at Level I just require more direct assistance, and the teacher must be alert to possible questions or problems.

Sound compositions should be simple in their requirements ("given" factors, criteria, use of materials) and in their procedures. They should not require very much time to complete or to perform. The teacher should provide maximum guidance without doing the work for the students. Songs, too, should be simple in their requirements (use only two or three chords, simple rhythms, highly metric poems, etc.) and in their procedures. The teacher must organize everything in advance, especially handouts that help the students organize their efforts effectively. Songs should be short; eight measures are plenty, since two eight-measure songs can be made into a sixteen-measure song, etc. The "given" information must be explicit and easily available for reference, and the teacher should be prepared, initially at least, to give considerable assistance.

Level I: Specific Examples

1. Behavioral Objective

Given their free choice of all sounds available in the room, the class will create an AB sound form by suggesting two contrasting groups of sounds, performing their work, and analyzing the tape-recorded performance.

Specifics

1. Have a "scribe" come to the chalkboard (or overhead projector) and record the suggestions.

2. Tell the class that they are going to compose, as a group, a composition that has two parts. The first part will be called "A," and the second "B." Tell them that the two parts should be different, and that they can suggest how to make them different. Have the chalkboard ready in this form:

3. Ask for sounds. As they are suggested, ask for symbols to notate the sounds. The scribe records the symbols agreed to by the class, one after the other.

    a. When section A has been completed, perform it and record it. Listen to it and discuss what kinds of sounds "B" should have if it is going to be different.

    b. Complete section B.

4. Perform the entire work after assigning all of the sounds to individuals or groups. Record it; listen to it. Discuss whether there is enough or too much contrast. Discuss how more or less contrast could have been achieved. Discuss whether or not the symbols used were effective. For example: "What other symbols might have worked well? Next time, we can use some of these new symbols for another work. Did you like the sounds? What other sounds could we use to replace those that were difficult to notate, perform or repeat, or that you just did not like? Can you get any other sounds from those objects? How could we notate those sounds?"

2. Behavioral Objective:

Given a C major scale, a staff with treble cleff, and four measures of rhythm each member of the class will create a tone-row melody by choosing pitches from the scale, and notating them on the staff in the given rhythms. Half of the groups' works will be performed by the teacher, and the class will agree on at least two general principles for improving these melodies.

Specifics:

1. Have a handout prepared with all of the relevant musical information and space to work. Have plenty of pencils available, with erasers.

2. Give the necessary directions and start the students on the activity. You move from desk to desk peering over shoulders to make sure that everyone is working (i.e., no one is so confused by your directions that he or she does not know how to begin) and seems to understand the criteria (i.e., everyone is using each note only once).

3. On a random basis, play half of the melodies. If possible or necessary, quickly notate each example on the chalkboard or overhead projector before playing it. Discuss each one quickly in terms of criteria established through leading questions: melodic directions, too many wide skips, or too many tones too close together are often good starting points. Have the class sing especially those melodies with wide, nervous leaps. Question: "Are they easy and pleasing to sing?"

4. Depending on which the class may prefer, agree to rework this set of melodies, or compose a new set during the next class if there is insufficient time to do it at present. Have a set of words ready that fit the rhythm of the tone row and sing several of the examples with these words.

Level II: General

This level includes activities of moderate challenge for students who have demonstrated appropriate though not extensive readiness. Creative activities for them should be based on (1) concrete goals of, (2) moderate scope, (3) a minimum of clearly defined "rules," and (4) *indirect* assistance.

(1) *Concrete goals* involve the *tangibility*, the *apparentness* of the projected results. While cognitions among this group are less dependent on the concrete than in Level I, their *goals cannot be abstract or ill-defined.* They are interested in results. wherever possible, *allow them some role in setting goals;* i.e., activities should lean toward "mixed" in the open-closed range of goals. (2) The *number of cognitions* and the *length of time* involved should be *moderate,* i.e., neither too short nor too long. If too short, the element of challenge is missing. If too long, the students will lose interest or give up. (3) *Minimum "rules" as to procedures and criteria are needed.* These minima should, however, be absolutely *clear* and *inviolable.* This provides structure and guidance, while allowing freedom or flexibility on the part of the students of the sort that increasingly breeds musical independence. (4) *The teacher's assistance is indirect.* The teacher assists by Socratic questioning, prodding, or hinting but not by directly solving the problem. "Given" factors need not be as explicit as with Level I, and Level II students can be expected to "figure out more" by themselves. *Sometimes this level does not respond well to having Level III students as peer tutors.*

Sound compositions can have several goals, but these should be relevant to, and accepted by, the students. They should deal with *broad cognitions* and should aim at developing a *positive feeling-response.* The scope should usually permit completion within one or two classes. *Restrictions should be kept to a minimum and should clearly guide the students in their efforts.* The teacher will only suggest and criticize without directly assisting the students by "showing them" anything. *They must be encouraged toward musical independence at this stage.*

Songs should deal with words and musical problems geared to the young people's interest. They can choose their own words, and you can choose the musical problems. Songs of from eight to sixteen measures can be done, and combined into longer works of thirty-two measures. "Rules" will amount to the general principles of how to derive a melody from chords, or the meter of a poem, etc., just as specified earlier. The students will be left mainly to their own designs, with the teacher redirecting their efforts and attention and clarifying principles through leading questions and the like.

Level II: Specific Examples

1. Behavioral Objective

Given their own choice of title, word material, and ten minutes, each group of (Level II) students will compose and perform a word fugue one or two minutes long by arranging the words in a four-part texture having a strictly *imitative* exposition, a development, and a recapitulation.

Specifics

1. Groups are tormed quickly. Suggest to the students that they choosse a title and words that they want to interpret—something that has meaning to the group.

2. By means of leading questions, the criteria are reviewed in terms of past lessons that have dealt with similar cognitions but have never "put it all together."

3. As students work, visit each group, reminding them of the criteria where necessary, and draw answers from them where problems appear. *Every few minutes announce the amount of time remaining for the activity.*

4. After the works are completed, perform and analyze each to validate whether or to what degree the criteria have been met. Solicit suggestions for improvement.

2. Behavioral Objective

Given the title "Spring," the use of body sounds and object sounds in the room, and fifteen minutes, each group of six (Level II) students will create and perform a unified work of less than a minute that freely interprets the title in terms of students' feeling toward the season.

Specifics

1. Groups are formed quickly; the title and all criteria are written on the chalkboard and quickly reviewed.

2. As the students work, move from group to group observing their progress, questioning them as to their "interpretation," and assisting them in actualizing it. Since no requirement for notation has been specified, some will not use it; others, whose ideas seem more complex, may need a suggestion for some notation as a minimal aid to the memory.

3. As object sounds become scarce, assist groups in finding more or alternative sources. Remind the groups of the time remaining.

4. Hear as many performances as possible during this class; promise the remainder for the next class. The "audience" is asked to guess the interpretation of each performance. Its interpretation of the performers' interpretation is confirmed or denied by the performers. Typically, the denials totally outweigh the confirmations. You can, then, begin a discussion about whether or not or to what degree it is possible to communicate *specific ideas* through music.

3. Behavioral Objective

Given their choice of one poem from among five poems on a handout assembled by the teacher, and ten minutes, each (Level II) student will determine its meter as being in two or three, will underline accented syllables, will put in bar lines, and will notate the rhythm of the poem based upon a given note value.

Specifics

1. Pass out the poems all on one sheet. There should be ample room on the bottom of the sheet for students to work.

2. They are asked to read all of the poems and choose the one that they like the best. Then they are directed to begin work according to past procedures with rhythmic activities.

3. As they do the first steps, place on the chalkboard the basic note value to be used in notating the rhythms, and the other note values as they relate to the basic unit (see page 158, chapter 3).

4. Move quickly among the students, checking to see if they are working and if they are on the right track, giving assistance where necessary. If anyone appears to be totally lost, he or she can be quickly grouped with someone working on the same poem who is proceeding well.

5. When the time is up, analyze one example of each poem according to the criteria, and agree to a single version. Have the students make appropriate corrections in their poems at their seats. Their work is retained for the following class (see below).

4. Behavioral Objective

Given their rhythmically notated poems already arranged on a handout with a staff line, a G clef, a chord progression (one chord per measure), and a G major scale with the appropriate chords already built, each (Level II) student will compose a melody by deriving pitches from the given chords and notating them in the given rhythms. Many of the works will be performed by the teacher and analyzed for melodic construction and accuracy by the class.

Specifics

1. Distribute the handouts according to the poems the stuents selected during the last class.

2. *Quickly review* the procedure for deriving a melody from chords and write it on the chalkboard.

3. The students begin work. Since no time is specified, begin the performance phase when you judge that most are through or nearly so.

4. As examples are heard and analyzed, encourage the students to make improvements of their own melodies as they discover ideas for form or melody construction that they had not previously considered.

5. Direct them to keep and refine their work even more for the next class. At that time, the works of those students whose songs were not performed during the last class will be heard.

Level III: General

Except for the intellectual challenges they often present, these students are usually rather easy to accommodate. They are the more advanced, "talented" youngsters, or those who have more than the usual readiness in certain concept-areas. Sometimes even a younger "prodigy" can be included with older students if grouping and scheduling permits. The requirements for Level III creative activities can be summed up in one expression: *increased musical and personal independence.* This does not mean no guidance or structure at all. It means that *"given" factors are mainly free or mixed* so that students have free choice of how they implement criteria. It means that *increasingly they should develop and state their own criteria, and to evaluate, independently, their own work in terms of their own criteria.* Teacher assistance, if any, should be very general; seldom, even, should it take the form of suggestions. *Highly stimulating questions designed to nurture natural curiosity are advised, as are questions that have no definite answer.* Aesthetic and other abstract considerations become more and more possible as these students progress. They must be continually though *realistically challenged* at all times. A major problem, though, involves the possibility of inflated egos, especially when these students are in a position to compare themselves with less advanced classmates. Such effects must be deemphasized and neutralized without, on the other hand, diminishing feelings of accomplishment. Another problem stems from the probability in middle school that often more girls than boys will be *in this group.* In the late elementary years, as adolescence approaches, this can discourage the equally able but slower-blooming boys. Encourage the boys—the girls can take it. By high school these differences in ability usually disappear.

Sound compositions often last longer for this group. Considerable if not most work may be done outside of class or school. The works of these young people are often complex. *Do not allow their goals to outreach their present abilities or they can become discouraged.* On the other hand, *do not let them set goals that are too easy, thus breeding laziness.* Many in this group can be easily interested in electronic composition. This is an especially effective means for involving bright but recalcitrant boys. Do all you can to gain their access to taping equipment. Start an "electronic music group" as an after-school affair, or as a single small-group activity unrelated to what others may be dong. Establish an "electronic music corner" where one or two people can work alone. If earphones are used this is generally a quiet, nondisturbing activity in an "open class" format.

Songs written by this group can often be musically satisfying. They can handle words of greater subtlety, and more refined musical concepts. They often can and will perform their own works as accompanied solos on the piano or guitar. Many of these works you should hear in relative privacy (e.g., before or after school), in order that Level I or II students in the class will not be discouraged. "Song clubs" can be formed as an after-school or special activity for this group, thus allowing greater scope of accomplishment. The better songs can be arranged and performed for concerts and other programs. Creative projects work well as independent learning activities structured as part of learning contracts or goal cards.

Level III: Specific Examples

1. Behavioral Objective
Given their own choice of title, materials, and until the next class meeting, each (Level III) student will compose a work whose form results mainly from timbre and tonal densities, and perform it for the class.

Specifics

1. Once these students have been identified, it is necessary only to asssign them their project, and to make yourself available for assistance should the need arise.

2. Depending on their experience with these criteria, you or they may wish to review previous work (cognitions) with timbre and tonal densities.

3. If this project involves an entire class (say, of very able students) they can all begin to work on their own projects. If they are mixed in with Level II children, place the Level III students in a "spurious" group where, though seated together and socializing or comparing projects, they are essentially working on their individual projects.

4. The performance and discussion of these works will be handled according to the same possibilities. If the entire class is at work on this project, all the discussion can be focused on it; otherwise discussion and performance will have to be mixed in with the work of others, thus benefitting the Level II groups with more refined works done by their peers.

5. The analysis/discussion should center around the degree of contrast attained in delineating the formal sections, and how apparent is the resulting form. Students are, as usual, encouraged to change their works as they benefit from the discussion.

2. Behavioral Objective

Given the use of five basic sound sources (tape recorder, piano, electric guitar, acoustic guitar, trap set of drums) each group of (Level III) students (assembled according to their choice, or the availability of the sound sources) will derive as many interesting and repeatable sounds as they choose and will compose, notate, and perform a compositions solely for its instrumentation. These works are to have sufficient unity and variety, and must make considerable use of the sound potential of the instrument chosen.

Specifics

1. Since grouping will be important here, take whatever time is necessary to allow for choices, and for each group to plan on how it will get, or get to use, its chosen instrument.

2. Groups may begin work immediately thereafter. Those who have chosen instruments already present in the room (i.e., the piano) may begin experimenting (e.g., making a "prepared piano" by sticking objects between the strings, etc.). The other groups can discuss and list ideas they want to try when they finally get to their instruments.

3. Where possible, allow them to bring their instruments to class. As work progresses, do what you can to make efficient use of time—e.g., "All of you ought to be somewhere near the end of experimenting with sounds, and getting ready to begin notating your compositions." As all the groups near completion, establish a cutoff time by which they must be ready to perform.

4. As performances are heard, focus on the criteria: the scope of derived sounds, their interest and repeatability, the notation used to control them, and the resulting unity and variety of the work. Since the students are faced with the inherent unity of only one instrument, the challenge will be to attain sufficient variety and contrast to make an interesting form.

3. Behavioral Objective

Given their own choice of poem and musical elements, each (Level III) student will compose a song by deriving rhythm and meter from the poem, writing a scale and deriving chords from it, establishing chord progressions for the poem, and deriving a melody that also contains unaccented non-chord tones. Each song will be performed—half for the class, half for the teacher (after school)—discussed, and refined on the basis of the discussion. All will be posted on the bulletin board.

Specifics

1. This is a rather independent activity and will require little from the teacher in terms of prior organization. Several sources of poems, however, ought to have been found and made available, as should pencils and music-staff paper.

2. The teacher, as usual, should pass among the class or group, asking questions to sharpen the understanding of those who may have some difficulty with a specific phase of the activity.

Without pushng, the teacher should encourage full use of the time by dispelling daydreaming and other distractions. If some students socialize a little, do not be upset. When socializing takes precedence over composing, then be firm!

3. If some students ask questions of neighbors that bear on the project, by all means, do not discourage it unless the students involved would end up in a "blind leading the blind" situation. That should not happen in most cases; if it does the activity is inappropriate, or the individuals involved ought to be completing a Level II activity. When one person seeks and receives real help from another on a project like this, both parties profit. The questioner receives an explanation at his or her level of understanding and frees the teacher to deal with other, more difficult questions; the student giving the answer has his or her knowledge extended or reinforced through this little moment of "teaching."

4. At random, perform about half of the works for the entire class. Hear the remainder by yourself. Post all songs—at once, if you have space, or a few at a time.

4. Behavioral Objective

Given the use of songs previously written and fifteen minutes, each (Level III) student will rewrite the song in a different meter (and thus with different rhythms) and make *more* or a *different* use of non-chord tones. Both the previous and subsequent versions will be handed in to the teacher for a critique and suggestions.

5. Behavioral Objective

Given the choice of any previously composed song, each (Level III) student studying an instrument will transpose the melody to a key that will enable him or her to perform it while it is sung by the class in the original key. All such performances by students who study instruments will be done on an assigned day.

6. Behavioral Objective

Given their choice of any composed song—either from music at home or from the song series—each (Level III) student will compose a new melody using the same words, meter, key, chords, and rhythms. Both the previous and subsequent versions will be performed; the composer of each will orally compare the two versions for the benefit of the class.

Specifics

1. Each of these, as is so usual with Level III activities, permits much individual choice and effort. The teacher must announce the general project, handle any questions, and get things started.

2. After that, your main responsibilities are to monitor the progress of the individuals at work on these higher-level projects and to coordinate their performance for the class.

3. Finally, the discussions that result are most important in clarifying, refining, and synthesizing all relevant cognitions. This can, of course, profit not only all Level III students, but can be of great value to Level II students, should they be mixed in or should they dominate the class in terms of numbers.

4. The question of timing is all-important. You must do all that you can to have most projects completed at around the same time. Students must not be allowed to finish too early: challenge them with ideas for further refinements. They must not be allowed to dawdle or waste time: visit them often, observe their progress, and make whatever remarks are useful in redirecting their efforts.

TEN PRACTICAL SUGGESTIONS FOR PLANNING CREATIVE ACTIVITIES

1. Always have plenty of paper and pencils available for student use.
2. Music-staff paper is very inexpensively prepared from ditto masters sold already prepared by various commercial firms. These usually come with eight, ten, or twelve staves per sheet. Use

305

eight staves for ages nine to eleven; ten for ages twelve to fourteen; and twelve staves per sheet for high school students. The younger the student, the fewer the staves (because *larger* spaces are needed to accommodate their stage of fine-muscle control which requires making larger notes).

3. Wherever possible, use the overhead projector instead of a chalkboard. Have your transparencies or overlays prepared so that their appearance is as close as possible to your handouts. Instead of preparing the "given" information (such as the scales, with pitches numbered and identified) on individual handouts, this information can be conveyed to everyone from the overhead projector.

4. If it is possible, *it is very useful to have creative activities,* including both songwriting activities and notated scores for sound compositions, actually *completed* by students *on individual transparencies* using a black grease pencil or the kind of felt-tip pen designed to be used on acetate. In this way, when sample compositions are analyzed or performed, it involves only a simple matter of bringing them up to the overhead projector. Erasures and changes are easily made with a tissue. Sheets of clear acetate are available at most art-supply stores or can be ordered along with art or audiovisual supplies through the school. You can cut the sheets into sizes appropriate for your projector.

5. Encourage older or more advanced middle school students to keep their compositions for easy retrieval. You should keep the works of others for future use. Much extra mileage (and time) is earned through such reuse.

6. If you think that you have a good idea for an activity but it *doesn't meet your expectations the first time,* keep trying to make it work by making small alterations and refinements.

7. When you develop a fund of activities that have succeeded in the past, keep varying them, if only by changing the contents or materials slightly. This avoids boredom on your part, and the tendency for you to expect the same results from current classes as those that you received in the past (i.e., keeps you out of a "rut"). But don't get in the habit of doing these activities for their own sake. Remember, activities are only *means* to your goals. They are used to cognitively strengthen the elements you choose to feature.

8. Mix up creative activities so that not too much of one kind of activity is featured for too long at a time. At all cost, avoid the kind of predictability that results in students moaning, "Oh, no! Not another sound composition!"

9. Integrate creative activities with other activities such as singing, listening, moving to music, and playing. Remember, these activities can often follow the creation of a sound product, so be sure to use student compositions as the basis for such activities. In this way, many aspects of your program are fully integrated. But also be sure to carry on these other activities using other musical sources; in this way you can assure plenty of student experience with the standard repertory of songs, listening activities, and movement activities provided by song series, record sets, and other sources. A fifty-fifty ratio between student-generated materials and teacher-generated or commercially available materials might be an ideal balance in many instances.

10. *Never stop trying* to devise new activities; to improve the effectiveness and efficiency of successful activities; to improve your own musical skills and insights necessary for more refined applications of creative activities.

"DISCIPLINE PROBLEMS"

Major insights relevant to the issues of problem behavior among pre- and early adolescents in school have been included throughout this text. In particular, the discussions of growth-typical characteristics of adolescents, factors that are involved in determining whether or not a person is interested in learning, and teacher and student attitude development are especially relevant to the general problem of maintaining behavior in the classroom. If you have not read these discussions, or have not studied them closely with the idea of their application to potential problems of misbehavior, make very sure that you do before you consider yourself fully prepared.

This section will present and discuss some of the other specific causes of student misbehavior, and will suggest various approaches for dealing with such problems. If you are looking here for infallible formulas of behavior control, forget it! There are no such techniques available, and if there were, their use would be questionable. Inexperienced teachers are often on the lookout for prescriptions: "What should I do when a student does such-and-such?" You should know by this point that any answer, except a very general one, is impossible. There are far too many variables involved: the school rules and regulations, the nature and problems of the individual student, the teaching approach and philosophy of the teacher, and so on.

CONSIDERING THE CAUSES OF MISBEHAVIOR

The point of view to be taken here is that *there exist certain causes or factors that create or condition the manner in which a student misbehaves on a given occasion.* It is plainly futile and counterproductive to treat *only the symptoms* of those causes or factors: the incident of misbehavior. While it *is* necessary on many occasions to immediately stem misbehavior, such action can only be a short-term "Band-Aid." In such instances "behavior may be *adjustive* without being *adaptive* . . . without in the least assisting the individual's long-term welfare. It may even be seriously injurious to it."[13] And, as was once pointed out, "Everyone knows that you don't rid your lawn of dandelions unless you get at their roots because sooner or later the problem will return." Since an act may have a variety of consequences, a teacher can induce immediate adjustive behavior (i.e., temporarily stemming the misbehavior) that in itself will have poor long-term results,[14] both for the student and for the teacher.

Such misbehavior will likely recur, and often, with increasing frequency and intensity, if the basic causes of that behavior are not uncovered and solved. Thus, the many "discipline techniques" that certain "hardheaded," disenchanted teachers may use are destined only to provide the teacher some degree of *external control* over students. The more often this is done, the less occasion or need there is for increases in *self-control,* self-direction, and self-discipline on the part of the students.

Ultimately, the purpose of every class should be to *foster or nurture increasing self-discipline and independence.* Education, no matter at what level, ought to wean the student of the need for a teacher. Students should increasingly "learn how to learn" on their own, and should learn how to be more inner-directed, self-disciplined, and self-actualizing. That, too, is Action

307

Learning. To give up on this ideal is to forfeit any chance for classsroom conditions that go beyond a prison or military atmosphere, and decent attitudes toward music, a humanistic pursuit, are not fostered in such overly strict atmospheres.

"LEARNED HELPLESSNESS"

Somehow school "teaches" students that learning is something a teacher does *to* or *for* you. Similarly, adolescents regard "discipline" as something that a teacher does to students. *The idea that learning or discipline is at least a major responsibility of the student is ineffectively taught in schools today.*

Learning requires activity on the part of the student as well as teacher activity. So ultimately, when "discipline" is entirely a teacher activity applied *to*, *on*, or *over* students, one of the major goals of human development is thwarted. What results inevitably is the "learned helplessness" of increasingly "other-directed" people who are entirely dependent for the quality and conduct of their lives on other people, on forces outside of themselves.[15] They flounder helplessly as they are pummeled by forces they can neither understand nor grapple with, and they adopt the helpless attitude toward their daily lives that more fully actualized people reserve only for the seeming inevitability of death and taxes.[16]

THE UNDERLYING CAUSE OF PREADOLESCENT AND EARLY ADOLESCENT MISBEHAVIOR

If teachers are to teach "whole people," then each teacher, regardless of "what" is taught, must attempt to break this vicious circle. It is all the more relevant that teachers of preadolescents and early adolescents come to grips with this problem, since the students in this age group are *seeking self-definition and self-esteem as individuals* at the same time as *they must learn how to fit their individual personalities into socially workable plans.* This dilemma—to find one's individuality and simultaneously to socially integrate the developing Self—accounts for the basic underlying cause of student misbehavior no matter what additional factors may be operative. It also explains the seemingly paradoxical behavior exhibited by most normal pre- and early adolescents.

At some moments their behavior—good or bad—is influenced by the peer group; at other times it is influenced by the desire for independent action. In any given class of preadolescents, both motivations are usually present. Thus when a few initiate independent action of a disruptive kind, those others under the group-think influence of peer pressures may very well follow. When many in a group are being independent, you may have a variety of mis-behaviors, each competing for the attention of the followers in the peer group.

Knowing whether behavior is prompted by a need for peer approval or for independence holds forth the possibility that the teacher can *use these manifestations* in pursuit of significant learning and personal growth among students. Independence is fostered when activities and learning lead to an increased sense of independence of action, to an increased realization of self-worth, of personal independence, of individual achievement. The social impulse is acknowledged in various small group activities.

VARIATIONS IN CAUSES OF STUDENT MISBEHAVIOR

With this in mind, we can now turn to the more specific causes of periodic or chronic misbehavior that may vary greatly from student to student. These are relatively limited in number, with unlimited variations.

1. Conditions and experiences in the *home* are a leading cause of students' behavior problems. Teaching self-discipline is only one among many other instances (home economics, industrial arts, driver education, sex education) of the home surrendering its former role and responsibility to the school.

2. The home presents *models* of various sorts that may influence a student's behavior or attitudes in school. Many of these, especially among boys, will deal with music. The home also involves a *neighborhood* and other environmental factors that the student is in contact with much more than with school. Behaviors and attitudes are learned here as well.

3. The *school* itself is a source of problems for some, perhaps many, youngsters whose home influences are not all that negative.

   a. The school is a microcosm of society and involves pressures, competition, situations that some students do not or cannot cope with adequately for a variety of reasons. A student from a warm loving home is often unprepared for the cold impersonality of some teachers. A student given much encouragement and support at home is unable to handle repeated failure. This does not mean that such students are spoiled—just that their lives to date have not given them the experience of having to deal with the learned helplessness of repeated failure.

   b. Whereas the home is a relatively informal and natural environment, the school is inevitably more formal and unnatural in comparison. The processes and procedures of schools are established for reasons beyond the understanding of many students: to adolescents many rules seem abstract, unfair, unreasonable, or unwarranted.

4. The student may be experiencing some kind of difficulty related to *intrapersonal factors* that are independent of either school or home influence.

   a. Some have *undetected perceptual problems*. Such students have difficulty seeing or hearing the visual or aural cues necessary for profiting from instruction. Their repeated failure and inevitable "giving up" often results in misbehavior, or the appearance of it when the teacher assumes that they are just "not trying."

   b. Other students have specific, though undiagnosed, learning problems or disabilities of one kind or another. These tend to maximize other desirable behaviors.

   c. Some students, frankly, have one degree or another of undiagnosed *psychological* or *psychophysical problems*. Among all of the causes detailed here, this group is the one for which professional intervention is usually recommended. *Teachers should not be amateur psychologists*. When they try to be, they are all too likely to identify repeated misbehavior as

309

"hyperactivity." Hardly! Fortunately, this group represents a very, very small percentage of students in most schools.

Of all these causes, the ones most subject to teacher influence are those stemming from school itself. Simply put, teachers are in the strongest position to eliminate or minimize in their own classrooms the major school-related factors that may be influencing a student to misbehave in one way or another. Generally, students whose problems stem from this source are problems in all or many classes. Among other things you are strongly warned against teachers' room gossip that influences your regard for and treatment of certain students identified as problems in other classes. At most, you should take such gossip as a warning against allowing the "self-fulfilling prophecy" to come true for the students in question when you have them in class; and you are encouraged to be aware of and sensitive to the individual problems of such students.

You can often exert some control over the effects of behavior stemming from home influence. Among other things, you and your classes should *provide another model* for students—if necessary, a positive alternative to the ones presented by parents and siblings. While it is unfortunate, you should not be surprised when adolescents come to you with personal problems, or when they have evidently gotten a "crush" on you (which in truth usually means they regard you warmly as a valuable model, as someone they look up to). In either case, you might prefer that the home or church be able to fill the young people's needs. But if students approach you with such personal problems it generally is a sign that you are having a positive influence in establishing an alternative model for their development.

The classroom and its related activities are best considered an environment. The teaching-learning environment can provide environmental influences that counterbalance other ones more characteristically encountered by the youngster in the home community. Thus cooperation, caring, open-mindedness, and noncompetitiveness in class can replace the "dog eat dog" existence provided by the pressures of certain environments or environmental influences. This would be especially true in inner-city or high-poverty, high-crime neighborhoods.

Finally, teachers do have considerable control over the first two of the three intrapersonal factors that can influence students' behavior. Be on the lookout for perceptual problems. Students who squint at the chalkboard, students whose nose almost touches the paper when they read or write, should be identified to school health officials. In the meantime, give them a seat where they can see or hear better, and assign them activities in which, for example, reading or writing words is minimized. Similarly, students who have reading problems (i.e., in school jargon, are "behind" in reading) will also have some degree of difficulty with certain verbal behaviors. Thus, note- or test-taking, or any other activities that involve considerable verbal skill, should be minimized. Some verbal behaviors can facilitate musical behaviors, but when they *interfere* with musical learning they should be minimized and conceived within the capacities of the student's verbal abilities. Certain musical experiences (e.g., directed listening—see page 232) can even assist in the development of verbal abilities.

310

In every instance cited so far, the teacher is well advised to *seek out the source of the difficulty and to try to eliminate the difficulty altogether*. Failing that, try to *minimize the effects of the problem,* and thereby to minimize the degree or incidence of misbehavior. In severe cases, this may entail research into the student's files, taking care not to be unduly influenced by negative reports of other teachers. But do attempt to find out about the home and any problems that are clearly the result of home relations or environmental influence. Take these into consideration in making plans, in devising activities, in planning for results. *Do not expect student behavior to be uniform within or between class groups.*

In addition to these general factors there are some other, quite specific causes of misbehavior that are not only within the teacher's power to control but *are often caused by the teacher as a result of faulty understanding*.

TEACHER-CAUSED MISBEHAVIOR PROBLEMS AND THEIR SOLUTIONS

Far too much misbehavior is unintentionally caused by the teacher rather than by the students. At the very least, the largest number of major confrontations and upheavals can be avoided or mitigated by the teacher. This doesn't mean that students have no responsibility. But the teachers are supposed to be wiser, and should be able to head off problems.

Instead, too often teachers precipitate their own crises. How? Unwittingly, in most instances, by not being aware of the operative factors in their own attitudes and teaching style and in the attitudes and personal natures of young people. A survey of some of these factors can give the outline of this process, but you ought to analyze them in terms of yourself until they become true insights rather than abstractions on the pages of a text.

1. *Teachers who run regimented classrooms under the sway of outdated and unrealistic beliefs create the largest majority of their own "garbage" misbehaviors.* Prominent among such beliefs is the one that requires students to be in their seats, quiet, paying unequivocal attention to the teacher's "chalktalk," and productively working each and every minute. Desks or chairs in such classrooms are usually in straight rows; books must be neatly arranged under the chairs. This attitude stems from the model of the lecture method of teaching in many college classes, where *such behavior is required in order for the teacher's lecture to be heard and understood.* Talking, movement, etc., disrupt the teacher's train of thought, or prevent others from "paying attention." It is considered rude, disrespectful, and unnerving! These teachers seek the lifeless calm produced by formal routine. It is reassuring to them because it is predictable. Related to this notion is the view held by such teachers that adolescents should be able to control themselves just as adults do.

Such antiquated beliefs go entirely contrary to the very nature of these students, who require movement and activity—both mental and physical—and who are just *beginning* to be aware of the stereotypical adult behavior of social conformity or "tact." Teachers operating within this unrealistic belief system can count upon many kinds of chronic minor disruptions, which—depending on other factors to be outlined below—can develop into fully blown confrontations; frequent trips to the pencil sharpener or wastebasket; passing notes; whispering; throwing paper wads and other objects; knocking books off desks; annoying other students; speaking out of turn or without raising the hand, etc., etc., etc.

Solution: The kinds of Action Learning activities and procedures recommended so far are calculated to take into consideration the growth-typical behaviors and needs of preadolescents and adolescents. Movement, talking, activity of all kinds, are part of the program. A teaching style that amounts to custody does not encourage spontaneity or creativeness. Only when such signs of "minds at work" begin to disturb other students or nearby classes should the teacher step in and "redirect effort." Students are often truly unaware of how loud or exuberant they have become. Only behavior that prevents learning or that disturbs adjacent classes is to be interrupted. Cross-talk between groups is generally unproductive and is best discouraged. Teachers should be better able to adjust to such a learning format designed for *students' needs* than can youngsters adjust to formats designed to make the *teacher* feel comfortable. The choice is yours: take the time and effort to master an Action Learning approach or spend all your time functioning as a police officer.

2. *Teachers who plan certain learnings because they are "good for students even though they do not appreciate it now" create multiple discipline problems for themselves.* Such authoritarian or "essentialist" beliefs presume to know what is best for children and take the form that "everyone *should* know about . . ." The usual content of such lessons is abstract facts and information believed to be characteristic of the so-called educated person or musical skills that require extensive and dedicated study before they become truly functional. The behavior problems that inevitably result all stem from boredom or frustration, from the natural adolescent resistance to the prescriptive, patronizing introduction of values by adult authority figures, from the need for relevance or immediacy of results, and from the need for a sense of short-term achievement. None of these needs can be met by such teaching, no matter how well the teacher is able to "keep the lid on" by heavy-handed means (e.g., threats, punishment).

Such learnings almost always seem to involve high-level abstractions, thus further impeding students whose verbal, intellectual or musical skills are limited. Altogether this kind of teaching leads to some of the most severe forms of confrontation. The question is not whether the teacher can handle the confrontation. When the teacher can and thus "wins," even further antagonism arises. The problem is to avoid any confrontation to begin with. Most students are neither unreasonable nor lazy. But *they do know when unreasonable or unrealistic demands are made of them.*

Solution: Learning activities that are "good for students" because *they are interesting, represent students' own present values and needs, are relevant, have easily observed short-term results and promote a sense of real achievement* (i.e., learning in itself becomes more personally rewarding), *as well as the avoidance of imposed or introjected values by the teacher*—all of these will minimize many if not most incidences of gross misbehavior. Again, the teacher's role will be to occasionally remind students of the activities at hand and to keep the "hubbub" down to manageable limits. Productive enthusiasm on the part of students is a sign of teaching success, not of mischief or lack of respect. One teacher has referred to such occasions as *positive discipline problems* in order to distinguish them from the negative discipline problems that end in confrontation and mutual antagonism between the students and the teacher. Just keep things within productive limits and do not overly stifle involvement.

3. *Music teachers who teach so-called objective content in order to emulate the efforts of other teachers, give objective tests and grades, and simplify (superficially) their teaching efforts will experience some of the most extreme forms of student misbehavior.* Such "content" often takes the form of separate "units" on instruments of the orchestra; musical notation; categorized and labeled varieties of rock, folk, and jazz music; and the historical periods of music (along with composers' names, dates, and important compositions), "enriched" with educational films and filmstrips of prepackaged lectures. The results of such teaching combine the unfortunate results of the first two types of teacher orientation sketched above: chronic minor disruptions and increased confrontation.

Because something seems relatively "objective" and is seemingly easily organized by the teacher does not make it appropriate learning for students in general music classes. Just the opposite is usually the case.

Solution: Adolescents require learnings that are personally interesting and relevant, subjective, dealing with feeling-responses—their personal and unique responses and their growing sense of *selfhood.* Since they receive more than enough (any is too much) so-called "objective content" in other classes, music should be and can be a kind of "oasis" in the school day where the natural strengths of the musical art for dealing with the affective domain is drawn upon and used to full advantage.

4. *Teachers who ignore the "emotional content" of what is learned, and the "arousal" factor needed in the learning process for adolescents, fail miserably in preventing strong outbursts of rebellion.* Such rebellion often takes the form of direct, overt action (e.g., "standing up to the teacher"). Sometimes it amounts to being passive (e.g., the "I couldn't do it" response really means "I didn't think I could do it so I didn't try!"). Both types of students view certain learnings or learning methods as threatening. Commonly their responses involve either "the typical flight-fight reaction"[17] or, equally problematic, "the appearance of aggression and anxiety."[18]

Teachers who provoke these reactions fail to appreciate that "the way in which an individual deals with a situation that is emotionally relevant . . . often depends on his past experience with the situation. For example, he will approach a situation if in the past the cognitive consequences—and thus the emotion—have been positive and pleasant. On the other hand, a situation that terminates in a negative unpleasant emotional response may be avoided or even reinterpreted."[19] Furthermore, an event may be appreciated depending on whether an individual anticipates that the outcomes are more likely to be positive or negative. "In particular the sense of control, whether or not the onset and offset of a particular event is under the individual's control, may be of particular importance."[20] Remember, "learned helplessness" is in part determined by an individual's feeling that he or she has no control over the outcome of events.

Thus, teachers who ignore a student's readiness for learning, and even more important, that student's own emotional appraisal of such readiness (e.g., "You can do it"—"No, I can't!") are courting disaster. Not only disaster in terms of disturbing the teacher or class, but in terms of the accumulative harm resulting for the individual.[21] Often, in these circumstances, the only way a student can maintain self-esteem is to intentionally "bait" the teacher, then to directly confront the teacher and not back down.[22] The teacher who forces a student into such a corner from which there is no graceful exit for either of them is to be especially condemned. Superficially, the teacher always "wins" (in his or her own eyes), but in the minds of all the students in the class it becomes just another example where the teacher's authority has not been *earned*—it has been abstractly *demanded* solely on the basis of the name "teacher."[23]

Solution: Properly assess learning and emotional readiness, learning styles, needs, and interest, and employ the three-level approach to readiness in a program of individualized instruction that never makes a student feel threatened or anxious about being able to succeed. Building up a fund of successful past experiences (by considering such readiness) increasingly allows the student to view the learning challenge as within the demonstrated potential of his or her control and mastery: "*I* think I can do it!"

5. *Teachers who use grades, extra work, and similar devices to "motivate" students are mistaken in their belief that failure can motivate. Failure motivates nothing but more failure. Nonadaptive problem behavior is the only thing available to the student who needs some sense of success at something.* As indicated earlier, a student's sense of control, of personal competence, influences his or her interpretation of any particular emotional situation. "Thus what may be frightening at one point may become amusing, not because there has been an objective change in the situation, but because a sense of mastery has drastically changed the cognitive interpretation of the same situation."[24] It is this increasing sense of mastery over their personal destinies that must be improved in students' minds, and the teacher must directly intervene and help them achieve such insight. Using punishment as a threat—as a consequence to be avoided—either intensifies anxiety without increasing mastery or arouses antagonism. Increased

anxiety will result in disruptive behavior as the teacher either must "force" passive students to work (which is about as intelligent as saying "Love me or else!") or keep actively misbehaving students "in line" (an apt expression for that kind of teaching, which can be compared to training circus elephants or military recruits).

Grades are unavoidable in many teaching situations, although not in the sense that they have any educational advantage: they do not![25] They are usually necessary because administrators insist upon them and because students and parents have come to rely on them in a variety of misguided ways. Use them if you must, but be very aware that they contribute greatly to student anxiety (rather than motivation) even with successful students, and generally do just the opposite of improving student performance.[26]

Solution: Deemphasize grades altogether. Do not use them as either motivation or punishment. Be honest with students about the usefulness of grades. Separate in your own mind three things: *evaluation, reporting* evaluation, and *recording* it. Grades are only one form of recording an evaluation, and a poor one at that. Be fair and consistent whatever system you use. Minimize the question of grades simply by not grading on a daily basis the products of student activities. If you do grade everything, they will become increasingly anxious, increasingly unsure of mastery or their control over the situation, and therefore much more inhibited or aggressive.

However you arrive at grades for "marking periods," be careful to explain as kindly as you can to students whose efforts have resulted in lower or unsatisfactory grades the reasons for this as you see it—not trying to "motivate" but simply to explain and clarify. When grades have no realistic basis in the minds of students, neither high nor low grades are respected as either rewards or punishments: they are simply ignored, except that there is an additional loss of respect for the teacher on the part of the students. An Action Grading process is suggested in Appendix A as a model.

6. *Teachers who either breed or fail to relieve "learned helplessness" must inevitably suffer the results of behavior in the one area over which the student feels he or she has some control and competence: misbehavior!* He or she can always do that well. "Learned helplessness" comes about in two ways. It occurs when a student's poor emotional readiness (i.e., fragile sense of control or mastery resulting in a negative prediction of success) makes him or her frequently anxious about situations that are known to be unavoidable. Another source is a student's attribution of failure not to personal causes but to external causes over which he or she feels there is little possibility of personal control.[27]

The results of learned helplessness can be twofold. At the least a person becomes depressed and increasingly unable to cope with work or responsibility. There is a loss of will, and the individual becomes passive, apathetic. There is a complete withdrawal (into oneself or from attempting anything) because the person feels no control over external forces (teachers, grades, other students, etc.). So, minimally, such a student "gives up" and accepts that he or she simply cannot learn, cannot succeed.

> They once tried to do their very best, but now give no more than halfhearted effort to anything. They are often very bright young people, potentially capable of high-level work; but they coast along on far lower levels of achievement. They usually don't know why: "The teacher's no good," or "I just don't care for school," may be the kinds of reasons that come to their minds. In fact, they are defending their self-concepts, and avoiding feelings of unworthiness by side-stepping any real test of what they can do. If they don't really try, if they don't do their lessons and their homework, then they might be called "lazy and "delinquent"; . . . it is far less painful—in terms of the terrible and deep anxiety we suffer when we feel insignificant—to be a "delinquent and lazy genius in the rough" than to be a conscientious "mediocrity." . . .[28]

But whether these traits arise depends on whether the student even attempts *to learn.* When the condition is particularly severe (well entrenched due to a chronic pattern of failure), the result is a general *anomie* (a disruption of personal or social value, of the ability to respond to norms, especially—in school—norms of behavior), and the student gives up trying altogether to learn. So "loss of interest, decrease in energy, inability to accomplish tasks, difficulty in concentration, and the erosion of motivation and ambition all combine to impair efficient functioning."[29] But alternately, students can rationalize the causes of such externally manipulated results and blame the teacher, the school, adults or society in general, other students, etc. "Where self-esteem is damaged, destructiveness is bound to be unleashed, to attack whatever is 'bad,' whatever is not 'significant.'"[30] An extreme form of this behavior will be severe or chronic rebelliousness—misbehavior intended to restore some part of the student's self-image or to "get back at" the threatening forces (teachers, authority figures) responsible for this helplessness. Such a person find it inwardly "more important to defeat the efforts or to thwart the possible success of the teacher . . . than to succeed himself."[31] Juvenile delinquency can be a result if this is carried to extremes.

Solutions: Tangibly improve the student's sense of mastery and successful achievement. Include appropriate measures of student independence so that the student can see success as the result of his or her own efforts. Minimize any sense of failure, especially chronic failure. Emphasize a "strengths and weaknesses" approach to evaluation so that the experience of "total failure" is not possible for the student. In this approach as many good points are noted as are weaknesses. Emphasize growth rather than absolute achievement: "This is getting better" replaces "This is not good enough." Carping criticism only creates more problems.[32] Since letter or numerical grades are absolutes, use an anecdotal commentary form of reporting evaluation as much as possible. Be accepting rather than rejecting; helpful and warm instead of cold. Above all, be responsive in positive ways, so that the student can learn that the environment (which in school includes most notably the teacher) is responsive to his or her initiatives. With this kind of teacher responsiveness comes the student's feeling of control—increasing control, at least—over the results of personal actions.

It is useful to note that teachers, too, are susceptible to "learned helplessness" when they feel that students have more control over a teacher's life and class than the teacher does. Many teachers thus leave teaching, although some effort along the lines suggested here could have helped them regain control of themselves and hence control of their teaching. And many instances of "behavior mod"—such as rewarding reluctant cooperation with the opportunity to listen to rock music—end up controlling or "conditioning" the teacher's behavior as much as, or more than, the students'.

7. *Teachers who fail to note that they are positively reinforcing aberrant behavior cause it to become increasingly chronic.* "Helplessness" is learned by students when their failures are continually reinforced by more failures, including poorer grades. Such students feel that they can succeed only in meeting the teacher's negative expectations. But other kinds of poor behavior are positively reinforced when the teacher is not aware of the student's intent (and the student may be no more conscious of intent than the teacher is). Thus students who disrupt by blurting out answers may be seeking recognition and often they are *positively reinforced* (rewarded) by a scolding from the teacher. This results in their doing it more, not less. Notepassing is similarly scolded and positively reinforced if it contributes to the satisfaction of having drawn attention to the offenders. Thus it continues. Many of the "garbage" varieties of behavior problems are positively reinforced in this way. If the teacher always "gets mad" at some small act of less than perfect behavior, the offender is positively reinforced if the (conscious or unconscious) intent was to annoy or bait the teacher—a common form of adolescent entertainment in boring classes!

Thus, in a very strange but sure way, students end up "conditioning" the teacher more and more.

The need to feel basically worthwhile *is* so vital that people (e.g., students) will harm themselves . . . [in order] to accuse the unloving parent and his surrogates (e.g., teachers) of a lack of goodness. Such a person may engage in what is termed "malevolent transformation." Since he unconsciously desires to perceive others as unloving and heartless, he may actually goad and provoke them (including the reasonably kind ones) to behave in ways which appear selfish, cruel, and malevolent.[33]

Some teachers—particularly student and first-year teachers—resent this as they find themselves becoming increasingly irritable, "bitchy," and defensive although they know that this is not the "real me." But not understanding how they are reinforcing such behaviors positively, such teachers continue to scold, cajole, and punish actions that are innocuous, and thus make such actions increasingly frequent and malicious. And such "malevolent transformations" also happen to teachers (see item 10 below).

Solution: Positively reinforce only those behaviors which are desirable. Be sure that scolding and punishment do not have the effect of positively reinforcing students' "teacher baiting" or their strategies for "getting attention." Nonreinforcement (ignoring, continuing without comment, doing nothing) has been shown to be the most effective means of stemming such minor misbehavior, especially if you are suspicious or unsure of its motivation. Above all, you must never lose your "cool" for if this is what the offenders sought, your reaction functions as positive reinforcement. Literally "count to ten" when you feel yourself losing control over yourself; literally "do nothing" until such group behavior is brought under students' self-control. Wait for the entire period if necessary—there is nothing more unnerving to this age group than doing nothing. This should be the only form of negative reinforcement that you use regularly. Doing nothing should be an aversive consequence that students will wish to avoid (this, not punishment, is negative reinforcement). Alternatively, if students are mainly engaged in one of the many "games" they play, often unconsciously, with teachers, the fun and thus the game ceases when the teacher identifies his or her awareness of the game: "Look! You folks are playing the 'Let's-get-the-teacher's-goat' game today, but it just can't work now that I'm on to it—so let's entertain ourselves instead by getting back to the songwriting and we'll listen to several before class is over" or, "What is this, 'Knock-books-on-the-floor,' 'Go-to-the-pencil-sharpener,' and 'Shuffle-our-feet' day in here today? Let's put all this restless energy to productive use and finish up the sound compositions you started yesterday."

8. *Only the stable child can accept punishment, and such a child usually does not need it to begin with. Teachers who fail to appreciate this intensify or worsen the misbehavior of unstable students.* Punishment only increases the aggressiveness or antagonism of adolescents—individually or as a group. And they are fully capable of holding a grudge!

Punishment is effective only with stable students and only when all offenders are treated equally. Often, however, punishment is directed at unstable students (and unfairly or inconsistently if the teacher errs in placing blame: e.g., does not pinpoint all offenders, or mistakenly punishes a non-offender). Such arbitrary punishment is widely recognized as a major cause of disciplinary problems.[34]

Punishment, therefore, *most frequently increases the antagonism between the teacher and students.* And so frequently even those students who are non-offenders in a given instance will help spread the antagonism through the class. The teacher becomes one more "enemy," one more arbitrary authority figure. Punishment can be effective only when it is very likely to entirely eliminate the *cause* (source) of the behavior and the symptom as well. This is not very likely in most instances, and even where it is, it has potentially bad side-effects. Most teachers use punishment only in dealing with the *symptoms*. Such teachers have the mistaken idea that when a student can anticipate punishment if he or she behaves in a certain way, that student will logically avoid behaving in that way and so avoid being punished. *Chronic misbehavior is not subject to logic!* Afterschool detention halls stand as daily proof to the inadequacy of such folk wisdom: they are filled with the same students repeatedly![35]

Solution: If you want students to be productive, the major technique that you have at your disposal is to create the kind of learning environment that they find unequivocally interesting and relevant, and in which they are aware (cognitively) of their own interests.[36] Furthermore, it is clear that the most successful way of inducing preferred kinds of behavior is to provide frequent models of the desired behavior. "Experiments show quite clearly that people tend to be euphoric in the presence of a euphoric model or angry in the presence of an angry model."[37] In the same way "the mood represented by the majority of a social group influences the mood of all its members."[38] Therefore, the frequent and miscalculated use of punishment, embarrassing students, denigrating them—in short, insulting their sense of self-worth in any significant way—will only result in an increasingly negative group-spirit.

You must, instead, *be a model of the kind of behavior you expect or desire from the class.* You must be energetic, enthusiastic, kind, fair, and considerate of the problems experienced by others. You can "joke off" half a dozen innocuous behaviors each class without their becoming more frequent because you didn't punish or react to them. In fact, since they are not reinforced, they are likely to be increasingly extinguished. If you want cooperative, responsive students, you must be cooperative and responsive to their needs and problems, as opposed to taking a hard-line attitude: "No one in my class gets away with that."

So often teachers misinterpret student behaviors as disrespectful when they are not. Verbal expressions that might have been "naughty" in the teacher's home or generation are widely accepted today as simple slang. It is the student's intent—as you can fathom it—that is important. Nonreinforcement will eliminate those responses intended to "get your goat." The net result can be a more friendly, cooperative classroom atmosphere and environment. This is the goal. To proceed otherwise jeopardizes the collective attitude, and often results in an increased cynicism on the part of the teacher, which in turn further antagonizes students.

9. *Teachers who use externally imposed disciplinary gimmicks ("crowd control" techniques) fail to realize that continued use does not result in increased student self-direction: the result is an increased need for using them, and for devising ever-new ones.* Students are not dogs or trained pigeons. They do not react as predicted to conditioning. You do not "train" students to be self-disciplined by disciplining them any more than you "train" them to like singing by forcing them to sing. You simply cannot force yourself on adolescents in this way; they are among the most resistant creatures on this earth to the simplistic techniques of direct behavior control. Even when behavioral control externally imposed does quell *symptoms* of behavior, it does not eliminate the *causes*. They continue to recur (as eventually do the symptoms). Unfortunately, one teacher often suffers as a result of such techniques applied by another teacher when students are "let loose" after being repressed by a "strong" teacher in the previous class.

The goal of education (as opposed, again, to training) is intelligent and increasingly free self-direction, self-motivation, self-actualization. You do not educate people (or even train them, for that matter) by doing something for them or by punishing them for not doing what they are supposed to do.

> Children . . . are often naughty "on purpose" so as to provoke punishment, and are quiet and relatively contented after chasstisement. . . . By provoking the outer world of parents or substitutes [e.g., teacher!] to inflict external punishment upon them, the child and adult save themselves from some of the severity of internal self-punishment.
>
> When punishment serves essentially to placate guilt, it fails as a disciplinary device. This is part of the tragedy implied in a penal system which metes out punishment without comprehending the psychological structure of the particular criminal.[39]

You do not educate people to be increasingly self-directed by doing all of the directing *for them*, by taking away all of the opportunity for self-direction, by relieving them of guilt through your punishment. Similarly you do not educate students to increased self-discipline by removing from them all sources of temptation to misbehave. Virtue exists only when such temptation exists and is consciously rejected by the student.

Solution: Begin any class by discussing with students what the minimal class rules of conduct shall be. It is important that students have this input: these will be, henceforth, *their rules.* Do not allow them to suggest rules which you know they cannot or will not possibly fulfill; don't accept unconscious "apple polishing" (the suggestion of rules that they feel *you* expect or want to hear).

When students are not holding up their end of the bargain (as individuals or as groups), have a low-key discussion with them of the incidents involved. When an entire class goes astray, similarly take the time to redirect their allegiance to "their rules." As time goes by, some rules may be relaxed or stiffened in this way by mutual consent. In some instances a given individual may agree to a stiffer standard of conduct in a certain rule-area than is adhered to for the rest of the class, with the promise that successful coping will result in the return to normal status or a relaxing of other rules. At all costs (even to your own sanity, if you are unusually "uptight") gradually—ever so gently—give students increased opportunities for self-direction. The earlier discussion of the various controls for creative activities is especially useful in this regard (see pages 291–295).

10. *Uptight teachers who are defensive, unsure, and lacking in self-esteem too often feel that student misbehavior is directed most of the time AT THEM PERSONALLY* (e.g., the students are "out to get me," are purposefully being disrespectful) and find that this self-fulfilling prophecy comes true with amazing regularity. Students inevitably behave up to our expectations. If we assume or expect the inevitability of misbehavior, it *will* occur! When a teacher is excessively "thin-skinned" and unsure of his or her personal worth, an aggressively defensive posture will be adopted that is largely responsible for generating exactly the kind of behavior that is not desired.

For this reason, if no other, teachers need to be "whole" individuals. They need be neither cocky nor defensive. They should have humility, should not be afraid of making and admitting to a mistake in front of students. They should have no fear of being wrong, of not knowing something, or of having typical human weaknesses. Often the best policy is simply to *tell the students what your problem is:* that screaming or running (or whatever) truly annoys *you*. In return for their consideration, you must be prepared to observe similar consideration for them.

Beginning or preservice teachers are in the greatest danger here. How often the best of ideals gives in to the fear that if external control, fear, threats, an "I mean business" approach is not immediately adopted, students will soon take control. While it may be true that students often will "test" new teachers (experienced or inexperienced, substitutes, etc.), this does not mean that you must begin like a Marine drill sergeant (i.e., "Don't smile until Christmas!"). Students are not easily fooled by such insincere approaches, and the first time that they see through your disguise—which is inevitable—they realize you for what you are: an actor playing an unnatural role.

Solution: Be yourself as much as you can, and be honest with students about it. Allow them, similarly, to be themselves—as long as that does not interfere with the similar attempts of others in the class, including the teacher. Use all of the above-stated solutions to establish and maintain an effective learning environment. There is usually no special need for a hardheaded or heavy-handed beginning. Begin and end with the same fairness and consistency, showing students that as they increasingly can accept responsibility for their own behavior you will allow and encourage such occasions. Above all, do not be uptight about any stage of adolescence. Students in this age group are no better or worse than anyone else.

They are not devils—bad or evil in any incontrovertible, innate sense. And if they were, they would require special help beyond what you are prepared to be able to offer. So give them the same "benefit of the doubt" that you would hope they would extend to you. As you get to know them and their individual idiosyncrasies better, employ any of the approaches so far and subsequently discussed that seem to fit the situation.

As you can see, there is a great deal teachers can do about the frequency and severity of misbehavior in their classes. Most notably, they can avoid creating or sustaining the conditions that lead to misbehavior. In the long run, teacher-imposed "strategies" (a term whose meaning originally implied warfare) for external control over students are doomed at best to dealing only with symptoms, which will in any case continue to occur. Depending on the teacher's attitude, such strategies can even intensify the aggressiveness of individuals or classes and thereby worsen the situation.

On the other hand, all of the techniques discussed so far should be directed to gradually increasing students' responsibilities for their own actions as much as possible in a given circumstance. At worst they punish themselves by not learning. But this is not a satisfactory conclusion, or one which we can easily accept. Our guiding principle should be to increase the occasions for, and hopefully the frequency of, responsible self-direction. However much this is improved, even if only a little, it is more than otherwise would have resulted from teacher-controlled strategies.

Ultimately, a good teaching "offense," one predicated on known and observed growth-typical characteristics and on the inherent nature of the musical art, will be a teacher's best "defense" (one that protects learning, if not the teacher's hide). The simple fact is that most pre- and early adolescents are quite normal human beings with typical strengths and weaknesses. They will respond positively to relevant instruction in just about any "content" area.

When musical instruction is not made dry and abstract they are even more likely to respond than in most "content" areas, since music is—whether they are conscious of it or not—one of their prime life-concerns. They take to it like ducks to water. But they usually do so on their own terms. To avoid discipline problems and to maximize the benefits of an education in music, students must be able to view the formality of a school program of music education as palatable and relevant. Then they can accept to some increasing degree the more formal terms of the schoolroom as their own. If or when this does not happen, or to the degree that it does not, problem behavior will result. Thus, once again, the teacher's task is one of attitude education: diagnosing present attitudes and planning to foster a movement or growth of attitudes in the desired direction.

Fortunately, from a psychological point of view, this is a readily possible goal. While students cannot have a full choice of seeking or avoiding all learning occasions, activities can be conceived and executed in ways calculated to make their inevitable participation increasingly less noxious, increasingly more rewarding, as they notice their own behavior and think, "Hey! This isn't that bad after all! In fact, its kind of interesting!"

> As the events unfold and actual mastery (i.e., control over the events) is observed, the experience of changing emotional tone, merely as a result of changing self-observation, is often dramatic. The euphoria of the underdog as he overcomes the favorite in sports, the soldier's joy at surviving a battle, and the child's delight at mastering a new task are all relevant examples.[40]

So when learning situations are viewed as a threat, the resulting anxiety and aggression can result in open confrontation. But when a learning activity is at worst "benign" (i.e., threatening no great harm) there is a greatly improved chance that students will reappraise it with a "What have I got to lose?" attitude.

This is especially true for the creative activities recommended throughout this text. Situations calling for creativity, whether "artistic" or simple problem-solving, are likely to induce some anxiety in almost anyone. They call for a solution in the future. The uncertainty of these two unknowns can arouse an anxiety that stirs the individual either to creative action or to withdrawal—giving up rather than gambling on the outcome. In the case of "creative coping" the old anxiety actually contributes to the degree of success ultimately experienced by the student. Any anxiety that leads to withdrawal or non-cooperation (often a form of resentment against being placed in such a situation) eventually results in ever more negative attitudes, an even more closed mind.

The teacher should not attempt to avoid entirely the possibility of students' not solving a problem adequately. *It is the potential that a creative solution might not work to some degree that makes creativity and problem solving exciting.* "To be free to succeed, one must be free to fail, for creative effort always occurs within the context of possible failure."[41] Thus, creative activities must be challenging in order to be interesting. But when "failure" to solve a problem becomes the predictable outcome of such activities for certain students, or when such a failure—chronic or not—equals "failing the coursse," then interest is destroyed. The negative self-concept of the student results in withdrawal or defensive aggression.

> When the one who is uncertain of the future attempts to create, his anxiety often drives him into some non-creative mode of tension reduction; this non-creative release provides still another instance of failure, or insult to self-concept. The very attempt at creative effort therefore comes to mean danger to the essential sense of personal significance.
>
> The child or adult who is reasonably confident of eventually receiving mediating rewards can apply himself efficiently over a considerable period of time; but one who is not finds himself beset by intense anxiety which clamors for immediate relief.[42]

Thus challenges that are in line with readiness, instruction that minimizes the crushing sense of inadequacy, can result in vitally interested, even excited students who find creative energy in the solution of the problems presented as creative activities. But because of the shortsightedness of this age group, *results should be relatively immediate.* They cannot sustain the anxiety, the tension of any lengthy efforts needed to solve a problem.

> The time lag between present effort and future reward—the suspense which adds spice to the creative efforts of the self-confident—severely depresses those whose anticipation of success is slight. They experience lethargy when they sit down to study or work at something requiring protracted effort.[43]

So each activity that elicits students' productive participation has involved an "I'll give it a try" attitude. This decision also implies that the challenge is interesting (difficult enough to generate suspense), that it can be solved without too great a time lag, and that the solution stands a good chance of being successful (gratifying; reducing the creative tension of suspense).

If such "gambles" result in punishment, poor grades, any sense of embarrassment or negative self-worth, or any fear of being put on the spot, subsequent opportunities for productive involvement will be viewed negatively (see number 4 above, page 313). Thus, when an activity receives "benign appraisal" (or reappraisal) by previously resisting adolescents, you must try your mightiest to insure success and gratification to whatever degree is humanly possible. Benign reappraisal

> changes the [threatening] situation into a benign one and thus eliminates the negative emotional experience in action. It is this benign reappraisal of the threatening stimulus that may, under conditions of arousal, produce some of the positive emotions that involve the mastery of danger. Danger can be mastered both in the real world and in the mind.[44]

But it is important that the "danger," the threat, the challenge of the activity be under the beneficent guidance and control of the teacher to some degree; otherwise the student is likely to retreat into his or her former emotional state of either learned helplessness or some form of aggressive defensiveness. This requires a very sensitive teacher who has the patience that results from understanding growth-typical behavior and the causes of discipline problems (see the Selected Bibliography for sources of more information on this topic). Most of all, it requires a teacher *who has a basic faith in the inherent goodness of young people* and the desire to help each of them realize this goodness. A feeling of negative self-worth on the part of a preadolescent or early adolescent is not only evidence of unsuccessful teaching; it is probably the most basic cause of all misbehavior.[45]

STUDENTS ARE HUMAN—SOMETIMES ALL TOO HUMAN

In summary, then, on the topic of student behavior you are reminded that students, especially preadolescents and early adolescents, cannot be expected to be fully competent, to be as entirely self-directed in terms of classroom behavior as, for example, college-age students. Students in the young-adolescent age group have many rough edges, many of which they protect as part of their uniqueness, as part of their last-gasp effort to not allow themselves to be socialized to the point of a robot-like uniformity. They are in a very tricky position, for they must learn how much they can be socialized without entirely becoming other-directed conformists. If anything, the preadolescents of special concern are not so much those who periodically *assert* their independence or individuality through misbehavior or resistance to authority. Of more concern ultimately are those who already have given *in* to other-directed control, and thus given *up* their own inner-directedness.

Such individuals are often perfectly mannered—at least around adults and authority figures—and can often seem to be model students. However, their misbehavior does seep through, and almost always in a very deceitful, sneaky way. Because of their need to be recognized as cooperative and conforming, they will lie, steal, and cheat. They haven't the character or personality that can be open and aboveboard in their relationships with others. Thus they resort to "stabbing their friends in the back," gossiping, and doing sneaky things to annoy the teacher. Nothing serious, mind you, but perhaps all the more pernicious for that reason.

Such youngsters often come from so-called good homes with strong, even domineering family members who may even be respected people in the community or are to some degree in public view. Girls are not immune from this. They have a special kind of poor adjustment that all too often results from a "sugar 'n' spice 'n' everything nice" attitude espoused at home. As objects of such culturally introduced sex-stereotyping these girls lose all assertiveness of any kind. They learn, often from female models, that boys are assertive and girls are supposed to be obeisant and compliant. While such girls seldom misbehave, they may internalize and repress their frustrations, and they gradually become less and less free to knowingly *choose* their own destinies. Thus, the same inner hindrances to learning occur, but the teacher is all the more mystified at their inability to make progress in class.

So be aware of students who seem to have the intelligence for progress but do not appear to be progressing, although otherwise they do not misbehave much. Any of the factors discusssed in this section—learned helplessness, emotional readiness for learning, etc.—can be operating against such students' best interest without much more indication on their part than inappropriate progress. The teacher should intervene in such instances, try to diagnose the difficulties, and do everything possible to put the students back on the road to success. Just because some boys and other girls are more noticeable in their misbehavior does not mean that other, quieter and more subservient types of students are not suffering similar problems. The evidence will be seen in your records of their progress. *All the more reason to keep such records.*

Finally, you are reminded that the music class presents a wonderful opportunity for "reaching" students who have been having difficulty in other areas of academic studies. The activities and Action Learning approach recommended so far are especially suited to maximizing success, to developing the kinds of personal relevance, feeling-responses, and the like that make a music-education program rewarding even for the student who has clear-cut academic deficiencies or difficulties.

This is one reason why music experiences or instruction are strongly employed in programs of special education, music therapy, and the like. Music education *can* be music therapy done early. Use the special magic of music to attract and sustain the interest of all your students. Do not accept the possibility that any one of them could possibly *not* be interested in music. When you are tempted to reach such a conclusion, do accept the possibility that the likely cause is that—for one reason or another, perhaps not your fault—*your music class is what they do not like!*

Speak to them privately (and sincerely! No con!) and determine the problem. Make every sincere attempt to provide them with a rich program that nurtures the kind of musical growth and success that allows music and music class to become increasingly self-rewarding. It may be the first or only occasion in that student's life where this has happened. You will have achieved one of the most significant goals for which many people enter teaching: to help individual students live fuller, richer, more productive lives. The responsibilities are great, *the effort required is tremendous,* and the public rewards and recognition are slight.

But the inner rewards are significant to just the same degree, and they daily fuel the energies of most successful teachers. Remember, you are entrusted with a very precious thing: the life of an individual human being. And by now you should be aware that you can have a profound impact on that life, for good or bad, even for the small number of minutes that you have that student in your class. Make every minute count in positive ways. Do not allow yourself to become cynical and progressively hardened. Maintain the joy of helping every student who spends time with you in your music classes. You, and they, and society, will be the better for it.

Above all, remember that your attitudes are often like an open book to your students. So try and give them every benefit of the doubt. Try to bring your attitudes under conscious control, for research shows clearly that students of all ages are aware of and concerned about how teachers feel about students:

> There was little reflection of a desire to get out of work. Children did not seem to feel that the "good" teacher was the "easy" teacher. The attitude of the student who praised her teacher by saying "Makes you study hard, and read books, do papers and homework, and write things about the subject" was not unusual.

> Finally, it was clear that students want teachers to be good observers. They want their teachers to pay attention to their needs, to understand their problems, to share their successes and to treat them openly, fairly, and with respect. In essence, the students said that the affective is more important than the cognitive; that personal, human qualities ultimately outweigh concerns with methods, materials and curriculum.[46]

ACTION LEARNING AND THE "OPEN" CLASSROOM: A BRIEF OUTLINE FOR USING MEDIA TO VARY INSTRUCTION

MEDIA DEFINED

Media are the *means* by which teaching is achieved. A teaching *medium* is a condition, a means, an intermediary for achieving ends. It is not necessarily to be equated with using audiovisual machinery or other technology. According to Marshall McLuhan, the famous theoretician of media influence in our society, media are much more influential than is ordinarily assumed.[47]

1. *A medium is an extension of man* (pages 19, 32). Media are those means which mediate between man and his objectives. They make it possible for him to extend his influence in or on the world. Media, thus, are any means by which man conducts his human affairs.

2. *The medium is the message* (pages 23-35). Each medium puts its own characteristic stamp or quality on its dealings. For example, if the medium of teaching consists of lectures on abstract, inert information, the "message" learned by students is that learning is the accumulation of verbal information (or something that teachers do to or for you—when you don't learn, therefore, it is their fault!). Thus the message of lecturing as a medium is *words*, not musical realities.

If, on the other hand, the medium involves the students' personal action with and use of relevant musical learning, the message is received in terms of *personal experience and use*. Where grades are a pivotal medium of teaching (i.e., for "motivation"), the message is that learning is pursued for, or only under the threat of, grades: remove the grades and students will no longer be motivated. When the medium of teaching instead involves other kinds of *evaluation* procedures, *recording* procedures (i.e., means of keeping a record of evaluation), and *reporting* procedures (i.e., means of reporting evaluation to students and parents), the message is that grades are superfluous. Thus bar graphs and vast numbers of other techniques are far superior to grades as means for accomplishing these purposes.

To rephrase McLuhan, *the method of teaching is the "message" or content that is learned*. Teach by using words, and words are learned. Teach by using music, and music is learned. Teach by allowing students certain degrees of self-direction, and self-discipline is learned.

But looked at in this way, *music itself is a medium*. To have a "musical message," the means of teaching—the medium—should be as musical and as closely related to actual musical function as is possible. If *music is a medium by which humanity expresses and contemplates the unspoken feelings and realities of life*, then real or realistic musical experiences will unfailingly bring "life" into your class. The more the methods of music education resemble the in-life "message" (eventual use), the greater will be their impact.

Teaching, too, is a medium. Therefore the teaching medium should not do the learning for the student (i.e., against his will, for his own good, without his knowing it). *Teaching as a medium implies teaching students how to teach themselves*. If teaching is the medium, "teaching oneself" is the message, and teachers do well to increasingly wean their students of the need for the teacher's intervention, motivation, and evaluation. The most important message of such teaching is complete student independence.

3. *The content of a medium is always another medium* (page 23). The content of writing is the medium of speech. The content of speech is concepts, ideas, thoughts, tendencies, and abstractions that are initially nonverbal neuronal messages of the brain. The content of music as a medium is those nonverbal concepts—nonverbalizable neuronal messages—that are otherwise not accessible to satisfactory externalizing (communicating, expression) through another medium. If these nonverbal neuronal messages can correctly be called feelings (or affects) and emotions, then these are the content of music, not facts and information *about* music.

4. *The true effect of a medium is seen in the "message" or change it produces in human lives or affairs* (page 24). Effectiveness in teaching, therefore, should if possible be judged in terms of some observable behavior or change in the frequency of a behavior. The effectiveness of teaching as a medium is not judged in terms of *what the teacher does*. Its value is seen in *what the student is now able to do or feel as a result of instruction*. The "message" of such teaching is Action Learning.

5. Media can be categorized as "hot" or "cool" depending on the degree to which the medium itself is active or passive (pages 36-45). *Hot media are those high in informational content*, well filled out with data. *They are, therefore, characterized by low levels of student participation or action*. Lectures are hot and so is the act of reading this book.

Cool media are those low in informational content. They do not contain much information but rather lead students to experience something and to derive information from the experience themselves. *Cool media, therefore, are characterized by high levels of student participation or action.* Action Learning is cool in this sense.

Generally, hot media lead to inactive students in terms of learning but all too active students in terms of discipline problems. Cool media involve student-centered classes where the teacher is responsible for creating the learning environment and situation, but where the students are increasingly responsible for learning.

6. *No medium has its meaning or existence in isolation* (page 39). Its meaning arises only in constant interplay with other relevant media. For example, teaching media are quite useless without some tangible relation to other necessary, facilitating media:

Philosophical Goals

Teaching Goals

Teaching Media

Evaluation Media

These, in turn, are related to similar considerations on the larger scale of schoolwide and community concerns.

7. *Media tend to transform one kind of knowledge or experience into another mode* (pages 63–67). Written words transform personal, previously nonverbal concepts into visually perceived symbols. In the process, the *flux* and *feeling-tone* of the ideas is made *rigid* and *objective*. In music, nonverbal neuronal messages are translated through notation and performance into the somewhat varied experiences of listeners; they retain some of the flexibility and feeling-tone of the original inner experience but are different in degree or kind from those the composer experienced.

In teaching, teacher-held concepts are transformed (not transferred!) into knowledge held by the student. The teacher's concepts are used indirectly to assist students in developing their own concepts. It is not possible for the teacher to simply transfer knowledge, since the medium (words, speech, notetaking, etc.) will distort or modify (transform) it in the process. Further, it is intended at least that the student's knowledge will be transformed into active involvement with music, and thus that music class will be the medium for causing this transformation (Action Learning).

VARYING INSTRUCTIONAL MEDIA

Overuse of any medium results in a static state: a standing-still where no improvement occurs. The *Hawthorne Effect* is a psychological principle predicting that simply modifying or changing a mediating circumstance will often produce some noticeable improvement. It implies to a certain extent, then, that *variety is the spice of life and is desirable for its own sake.* However, the change involved in variety must be continuous; otherwise each past change runs the risk of becoming the new status quo. The need for change is related, in effect, to the psychology of learning curves (see Fig. 5:7).

The "moral" is this: no one "method" (medium) is ultimately successful in inducing or producing continuous growth. Only the method that has built-in variety (e.g., sound compositions) will not become stale and predictable. Thus the greater the number of media a teacher has to employ, the greater the chance of reaching more students with more learning more of the time.

325

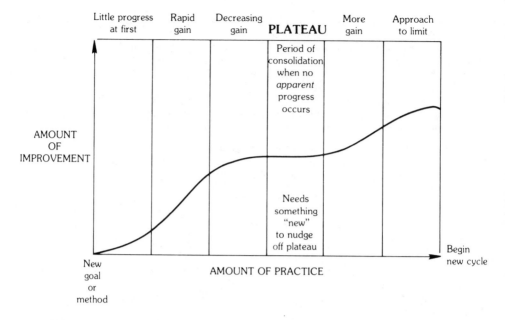

Fig. 5:7

Speech

Speech is useful when clear designations of meaning are generally possible and agreed upon. It is not useful when students don't understand words, or in spheres which depend on nonverbal media. Some problems:

1. *Vocabulary differences between students and teacher.* Speech is most effective when students do most of it (e.g., discussion).

2. *Connotation and denotation.* The former is rich, metaphoric, subjective, and expressive. The latter is technical, objective, and often abstract and cold. Some words have greatly contrasting connotations and denotations. What does the word "freedom" mean to a prisoner, to a minority person, to a student in your class, to you as a teacher, to your principal?

3. *Language is circular.* It always refers back to itself. Look up a word in the dictionary and choose a word from its definition. Look up that word, and so on until you inevitably arrive back at the starting words. Words refer to and define other words. They have a relevance only when they have a *living meaning* (connotation) for the people exchanging them. Words are abstractions and are not the same as the things to which they refer. A menu is not the meal and the map is not the territory. Similarly in music, the term (label) is not the musical experience.

4. *Language-arts skills.* Aural comprehension of lectures, reading problems, and writing (notetaking) introduce too many irrelevant variables into the music class. They all involve skills which need to be learned before being applied to other kinds of learning. Students having difficulty in *verbal literacy* need not have problems in developing *musical literacy*. Therefore, do not make verbal literacy a major condition for acquiring musical literacy. The music teacher who deemphasizes the role of language-arts skills as preconditions to learning maximizes the musical potential of the learner.

Multiple Means

The key to opening up music instruction is multiple means (or media) of instruction. Three factors tend to control this aspect of learning through media.

1. *Frequency:* multiple means allow for repeated contacts by students with the learning in question.
2. *Intensity:* individual learning styles are more receptive to certain media and thus the intensity of impact is greatest for a student who has the opportunity to work in a favored medium.
3. *Variety:* The Hawthorne Effect applies here. But breadth of musical offering also stands the greatest chance of broad application by the student in life (i.e., Action Learning).

Individual Learning Styles

All of the following are mutually interactive and influence the efficiency and effectiveness of learning.

1. *Time.* People are more responsive to learning at certain times of the day; also, the student's "mood" is an important timing factor. Learning when the student is in the mood for it is always more rewarding.
2. *Schedule/attention span.* Students have varying lengths of attention span. Rigid schedules seldom take this into account.
3. *Interference capacity.* Some students work best when the room is quiet, others don't mind, or thrive within a bustling atmosphere.
4. *Perceptual preference.* Some students respond better to certain kinds of stimuli: visual, sound, printed, multimedia, physical involvement, etc. Some, though few, are flexible and can profit almost equally from all.
5. *Working style.* While some work well alone or in groups, others work best in one or the other but not both.
6. *Teacher direction needed.* Some are more self-directed than others, who need more external direction (at least at first).
7. *Motivation.* Some are self-motivated; others need some view of personal gain, some inducement—hopefully of the intrinsic type (i.e., musical rewards).
8. *Classroom environment.* Must students remain in chairs? Need chairs be in straight rows? An overly formal environment can influence learning as much as an overly informal one.
9. *Responsibility.* Can the student be counted upon and trusted?

Individualized or Personalized Instruction

This kind of instruction does not necessarily have to be *independent study.* It is *individualized* when the *learning activities are made or prescribed especially for a given student and his or her learning style and needs.* There is no reasons why students with similar problems and learning styles cannot, therefore, work jointly on the same individualized study projects. Most sound compositions lend themselves to this kind of activity.

Variables here include the knowledge and interest you have in mediated instruction, and the time you have available. Several different kinds of mediated instruction, such as contract learning and goal cards, will be suggested later. Students' learning styles and the physical facilities and resources also have to be considered, as does the attitude of the school administration to such approaches.

Small-Group Formats

Often small groups combine the advantages of individualization with some greater degree of independence than is available in traditional large group instruction.

1. *Learning groups.* Up to seven or eight students with similar projects try cooperatively to acquire the learning needed to complete their respective projects. The teacher "steers" them to appropriate learning sources or means. Example: learning to do tape manipulation in order to compose a sound collage individually.

2. *Jigsaw groups.* These combine students of unequal ability or having specific things to contribute to the solution of a group problem or project. Each contributes to the solution of the problem or project. When necessary, the teacher can prepare students to make a specific contribution. Example: instrumental students are grouped together for a sound composition requiring each of their instruments.

3. *Simulations.* Small groups study certain hypothetical situations that have a realistic chance of happening to many people. The group considers alternatives and "acts out" their solutions. Example: "If you were buying several record albums of your favorite groups and another customer your own age volunteered the opinion that your purchases were in poor taste and gave you reasons for this opinion, what kinds of reasons would you expect and how would you answer them?"

4. *Knowledge teams or circles.* Similar to learning groups or jigsaw groups except that here special attention is placed on grouping students of equal ability. Here, too, students are working on the same project or problem, but the result will be prepared and presented individually. Example: learning how to play chords on the guitar.

5. *Cross-peer tutoring.* Students of unequal ability are placed together. The more advanced, or those with specific skills, are expected to teach or help the other students *in order to successfully complete a mutual project or problem.* Example: One student teaches rhythmic notation to others in order for them to be able to notate and perform a sound composition requiring the use of standard rhythmic notation.

6. *Brainstorming.* A group freely explores many possible solutions to a given problem or project before deciding on one course of action. All alternatives are presented along with the chosen solution. Example: "What factors have to be present in an effective system of musical notation that can be used by a performer other than the composer?"

7. *Role playing.* This is a specific kind of simulation. Members of a group are placed in a hypothetical situation requiring them to "act out" their thoughts, usually without benefit of enough time to work out "scripts" but with enough time to prepare themselves generally. Example: Given an obscure recording by an otherwise popular recording group or star) one person plays a reluctant recording company executive and the remaining group members try to convince him to produce the record as though they were the performing group or artistic agents. Emphasize musical arguments.

Individualized Learning for Independent Study
or Groups of Two or Three Students

These kinds of activities largely involve student *exploration* of a variety of learning possibilities in music.

1. *Interest centers.* These are specific locations where students can go to study, explore, or experiment with a variety of resources collected or assembled on the basis of a single topic, area of interest, or skill.

a. *Free:* Truly exploratory and therefore the free choice of students. Free-choice interest centers are designed to stimulate interest in an area totally unfamiliar to students. Example: students read the story synopsis and listen to highlights of musical-theater productions you judge to be relevant to their tastes.

b. *Elective:* From among several options, the student elects to pursue certain ones (perhaps a required number). Examples: record collecting; how to choose a stereo system; musical "hits" from the Renaissance; careers in music.

2. *Learning stations.* These are places where students master certain specific learnings or skills. They usually require highly organized learning materials such as programmed learning aids, tape-slide or filmstrip sets, etc. Examples: tape-manipulation techniques; playing the recorder; playing the electric chord organ; playing the guitar; how to transpose music for your instrument.

3. *Media areas or centers.* These are places where media can be used, especially such things as tapes, recordings, slides, programmed learning, and video cassettes. Obviously it is not the simple use of this technology that counts, but rather the use to which these media are put. Therefore preview, select, or organize materials carefully to suit bona fide musical ends. Filmstrips about music in the Revolutionary War will seldom make a lasting or useful impression. Examples: a mini-concert video cassette of the high school percussion ensemble; a tape-slide presentation you have developed showing "the ease and fun of playing a Recorder."

4. *Game tables.* These are learning activities designed as independent or small group games. These should not involve meaningless information, but should encourage significant musical pursuits. Example: "Rhythm-muddles," a commercial game dealing with arranging rhythms, which provides a "Scrabble"-like challenge.

Independent Learning

This is learning which a student works on independently. It may be individualized to suit the special needs of the student. But it need not be: often projects suitable for many in a class can be done individually over time by virtually every one in the class. The media involved are used according to specific needs of a given learner. However that does not mean that such projects may not be suitable for another learner in the future who has similar qualities or needs.

1. *Learning contracts.* These are best organized around a single musical skill or area of knowledge that is clearly relevant to the learner and that can be clearly evaluated. Learning contracts should provide multiple means of learning (reading, listening, watching films, etc.) in order to involve one or more of the student's preferred learning styles. A contract usually should involve:

a. A behavioral objective, paraphrased for the student, that specifies what the student is to learn.

b. The criteria by which the student's work will be evaluated.

c. The methods of assessment to be used.

d. The level of achievement required to successfully complete the contract (or the specific levels of achievement needed to earn a certain grade).

e. The listing of the learning media the teacher has organized and their location.

f. A realistic time limitation; or when a project involves multiple stages, provide a time-line specifying completion dates.

g. Where useful, a specification or choice of means by which the student's result will be shared with the class. Example: Learning how to generate sounds using a mini-synthesizer (print and other materials are organized for the student to use in active individual experimentation).

2. *Contract-learning activity projects* (CLAPs). These are similar to learning contracts in for-

mat except that they emphasize tangible *projects* (while learning contracts tend to result in a demonstrated learning or skill of a more general nature). A CLAP should be preceded by a diagnostic determination of the student's readiness for pursuing it. This may involve a special "pretest" or the recent completion of a prerequisite step. Finally, CLAPs should clearly describe or specify the final product. This should be detailed enough to guide the student's efforts and to serve as the criterion of evaluation. Items (a) through (g) under the section on learning contracts should be specified here as well. Example: taping an actual synthesizer composition using skills acquired in the learning contract above (and a readiness for using the tape recorder).

3. *Goal cards.* For all practical purposes, goal cards are mini-learning contracts or mini-CLAPs. They are short-term: they will take only one or two class periods at most. They are useful in preparing students for learning contracts (i.e., by generating interest) or CLAPs (i.e., as prerequisites). It is a good idea to place them on 4″ by 6 ″ cards and to file them according to category. Keep multiple copies for instances where more than one student may wish to work on the same activity (and to replace lost or destroyed cards). Provide as much of the information listed under the section on learning contracts as is necessary or realistic. Sequences of goal cards can be arranged to teach a composite skill. Example: the example given for learning contracts above (p. 329) could be broken into multiple goal cards. The student who needs short-term results benefits from this rather than from the longer-term learning contracts or CLAPs. *Goal cards are the best way of making interest centers, learning stations, and media corners work effectively.*

Self-Designed or Custom-Tailored Independent Study

These activities are especially useful for advanced or weak students; for students who have missed school due to illness or other reasons; or for those who transfer in and find themselves "behind." They are always planned especially for the needs of a specific individual. They should adhere to as many of the specifications of a learning contract as is possible or relevant and should be addressed to the student's learning style, however determined. Since they are time-consuming to make up, use them only when none of the other methods listed above will work as well. But even though they are designed with specific students in mind, *keep them.* Some future student may also fit the bill, or with minor changes the activities may be used by a learning group or in some other way. Try not to appear to use these as a reward or punishment.

Summary

Any teacher who does not seriously and actively consider using some of these varied means of instruction is simply ignoring most of the available known means (methods, media) of a significant music education. No teaching circumstance is so restrictive as to prohibit some significant use of many of these ideas. In fact, just the opposite is often true! The more restrictive a situation may appear to be, the more some of these media techniques will make up for deficiencies in staffing, available time, and other conditions.

Any planning by a teacher beyond large-group planning only *seems* extra. It is extra only when the teacher is used to thinking that large-group media are the only ones, or are the best. Otherwise, planning of this kind should be par for the course in the same way that other professions must attend to individual details. This is, in fact, one of the characteristics that distinguishes a *profession* from a *mere job*. Careful and thoughtful planning of the instructional considerations described here will maximize learning productivity and will minimize discipline problems. Readers interested in more details should refer to the "Instructional Media" section of the Selected Bibliography.

NOTES: CHAPTER 5

1. Ernest Cassirer, *The Logic of the Humanities*, Trans. C. S. Howe, paperbound, (New Haven, Conn.: Yale University Press, 1966), p. 111.
2. "Individuals are more highly persuasible by messages arguing in a direction which increases consistency and are more resistant to those arguing in a direction that increases inconsistency. . . . The preferred solution to a belief dilemma is one involving the least effortful path."—Milton J. Rosenberg et al., *Attitude Organization and Change* (New Haven, Conn.: Yale University Press, 1966), pp. 204, 208.
3. See Felix Greene, *Freedom from Fear* (Pacifica Tape Library, 5316 Venice Blvd., Los Angeles, Calif. 90019). This twenty-seven-minute tape is well worth the attention of every teacher and is highly recommended.
4. Rosenberg et al., *Attitude Organization and Change*, pp. 2, 1.
5. Ibid., p. 1.
6. Ibid., p. 4.
7. Robert Powell, *The Free Mind* (New York: Julian Press, 1972), p. 53.
8. Greene, *Freedom from Fear;* articulated at the beginning of the tape.
9. It would seem useful that music, which is one of the "humanities," should be taught by "humanistic teachers"!
10. Charles M. Rossiter, Jr., "Maxims for Humanizing Education," *Journal of Humanistic Psychology*, vol. 16, no. 1 (Winter 1976), p. 78. "The orientation with which a teacher approaches the classroom is far more important than any technique he or she might use" (p. 75). "A humanistic orientation does not present a dogma to which one must rigidly adhere if one is to be a humanistic teacher" (p. 77). Generally, this brief article advocates the following: (1) Be concerned with the whole person; (2) treat students as persons; (3) interact with students in a manner conducive to their psychological growth; (4) know and be yourself; and (5) *do not teach by formula* (pp. 75-78).
11. For example, humanistic psychologist Carl Rogers urges "teachers to determine the amount of freedom they feel comfortable with in the clasroom and to run their classes in accordance with those feelings." See Rossiter, "Maxims for Humanizing Education," p. 77.

12. For more detail see Thomas A. Regelski, *Principles and Problems of Music Education* (Englewood Cliffs, N.J.: Prentice-Hall, 1975), pp. 112, 115-18.

13. Samuel J. Warner, *Self-Realization and Self-Defeat* (New York: Grove Press, 1966), p. 173.

14. Ibid., pp. 178-79.

15. See Martin E. P. Seligman, "Fall into Helplessness," *Psychology Today*, vol. 7 (June 1973); also George Mandler, *Mind and Emotion* (New York: John Wiley & Sons, 1975), pp. 207-12.

16. See Julian B. Rotter, "External Control and Internal Control," *Psychology Today*, vol. 5 (June 1971).

17. Mandler, *Mind and Emotion*, p. 152.

18. Ibid.

19. Ibid., p. 150.

20. Ibid.

21. "Insults to self-esteem, however subtle, tend to be cumulative and to mount in pressure."—Warner, *Self-Realization and Self-Defeat*, p. 162.

22. "It is as if a point of 'honor' were involved. To cooperate carries for such people a deep sense of repugnance. To cooperate is to 'give in,' to 'make up,' in a situation where self-respect can be nurtured only through a continuing fight."—Warner, *Self-Realization and Self-Defeat*, p. 150.

23. "At those times when authority is particularly provoking and frustrating, the self-damage to personal efficiency is perceptibly increased."—Ibid., p. 40.

24. Mandler, *Mind and Emotion*, p. 150.

25. See Howard Kirshenbaum, Sidney B. Simon, and Rodney W. Napier, *Wad-ja-get? The Grading Game in American Education* (New York: Hart Publishing Co., 1971).

26. See Eric Gaudry and Charles D. Spielberger, *Anxiety and Educational Achievement* (Sydney, Australia: John Wiley & Sons, 1971), chapters 3, 4, 5. Also see Mandler, *Mind and Emotion*, pp. 186, 189.

27. See Seligman, "Fall into Helplessness," p. 43; and Rotter, "External Control and Internal Control," p. 37.

28. Warner, *Self-Realization and Self-Defeat*, pp. 142-43.

29. Seligman, "Fall into Helplessness," p. 45.

30. Warner, *Self-Realization and Self-Defeat*, p. 160.

31. Karen Horney, quoted in Ibid., p. 148.

32. Warner, *Self-Realization and Self-Defeat*, p. 140.

33. Ibid., p. 147.

34. Ibid., pp. 28-29.

35. Such "punishing features make their appearance so very long after the act which brings immediate reward [the "reward" perhaps of decreased boredom, or of getting the teacher mad] that this time factor causes the slight immediate reward to outweigh the greater but more remote punishment, and *works toward*

. . . *repeating and perpetuating the self-defeating habit pattern* [italics added]."— Ibid., pp. 179-80.

36. Mandler, *Mind and Emotion*, p. 91.

37. Ibid., p. 75.

38. Ibid., p. 76.

39. Warner, *Self-Realization and Self-Defeat*, p. 121.

40. Mandler, *Mind and Emotion*, p. 150.

41. Warner, *Self-Realization and Self-Defeat*, p. 80.

42. Ibid., pp. 166-67.

43. Ibid., p. 166.

44. Mandler, *Mind and Emotion*, p. 152.

45. Warner, *Self-Realization and Self-Defeat*, p. 93.

46. Marjorie Seddon Johnson, "I Think My Teacher Is A . . . ," *Learning*, vol. 4, no. 6 (Feb. 1976), p. 36.

47. Marshall McLuhan, *Understanding Media* (New York: New American Library, Signet Books, 1964).

6

Bases for General Music Education

334

☐   Creative Teaching for Action Learning

☐   Chapter Notes

THE PROBLEM

A number of years ago in summer school the writer taught to graduate students a course dealing with Action Learning. Since time was limited, only the "methods" were dealt with; there was no explanatory context. Just the "recipes." The upshot was that these teachers learned how to run individual activities but were unable to successfully integrate them into a meaningful program. All of a sudden, "units" on sound composition spurted up. Directed listening was done for a week, then dropped for the remainder of the term. Songwriting, too, was treated in an all-at-once manner, and was made into a mere academic study of music's rudiments.

All this was terribly disconcerting, for the overall effect was to negate all the strengths of the Action Learning approach and to render the activities as ineffective as many other more traditional methods had become in the hands of thoughtless teachers. Never again, it was vowed, would the "methods" be taught in isolation! These methods succeed best when the teacher is mindful of such broader considerations as: (a) why the methods work; (b) what alterations should be made when they are not as successful in a given situation as they might be; (c) when and how they should be employed in a thoroughly effective program; (d) how music learning occurs in conjunction with these methods; (e) how the implications of such methods and the assumptions about them are contrasted with those of other or traditional methods; (f) which philosophical and teaching goals are warranted in a program designed to promote the synergetic aspects of the musical art.

Many of these questions have been discussed in conjunction with the related methods throughout the text so far. In addition, there exist several more considerations of a general nature that affect the program recommended as a whole and that deal with the process of musical learning itself. This chapter is concerned with these factors. Here you will receive insights into "how to put it all together."

SOME TRADITIONAL ASSUMPTIONS AND THEIR PITFALLS

1. ASSUMPTION: MUSIC CLASS SHOULD BE FUN

This is an assumption you often hear; in fact it is often made about all school experiences. But since music is basically an enjoyable pursuit—more naturally so for most people than arithmetic is, for example—this attitude of

335

fun at all cost often causes more problems in music education than it does in other aspects of the school day.

There is little doubt that music class should not be *not* enjoyable or interesting! But *music class doesn't have to turn into a recess or recreation period.* The word "fun" is usually used to refer to moments of frolic, gaiety, and merriment. It implies an intensely entertaining or amusing event. And therein lies the problem. It is a serious mistake to assume that all musical experiences need to involve intense entertainment or amusement value for youngsters.

Just as physical education entails far more than entertaining games played as a divertissements, so music education involves more than entertaining musical "games" played in the classroom. Neither pursuit is included in the process of education for the pure entertainment of children. Nor are they intended as mere study-breaks. Both have serious purposes.

On the other hand, *music classes ought to be pleasing, interesting, or engaging in some way.* This need not involve the intense joy of out-of-school games. Adolescents can find many degrees of satisfaction between the extremes of exhilaration and boredom. In fact, the successful teacher is the one who manages best to create activities that achieve a synthesis of pleasure with seriousness.

This is a difficult status to achieve in instruction, however. While pleasure and purpose are not mutually exclusive positions, they do not always seem to go together readily in our daily lives. Therefore a synthesis of "pleasure with purpose" or "work and play" will not be a singular, once-and-for-all-times accomplishment. Rather, it will be an ever-changing, evolving, fluctuating condition of tension, shifting or leaning a little more this way, then a little more that way between the two aspects. The result of such activities should be *a sense of satisfaction: a gratification that arises from a task undertaken with relevant goals in mind and brought to successful completion.* Students should virtually be disappointed when the time for musical instruction comes to an end, as it must.

Nothing is really "fun" unless there is some challenge or difficulty to overcome. It is especially "fun" if the difficulty to be mastered is relevant or important, as opposed to meaningless on inconsequential. Avoid those kinds of classes that run afoul of social attitudes and roles acquired by youngsters as they approach adolescence. Boys in particular often shy away from classes that conflict with their developing sense (stereotypes) of masculinity. They are neither interested in the challenges or difficulties presented nor would they consider overcoming such difficulties relevant or important if they did succeed.

The question of fun is thus an odd problem. The elementary years begin with the problem of maintaining a certain atmosphere of seriousness to go along with children's natural pleasure from musical involvement. A certain tempering of their overenthusiasm for music is required. In the middle and junior high school the problem becomes just the opposite. The child has grown into a more complex physical, mental, and social being. Competing interests, a greater capacity for looking ahead, changing patterns of social interaction, and other important growth characteristics can cause these older children to appear less interested in musical activities other than social listening and dancing. And high school students often have to be encouraged to be *more playful* since they often feign, however unknowingly, a sophistication that can result in a quasi-adultlike aloofness.

Music activities for all high-school-age adolescents must be especially relevant in application to their present and future lives, must be especially invigorating and challenging, and must result in significant personal accomplishment. Unfortunately, if their musical education to this point has been boring, irrelevant, and abstract, their preliminary attitudes will be all the more solidified and the teacher will have to make special efforts to open them up once again to the benefits of instruction in music.

So as children grow physically, mentally, and socially, and as their interests and abilities are sharpened, the problem becomes less one of tempering uncontrolled fun and more one of making certain the music class is interesting and in line with students' evolving image of themselves. Care must be taken to ensure that they do not develop poor attitudes toward musical instruction which are then generalized to all of music.

2. ASSUMPTION: MUSIC LEARNED IN SCHOOL SHOULD BE THE STANDARD REPERTORY

One of the things that can "turn off" pre- and early adolescents is the kind of music the teacher chooses to have such students sing, play, or listen to. Traditionally this has involved the standard repertory of folk and patriotic songs, the art music of the western cultures, and even some popular music of these cultures.

Often all that learners encounter in school is similar to what they have encountered at home—generally music from the seventeenth to the nineteenth centuries, and a touch of twentieth-century music mostly in the more popular, commercial vein. Song series and other materials consist almost entirely of this same fare, as do listening lessons. None of these kinds of music are due any special criticism. *The mistaken assumption is that this kind of music should be the only kind studied in music classes.*

Such a music education would consist solely of the music of the *past,* and would be solely concerned with our cultural heritage and how music has developed over the ages. It is doubtless true that much of the standard repertory is important and will continue to be available in some form. Much of it will in time, however, be relegated to a secondary, perhaps purely historical niche, and will receive few if any performances in the future.

Excessive preoccupation with such music does not prepare the student to respond to the music of today and tomorrow. Most of the music of the present is (and presumably most of the music of the future will be) of an entirely different character than the traditional music of the standard repertory. What is avant-garde today will be passé tomorrow.

Many learning theorists have repeatedly emphasized that learning is expanding at such an incredible rate that people will no longer be able to actually learn in school all that needs to be known. They must be led *to learn how to learn; they must learn the general or basic structures and principles constituting various areas of knowledge.* When the time arrives that specific knowledge is required in later life, the individual is thus prepared to acquire it as the situation demands.

The various contemporary forms of music still manifest most of the same elements, principles, and techniques as more traditional music. But they do so in new ways, using new sound sources and combinations, and often for different purposes than has been true in the past. If your program of music education includes a large proportion of newer music, such as sound compositions, you will find that what is learned through experiences with it is easily transferable to other kinds of music. Similarly, your classes are not locked in a closed system that involves mainly the "given facts" of a historical tradition. They can begin to gain insights into music directly from their experiences with music and musical elements and techniques, unburdened with having first to learn the historical preconditions.

This is not very far removed in actuality from the activities of very young children with music. The "melodies" they hum or sing to themselves while playing are often not "tunes" in the traditional sense. A child at the piano is usually engrossed in simply exploring sound—sound patterns, combinations, volumes, etc.—and profits well from this kind of activity prior to the formal study of piano. In fact most of our early learning is freely exploratory in just this way. Upon such experiences, a formal educational program can grow.

This "exploratory phase" involves experiencing the attributes of music without having first to master specific techniques, notational symbols, and other elements. With no such absolutes to be learned first, children can proceed naturally in acquiring the readiness for other kinds of music and musical instruction. Failure is thereby minimized, and there is also a final benefit of incorporating much nontraditional music: positive attitudes arising from a history of success in music activities. The kind of "discovery" that is possible with this kind of music is quite different from the "work" involved in learning a preexisting musical language.

It seems almost certain that much of the music of the future—if it continues on its present course—will never involve the *singular* musical systematization that was characteristic of the standard repertory over the last three centuries. In other words, composers in the future will always be involved to some degree in "discovering" new techniques and processes, new sounds and notational systems, new performance practices and reasons for composing.

Thus there are many reasons to balance your program equally between the more standard repertory and the ever-evolving concerns of contemporary composers:

1. Learners are prepared to cope with the music of the present and future.

2. They are deriving very solid and basic musical concepts that have equal application to both the past and the present.

3. Without the absolute "rights and wrongs," "shoulds and should nots" attached to learning a tradition, individuals can achieve greater success and thus develop a positive attitude toward music and music instruction.

4. The techniques and results of contemporary music are natural to youngsters whose concepts and attitudes are not yet frozen and whose minds are still open to all of human experience. It is adults whose minds have been overconditioned to the standard repertory and who find new music less interesting or enjoyable than do younger people.

5. New music encourages teachers to think and plan in terms of observable student growth, since children can from the very beginning create, perform, and respond fruitfully. Thus as a beneficial byproduct it allows active involvement in all phases of music from the very first class.

6. Lastly, this kind of music is very well suited to the adolescent's imagination and feelings. The cognitive aspects of musical learning will thus follow naturally the development of each student's feelings for and valuing of music. These are always important prerequisites to any learning that will last.

3. ASSUMPTION: MUSIC EDUCATION MUST BE CARRIED ON IN LARGE GROUPS

Traditionally children have been herded together for music class and all instruction has been carried on with them simultaneously. Since most of the purposes and techniques of instruction in other subjects were designed to facilitate this arrangement, this all seemed very natural.

Today, everywhere, this is less and less true. Instructional formats are being broken down into a variety of teaching formats. Today we have so-called open classes and tracking, "teaching as learning" (i.e., peer teaching), individualized instruction using teacher aides and, as we saw in the previous chapter, a variety of mediated instruction using programming, learning contracts, goal cards, media centers, and independent study corners or areas. If music education is not to go the way of the dinosaur, the forms of instruction in music must more closely match or even improve upon the forms of instruction in other subjects.

While certain kinds of musical experiences—such as bands, choruses, and orchestras—will always require large groups, the learning experiences in other areas of a program need not. The solution is not simple, but a solution does exist and is being used with success in many schools. It necessarily takes different forms according to the contingencies of the local situation, but all solutions seem to have one thing in common. *They all have extended music education beyond the traditional singing/music reading approach, which was the major factor in imposing the need for large-group instruction.*

Generally this new solution involves working with youngsters in various smaller groups. Smaller groups can be convened for most kinds of music activities and give the teacher more flexibility in meeting student needs. In an open middle school:

1. Music education is seen as a more natural event.

2. Music instruction of this kind can be kept relatively short, but many short experiences a week can easily add up to more learning than the typical approach of reserving a "period."

3. When activities involving composition, performance, and listening result in observable learning, then various kinds of more independent work or work in smaller groups is possible.

    a. Individual projects can be carried on in the same way that, say, science experiments are handled.

    b. Mediated imstruction may be used. Programmed materials, audiovisual materials, learning contracts, and goal cards can be established in learning centers, study carrels, or music corners.

    c. True creative work is best done individually or with a few other students. This leads to musical independence.

Proceeding in this way usually results in more tangible, observable indications of learning. And for an art form that is a mainstay of a humanistic education, such individualized work and attention maintains the intrinsic "human" character of the musical experience.

Similarly, high school classes in music theory, musicianship, or music appreciation are best regarded as an open "laboratory" for full musical involvement by students. Whatever other traditional activities are pursued, *all the Action Learning activities and principles covered so far are easily adapted to the higher levels of challenge, sophistication, and productivity characteristic of high school students.* Boring lectures, note taking, and test taking are out; a high level of musical involvement is in!

A special premium of this kind of instruction is that the teacher is not always *directly* involved in the learning process. This affords the teacher a greater variety of teaching approaches, since a variety of activities can be started simultaneously or interwoven in many ways. The students have not been taught. *They have actively learned!* And this is the prime difference between large group and Action Learning methods of instruction.

4. ASSUMPTION: WHAT IS LEARNED IN MUSICAL INSTRUCTION IS NECESSARILY MUSICAL

Any kind of formal learning involves goals. And goals involve questions and problems of motivation and the correspondence of the teacher's goals with the goals and needs of students.

Psychologist Abraham Maslow spent a lifetime studying the needs that stand behind motivation. Fortunately, his conclusions not only meet the test of common sense; they also result in a point of view that is very compatible with the arts (see Fig. 6:1). He determined that there are two kinds of needs—states that are somehow unfulfilled and thus seek satisfaction. The subsequent quest for fulfillment or satisfaction is responsible for the propelling force we call motivation. At the lowest level are the most basic needs, called *Deficiency-Needs* or *D-Needs*. These, when unfulfilled, involve some kind or degree of psychological or physical "illness." The person feels "deficient" as long as such needs are unmet. The fulfilling of Deficiency-Needs prevents or cures such conditions and brings about a more satisfactory life situation. D-Needs, therefore, are not a concern of typically healthy persons.

D-Needs are fundamental to motivation, for there is a "tendency for a new and higher need to emerge as the lower need fulfills itself by being sufficiently gratified."[1] This process of fulfilling lower needs, then seeking fulfillment of the next highest need, results in *personal growth* as the individual conquers one

Fig. 6:1

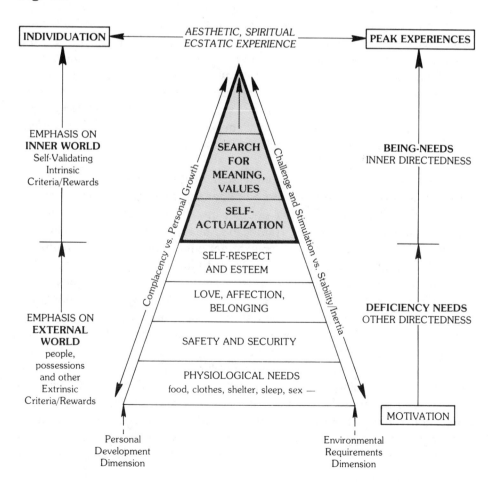

stage after another. Thus seen, students in schools will not be able or motivated to learn as long as they are, for example, hungry or tired. Once such deficiences are no longer a problem, students need the *stability* of feeling safe and secure in the learning situation if they are to profit from it. With a growing sense of *belonging,* students earn the measure of *self-respect* and *self-esteem* that makes possible the higher motivational states.

Notice, however, that to this point the D-Needs "for safety, belongingness, love relations and respect can be satisfied only by other people, i.e., only from outside the person. This means considerable dependence on the environment,"[2] and thus on the *external world* of other people, possessions, etc.—all of which can be called *extrinsic criteria* or *rewards* that motivate behavior. Complacency sets in when a person has become too easily satisfied with any stage of D-Needs (say, when basic physiological satisfactions, security, and love are all that the person desires in life). Smug contentment prevents such a person from looking to higher horizons. The person is unmotivated to grow into a fuller being and remains *inert.*

Such a person, moreover, is not *self-directed,* since he or she is overwhelmingly dependent on other people, possessions, etc., for satisfaction of basic needs: love can always be withdrawn, those people or possessions that provide safety and security can be lost, and the food on the table may depend upon being polite to a hateful superior at work. To a greater or lesser degree, then, unmet Deficiency-Needs result in some serious degree of other-directedness, of having the quality of life or one's actions determined or controlled in some way by other people. The deficiency-motivated person either requires other people or things to fill the lack or acts always having in mind the impression made on other people.

"In contrast, the self-actualizing individual, by definition gratified in his basic needs, is far less dependent, far less beholden, far more autonomous and self-directed. Far from needing other people, growth-motivated people may actually be hampered by them."[3] Rather than being controlled or motivated by extrinsic criteria and rewards in the external environment, self-actualizing individuals control and use their environment to fulfill their growth potential.[4]

Such personal growth beyond D-Needs brings forth the potential of the *Being-Needs, or B-Needs.* Being-Needs are self-validating, self-justifying, and self-sufficient. They fill no particular deficiency and they require no "significant others" to provide them or approve of them. What is more, they add to and affirm our Being, our Existence, our lives. They make the difference between merely "getting by" in life and living a full life—a life that celebrates that we Are who we Are doing what we Are with our Being. Thus Being-Needs are characterized by inner-directedness: the motivation for fulfillment comes from within and remains the same whether or not the world or people in it are watching! At this stage, people are no longer "owned" by their possessions, since life's meaning is increasingly for them an inner state or value. Thus personal and *intrinsic criteria and rewards* are the source of motivation for such people; and fully developed, the process results in the functional *individuation* of the person: the stage at which the individual—as a unique person rather than as a biological entity—truly comes into Being. It is the stage at which one is fully distinguished from others: now the person is truly unique, at least as he or she comes to appreciate.

It is significant that Maslow puts at the very top of this "Hierarchy of Needs" the *aesthetic experience*,[5] which he also describes as being closely related to moments of profound spiritual insight, and which can be compared favorably to experiences of ecstasy—even sexual ecstasy! These experiences he calls *peak experiences:* they are intense moments when we feel most alive, most unique (individuated), and most fulfilled or at "one" with ourselves. Thus at these moments we are most "whole" and most aware of it!

If the *complacency* of low or no motivation towards *personal growth* is to be overcome, the *stability* and *inertia* characterizing D-Needs must be replaced by *challenge* and *stimulation*. It is heartening, too, that once they are experienced, B-Needs themselves provide one kind of challenge and stimulation as well as responding to other kinds.

It stands to reason, then, that aesthetic growth is not only a valuable goal in its own right but is also at the very heart of "basic education." Understood in the manner that has been described, it is the ultimate goal of education and thus provides direction and motivation for all learning. "Growth takes place when the next step forward is subjectively more delightful, more joyous, more intrinsically satisfying than the previous gratification with which we have become familiar and even bored."[6] For many people experiencing such growth, motivation is no problem. Growth *is* motivation and thus they grow naturally to ever-higher levels of B-Needs. But what happens if this positive progression is not nurtured properly, stops, or is hindered in any way from any source?

The result is often euphemistically called "motivation problems" or a "bad attitude." Rather than experiencing the motivating potential of anything even close to an aesthetic response (or even participating in lower-level activities that nurture the D-Need for self-respect, thus providing the basic potential for self-actualization and the discovery of meaning and values) students too often learn to dislike music class. They do not, you should note, learn to dislike *music* as such. Music continues to be sought—generally outside of school—at a level that *at least* gratifies basic D-Needs such as belongingness (through peer approval). Since music paradoxically contributes as well to a greater sense of individuation—a growth need of all adolescents—it is an absolutely essential aspect of adolescent existence in our culture.

In school, though, teacher attitudes and class lessons that contribute to insecurity, alienation, learned helplessness, and a poor self-concept all conspire to destroy motivation. Oh, students may sometimes *seem* to cooperate; but

343

they are doing so only in response to extrinsic motivation in such forms as threats by an authoritarian teacher, fear of failure, or anxiety about being made a fool of in front of peers. These are all techniques used by so-called disciplinarians, those teachers who earn their fame *controlling students by threatening or violating D-Needs rather than by providing the challenge and stimulation of musical activities that draw upon the natural motivation of B-Needs.*

In the meanwhile students may appear on the surface to be "paying attention" in some ill-defined way. What they really may "learn," however, is a poor attitude toward music class because it fulfills no particular Deficiency-Need (in fact, classes taught this way often overemphasize deficiencies) and results (in school, at least) in no particular self-actualization or peak experience (Being-Need). That may be the reason why students seem so self-actualized in a certain sense when they encounter "youth music" freely outside the confines of school. Then it is a self-validating experience for them sought actively and freely for that reason.

This seems particularly likely in considering the attitude of adolescents and preadolescents towards the accepted youth music. While it is difficult to assess how much aesthetic fulfillment, if any, may be obtained by such involvements, it is readily apparent that *very important needs of some kind are fulfilled by contacts with youth music and that youngsters do feel varying degrees of self-actualization as a result.*

It is perhaps simplistic to affirm that among the learning to result from musical instruction, the most beneficial to the learner is the kind that is positive, leading to increasing self-actualization and to the richer fulfillment of basic aesthetic needs. Learning that results in or from feelings of deficiency is not conducive to positive musical growth.

While it must be admitted that not all children have the same potential for growth in music or other aesthetic spheres, none have developed their potential fully. Instruction that emphasizes weakness or failings in specific skills is very likely to induce feelings of failure, of learned helplessness, of a poor or deficient sense of self-worth. This becomes all the more crucial, it seems, or all the more apparent, in any case, with pubescence and adolescence. One of the most important growth tasks at these stages is to arrive at a *positive self-image, a sense of self-esteem.*

If instruction is to emphasize the realization of whatever potential for growth and response exists in a student, it will *not* put a premium on the acquisition of ungratifying skills designed to rid the individual of skill-deficiencies (as defined by the teacher) —skills which the student does not recognize or accept as important or relevant. Effective instruction does put its emphasis on those aspects of musical growth that are most conducive to the positive experiencing of music; to the kind of musical response that comes closest to a peak experience; to the kind of self-image that results, at the very least, in seeing oneself as having an affinity for the musical experience. Such growth arises from within, and is not imposed from outside the individual.

In short, *musical experiences undertaken as part of the school music program should lead to a positive attitude and positive motivations with regard to the musical art.* Achieving this condition requires specific attention to the needs and characteristics of individual students, the processes of human motivation, and the character of the musical art. With any less of an effort, classes may seem to temporarily "learn" certain musical concepts, facts and informations, or even skills. But they will also "learn" how to make the teacher *think* they are learning in music class, or even liking music class. They can learn that music is only singing, or all listening, or ("God forbid," says Johnny Roughneck) dancing.

Yes, *students "learn" more than is actively taught about the music being learned.* This "hidden curriculum" is why the teacher must be perfectly aware of what is being taught, and more importantly, how it is being taught. Keep in mind the maxim that how a child feels *about* what he learns can have a more enduring effect than *what* he learns. Often the attitudinal and emotional by-products of instruction have a more permanent effect than specific cognitions and skills. These specific learnings must be used, reinforced, refined, to be sure. This helps insure their retention. But even with such efforts, *instruction will have had no positive or long-term impact unless attitudes well disposed toward music are developed.*

This will not result unless the teacher takes specific steps to foster this condition. Such steps are the most difficult aspects of musical instruction and therefore constitute one of its greatest hazards. As a potential pitfall this aspect of instruction is second to none in importance. Its misuse must be avoided with all your human wisdom and insight.

5. ASSUMPTION: ALL STUDENTS LOVE MUSIC EQUALLY

While it is no doubt true that everyone has some natural inclination toward music, *it is a false assumption to believe that music has the same thing to offer each person, in the same way, and to the same degree.* By virtue of their environment and genetic endowment some students are more receptive to music learning or more able to profit from it. They have a certain potential that other children do not seem to possess by the time they reach school. These other children will develop abilities in the visual arts, dance, or perhaps theater. Still others will be inclined to manifest their creativity in electronics, automobile mechanics, or homemaking. Some will become athletes, or will specialize in industrial arts. Some will be quite well rounded, and others will be single-minded and tenacious in their pursuits.

This involves somewhat more than what is ordinarily called "individual differences." That catchall expression is usually used to refer to individual abilities in readiness, learning styles, or learning rates *within* a given subject-area that must be learned by everybody in a more or less uniform style. It is considered important, therefore, to allow for individual differences in a manner that leads to a more complete mastery of the subject.

The musical experience, the musical response, is not the singular thing that the principles and operations of mathematics are. While a carpenter must have specific skills in arithmetic, we cannot and should not expect the same kind of singular need to exist in music in order for people to respond fully to music and to seek its peak experiences.

Musical talents and potentials, whatever they may be in a given individual, are not singular or reducible to singular qualities. They are infinite in their variety, and the requisites for fulfillment and actualization are equally as infinite. This does not mean that students are allowed to drift along on the vagaries of self-defined interest. It does not mean that the teacher must cater to every apparent whim and desire.

It does mean that *experiences must be devised that enable students to take from them everything they are capable of deriving, and in the way they are capable of deriving it.* It means that musical experiences ought to be planned with sufficient breadth of possibility and that somewhat diverse degrees and qualities of achievement and progress are possible. *It is possible and desirable, therefore, to structure lessons in which students are able to reach their own level of ability and interest, whatever it may be* — i.e., what might be called *multiple outcomes* are possible. It is in this area that singing and music reading must be handled with great caution, since they are perhaps the most rigid and singular of musical learnings. The expectations for singing and music reading seem to be more rigidly applied by teachers than for other aspects of music. Certainly no areas of music will be found where there is greater individuality in readiness, prior accomplishment, talent, and potential, and where there is greater individuality in readiness, prior accomplishment, talent, and potential, and where there is greater chance of paying only ineffective token attention to such differences.

The trick of proper instruction is to nurture the seed of interest that all people have for music without expecting that each seed will yield identical growth. You must build on students' natural interest in music by structuring activities that encourage and facilitate their ability to operate at their own level and to profit in relation to their potential and intrinsic interest. *Above all you must not kill the plant for the love of an orderly garden.* You must not diminish in any way students' interest in music by unwarranted expectations of uniformity or by the nature of your teaching.

How well students learn is a matter of extending individual potential to its fullest growth without pushing it beyond. Here it will be equally true that *how* you teach will often be more significant in its ultimate impact than *what* you teach. The question of individual talents and potentials is in part a social difficulty as well as a pedagogical difficulty. Adolescents tend to judge their progress and derive some of their satisfaction in terms related to the achievement of their peers. Thus *motivation eventually narrows down to the need for as much intrinsic motivation as is humanly possible, and a deemphasis of competition or any other form of extrinsic motivation.*

To be sure, you will have occasion to prod, cajole, even to push. These occasions, however, must be either relatively infrequent or appropriately balanced with more intrinsically motivating learning experiences. To do less is to make your students musically dependent on extrinsic forces, and to deny them the intrinsic benefits of music experienced for its own sake. To do less is to run the risk of interfering with the natural growth processes that result in self-actualization and the meeting of aesthetic Being-Needs.

6. ASSUMPTION: MUSIC EDUCATION IS EASILY SUSCEPTIBLE TO THE TECHNIQUES OF BEHAVIORISM

Music is peculiar with regard to behaviorism, since in its performance aspects it deals with very *overt*, observable behaviors. On the other hand, performing and listening to it traditionally has been said to involve feelings, emotions, and thoughts. These are all conditions that are *covert* and not too susceptible to empirical observation and therefore their existence is largely denied by many behaviorists.

A brief general review of behaviorism and its contentions can help clarify this situation. In general, the behaviorist takes a very empirical attitude toward human functioning. *Only overt behavior which can be empirically studied is considered valid.* Anything else is either regarded with extreme suspicion and skepticism or is denied. *A person's behavior is attributed solely or mainly to the external influence of the environment.* "When a bit of behavior is followed by a certain kind of consequence, it is more likely to occur again, and a consequence having this effect is called a reinforcer."[7] Thus behavior depends upon the consequences brought to bear on it by the environment.

> The environment not only prods or lashes, it selects. Its role is similar to that in natural selection, though on a very different time scale, and was overlooked for the same reason. It is now clear that we must take into account what the environment does to an organism not only before but after it responds. Behavior is shaped and maintained by its consequences.[8]

Man is not free in this sense, the behaviorist contends, because behavior is caused by factors *outside* the individual. It is not caused by "inner" forces related to emotions, feelings, will, etc.

All these questions about purposes, feelings, knowledge, and so on can be re-stated in terms of the environment to which a person has been exposed. What a person "intends to do" depends upon what he has done in the past and what has then happened.[9]

In this sense, things or events are experienced as good or bad depending on the nature of the reinforcement, the consequences of such an interaction with the environment. "To make a value judgment by calling something good or bad is to classify it in terms of its reinforcing effects."[10] Things that reinforce positively are good; things that reinforce negatively are bad. *Reinforcements* "feel" good or bad, not *feelings*.

> Men have generalized the feelings of good things and called them pleasure and the feelings of bad things and called them pain, but we do not give a man pleasure or pain, we give him things he feels as pleasant or painful. . . . What is maximized or minimized, or what is ultimately good or bad, are things, not feel-ings, and men work to achieve them or to avoid them not because of the way they feel but because they are positive or negative reinforcers.[11]

Through this line of reasoning, the behaviorist arrives at what is essentially a view of *deficiency* or *deficit motivation*. People behave as they do, it is claimed, to *avoid any negative* (unwanted) *consequences* of their actions. Compare this to Maslow's assertion:

> Man is ultimately *not* molded or shaped in humanness, or taught to be human. The role of the environment is ultimately to permit him or help him actualize *his own* potentialities, not give him potentialities and capacities; he *has* them in in-choate or embryonic form, just exactly as he has embryonic arms and legs.[12]

To Maslow, Deficiency-Needs are biological or physiological in nature and are the lowest needs in the hierarchy of motivation. On the other hand, deficit motivation—avoiding unwanted consequences—is seen by the behaviorist as the basis for most behavior. When properly reinforced (i.e., when feared con-sequences are avoided and thus the results of one's behavior are found to be pleasant or gratifying) such behavior is retained.

In this way the behaviorist, in effect, denies the existence of an autonomous person acting on the basis of inner states of mind, feelings, and the like. All at-tention and importance are attached to reinforcements present in the environ-ment. Feelings, as such, are relegated to almost an equation with sensory perception. Only observable behavior is accepted as evidence of psychological functioning.

In the mind of not a few psychologists and philosophers, this position is untenable.

> The chief motive of [behaviorism] is to establish psychology as a natural science distinct from physiology, biochemistry, or any other physical science, yet to give it the virtues of experimental research and so-called "objective" truth . . . ; and no scientific research can restrict itself to any set of phenomena having causal connections with some other set, yet leave that set alone. So the blessed

word "behavior,"—while purporting to supply an "objective correlate" for the mental phenomena—feelings, thought, images, etc.—which are the original material of psychology, but stand condemned as "subjective," really creates methodological difficulties of its own.[13]

These "methodological difficulties" create special problems of their own in musical instruction.

If musical instruction is regarded entirely in terms of observable behavior by assuming that overt behavior is the goal of learning or that mental phenomena *always* result in overt behavior, then serious difficulties can arise. These difficulties arise because a strict behavioral interpretation of musical learning conflicts with the nature of the musical response or experience as confirmed over the history of mankind. *Behaviorism stresses the overt (outer); the musical experience or response has been regarded historically as covert (inner).*

On the surface there seems to be much merit in believing that the pleasure of the musical response is a positive reinforcement resulting from the organism's contact with a musical stimulus. But to deny the existence or relevance of "feelings" by contending that it is not feelings that are "felt" but the reward seems to ignore the complexity of human mental functioning almost entirely. It ignores the incredible complexity of such a stimulus-response situation as a musical experience; it equates feelings with sensory awareness, as if such perceptions were singular or simple. It reduces the quest for musical experiences and responses to a matter of avoiding unwanted consequences and, most significantly, *it fails to explain how the arts arise in the first place.*

Taking a broader view, *other psychologists and philosophers ascribe an active character to the mental experience.* They regard it as central to human functioning. For example, noted psychologist Arthur W. Combs writes:

> There is a vast difference between knowing and behaving. Knowing comes from getting new information. Change in behavior is a people problem, the human side of the learning equation. It comes from the discovery of meanings. *The most important aspect of learning lies, not in the giving of information, but in the discovery of its meaning.* Some of the most important learnings we have, have nothing to do with new information but have everything to do with the deeper and deeper discovery of the meaning of things we already know.[14]

To Professor Combs, feeling or emotion "is a question of personal involvement, an indicator of the degree to which ideas are likely to affect behavior." "Things which have no personal meaning arouse no emotions," so "the discovery of meaning and its accompanying emotion is at the very heart of learning. Education which rules out caring, of necessity makes itself ineffective."[15] Thus he is not totally unconcerned with the observable responses known as behavior; these are important. But he is also concerned with the less observable *prior conditions* of certain behavior, and with the *motives* that determine the behavior itself.

349

This "feeling" aspect of the mind is extremely personal and not entirely susceptible to the kind of generalizing preferred by behaviorists. Feeling is a kind of *mental action*

> *which is presented only within the organism in which the activity occurs.* Each organism, therefore, feels its own *actions* if they enter this phase, and not any other creature's. . . .[16]

> . . . The result of this heightened and largely self-perpetuating *activity* is that we continuously feel our own *inward action* as a texture of subjectivity, on which such objectively felt events as perceptions impinge, and from which our more sustained and complete subjective acts, such as concerted thought or distinct emotions, stand out as articulate forms. That psychical continuum is our self-awareness.[17]

Thus overt behavior may only *appear* to be objective. But the causative factors which lead to it are personal, subjective, and determined entirely by the *unique mental actions* of each person. *Meaning is actively created within the person and is not simply a quality of the environment or "in" the particular stimulus.*

> Meaning is not something that lies within an object but a description of the way the object affects the mind, the way it brings about or fits into a pattern of thought. This pattern of thought may already exist or it may swiftly grow around the object to give it a context and therefore a meaning.[18]

Therefore from this point of view *meaning determines behavior.* Put another way, *behind similar or identical overt behaviors there are unique meanings, feelings, mental actions that may not be apparent because they are covert.* In addition, *not all mental action results in overt behavior.* Most mental activity results in a chaining with other mental acts. Some mental activity is stored for future use, and some is ignored, repressed, or forgotten. And overt behavior is not necessarily the *only* evidence to be used in assessing the quality, kind, or scope of mental experience.

Overt behavior is not a normal consequence of musical consumption. The overt behavior of most people involves mainly the act of actively seeking musical involvements. But once they are experienced, overt behavior is not called for. Langer affirms this clearly in setting forth the purpose of art.

> The primary function of art is to objectify feeling so that we can contemplate and understand it. It is the formulation of so-called "inner experience," the "inner life," that is impossible to achieve by discursive thought, because its forms are incommensurable with the forms of language and all its derivatives (e.g., mathematics, symbolic logic). Art objectifies the sentience and desire, self-consciousness and world consciousness, emotions and moods, that are generally regarded as irrational because words cannot give us clear ideas of them. I believe the life of feeling is not irrational; its logical forms are merely very different from the structures of discourse. But they are so much like the dynamic forms of art that art is their natural symbol.[19]

350

From this we can see—if we ever doubted it—that music deals inherently with *human feelings,* and with all that these entail. Music education, therefore, should deal with the feelings and self-awareness that are evoked by music. The overt aspects of musical instruction exist in order to enhance the adolescent's ability to "feel" music, to "feel" the texture of his or her own self-awareness, and to "feel" the positive benefits of this mental activity. Thus inner states are the goals, and overt acts are only their manifestations.

This poses a dilemma. There are important benefits in having learners actively involved in pursuits that result in some form of overt behavior, yet we must remember that the overt aspect only facilitates learning; it does not fully constitute it.

> The results of active experiencing can be summarized approximately in the following way. There is physical, emotional, and intellectual self-exploration of one's abilities; there is initiation of activity or creativeness; there is finding out one's own pace and rhythm and the assumption of enough of a task for one's abilities at that particular time, which would include the avoidance of taking on too much; there is gain in skill which one can apply to other enterprises, and there is an opportunity each time that one has an active part in something, no matter how small, to find out more and more what one is interested in.[20]

Thus, to some limited extent, *active learning involves (a) changes in behavior and (b) changes in the frequency of behavior that can be noted as prime though not the sole evidence of learning.* What is not as easily observed in such occurrences is the quality or specific nature of such learning. Any number of motives may stand behind the *apparent* musical behavior of any student in your class.

Students often do some things, as do all people, more to *avoid* unwanted consequences than to positively *seek* pleasant ones. In music classes this situation arises when students do not respond to or for the benefits of music as music. Sometimes they respond to the situation—the environment, in the behaviorists' terms—in which music is presented. *Then the conditions under which music is encountered in class may tend to affect their responses rather than the music itself.*

Students in these situations may also, by virtue of the pressures inherent in the learning situation itself, be inclined to *copy the musical behaviors of others* (as when they imitate the movements of others during free-movement activities). They may be inclined to derive cues (clues) as to what they think the teacher "is after" by studying the teacher rather than the musical stimuli. Middle school students may even be inclined to cheat to acquire the "expected" musical behavior.

In other situations their participation may reflect a desire to impress friends, to be with friends, or to accomplish something (anything) successfully, and they may tend to derive positive reinforcement more from this than from actually experiencing the music as music. *All of these difficulties are especially prevalent when inordinate emphasis is placed on cognitive learnings or psychomotor (performance) skills.*

The cognitive and psychomotor domains inherently tend toward objectivity; toward ideas of right and wrong, success and lack of success. However, since understanding and perception, just to name two cognitive qualities, are unique from person to person they are not really as objective as some teachers believe. Overemphasis on these two domains puts students in the position of having to master these things in the "correct" way—otherwise the teacher makes it clear that they have not learned from their musical instruction.

In point of fact, however, the purpose of becoming involved with music is to respond positively to musical stimuli, be they aural (as in listening) or visual (as in performing from notation). The *experience* of this response *within the student* is what counts! The teacher, as a result, should neither *impose* experiences on the student, nor *direct* (help or steer) the student too much in completing activities.

> Whatever he may subsequently do by himself will look small and mean compared to what had been made for him by someone else. He has not added to his total experience for coming up against something new for the next time. In other words, he has not grown from within but has had something superimposed from the outside. . . . Each bit of active experiencing is an opportunity toward finding out what he likes or dislikes, and more and more what he wants to make of himself. It is an essential part of his progress toward the stage of maturity and self-direction.[21]

The central domain in music, then, is the affective domain, the feeling domain. All cognitions and psychomotor activities are but means for the enhancement of the learner's ability to respond to music fully in terms of feeling-responses. However, the behaviorist largely disclaims the affective domain. It is explained away in terms of overt behavior. But you have already seen that *overt behavior is not the central goal of music education,* especially of general-music education. *At best, overt behavior is a very general indicator of whether or not your instruction is enhancing the student's inner ability to respond to music,* the student's ability to contemplate the experience of life ("felt life") embodied in music. Without frequently repeated overt "demonstrations" of such *inner learning,* overt behavior can often be misread.

The real goals of musical instruction, the inner changes and meanings, are not too easily observable on a day-to-day or class-to-class basis. Since the inner, or covert, phase of learning can only be inferred from overt behavior, overt behavior becomes a reliable indicator only over time, after many varied overt indicators have been "read" under different yet related circumstances. It is in this sense and for this reason that the unique style of behavioral objectives outlined in chapter 5 are advocated.

A certain few overt signs of inner states of mind, may be dependable in a general short-term sense, even though they do not provide much specific information. For example, unbounded joy is not easily feigned or directed to extrinsic reinforcements (such as pleasing the teacher). Reluctance to conclude musical activities can indicate acceptance of these pursuits.

A particularly reliable long-term sign involves students' choices with regard to nonrequired music. Do they seek musical involvements? Do they come in with questions or projects that they have conceived of independently of your own designs? Do they *willingly* and for *musical reasons* volunteer to sing in choirs, and enjoy the activity as such? Do they listen to music as an end worthy in itself? Most important, do they enroll in high school music electives? Of course, the teacher is often limited in the extent of observation of this kind that is possible. But open-style classes and others of this general variety tend to facilitate such observations.

You are once again reminded that music education involves two aspects. They are often regarded as related, but emphasis is not always accurately placed. On one hand are the so-called objective learnings heavily involved in cognition and psychomotor skills. On the other hand are the so-called subjective learnings of the affective, or feeling, domain.

The proper point of emphasis should be the affective domain. *Cognitions and skills that actively and directly contribute to the ability of the student to respond with "feeling" to music (either as a listener or as a performer) are the most appropriate ones to teach.* Judgments about progress in the affective domain are made in more general terms, and repeatedly over longer periods of time, than judgments about specific cognitions and skills that contribute to the feeling-response (but are not the same as it); the latter can be based on the overt aspects of fewer lessons because they are more specific. *If such overtly demonstrated cognitions do not in the long run enhance the student's ability to respond to the music more fully, then musical self-actualization, is not occurring.*

> The notion of the human being as essentially reactive, the S-R man, we might call him, who is set into motion by external stimuli, becomes completely ridiculous and untenable for self-actualizing people. The sources of *their* actions are more internal than reactive. This *relative* independence of the outside world and its wishes and pressures does not mean, of course, lack of intercourse with it or respect for its "demand-character." It means only that in these contacts, the self-actualizer's wishes and plans are the primary determiners, rather than stresses from the environment.[22]

Nowhere is this more true than with regards to our desire for and response to music.

The overt signs of learning in music, therefore, must be regarded *carefully*. At best they constitute extremely small bits of information for the teacher's use. *Consistency* over the long run in inspiring an even greater love and capacity for musical response *will be the final determinant of success.* This will never be "scientifically" or "objectively" definable or quantifiable as to degree. It will be successful to the degree that the student has progressed under your instructive efforts to a stage closer to fulfillment of his or her potential for musical peak experiences that are self-validating and self-justifying.

And this, in essence, is not really a process that is unique to music. As Dr. Combs writes:

> The problem of learning . . . always involves two ascepts. One is the provision of new information or experience; the other has to do with the individual's personal discovery of the meaning of information *for him*. The provision of information can be controlled by an outsider with or without the cooperation of the learner. It can even be done, when necessary, by mechanical means which do not require a person at all. The discovery of meaning, however, is quite a different matter. This only takes place in people and cannot occur without the involvement of persons in the process. . . .[23]

> Meanings lie inside people and are not open to direct manipulation. When we talk of change in personal meanings, of growth of the student's self, it is the *student who knows* and the *teacher who does not* and that is exactly the reverse of the model we have been used to.[24]

It is also the reverse of the gospel according to the pure behaviorist.

HOW MUSIC IS LEARNED

As Dr. Combs indicated above, music learning (like any learning) arises from the provision of new information or experience, first of all, and then from the learner's personal discovery or construction of meaning. Therefore the general music teacher must *provide new information or experience* which, in turn, must promote the *inner act of meaning-construction or discovery by the student* as a natural consequence. Now, most readers are all too likely to regard the lecture or lecture-demonstrattion as the best means of providing information, but in general-music classes at all levels it is about the worst form and contributes to the largest number of discipline problems. It requires that students sit still and "pay attention." Thus it runs contrary to their natural inclinations to be active and to the nature of music, which always requires an active response.

Information is best given in general-music settings *in the form of experience* (i.e., through activities) designed to lead to the acquisition of necessary information, ideas, concepts, skills, and other such related gains. This experience, then, provides the bases for subsequent activities in which even more is learned while the earlier learnings are further integrated and reinforced. Simultaneously, the active nature of such activities will—to the degree they have been well conceived in terms of students' needs and interests—encourage or enhance the likelihood of students' inner "meaning making." Especially when viewed from the students' point of view as successful, these kinds of activities also provide future motivation at the same time as they serve the teacher in evaluating the success of instruction and learning.

The net effect of such experiences will be a cognitive strengthening where the learnings (information, concepts) and inner meanings are used, applied, or demonstrated in future activities. Such learnings and meanings will have become more "attensive" for the learner. These musical qualities, in turn, will be perceived more easily, more often, and more richly. As a result, the satisfaction provided by these newly enriched perceptions can contribute even further to new levels of inner meaning. Since this inner meaning is brought about by each student in his or her own way and to a unique degree, the "feeling qualities" of such learning begin to become self-enhancing. And when this aspect of "felt" importance occurs, the learner is at a stage where *a preconscious act of meaning analysis, of cognitive appraisal, or of qualitative valuing is happening,*[25] and is happening in a positive way.

In the earlier chapter on listening, this preconscious meaning analysis, cognitive appraisal, or qualitative valuing was described in terms of *subception,* the subconscious counterpart to conception. As subception progresses, all learning encounters, all new perceptions, are "subject to transformations, and the specific transformation that is given to a particular input is its appraisal."[26] *Cognitions* (knowledge abstracted from past experiences) and *affects* (derived feelings, meanings, and subjective appraisals) work together because subception allows these two aspects to function virtually simultaneously.

The area in which cognition occurs is determined by the teacher, who, you will remember,

(1) must *provide new information* (as in the songwriting information provided for students) *or experience* (as in directed listening and song composition activities).

But the affective aspect results from the ability of learning experiences to

(2) *promote construction or discovery of meaning* by the student as an inner act.

In order to insure both conditions, the problem of novelty becomes crucial.

(3) Each new activity or experience must *hold forth enough novelty to arouse and sustain interest;* it must foster a positive cognitive appraisal on the part of students.[27]

This judgment is usually made preconsciously by the learner in subception according to one or more of the following conditions:

a. The student's anticipation of *success* or *failure* based upon past experience.

b. The sense of *interest* the task portends for the student. This is a judgment of *relevance,* meaning that the student seeks to determine some relationship to his or her life in the proposed learning.

c. The degree of *challenge* involved: if it is too easy or too difficult, problems will be experienced.

d. The sense of *personal need,* in terms of the student's Deficiency-Needs or Being-Needs.

355

It is not possible to influence these criteria *directly*. Only over the long run can a teacher expect to *indirectly* improve the way students apply these criteria to new learning experiences. Therefore, the teacher will need perseverance, creativity, cleverness, and maybe even some luck before the effects of past learning become such that students more and more "appraise" prospective learning occasions in positive ways.

4. But *new activities must not be too novel;* too much novelty runs the risk of seeming unrelated to the student's past, present, or future life and may also be threatening to less secure students.

   a. New experiences must be capable of *assimilation* with familiar past experiences. This means that the experiences must be varied, but not so dramatically different that they appear altogether strange.

   b. Experiences capable of *accommodation* by means of a slight reinterpretation of past experience are the farthest a teacher should go in the direction of novelty.

Experiences that are new enough to represent a different (though refined or extended) example of some previous learning facilitate *assimilation* of the new learning with the old and thus encourage *transfer of learning*. Experiences that are novel enough to encourage the learner to reinterpret previous learning in terms of new experience foster the process of *accommodation* and are another example of transfer of learning. In both cases, the student senses some kind of "fit" between the old and the new. This sense of "aha" or "eureka" is the kind of personal discovery or creation mentioned earlier in point 2. Without this inner meaning no effective learning has occurred. If the "fit" that constitutes "meaning" does not occur, the student will usually ignore or reject the new experience. At best it is benignly stored for "future reference." But this happens only with an already developed positive attitude.

As a result of a positive "fit" between past and present experiences, the student is more likely to appraise future instances of similar learning opportunities in a more positive light (according to the criteria given earlier under point 3) because such a "fit" is what constitutes meaningfulness and personal relevance. Negative experiences, on the other hand, will lead more often to the opposite result, especially if the student has a history of such experiences, and no or few positive ones to counterbalance an occasional nonproductive effort (or nonproductive lesson concocted by the teacher).

Either way, the student's *selective attention* in the future will be determined by whether similar past experiences have achieved the "fit" that amounts to a sense of personal meaning. Through a synthesis of past experiences in memory, positive effects of this kind make possible the student's improved ability to notice more in music. Thus it is possible to feel the music more intensely. Music in general becomes more attensive for the student.

5. *The more inclusive concepts become* (i.e., the more they synthesize past experiences through assimilation or accommodation), *the greater is the possibility of an enriched response.*

What was noticed today in isolation (e.g., melody) can be in the future noticed in conjunction with, or as conditioned by, one or more additional musical elements (e.g., rhythm and harmony):

> The very complexity of inputs in the emotional situation is exactly the factor that makes for the complexity and richness of emotional experience and emotional meaning. The structure of a particular input and its relation to other contemporary simultaneous inputs as well as to existing mental structures provide the "meaning" of the situation.[28]

This, too, happens as subception, when many simultaneous inputs interact in the model described earlier in chapter 4 (see Fig. 4:2, page 194). In addition, subception also contributes a degree of "feeling" to the simultaneous inputs and combines with them in a "wholistic" or synergic result.

6. In effect, *the feeling-tone from past experiences conditions or colors any similar new response.* What this means is that emotions and feelings experienced along with past learning are remembered along with the learning and are "felt" again in the new learning situation.

> The contents of the stream [of consciousness] are recorded in the brain, including everything to which the man . . . paid attention, but none of the things that he ignored. His thoughts are recorded with the sensory material that he accepted. His fears are there, and his interpretations are there as well—all recorded by this extraordinary mechanism within the brain.[29]

In this way subception brings to bear on each new experience the joint cognitive and affective experience with the perception or learning in question from the past. Not only, then, does this process allow simultaneous effects to be combined mentally; it also contributes the feeling of satisfaction or frustration that represents the mind's "appraisal" of such a new experience, and *the awareness we have of our awareness* will also be assimilated or accommodated along with the perception or learning in question. Students' self-awareness of negative appraisals account for many difficulties some teachers have with discipline problems, "bad attitudes" toward music learning, and the like. But if this self-awareness is of a positive feeling, the learner becomes increasingly capable of being more responsive to music and more "appreciative" of or gratified by the perception of his or her *own* "inner life." The ongoing awareness of one's own subjectivity (self-awareness) colors the response and further enhances the ultimate profoundity of that response.

Because this subjective appraisal is so important a component in learning, and because a student's self-awareness of his or her feeling-tone during an experience is ultimately more important to the success of learning than any other factor, it can be seen that, in all practical reality, *there is no such "thing" as a pre-existing "body of knowledge" that can be simply transferred into students' minds.* Each learner "constructs" (organizes) the perceived reality uniquely, and in so doing creates personal, inner meaning.

Dramatic evidence exists to demonstrate this pervasive role of personal experience in structuring our reality.[30] Pioneering biologists studying vision in kittens discovered that perceptual abilities do not develop automatically.

> Instead, the researchers have found, our visual machinery is strongly shaped by our early experiences—experiences that drastically affect the way we see the world in later life and that may even determine how gifted we will be musically and linguistically. It may be that areas of great potential in child development are being wasted simply because we don't teach the right things at the right time, the time when children's brains are most receptive.[31]

In other words, there exists a particularly critical period for certain kinds of learning and experience in young kittens (and young children) when there is a particular flexibility and plasticity of the developing perceptual systems: external influences during this time will play such a large part in developing the "world view" acquired that dramatically conflicting views of reality can arise.

> For instance, the Cambridge kittens were reared in visual environments consisting only of vertical stripes or horizontal stripes, not both. When the animals emerged from their striped worlds into the real visual world, they behaved in a most extraordinary way. "Horizontal" cats were perfectly capable of jumping onto a chair to settle down for a sleep; but when walking on the floor, they kept bumping into the chair legs, just as if the legs were invisible. In contrast, "vertical" animals had no difficulty in negotiating the chair-leg hazard, but they never tried to jump onto a chair; it was as if the seat were not there.[32]

In every functional sense, then, kittens reared only with horizontal visual stimuli did not see verticals: for these animals, vertical lines and objects *did not exist!* The opposite was true of kittens reared in vertical environments: they were totally unaware of horizontals. It was discovered that the kittens' brain structures had been affected to the degree that it was impossible for them to perceive the structures not encountered in their training environments: "These animals really were blind to things in their environment that were perfectly visible to you and me and to any self-respecting cat, all because of their unusually early experience."[33]

Further researches indicate that the feature detectors of the kittens' visual system required about one hour to be affected permanently by such stimuli. But, you may ask, does this research really apply to human beings? Most definitely it does. Subsequent researches in Canada uncovered precisely the same effects in human beings. Researchers compared the visual abilities of Cree Indians living in tepees in the wilderness with those of city-dwellers:

> In the past researchers had found that "normal" people have better visual acuity (can see most sharply) in the horizontal and vertical axes. But what [later researchers] found throws into question this concept of normality. They discovered that the Cree Indians have no particular axis of high visual acuity and are not especially attuned to horizontal and vertical lines. These people had, of course, been brought up in the country and away from the city, which is dominated by rectangular shapes. It may well be that the normal horizontal and vertical visual acuity preferences are imposed on us simply because we live in a

rectangular world. If houses were spherical instead of boxlike, things might be different. . . . The crucial point is that human vision does appear to display the same kind of plasticity found in the experimental cats. *And what is true of vision probably applies to our other senses as well.*[34]

This last idea is important for music education. It strongly suggests that the perceptual process is similar for music or vision. Not having had certain aural experiences, the mind is literally unaware of them. Only when musical-stimulus experience is presented to students and their attention is directed toward it can the brain (and mind) develop those mental structures that can increasingly notice and be influenced by such novel aural stimuli. Facts and information can never replace such direct musical experience.

> Musical talent very often runs in families. It may be "in the genes," of course, but there is undoubtedly a large environmental element, too. Children exposed to a lot of music when young are almost always more musically talented than average; how much this development is due to encouragement and opportunity is difficult to tell. But evidence that the musical brain becomes keyed in to its early experiences comes from the observation that people who develop perfect pitch while exposed to a slightly out-of-tune instrument always match their pitch to the instrument's. Although playing Beethoven to one's infant will probably not cause an environmentally generated reincarnation of the grand master, it may well produce a more-than-usually musically talented child.[35]

While such aural stimulation is especially important for the very young child during the critical periods of musical development, it is no less important the older a person gets: *just more difficult!*[36] There probably is some truth to the old saying about teaching old dogs (or cats) new tricks. But throughout life we are all still subject to learning in this manner.

The essential point is that a person's view of or ability to perceive "reality"— and we are interested in *musical* realities—is nothing more than a schematic representation of the world that is derived from his or her personal experiences (environmental inputs or percepts) and the way in which the person internally processes and organizes these experiences:[37] "The most important aspect of the *quale* [experienced quality] of an emotional experience and its accompanying behavior is the interpretation of the environment, the events that are the occasions for particular emotions."[38] And this is no less true with musical responses than it is with so-called discipline problems: how an experience is *interpreted* determines its emotional quality and thus the accompanying behavior (desirable or not desirable).

Pre- and early adolescents thus need learning through tangible experiences with music every bit as much as do younger children. Even though the young adolescent is increasingly able to think abstractly, it is still necessary to provide musical activities, and to direct attention as much as possible to relevant aspects of the musical experience. Finally, you must provide the opportunity for adolescents *to act upon or with their perceptions:* they need the chance to make their own meaning, their own interpretation. Telling is not teaching. This point is clearly made in conjunction with the perceptual research done with the kittens:

> Probably the most important skill that children learn is *how* to learn. The mark of intelligence is the facility for solving problems. *Too often we give children answers to remember rather than problems to solve. This is a mistake.* Unless children develop the art of problem solving—whether by analytical logic or by non-sequential intuition—their brains will remain underexploited. Everyone knows that infants go through a period of being intensely curious. This curiosity is probably a behavioral expression of the brain's most sensitive period for acquiring knowledge and learning techniques.[39]

As you have seen, the onset of adolescence is also an important developmental stage as far as intellectual curiosity is concerned. It is the stage at which conceptual learning responds less to external percepts than to internal percepts or organization. With adolescence comes the increased ability to make connections between already existing concepts without a need for new external perceptual input. As the teacher you must provide the occasions that set this thinking process into operation for your students.

The types of occasion that have been recommended throughout these pages, and in the quote directly above, are the problem solving, creative activities. An additional benefit is that the *overt* results of these activities also provide *new perceptual input to further expand and refine the concepts being manipulated.*

The position taken throughout this text is not a *philosophical* point of view. It is based on recent research in neurophysiology and neuropsychology, learning psychology, and the psychology of emotion. Many methods used by music educators fail to take into account the relevant known facts of human learning and mental development and have progressed on a track and train of their own. *They* can be criticized as "ideal" and philosophical, since they too often bear only tenuous relationship to the problems of human development, and have not always been successful.

> Almost certainly, the learning capacity of the human brain has not been exploited to the full by current educational approaches. The essential point is the possible existence of sensitive periods not just for visual development, but for music, language, logic, and artistic talents.[40]

The approach of adolescence, with its many social, psychological, and physiological growth-typical characteristics, is most certainly such a "sensitive period." All the research points to the need for an Action Learning process in which experience is *acted upon* mentally, then overtly, thereby making mental use all the more effective. Although early experiences are very important in learning, the late elementary school and adolescent years are crucial too. At this time a synthesis of music learning must begin (it never should end!) if music is to serve a positive growth role for students, now and in later life. So this is the time of the music educator's *last chance* to "open" these young minds to the potential of music. What might be called "musical literacy" must stem from this critical period, for *it is usually by the age of ten that the specialization of the two brain hemispheres is completed:*

> By the age of ten, dominance for speech—and probably for other skills as well—is fixed. Tasks of synthesis (synergy), spatial perception, and music apparently go to the right side. The left side gets all the sequential, verbal, analytical, computerlike activities.[41]

And with this specialization comes the unfortunate tendency of the hemispheres to work at cross-purposes.[42] Thus after the age of ten you must nurture the musical potential of the brain (the right hemisphere) without so overusing the left hemisphere that there is a resulting imbalance of cognition-capacity development over feeling-capacity development. It is for this reason that such emphasis has been given to the middle school and to the need there for Action Learning. For if we fail to open or develop musical minds at this critical stage, the beauties of the musical art may very well be lost to such students forever.

The following description of the process by which psychotherapy can be effective provides a point-by-point parallel to the problems of music education with this age group. In our case the ultimate result of instruction should be a change in mental acts related to music that causes the student (even as an adult in later life) to overtly seek out and profit from musical contacts. Indeed, even the general goals of the music teacher and therapist are similar: to improve the quality of a person's life.

> When a psychotherapist [diagnoses the problem] and then tells the patient, his "telling the patient" is not equivalent to the patient's inspection of the cognitive system; it is just another input. . . . It is necessary to encourage the patient to test and elaborate on what the structures might be that mediate certain actions. . . . In other words, by *"knowing and using"* these structures, first insight might be developed, and change can then follow. *Changes will occur to the extent to which the patient can use the experience and action system as his private laboratory for generating and testing hypotheses.* Once again, *cognitive structures are changed and generated by action.*[43]

These points could not be more true or important of music education. The goal of an education in music is to *know and use* what is learned. Changes of behavior (i.e., effective learning) will occur to the degree that the student can *use* what is learned. Furthermore, such a use of learning constitutes "learning how to learn": a student can "use the experience and action system as his private laboratory for generating and testing hypotheses" about music and musical responses. This is what the act of inner "meaning-making" really amounts to. And, as can be seen in the quotation above, cognitive structures (concepts) are "generated by action": mental and overt acts of meaning-making *by the student* that amount to acting on and organizing personal experiences. It is useful, too, that students' mental actions (covert responses) have an overt manifestation in order that teacher and student alike can observe the fruits of learning. Such overt demonstrations are, as well, *new experiences* that contribute their own part to the ongoing learning process.

COVERT MUSICAL ACTIONS

The gamut of covert musical actions is summarized in Fig. 6:2.

Cognition, as we have seen, deals with what people loosely call "understanding," although it really amounts to the cognitive structures that are created by personal inner meaning-making. The psychomotor processes are those mental actions which make possible a musical performance or any skill such as playing football or typing. They are the prior conditions for a *conscious skill.* In order for a performance to be done *knowingly* so that it can be repeated or analyzed in the event something goes wrong, these mental processes need to be working effectively.

"Hearing inwardly," the first item in the psychomotor list, refers to the

Fig. 6:2 Covert Musical Actions

Cognitive	Affective	Psychomotor
perceiving	responding intuitively	hearing inwardly
analyzing	interpreting freely	attending to cues
comprehending	preferring	monitoring self
remembering	enjoying	following instructions
identifying	characterizing in terms of	fixating in practice
comaring	feelings	refining
differentiating	creating in subjective terms	coordinating acts and cues
evaluating	choosing on the basis of	acquiring speed in
judging	feelings	performance
synthesizing		lessening time to learn
		perfecting

These inner actions are *processes* by which new percepts are processed by assimilation and accommodation into existing mental structures. As such they do not result in any concrete thing beyond the vague "aha" reaction, assuming that processing has seemed successful to the student. As a result, they require some externalizing as overt acts in order to result in something tangible that both the student and teacher can observe as some indication of the success of the process. They are separated into three groups only for convenience. Even within groups the borders between individual responses are overlapping. Nonetheless it is recommended that you *emphasize only one of these inner actions at a time* and seek to make it in some way overt.

operation of the musician's "inner ear" that makes possible the purely internal image or perception of sound (percepts) when none is externally present. It is the ability to "sing" or "hear" a melody "in one's head." Thus the inner ear is responsible for covert "aural images." The inner ear is the absolutely prior condition of all musical performance: for example, it is this faculty that is at fault in children who cannot match pitch.[44]

The affective processes deal with the values, attitudes, and other subjective "feelings" that arise along with all our various learnings.[45] Therefore affective responses do involve and do demonstrate the concepts that allow the feeling to arise in the first place (i.e., you have to know of and perceive a musical factor in order to respond to it feelingfully). Such externalizing of feelings is, perhaps, most practically done through discussion and the use of expressive speech such as metaphor and analogy. The realm of subception is definitely not very susceptible to normal speech. Certain affective states can be *directly expressed*, as in composition or in moving freely to music.

The synergic musical response is clearly a synthesis, a blending of knowledge (condition) and feeling (affect), and is the ultimate goal of all musical behaviors and instruction. A program of education in music ought to center far more often and far more vividly on these synergic responses and processes than on any other single mental process. In musical synergy, cognition and affect are interdependent, but with an emphasis on the feeling response as an *end*. Feelings and concepts are interdependent in cognition too (cognitive ap-

Fig. 6:3 Importance of the Affective Realm in Musical Cognition and Performance

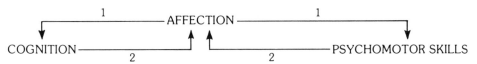

Affection—values, attitudes, and feelings—makes possible musical cognition and performance by first (shown as 1 above) finding enough meaning, relevance, or challenge in musical pursuits to "inspire" the student to want or intend to acquire musical knowledge or performance skills. Second (shown as 2), as knowledge and skills develop, the affective rewards of musical involvement are further enhanced by cognitive appraisal, and so on in a mutually rewarding circle controlled at all times by the affective realm. Thus the real contact between skill development and the cognitions which further it is the affective realm, and the value the student places on such learnings (i.e., the appraisal that such learnings will improve performance and thus increase the pleasures of performing). In effect, then, all instruction aims at enhancing the feeling-response to music in all its aspects—listening, performing, and composing.

363

praisal results in feeling-states), but the emphasis is usually on using a concept as a *means* of cognitive strengthening. But *this does not warrant emphasis on knowledge for its own sake.* Knowledge for the sake of enhancing cognitive appraisal and thus feeling-responses should be the emphasis, as illustrated in Fig. 6:3.

Remember that each of the mental actions constituting learning, skill, and musical responsiveness are purely inner or private phenomena. We sometimes speak of them as though they are overt, because they *sometimes* have observable consequences. But "understanding" something or "feeling" something does not ordinarily or necessarily have some direct, observable phase. In daily life we experience many cognitions or affections without manifesting them outwardly. Therefore it is useful to list the various kinds of *overt manifestations of covert mental processes* that are common in music education. These are found in Fig. 6:4.

Remember, the teacher cannot "teach" directly by telling. The teacher must involve the student *actively* in the operations and processes of music and the perception of music as phenomenon. Fig. 6:4 represents the general types of overt behavior that are used in creating musical activities. The teacher facilitates the formation of concepts and general responsiveness to music (in terms of feelings) through discussions and other clarifications. But in the end each

Fig. 6:4 Overt Behaviors in Music

Verbal Behaviors	*Making Behaviors*	*Performance Behaviors*
speaking	composing	playing instruments
writing	creating	singing
	arranging	conducting
	rearranging	moving to music
	organizing into	dancing
	something new	
	notating	

In the long run these overt musical behaviors provide reasonable (though not completely reliable) evidence of success and musical growth. For example, the student's ability to "comprehend" a musical form can be dealt with by having him or her compose a sound composition in that musical form. This is a musical behavior, as such. It does not involve passing a test on musical form. A student's ability to "perceive" certain musical elements can be dealt with by having him or her verbally indicate what was heard. The key in each instance will be that you seek to reveal covert mental activities by having an overt consequence, an overt manifestation of inner mental behavior. By "reading backwards" from this overt behavior you have *some* evidence of learning, if only by inference.

student, tempered by his or her environment and genetic assets, determines through inner meaning-making what is learned and to what extent. Your activities must, as has been indicated many times already, also provide for this meaning-making phase.

IMPLICATIONS OF CONCEPTUAL LEARNING

It is important to remember that a concept arises when one or more previous experiences can be related to a present experience. The insight ("aha") or matchup ("fit") that results is a concept, no matter how tentative. Such a concept is thereafter subject to the influence of each new experience provided by instruction. These new experiences are *assimilated* with or *accommodated* to previous concepts under favorable conditions. Or, if the student has generally had a history of successful experiences in class with this kind of learning, the experience may be held in a "ready" state waiting for the clarification of new percepts.

But when prior experiences have been generally negative or unrewarding, when attempts to fit new experiences into existing concepts have often resulted in frustration, failure, or in no sense of accomplishment, then a negative experience will result. In the future the student will likely demonstrate increased resistance to learning, an increase of poor or negative attitudes toward music class, and misbehavior—this latter as a substitute for the lack of gratification gained from the learning experience.

Whether the experience is positive or not, learning is never complete as long as the individual has new experiences to process. Thus it is most natural for concepts to continue to develop and change. They never arrive at a "finished product," a once-and-for-all-time state of completion. Therefore learners do not acquire *the* concept of rhythm at any given time in their musical concept. There is no such "thing" as "*the* concept" of anything. With adult and child alike, musical concepts change and grow according to the nature and number of ongoing musical experiences—whether these are formal studies in school or informal activities outside of school. Since peoples' musical experiences differ in a variety of ways, so do the concepts developed vary to some degree from person to person.

Concepts, thus, are not singular, one-time acquisitions or accomplishments. They are dynamic and reflect the ongoing process of mental development (see Fig. 6:5). Only in the event of a "closed mind" (or a dead one), can the process stop. In live people, "frozen concepts" are a sure sign of a calcification of their mental potential and usually indicate a bias, a prejudice, or—especially when they are extreme—a more serious mental problem (neurosis, psychosis, etc.).

Because concepts have no singular form or manifestation, and because

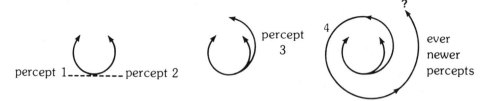

As though from a seed, concepts are constantly expanding, more inclusive. With the continued input of new percepts, concepts grow as shown above.

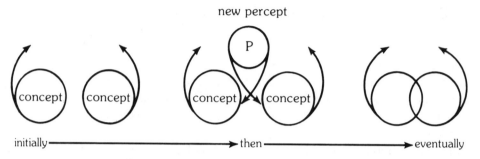

Concepts are not isolated or unrelated. While they may seem to be at first, some percept will "fit" both of two unrelated concepts and thus, as shown above, will bring them into continued functional interdependence (synergy).

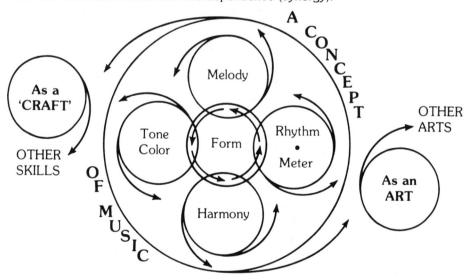

From a network or web of such interdependencies arises a concept of "music" in general, as shown above. This concept continues to change and evolve as its component parts change and exert continually new influences on other parts. Thus this larger concept is equally fluid and flexible. And it, too, may be related to an even larger network of concepts that constitute a person's concepts of "art" or the "aesthetic response" to art objects. Thus human mentality is constantly changing and extremely complex. In a sense, at least with regard to music and the arts, the more complex the conceptual bases, the richer can be the musical response.

Fig. 6:5 Growth and Relationship of Concepts in Normal Functioning

their refinement and modification never ceases, *concepts cannot be passed around*. They cannot be passed from the teacher to the student directly, as though they were simply a definition or an explanation. They cannot effectively be "told" to anyone—not, that is, if the teacher expects the concept to have effectively entered the student's mind. Concepts result from and as the learner's *personal experience* (involvement) and subsequent inner meaning-making.

Teaching general music, therefore, is largely a matter of selecting and arranging musical experiences, which are the *means* of reaching the *goal* of nurturing musical concepts through students' active involvement. Furthermore, the actual process of teaching involves *guiding students' perceptual and conceptual involvement during their participation* in such learning activities. The experiences and guidance thus provided should be aimed at *the creation of individual relevance or inner meaning by each student.* This is a slowly developing process. While it is always possible for the teacher to increase the efficiency of the activities by which new experiences are provided for students, "the problem of changing meaning . . . is a slower, more difficult human task which cannot be done by an outsider. It has to be done by the learner himself."[46]

THE IMPORTANCE OF THE FEELING-RESPONSE

Often, in the past, it was assumed that learning information would automatically lead to the kinds of "changing meaning" that result in what was called "appreciation" of music. We can no longer regard this attitude as practical. Instead, keeping in mind the conditions of motivation, we must realize that *affects (feelings, attitudes, and values) are stored and grow simultaneously with concepts.* How a person "feels" about what he is learning, or how he is learning, will be "learned" at the same time the concept is learned (see Fig. 6:6). In fact attitudes are, in a certain sense, feeling-laden concepts of how a person perceives himself in relation to something.

Attitudes deal in part, then, with a person's self-concept: how a person understands himself on various occasions under a variety of circumstances. *Concepts of one's musical self in the form of attitudes, values, and feelings are inseparable from the process of developing concepts of the "content" that constitutes music.*

Therefore certain affects will always be associated with conceptual learning. In fact, these *affects will condition whether, what, or to what extent a person can or will learn.* Most efforts, motivations, and needs will be more under the control of the affective component (which is personal) than the conceptual component (which, in comparison, seems quite abstract and impersonal). *If the adolescent does not feel gratified or rewarded in some way by the ac-*

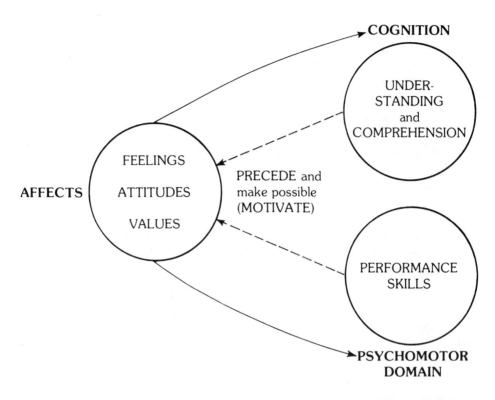

Affective learning is a central and pervasive force. It motivates students to learning in the cognitive and psychomotor domains. Success in these areas further intensifies good "feelings" and can thus inspire further learning. Affective learning also effectively makes possible those cognitions necessary to psychomotor learning and those cognitions which arise from the act of performance (notice the broken arrows above). In other words, when the affective component is positive, students are willing to learn those cognitions necessary to performance or to take part in those skilled acts useful to cognition.

Fig. 6:6

complishment of what is learned, or by the effect of what is learned, the affective component develops negatively. This will have an interference effect, and can lead to increasing resistance to such learnings in the future. If, on the other hand, the learner is gratified or rewarded in some way by the learning, the affective component will develop into a positive musical self-concept, and can be conducive to more positive learnings in the future (see Fig. 6:6).

Good attitudes, positive values, and gratifying feelings will be retained long after specific facts are forgotten. Ultimately the feeling-component constitutes a natural musical response.

MUSICAL LEARNING THAT IS ENDURING

Specific knowledge that has faded in memory can be more easily reconstructed by virtue of the conceptual framework established at an earlier time. A network of interrelated concepts assists the learner in dealing with such specifics, since it provides a context, a structure to which things can be related and from which they can be derived by deduction.

As children grow to adolescence they can begin to draw deductive conclusions from, and find relationships between, previously learned concepts even without the need for direct, concrete experience. They are reasoning *from* the generalizations represented in the concepts *to* the particulars represented in their discoveries. The learning cycle, thus, can come full-circle. The new specific conclusions become the impetus for new experiences necessary to the development of totally new concepts (or the continuing refinement of earlier, more basic concepts).

With these new or refined concepts come, again, new opportunities for deduction and hence, again, new opportunities for inductive learning. Figure 6:7 presents this cycle in a more graphic form.

The teacher creates the activities through which this process begins to unravel, but you can only lead a student to learning; you cannot make him "drink" from it.

It is hard to see how [effective learning] can be accomplished without far more interaction and participation on the part of students than we have ever known in the past. It means taking the learner into partnership and respecting and encouraging his own human qualities. It calls for commitment and involvement of students in every aspect of the educational problem. It means giving a great deal more self-direction and responsibility to students themselves. . . .

Responsibility and self-direction are learned. They must be acquired from experience, from being given opportunities to be self-directing and responsible. You cannot learn to be self-directing if no one permits you to try. . . . If young people are going to learn self-direction, then it must be through being *given* many opportunities to exercise such self-direction throughout the years they are in school.[47]

THE SYNERGIC MUSICAL EXPERIENCE

Music is an experience. It is a total experience. It is not just the result of concepts like melody or harmony or rhythm or intensity or form, or for lack of a better word, "expression." It is all of these things in mutual interpenetration and interdependence which synergically create the "whole." And some music, like the newer contemporary forms, sometimes seems to be none of these things. New music often requires entirely new concepts.

Because the novice, for all practical purpose, can concentrate on only one

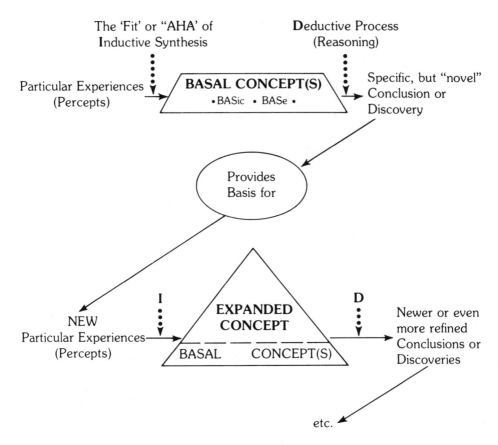

The 'Fit' or "AHA" of
Inductive Synthesis

Deductive Process
(Reasoning)

Particular Experiences
(Percepts)

BASAL CONCEPT(S)
• BASic • BASe •

Specific, but "novel"
Conclusion or
Discovery

Provides
Basis for

I

**EXPANDED
CONCEPT**

BASAL   CONCEPT(S)

D

NEW
Particular Experiences
(Percepts)

Newer or even
more refined
Conclusions or
Discoveries

etc.

Each separate experience stimulates the "aha" synthesis that results in concept formation. The term "basal concepts," as used here, refers to the formation of a broad base. Concepts can be compared to a pyramid; they are refined and become more specific, though unlike a pyramid, they never reach final completion. In time, reasoning (deduction) can derive new discoveries from basal concepts which in turn becomes a basis for new inductive experiences. An expanded concept results through the processes of assimilation or accommodation. This, in turn, can breed newer or more refined discoveries.

Fig. 6:7 Inductive/Deductive Learning Cycle

or a very few things at a time, it is necessary to focus artificially on specific smaller components of the musical experience. But these are only *moments of emphasis* and not end-products worthy of such emphasis in and by themselves. Only the total musical experience is due such singular emphasis.

When breaking the musical experience into its components for a moment of temporary emphasis you must not oversimplify it or reduce it to the meaningless trivialities sometimes encountered in commercially available materials. The following position of Jerome Bruner, while referring to the appropriateness of "subjects" of instruction, also applies equally to the question of what within a subject is worth learning:

> If one respects the ways of thought of the growing child, if one is courteous enough to translate material into his logical forms and challenging enough to tempt him to advance, then it is possible to introduce him at any early age to the ideas and styles that in later life make an educated man. *We might ask, as a criterion for any subject taught in primary school, whether, when fully developed, it is worth an adult's knowing, and whether having known it as a child makes a person a better adult. If the answer to both questions is negative or ambiguous, then the material is cluttering the curriculm.*[48]

Following Bruner's urging that "any subject can be taught effectively in some intellectually honest form to any child at any stage of development,"[49] it is necessary to not allow young people to associate music or musical instruction *solely* with those enjoyable activities with which musical instruction usually begins. As children grow older they frequently regard many of their previous experiences as childish. If some major facet of instruction is overemphasized or is intellectually or musically unworthy, it is little wonder that they become increasingly disenchanted. It no longer fits their developing self-concept, and, once again, the self-concept is pivotal to learning.

> We know of the crucial role it plays in every aspect of human behavior. We know, for example, that it is a basic cause of failure in all the school subjects. It determines in high degree whether a person will be well-adjusted or maladjusted, effective or ineffective in his dealings with life and it plays a primary role in the achievement of self-actualization. It is even fundamental in the growth and creation of intelligence itself. . . .
>
> Students do not park their self-concepts at the door, they bring them right on into the class with them. What we do with these students, even when we are teaching math, or science, reading, geography, music or physical education is also teaching them *who* they are and *what* they are, for it is people we teach, not just subject matter. . . .
>
> If it is personal meaning which produces change in behavior, then it is the selves of our students with which we must deal in our classrooms or pay the penalty of making our teaching ineffective.[50]

In the same sense, if the musical experiences you deal with are truly relevant and intellectually honest for the learner at his present stage of readiness, then such activities will be more inclined to be self-validating. They will require no great efforts of "disciplining" the group. They will be much more naturally received for their merits.

TEACHER ROLES IN FACILITATING LEARNING

A teacher is part of the learning environment. The teacher is a part of the social interaction involved in group processes of education, and the role adopted by the teacher, therefore, can have great bearing on the success of in-

371

struction no matter how well planned and otherwise executed that instruction may be.

Teacher roles are varied and multiple. Many exist, and a teacher may wear more than one hat in succession depending on certain variables. Knowing this to be true, some teachers change from "superconscience" to "enemy" to "devil" and the like. This is hardly the kind of variety that facilitates successful instruction.

The superconscience role is provided by the teacher who nags and reminds, cajoles and "motivates," scolds, worries, and coerces the student into action. The enemy is distrusted, and disliked, and feared; students avoid contact or volunteering if possible. Whatever apparent *work* is accomplished is done out of fear of punishment. The devil is a fun-spoiler, a teacher who may be boring, thus leading students to invent their own fun, which then results in "discipline problems." A devil also finds serious fault frequently with innocent behavior like whispering or with occasional daydreaming.

No, these roles are not what teachers should attempt! The teacher should attempt a role of "active group member." This is not quite an attitude of "one of the boys" (or girls); that can lead to problems. Rather, it is along the order of "an older person who is doing this along with us"—a *friend*. This role permits and encourages the teacher *to learn* along with the group. No ultimate font of total musical wisdom here. Just one more voyager on the road to increased knowledge, albeit a somewhat more experienced voyager. A similar beneficial role is that of "clock-winder." A clock-winder gets things started and rewinds them periodically when they start to run down. Otherwise the clock-winder stays mainly on the sidelines.

The "resource/programmer" is the role played by the teacher who creates and collects material for independent or individualized study. Sometimes the resource/programmer must mutate into a kind of "tutorial clock-winder." Students need periodic help or redirection in completing such work or using the materials or media. Perhaps the most all-embracing role a teacher can create is that of "driver-education teacher."

In the role of driver-education teacher, you give directions, talk and call attention to the fine points of things, issue warnings when necessary, but do not steer for the student. All you can do is put on the brakes when circumstances require. Then you collect yourself (or your nerves) and proceed to get back on the road again.

This role is perhaps the most useful: you can give considerable direction to what is happening, yet are not in total control to the detriment of students' personal involvement and benefit. One learns to drive a car, in the final analysis, by driving a car. Beyond a certain point, no amount of cognitions, lectures, or demonstrations are going to help. One has to do it. The role of driver-education teacher helps induce the appropriate classroom atmosphere for such learning. It is a well-rounded role and the one that often seems to be generally congenial to a variety of personalities. But like a real-life driver-education teacher, you must expect a certain number of scrapes, dents, and harrowing experiences.

A final role that deserves some mention is that of "beneficent dictator." This, too, has some small application, mainly in performance ensembles. The role is best created, however, with a heavy enough emphasis on the beneficent aspects to encourage the students not to pay too much attention or care too much about the dictator components. Some teachers get this backwards: they create the role of dictator and then claim to be beneficent because "it's for your own good!" This seldom works with either young children or adolescents.

Teacher roles are part of your instructional strategy! But they are *not acting jobs* that require you to be someone you are not. Adolescents can usually smell a phony at ten paces. You must be yourself, even when, for instructional reasons, you emphasize a particular part of your personality as your "teaching role." Never was it more necessary to affirm the need to "be yourself" than in teaching.

Many teachers tire easily and become cranky or touchy, lazy or apathetic, not by virtue of the act of teaching, but by virtue of the act of putting on an act all day long. They never feel "themselves" or perhaps they adopted a phony role-playing technique before they found out who in reality they were. They have no secure self-image.

> Those attitudes which appear effective in promoting learning can be described. First of all is a transparent realness in the facilitator, a willingness to be a person, to be and to live the feelings and thoughts of the moment. When this realness includes a prizing, a caring, a trust and respect for the learner, the climate for learning is enhanced. When it includes a sensitive and accurate empathetic listening, then indeed a freeing climate, stimulative of self-initiated learning and growth, exists.[51]

The realness or honesty of self-image that stands as prerequisite to teaching success should not be confused with the roles a teacher can adopt on a changing basis to facilitate certain kinds of instruction. First and foremost you must *know* who you are and *be* who you are. Then you are in a position to adopt those attitudes that require a slightly different type of participation, or role, on your part, depending upon the requirements of the instruction you will undertake.

The first commandment of teaching is to avoid being predictable. Young people prey on predictability—not out of malice but because they are too easily bored, too easily routinized. The nature of the brain demands change and variety in order for learning to occur. If the teacher does not offer it students are very well able to invent it themselves. Boredom and getting in a teaching rut go hand in hand with predictability.

METHODS: FLEXIBLE OR STATIC

French novelist-philosopher Albert Camus wrote in his novel *The Fall,* "When one has no character, one *has* to apply a method."[52] This sentiment might apply as well to teachers whose character and professional determination is such that they expect to be given mindless, static prescriptions for invariable application in all teaching situations.

There are probably only two sources of instructional methods. There are those that are derived from some interpretation or application of psychology. These, often, are devised by "master teacher" specialists and later applied by other teachers. Other "methods" are simply created according to trial and error by individual teachers. When these "work" they are often repeated and are frequently passed around from teacher to teacher. Eventually they may find their way into a "methods" text.

In either kind of approach what is involved, at best, are certain *general techniques.* They are not intended to be regarded as prescriptions or formulas for step-by-step, invariable procedures. All teaching techniques require careful and considered thought by the individual who is using them. They must not be just adopted. They must be *adapted* to the contingencies of the teaching circumstances. The contingencies influencing this flexibility are many and varied.

1. The age of your students.
2. Their readiness in terms of environment and endowment.
3. The nature of the community; its attitudes towards, and support of, the arts.
4. The physical nature of your classroom.
5. The general teaching format favored in your school or classroom (e.g., open vs. traditional).
6. The materials you have available for musical instruction: musical instruments, independent study materials and media, etc.
7. Whether you are a music specialist who works directly with non-music classroom teachers in preparing them to teach music or whether your work is directly with students.
8. What the attitude of your administration is towards musical instruction.
9. What do teachers with classrooms on either side of yours feel about what you do—do they find their classes interrupted by musical activities in your room?
10. Your commitment to the importance of music in your life and music education for all children.

All of these variables cry out for a flexible approach in which certain general techniques, regardless of where you have learned them, are adapted to suit the needs of the situation.

The teaching approaches outlined in this text should be regarded only as guidelines, as general techniques. Each will require considerable thought on your part as to how it can be implemented best. It is unfortunate, in a way, that they are learned largely in the abstract and applied only after you are involved in student teaching. But in a way some real good is served. Very often teachers who learn only by direct imitation or observation of an experienced teacher learn *only* his or her "methods."

Therefore the suggestions made here are only guidelines or starting points for your creative variation. You must invent the rest. You must fill out the skeleton represented by the Action Learning "method." This, in addition to the variables listed earlier, will depend to large measure on your growing understanding of your students' musical needs and growth. There is, however, one rule which is not susceptible to variation. *Whatever "methods" you use, or however you adapt them to your situation, they must be consistent with (a) the learning abilities and developmental nature of your students and (b) the nature of the musical art.*

The important thing is to enhance, by whatever means, students' abilities to respond to music fully in terms of their capacities, and to thereby further incline them to integrate music into their lives now, and later as adults. Hopefully, *you* personally find music rewarding. It will be this perception of the importance of music in your life that will provide the final spark that brings your "methods" to life. As a teacher you must understand in the deepest recesses of your being the special relevance of music to a life well lived. Only in this way can you convey your own enthusiasm and serve as a living guide through the musical explorations of your students.

While this is certainly true in many areas, nowhere than in music is it more necessary to

> encourage teachers to stand forth, and declare themselves in any way that time, money, versatility, and electronic hardware have made possible. Let teachers disclose, not just the techniques for chemical analysis, or the rules for declining verbs—but also what all this means, how it challenges them in the meaningful pursuit of their lives. Let education approximate to dialogue, and not shaping. . . .[53]
>
> . . . Teachers illuminate what is; they are existential explorers, groping for new meanings as they challenge old ones. They are not solely repositories of a skill or corpus of information.[54]

Music education is the experience of music, and the experiencing and contemplation of life and its meanings through music. If these meanings are not derived from and related to the life of the student, if they do not have what has been called "felt life," they will have no role in the student's present or future existence. It is in this very direct way that music educators are "existential explorers," and that Action Learning is so desperately required.

CREATIVE TEACHING FOR ACTION LEARNING

It is precisely in the sense that teachers are "explorers, groping for new meanings as they challenge old ones," that teaching itself must be creative. It is first necessary to challenge old beliefs, attitudes, and meanings in students, other teachers, and the educational establishment if these forces conspire to prevent the kind of teaching that puts knowledge into action. From such challenges can arise the new meanings that result daily from creative teaching.

It has been observed that "creative work . . . requires an act of destruction of the existing forms and structures."[55] This no less true in teaching than in art or science. Individuals who attempt to break new paths should realize

> that by that very act they are destroying or at least undermining existing struc-
> ture, structures that have been accepted by their colleagues and by society at
> large. Thus the creative individual must be able to tolerate and even seek out
> the destructive consequences of the creation. In a sense, that destruction must
> not be "aggressive" in the normal sense of intending to hurt someone but, in-
> stead, must be seen as neutral . . . and destructive only of ideas in the service
> of creating new structures.[56]

In comparison, noncreative individuals avoid such challenges of existing structures because they cannot tolerate the resulting state of creative tension. They
are not able to survive the suspense or sustain the initiative, and to be fulfilled
by overcoming the difficulties and feelings involved.[57]

But teaching today requires a creative approach and the direct involvement of teachers everywhere to renew themselves and the profession in order that young people everywhere may be better able to integrate their learnings into the actions of effective life-plans. From a practical point of view such creative teaching is needed in order to "reach" young people, especially adolescents, and to preserve the teacher's sense of accomplishment. Nothing is less re-warding than struggling daily with adolescents and following mindless pre-scribed plans for methods. This only perpetuates the status quo of those un-happy and unfulfilled teachers who many years ago gave in to the subtle pressures of burnt-out colleagues.

The suggestion that creative teaching necessitates some destruction of the existing forms and structures of teaching requires a teacher to be able to tolerate the emotions involved in breaking new paths, and to derive direct sustenance from the feelings of overcoming difficulty and succeeding. But for many readers there may be a double difficulty of which you should be aware in order to more successfully commit yourself to such creative goals.

1. Each of us to some degree is a socially conditioned creature. One of the things that society at large, and especially its representatives in the school "Establishment," tries to maintain is
the "sacredness" of existing forms and structures. Such a shared set of assumptions or beliefs
about "truth" or "reality" is called a "paradigm."

> Paradigms do not change easily. . . .
> The Establishment is always invested in the old paradigm. So the new paradigm does
> not get adopted just because it is neater and works better than the old one. The old crowd
> wins the first few battles, and in fact the paradigm doesn't change until the old crowd dies
> and the new young crowd grows up and rewrites the textbooks and becomes the
> Establishment itself.[58]

Thus it is difficult at first for individuals to realize that if society is to grow, to improve, it requires growth and change—just as do concepts. Society in any event cannot and will not be frozen in one conceptual frame of mind. It *will* grow, it *will* evolve, as a result of the actions of many solitary individuals who are committed not to social norms but to the improvement of social structures. "Sometimes the paradigm bends, and sometimes it falls apart and gets replaced."[59] Education is indispensable to such change.

2. In the face of society's natural resistance, those individuals who will be creative will have to work hard; they will have to allay the concerns of other teachers or educators who fear the destruction of the "old" with all the security it seems to represent. They also fear the "new" because it can make them look bad in students' eyes and thus forces them to work harder in maintaining their own stature. But this is, of course, useful and is one of the many reasons for encouraging truly creative teaching: it has a spreading effect throughout the school structure and establishment.

Without a doubt, creative teaching is the most rewarding activity available to teachers. It enhances their relationships with students and the effectiveness of their teaching. But it also holds forth a great deal of personal satisfaction on the part of the individual teacher, who indeed comes to feel personally creative, alive, and vital. For such a teacher the school day is not merely survived; it is enjoyed in the same way that the artist "enjoys" his or her "work." The fact that it is work, often hard and demanding work, does not negate the possibilities of such pleasures. It is not, as some people maintain, impossible to enjoy work. One does not have to invent hobbies in order to enjoy life.

The path of Action Learning proposed and described here holds forth special potential for promoting such feelings or creativity in the teacher. The teacher will not be an "educational pharmacist" who rigorously executes the prescriptions of curriculum merchants. There is little joy, little sense of accomplishment or creativity, in such teaching. Even when prepackaged lessons and methods appear to succeed to some degree, the teachers who use them have difficulty accepting credit since they seldom even know *why* the method works. Above all, when things are not going well they seldom understand why the method *doesn't work* and thus cannot make appropriate adjustments; so they continue in the way they were trained, in hope that whatever is wrong will adjust itself or that conditions (i.e., "fate") will change for the better.[60] Some even consider getting a new position, thus attributing their lack of success to the contingencies of the particular teaching situation.

With the guidelines and suggestions provided throughout these pages, the basic skeleton of an approach based on research and experience has been provided as your "theme." *You* must create the method you will use, the "variations" of the "theme," according to the special circumstances of your teaching situation. Furthermore, you have been given the opportunity for the kind of understanding of the "theme" that can enable *you* to "learn how to learn," to "teach yourself how to teach." If you capitalize on such understanding you will continue to grow and evolve as a teacher and your efforts will never be outmoded. In contrast to "cookbook" methods, you can make up your own cookbook, your own recipes, from the suggestions and rationale provided here. Thus *you* can take all the credit due any creative success that results from your efforts.

It is not easy, nor is it without its temporary setbacks. But no goal easily won is very highly valued by most people. Only goals involving considerable challenge and risk are viewed as important and satisfying victories. Teaching, and teaching *general music* especially, presents such a challenge. You can gain insight and strength from the thoughts of Albert Camus, in his essay "Create Dangerously":

> "Every wall is a door," Emerson correctly said. Let us not look for the door, and the way out, anywhere but in the wall against which we are living. Instead, let us seek the respite where it is—in the very thick of the battle. For in my opinion . . . it *is* there. Great ideas, it has been said, come into the world as gently as doves. Perhaps then, if we listen attentively, we shall hear . . . a faint flutter of wings, the gentle stirring of life and hope. Some will say that this hope lies in a nation; others, in a man. I believe rather that it is awakened, revived, nourished by millions of solitary individuals whose deeds and works every day negate frontiers and the crudest implications of history. As a result, there shines forth fleetingly the ever-threatened truth that each and every man, on the foundation of his own sufferings and joys, builds for all.[61]

NOTES: CHAPTER 6

1. Abraham Maslow, *Toward a Psychology of Being*, 2nd ed. (New York: Van Nostrand Reinhold, 1968), p. 55.
2. Ibid., p. 34.
3. Ibid.
4. Ibid., p. 160.
5. Ibid., pp. 103-114.
6. Ibid., p. 45.
7. B. F. Skinner, *Beyond Freedom and Dignity* (New York: Random House, 1972), p. 25.
8. Ibid., p. 16.
9. Ibid., p. 68.
10. Ibid., p. 99.
11. Ibid., p. 102.
12. Maslow, *Psychology of Being*, p. 160.
13. Susanne K. Langer, *Mind: An Essay on Human Feeling* (Baltimore: Johns Hopkins Press, 1967), pp. 16-17.
14. Arthur W. Combs, "Humanizing Education: The Person in the Process," in *Humanizing Education: The Person in the Process* (Washington, D.C.: NEA, 1967), p. 76; italics added.

15. Ibid., p. 74.

16. Susanne K. Langer, *Philosophical Sketches* (New York: New American Library, Mentor Books, 1964), p. 17; italics added.

17. Ibid., p. 27; italics added.

18. Edward DeBono, *New Think* (New York: Avon Books, 1971), p. 162.

19. Langer, *Philosophical Sketches*, pp. 80-81.

20. B. Zugor, "Growth of the Individual's Concept of Self," *A.M.A. American Journal of Diseased Children*, vol. 83 (1952), p. 179.

21. Ibid.

22. Maslow, *Psychology of Being*, p. 35.

23. Combs, "Humanizing Education," p. 73.

24. Ibid., p. 82.

25. George Mandler, *Mind and Emotion* (New York: John Wiley & Sons, 1975), pp. 72-82; C. E. Izard, *Human Emotions* (New York: Plenum Press, 1977), pp. 30-35; 38-39.

26. Mandler, *Mind and Emotion*, p. 106.

27. Ibid., p. 172.

28. Ibid., p. 73.

29. Wilder Penfield, *The Mystery of the Mind* (Princeton, N.J.: Princeton University Press, 1975), p. 49.

30. Roger Lewin, "Observing the Brain Through a Cat's Eyes," and Albert Rosenfeld, "How Real Is Our Reality?" in *Mind and Supermind*, ed. Albert Rosenfeld (New York: Holt, Rinehart & Winston, 1977), pp. 137-43, 144-47. Readers are encouraged to read the full account.

31. Ibid., p. 55.

32. Ibid.

33. Ibid.

34. Ibid., italics added.

35. Ibid., p. 56.

36. Maya Pines, *The Brain Changers* (New York: New American Library, Signet Books, 1975), pp. 115-16.

37. Mandler, *Mind and Emotion*, p. 200.

38. Ibid., p. 71.

39. Lewin, "Observing the Brain Through a Cat's Eyes," p. 56.

40. Ibid., p. 56.

41. Pines, *The Brain Changers*, pp. 138-39.

42. Ibid., p. 139.

43. Mandler, *Mind and Emotion*, pp. 221-22; italics added.

44. In order to "match pitch" the following steps are required. First the learner must be able to perceive adequately the externally generated pitch (i.e., "normal" hearing). Next the student must compare his impression of this external pitch

with pitch experiences stored in "tonal memory" as *aural images;* this involves the "inner ear." Third, this (inner, stored) aural image is the basis for creating a vocal sound that "matches" the external pitch. When this does not occur, the student is not stupid or untalented. He simply has not had enough experiences to build up a sufficient accumulation of mental aural images; or he might have neurological problems that prevent the processing of stimuli with sufficient accuracy (Pines, *The Brain Changers,* p. 141). Either problem requires a vastly increased number of such experiences. This is difficult to do without extreme efforts at individualization, since most children already arrive at school with a fairly sufficient fund of such experiences (playground singing, hearing and singing music at home, and other such environmental contacts during the "sensitive period"—as with the kitten's sensitive period for vision development). Overemphasis on this retraining too often results in negative experiences and attitudes on the part of so-called "pitch-deficient" or "monotone" youngsters.

45. See point 6, pp. 347-354
46. Combs, "Humanizing Education," p. 76.
47. Ibid., p. 81.
48. Jerome S. Bruner, *The Process of Education,* (New York: Random House, Vintage Books, 1973), p. 52; italics added.
49. Ibid., p. 33.
50. Combs, "Humanizing Education," pp. 80-81.
51. Carl R. Rogers, "The Interpersonal Relationship in the Facilitation of Learning," in *Humanizing Education: The Person in the Process* (Washington, D.C.: NEA, 1967), p. 16.
52. Albert Camus, *The Fall,* trans. Justin O'Brien (New York: Random House, Vintage Books, 1956), p. 11.
53. Sidney M. Jourard, "Automation, Stupefaction, and Education," in *Humanizing Education: The Person in the Process,* p. 51.
54. Ibid., p. 48.
55. Mandler, *Mind and Emotion,* p. 246.
56. Ibid.
57. Ibid., p. 247.
58. Adam Smith, *Powers of Mind* (New York: Random House, 1975), p. 21.
59. Ibid., p. 23.
60. A leading sociologist of education, in an influential book, notes with alarm that most teachers seem to attribute both their successes and their failures to "fate." A good day for most teachers is attributed to the students' behaving well—for reasons the teachers do not pretend to know or identify. A poor day is chalked up to upcoming vacations, the weather, and a host of other poltergeists. Teachers, it seems, are to be pitied; they seem to feel they have almost no control over their own teaching successes and destinies. See Dan Lortie, *Schoolteacher* (Chicago: University of Chicago Press, 1975), pp. 168-75.
61. Albert Camus, *Resistance, Rebellion, and Death,* trans. Justin O'Brien (New York: Alfred A. Knopf, 1961), p. 272.

Appendix A:

Curriculum Planning and Use

A curriculum consists of the statement of long-term objectives that are to be accomplished in large part by each individual student. It is expected that each student will manifest a different pattern of strengths and weaknesses, attitudes and interests in accordance with his or her readiness at the beginning of study. Therefore, at the completion of the program there will be multiple or varied outcomes in terms of particulars, but all students generally should display significant mastery of each musical competency. Notice in the sample curriculum that follows how long-term objectives are stated in the general format of behavioral objectives in order to serve as the basis for short-term (daily) objectives. The italicized words in the outline are the covert actions (mental processes), the cognitive strengthening of which are the goals of instruction. They are drawn from the lists in Fig. 6:2, page 362.

I. *Melody*

A. Each student will demonstrate the ability *to perceive, analyze, identify, differentiate,* and *compare* melodies by:

1. Writing appropriate answers for listening lessons involving melodies and discussing these answers for the benefit of the teacher and class.

2. Notating short melodic patterns featuring diatonic intervals up to a perfect fifth, using dots and lines to show melodic direction and whether the pitch is repeated, a step, or a skip.

3. Singing melodies at sight from a "guess that tune" melody notated on the board.

B. Each student will demonstrate the ability *to synthesize, apply abstractly, evaluate, elaborate,* and *decide on* melodic elements by:

1. Composing melodies in parallel and contrasting phrase and period forms of varying lengths.

2. Composing sound compositions of varying lengths in which the linear elements are controlled and manipulated in a melodic manner by employing techniques of melody writing: augmentation, diminution, motivic development, inversion, retrograde, and retrograde inversion.

3. Arranging preexisting melodies into song cycles, theater pieces, etc., of an extended nature.

4. Composing songs that show a variety of usages in melodic direction: steps, skips, repeated notes, beginning and ending pitches (melodic cadences).

5. Composing songs or using linear sound composition elements based on "given" material and according to certain specified principles of melody writing (as in item 2 above).

C. Each student will *identify in terms of concepts with* melodies heard aurally by:

1. Overtly reflecting his or her feelings about the melodic elements present by choosing pictures or descriptive adjectives; by original graphic design, media projects, humming and whistling, etc.

2. Discussing the expressive role of melody in given or freely chosen examples.

3. Discussing the formal role of melody in given or freely chosen examples.

D. Each student will respond to melodies *intuitively* and *interpret* them *freely* by:

1. Singing a *controlled improvisation** to a blues progression played at the piano by the teacher.

2. Singing freely along with recordings selected by the teacher for that purpose.

3. Writing about or describing personal feelings about the relationship between the melody and words of a song.

E. Each student will *prefer, enjoy,* and *choose on the basis of feeling* certain melodies by:

1. Writing an informal listening lesson for the class that uses a personally chosen recorded song; discussing his or her own feelings about the melody.

2. Asking for in-class performances of certain songs that are personal favorites—i.e., asking to hear or to sing these songs.

F. Each student will *characterize, create,* or *subjectively organize* certain melodies by:

1. Composing songs, in an out of class, assigned and not assigned, which have no teacher-specified criteria.

---

* Using only tones of triads.

2. Discussing personal creations and those of others (classmates and commercial) in terms of personal feelings.

3. Composing freely, in sound compositions and songwriting, all those melodic (linear) elements not otherwise given or established as criteria by the teacher.

G. Each student will *hear* melodies *inwardly* by:

1. Singing melodies by ear.

2. Singing countermelodies by ear.

3. Singing portions of melodies "silently" by ear, then reentering correctly on cue.

4. Verbally identifying a notated melody without hearing it played aloud.

5. Identifying in writing one among several examples as the melody that was played.

II. *Harmony*

A. Each student will *perceive, analyze, identify, differentiate,* and *compare* harmonic elements by:

1. Writing appropriate answers for listening lessons involving harmony, and discussing these answers for the benefit of the teacher and class.

2. Singing chord progressions used in songwriting melodically (arpeggiated), with accompaniment by the teacher (on the piano, guitar, etc.); or playing them melodically on an instrument.

B. Each student will demonstrate the ability *to synthesize, apply abstractly, evaluate, elaborate,* and *decide* with regard to harmony by:

1. Composing successful songs to given harmonic progressions.

2. Arranging or rearranging harmonic progressions for the purposes of original song compositions.

3. Employing harmonies of established songs in the composition of original songs.

4. Reharmonizing a personally composed melody with largely new, yet correct chords.

C. Each student will *identify in terms of concepts with* harmonies heard aurally by:

1. Discussing the expressive role of the harmonic elements heard in given or freely chosen examples.

2. Discussing the formal role of the harmonic elements heard in given or freely chosen examples.

3. Discussing in all music, including sound compositions, the effectiveness (formally or expressively) of tension-release created by harmonic (simultaneous) elements.

4. Discussing the elements and effect of tension-release in daily life.

D. Each student will *respond* to harmonies and harmonic usage *intuitively* and *interpret* them *freely* by:

    1. Singing harmony parts by ear during class singing sessions designated for that purpose.

    2. Discussing the effectiveness of harmonies employed in terms of "pure" music; in terms of "programmatic" music.

E. Each student will *characterize, create,* and *subjectively organize* harmonies by:

    1. Composing songs to his or her own chord progressions.

    2. Discussing the effectiveness of his or her own original chord progressions and those of classmates.

    3. Discussing the effectiveness of chord progression used in popular music.

F. Each student will *hear* harmonies *inwardly* by:

    1. Singing specific harmony parts by ear during class singing.

    2. Identifying in writing the number of different harmony parts (or vertical elements, in the case of sound compositions) heard in a given performance.

III. *Rhythm/meter*

A. Each student will *perceive, analyze, identify, differentiate,* and *compare* rhythmic elements by:

    1. Writing appropriate answers for listening lessons involving rhythm/meter, and discussing these answers for the benefit of the teacher and class.

    2. Identifying in writing, from choices given, rhythmic/metric patterns employed in a composition.

    3. Verbally identifying duple and triple, compound and simple meters from given aural examples.

B. Each student will demonstrate the ability *to synthesize, apply abstractly, evaluate, elaborate,* and *decide* with regard to rhythms/meters by:

    1. Composing songs and sound compositions that employ such factors successfully.

    2. Organizing a variety of different rhythms possible in a given meter using whole through sixteenth notes.

    3. Composing or organizing compositions whose major formal element is based on rhythm/meter.

    4. Composing songs with *rhythms* arranged into parallel and contrasting phrases/periods.

    5. Composing, arranging, or organizing rhythmic variations of given melodies or rhythm scores (i.e., "rhythm bands") having a set starting rhythm.

C. Each student will *identify in terms of concepts with* rhythm/meter heard aurally by:

1. Moving or conducting in such a way as to reflect a rhythmic/metric "interpretation" clearly based on the rhythm/meter of the music.

2. Discussing rhythmic/metric elements in terms of their expressive role in given or freely chosen examples.

3. Discussing rhythms/meters heard in daily life, or creating compositions using such rhythms/meters.

4. Discussing the "rhythm" of daily life: especially, a single day, how such single days organize into larger periods or units—e.g., the rhythm of school at different times of the year.

D. Each student will *respond intuitively* and *interpret* rhythms/meters *freely* by:

1. Improvising rhythmic patterns within given meters.

2. Performing rhythmic improvisations on rhythm instruments or by making body sounds, etc., to aural examples chosen for this purpose by the teacher.

E. Each student will *characterize, create,* or *subjectively organize* rhythms/meters by:

1. Composing songs and sound compositions employing freely chosen rhythms and meters.

2. Discussing the effectiveness of his or her own and classmates' original rhythms or choices of meters.

F. Each student will *hear* rhythms/meters *inwardly* by:

1. Singing rhythms/meters by ear correctly from given examples played by the teacher.

2. Identifying in writing rhythms played from among visual examples given.

3. Identifying verbally the title of an example simply by being given its rhythm aurally.

IV. *Timbre*

A. Each student will *perceive, analyze, identify, differentiate,* and *compare* timbres by:

1. Writing appropriate answers for listening lessons involving timbre, and discussing these answers for the benefit of the teacher and class.

2. Identifying in writing certain timbres or combinations as prespecified by categories (e.g., metallic vs. wood; strings vs. woodwinds) in examples heard aurally.

3. Discussing different performances of a composition done by performers on different instruments.

B. Each student will demonstrate the ability *to synthesize, apply abstractly, evaluate, elaborate,* and *decide* with regard to timbres by:

1. Composing sound compositions, and song accompaniments, that effectively employ timbre expressively as a means of creating given forms.

2. Notating a score for an electronic sound collage (*musique con-crète*) based on school sounds, city or town sounds, or personally chosen environmental sounds such as farm or highway sounds.

C. Each student will *identify in terms of concepts with* timbral usage by:

1. Discussing timbral elements in terms of their expressive role in given or freely chosen examples.

2. Discussing timbral elements in terms of their formal role in given or freely chosen examples.

3. Discussing the role of timbre in the conduct of everyday life, identi-fying specifically what and how timbres are involved (e.g., recognizing people by their voices).

4. Discussing the role of electronics in music today and in people's lives in general, and the timbral possibilities for musical composition that are now available.

5. Discussing the effect of electronic recording on the nature, role, and practice of composition: in rock and other "popular" forms of music; in "art" music (e.g., what does it portend that much of this music is not notated?)

6. Discussing the effect of acoustics and listener placement on timbre when one is listening to music; the question of "live" vs. "recorded" music and the impact of each on timbre.

D. Each student will demonstrate a variety of affective responses to tim-bre by:

1. Composing, arranging, or organizing music that uses timbre in sub-jective ways.

2. *Characterizing* responses to timbre heard in listening lessons.

3. Discussing personal *preferences* for kinds of timbres often em-ployed in music.

4. *Choosing freely* or *preferring* to manipulate timbre as an important ingredient in composing.

V. *Texture*

A. Each student will *perceive, analyze, identify, differentiate,* and *com-pare* textures in music by:

1. Identifying in writing whether examples or sections of music heard were monophonic, homophonic, or polyphonic.

2. Verbally analyzing texture by reference only to a score.

B. Each student will demonstrate the ability *to synthesize, apply ab-stractly, evaluate, elaborate,* and *decide* with regard to texture by:

1. Composing sound compositions that employ specified textures.

2. Composing sound compositions whose forms result from texture.

3. Composing sound compositions whose expressive elements are significantly influenced by texture.

4. Composing sound compositions in which timbre and texture are

combined effectively to meet either freely chosen or given requirements (form, expression, programmatic content, etc.).

5. Composing sound compositions in which both the texture and rhythm/meter are combined effectively to meet either freely chosen or given requirements.

6. Composing songs to harmonic patterns that can result in effective rounds or canons.

C. Each student will *identify in terms of concepts with* texture usage by:

1. Discussing the role of texture with regard to text setting, effectiveness, musical expressiveness, musical form of music heard in class.

2. Discussing the effect of combined environmental textures on us in our daily lives (i.e., simultaneous sounds resulting in different textures, such as birds chirping periodically against the constant sound of a stream or lake).

3. Discussing the textures of: daydreaming, a party, a football game, a telephone call, etc.

D. Each student will demonstrate a variety of affective responses to textural elements by:

1. Employing texture in free composition effectively.

2. *Characterizing* responses to texture heard in listening lessons.

3. Discussing *preferences* for kinds of textures often employed in music.

4. Composing and/or devising listening lessons that show increasing frequency of usage, over the course of time, texture other than homophonic.

VI. *Form*

A. Each student will *perceive, analyze, identify, differentiate,* and *compare* the following musical forms/processes:

simple binary	rondo	sonata principle
simple ternary	theme and variations	eclectic forms
complex binary	fugue	song form and trio
complex ternary	sonata rondo	unity and variety
		unity in variety

1. By being able to identify, or to describe in his or her own words, the forms/processes of selected aural examples.

2. By writing or discussing a personal analysis of these forms/processes from the musical score without aural examples.

3. By using music listened to outside of class to compile a list of examples of each form/process, for comparison with the choices of classmates.

4. By applying these musical forms to such visual examples as diagrams and other graphic representations, photographs, and paint-

ings—and vice versa; by responding appropriately to listening lessons featuring these forms.

5. By discussing with the class the appearance of these forms in nature, in the town, and elsewhere in the environment.

B. Each student will demonstrate the ability *to synthesize, apply abstractly, evaluate, elaborate,* and *decide* with regard to form/formal processes by:

1. Composing, arranging, and organizing sound compositions, songs, or extended works (song cycles, etc.) in each.

2. Composing, in free situations, in many of these forms (as opposed to feeling comfortable in only a few).

3. Showing increased sophistication over the course of study in the manipulation of all relevant musical elements used to achieve a form.

C. Each student will *identify in terms of concepts with* formal processes by:

1. Writing about or discussing the "form" or "formal process" observed in one recent day of his or her life—and over larger periods of time.

2. Writing about or discussing the "formal process" involved in examples of architecture, the visual arts, and literary and theatrical arts regularly encountered by most people: e.g., buildings in the town; paintings or sculpture in the town; TV shows, movies, plays, or musicals seen locally.

3. Discussing the "form" or "formal processes" in anyone's attempt to organize otherwise unstructured time: e.g., a rainy Saturday, sitting in the dentist's office, waiting to be asked to dance, a long trip.

4. Discussing the "form" or "formal processes" of athletic or other games: the role and importance of these formal processes in the enjoyment of such activities.

5. Discussing how unity and variety influence the quality and nature of our daily lives.

D. Each student will demonstrate a variety of affective responses to form and formal processes by:

1. Discussing current personal *preferences* for unified or diversified activities; teaching styles preferred; preference for watching one sport over another, etc. Over time a progression of enriched insight with regard to unity and variety should be observed.

2. Same as above with regard to musical preferences, attitudes, values, and tastes.

3. Being able to identify and discuss music that is very basic (simple) in terms of form and formal process, and *to characterize* personal *preference* for it in comparison to music identified as complex in terms of form and formal process. The teacher should look for progressively

greater insight. (N.B.: This should not infer *greater insight as to reasons for the choices involved:* very simple music can be very effective, and very complex music can be ineffective.)

4. Organizing a list of songs heard in and outside of class that are especially liked, at least in part, because of the form or formal processes involved (which should be identified too). The student should explain how or why the form or formal process involved is attractive.

VII. *Style*

You may deal with this question in any of several ways. It could be a separate element in your curriculum, and thus would be numbered VII if you were following this format. In this case you would probably want to deal with the following considerations:

Personal style: Composer's or group's—in clothing, etc.

Geographical: Western European vs., for example, Oriental.

National: Style idiosyncratic to certain nations.

Ethnic: Ethnic groups, styles, i.e., black, American Indian, Afro-Cuban.

Appeal (constituency): folk, popular, "art."

Historical: Chronology of stylistic change within a given area (rock, jazz, art music, etc.).

As you can see, this is a very complex issue all by itself. Therefore, it is recommended that you not try to pin down such questions as the romantic style, etc. It is far easier and more effective to choose each musical example for any of your activities according to its attensive qualities. But choose as wide a variety of styles as possible. Deal with each notable stylistic characteristic *as you encounter it* in the examples you have chosen.

Granted that this may seem to be a bit hit-or-miss, but it does have many points in its favor.

1. Much information concerning historical style is irrelevant to commonly encountered listening. It is not necessary to understand the historical development involved in the styles of jazz and rock in order to respond fruitfully to a current example. Therefore, deal only with the relevant stylistic aspects of the current example.

For example: A listening lesson might feature a romantic-era composition, and *some* of your questions might focus on those elements that contribute to its style. This can be followed by an activity in which students compose a "romantic style" sound composition.

2. If you cannot present a comprehensive selection of styles in the pursuit of your other goals for the class, the chances are not good in any event that you could organize a separate goal solely to teach style. If you can utilize a

wide variety of styles, then the question of style will be appropriately dealt with in a musical context, since style is always relevant to any musical perception.

3. Style is a very difficult issue to deal with, even in college instruction. It is vague and elusive at best, and not given to systematic organization other than arbitrarily from the point of view of the teacher.

4. Style, organized systematically, will lead you to do a great deal of lecturing. You understand style to whatever degree you already do, due to your own vast prior experience (readiness). Your students simply have not had enough experience to make what seems to you to be very simple distinctions.

5. The main thing about style that needs to be known is that it is the result of a complex chemistry of cause and effect, and not a little accident. Instead of always emphasizing those traits that are *common* among works, we might better emphasize—at least in equal measure—those qualities that make a piece or class of pieces *unique*: i.e., the source of the chemistry of a *particular piece or class of pieces*. Thus, it is not simply a question of why Beethoven is a romantic or classical composer, or why his pieces can be grouped according to periods, but why any two adjacent or widely separated opus numbers are effective *music*. The same holds true for contemporary performers of rock and pop music.

6. Thus, each piece can be its own "exercise" in stylistic understanding. In fact, if each piece encountered is so treated, it is all the more likely that it will have been effectively "experienced."

In high school theory, history, and appreciation classes, the more specific factors may be more systematically treated against this background of general readiness for stylistic "appreciation" or understanding.

POINTS TO REMEMBER IN USING THIS CURRICULUM OR OTHERS BASED ON IT

1. Any curriculum is hypothetical, tentative, an educated guess, or wishful thinking. Each must be adjusted to reality. Therefore, you begin with something such as exemplified above, and after working with it for *several years or classes*, adjust it to fit the needs, interests, and abilities of your students, in your school, with your materials, room, and administration.

a. Any number of long-term objective items may be omitted for future classes when it is apparent that they have been unreasonable, unfruitful, or impossible to attain.

b. Other items or variations can be added according to your insight, student interest, or new developments in music, methods, materials, etc.

c. *Specific criteria* are not specified in the curricular objectives: *include them* in the short-term (daily) objectives you use in teaching. Criteria should be adjusted according to the grade level (in graded schools) or ability level (in ungraded situations).

Therefore, this sample curriculum could be used for grades 5-8 or grades 6-12, for example, but each level would have slightly more sophisticated and refined requirements to meet. And even within this general alteration according to level, you may still have to plan carefully for the kind of *multiple outcomes* that can evidence success—at varying levels of achievement for various students according to their readiness or ability. Thus two students can both meet an objective, but one does it by means of quite-sophisticated composing while another's composing is naive though technically correct.

2. Evaluation should be ongoing if possible. That is, your daily activities should provide the ongoing evidence of learning. As daily, short-term objectives are successfully met by the class, it is your task to continually upgrade the level of difficulty until the class and the individuals constituting it have generally progressed to a certain level.

This level, the first time it happens, becomes your *target level*. It should be considered "A" or its equivalent in numerical grades. Subsequent classes you teach will aim at this level, and theoretically the target level will gradually expand in most areas as *you* come to understand the curriculum and your teaching methods better. (See pp. 398-399 for a recommended means of Action Evaluation).

3. If administrators insist on marking periods or weekly tests or grades or other "administrivia," play along. Hedge if you have to. If you cannot avoid it, give "tests" in the form of activities built around one or more long-term objectives and indistinguishable to your students from most other class activities. Evaluate these after putting all the blame for having to do so on "the system." It is important that students know that you do not enjoy or approve of such **grading** (if in fact it is true that you don't). It is also important that they know that you *are* in favor of **evaluation,** and that you carry this on daily.

5. *Warning:* do not atomistically reduce music to nuts and bolts by regarding any one long-term objective as self-sufficient or as standing alone in any way. Each musical element is always interwoven with, or related to, other elements. A curriculum exists only *to emphasize one or a few elements at a time.* Never allow students to get the idea that each element is functionally separate; be sure you always take some time or effort to facilitate their seeing the relations that exist between musical elements.

Similarly, do not think that an activity is one hundred percent cognitive, affective, or psychomotor. All musical behaviors involve all three in some amount. Again, some lessons/activities emphasize one of these kinds of behavior, but not to the exclusion of others. The affective element is the most important of the three.

All of these interrelationships can be shown in the following manner (Fig. A:1): all elements intersect at all points on the cube. Teaching, like

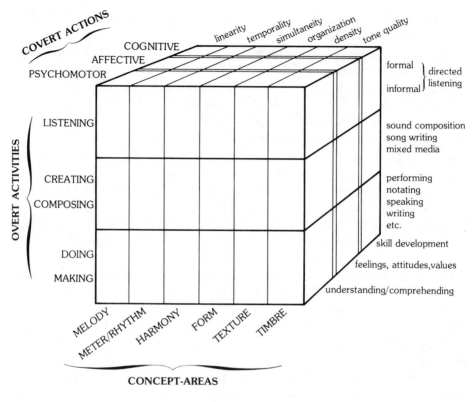

Fig. A:1 Instructional Gestalt for Action Learning

music, is a gestalt. The whole determines and controls the number, nature, and behavior of the parts. If the "parts" are your teaching "methods," the whole is the effective learning specified in your behavioral curriculum. Thus the curriculum regulates how the various parts interrelate and function to produce the greatest wholeness of result.

CURRICULAR STYLES

A curriculum is not something you "cover." You teach *with* a curriculum, using it to ensure organization. This organization should establish relationships between all separate facets of the curriculum and should impart to students a sense that instruction is goal-directed, is going and getting somewhere. Students are the first to appreciate that, as someone has said, "if you don't know where you're going, you're likely to end up someplace else." Thus a curriculum is your guide to the long-range goals you seek to achieve.

Your goals involve three ingredients. First, they imply your philosophy of education and music education. They also imply your general teaching "style." Finally, the nature of how you evaluate students, your own teaching, and the curriculum are also involved. These three aspects make possible four different curricular styles, not all of which are very desirable for general music instruction in the middle and secondary schools.

1. A *basic skills curriculum*, for example, usually stresses performance skills, music reading, and musical information in the belief that students might use these somewhere or sometime in life. Instruction here usually involves "observational learning (i.e., watching demonstrations), "rote learning" (learning through imitation), drill (repetitive practice), and memorization and recall of information. This text has warned you that this curricular style is the most likely to run afoul of poor student attitudes and discipline problems in middle and secondary school general-music classes. With the exception of stressing abstract information, this curriculum is best suited to elective performance ensembles where, by the very fact of their presence, students indicate an interest in, and therefore some desire to work for, such goals.

2. A second and equally problematic type of curricular style stresses our *cultural heritage*. It emphasizes an understanding and appreciation of our musical heritage as an objectively enduring "good." It almost inevitably stresses *verbal knowledge about music*, and thus features mainly lectures, lecture-demonstrations, research or other kinds of library reports, notebooks, and similar means as the predominant mode of instruction. Written tests are especially likely as a regular feature of this kind of instruction. Most high school "music *appreciation*" courses, and many junior high "*general* music" classes are really misnomers for this kind of instruction. Again, this curricular style violates virtually every recommendation and piece of evidence outlined in describing Action Learning.

It is a fact of life that new information is seen as relevant under two conditions: (1) where it leads an individual closer to goals he or she recognizes as being of personal value; (2) where it is forced on unwilling subjects under the threat of grades, punishment, and other authoritarian forms of extrinsic control. The first instance is highly unlikely to occur in public school: after all, most music educators in their own college experience found it difficult to retain motivation in many of their lecture classes (e.g., music history). We have already seen how the second instance contributes to the great likelihood of confrontation and other severe forms of discipline problem.

3. *Essentialism* is the style of curriculum set up in the belief that music is essential in the preparation of a "well-educated" person; that everyone should "know something" *about* music if they are to be considered competently educated. Taken to its extreme, some teachers have students memorize names and dates of famous composers, and the titles of several representative compositions—as they put it to students, "in order not to appear ignorant about music when somebody discusses it with you at a cocktail party someday." Other, somewhat more realistic teachers recognize that musical involvement *is* "essential" to the well-being of all people and that music listening is the most accessible mode of musical involvement. Thus they stress listening skills and conceptual learning. This latter version of essentialism is more commendable than the first style for obvious reasons. Both, however, impose goals on the students who, for their own part, are not at all necessarily in agreement with, or care about, such goals. Thus when any mismatch arises between the teacher's goals and expectations and students' motivations, some degree or form of continuous discipline problem is assured.

4. *Action Learning* is one variety of humanistic-existential-progressive curricular orientation. It is predicated on greater individual instrinsic motivation and self-motivation on the part of students who come to see for themselves that the activities and goals the teacher chooses are in some way and to some degree related to their lives now and in the future. Thus the student's inner world is both the starting and the ending point of all instruction. Instruction is predicated on a challenging and interesting involvement where music is acted upon and acted with in the pursuit of goals *the students* find rewarding. To the degree that it is successful, this style of curriculum enhances the likelihood that some of the more laudable aspects of the other three curricular styles are actually incorporated into students' lives: (1) from the basic skills type, that some relevant and useful skills are learned (e.g., writing and performing one's own songs via

Songwriting Activities); (2) from the cultural heritage orientation, that students will have become more familiar than they otherwise would have been with the major aspects of our musical heritage, and that this learning will have been acquired in a manner that increases their regard for and attitude toward it (e.g., directed listening lessons; learning traditional means of composition by doing sound composition activities); (3) and from essentialism, that such music learning is more likely to become an "essential" part of their lives in the future; the "essential" role of music in general education is also assured in truly pragmatic terms.

RECOMMENDED "FINAL" GOALS FOR GENERAL MUSIC IN THE MIDDLE AND SECONDARY SCHOOLS

1. A sustaining or improving of attitudes toward music, resulting in an increasing desire or intention to be musically active in some way.

2. Increased accuracy and richness of perception of formal and expressive aspects of music.

3. Increased familiary with a wider variety of musical media, types, and styles of music than students can otherwise acquire informally in the home or community.

4. Identification and nurturing of the musical ability and interest in all children, and of especially talented or interested youngsters, for purposes of encouraging full development of such potential.

5. An understanding of the role and importance of music in history and in one's present and future life.

6. The development of specific and long-lasting musical skills for those who have the ability or interest.

7. An increased ability to make independent value judgments in music based upon discrimination of musical elements.

8. A positive contribution to each student's overall education, especially in the areas in which music can be central, namely, in nurturing positive self-concepts, explorations of the feeling-life, and as an opportunity for social interaction in pursuit of mutual goals.

Administrators will appreciate and be impressed by the inclusion of such goals along with any curriculum submitted by the teacher. Students will appreciate and be impressed by any teacher who actually works toward and achieves some measure of success along these lines.

KEEPING TRACK OF YOUR CURRICULUM

Assuming you have prepared a curriculum based on long-term objectives and operational goals, you will easily be able to derive meaningful day-to-day instruction. However, it is something of a problem to ensure that day-to-day lessons are related to each other and that you adequately address yourself to all or most of the long-term objectives you set for your curriculum.

In order to do this, it is first useful to distinguish some of the aspects of your day-to-day teaching. In Fig. A:2, the differences between activities, lessons, and units are explained and shown.

Fig. A:2

 ACTIVITY: narrow focus; its *very short-term goals* are *MEANS* to *larger ends.*

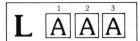 LESSON: Synthesizes several activities in order to reach *intermediate goals* which themselves are *MEANS* to *even larger ends.*

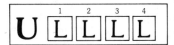 "UNIT": A grouping of lessons around a common focus or theme. This maximizes *unity* of learning as the *focus* or theme becomes an *even larger intermediate goal.*

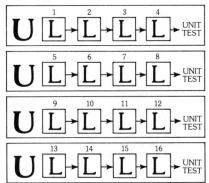 Traditional LOCK-STEP *UNITS* where each earlier grouping is regarded as self-sufficient (i.e., once "covered" is falsely believed to be sufficient) and where *no relationships or unity* exists between the UNITS or the lessons that make them up. *This is to be avoided.*

In truth of fact, teaching this way results in each earlier grouping becoming more remote in memory and thus in fact. Earlier learnings are ineffective because they are no longer present at the end of instruction.

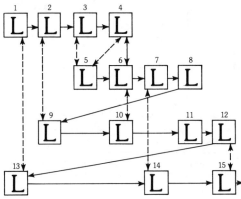 INFORMAL SEQUENTIAL "UNITS" are *informal groupings* of lessons around a common individual focus. Here not only are the lessons within the "unit" unified and related (see the solid arrows) but they stem directly from or are related directly to lessons in previous "units" (see the broken arrows). Each grouping is also directly related somehow to a previous "unit" grouping. Thus *subsequent lessons in later "units" expand upon learnings that were part of but not stressed or emphasized in earlier lessons and units.*

Notice how L4 and L6 directly connect and relate the first two groupings. The last lesson of a group need not always lead directly to the first lesson of a new group.

With these distinctions in mind, the following suggestions can be made for your day-to-day planning and record keeping.

1. Keep all your daily plans in a ring-binder notebook. It is strongly recommended that you use the Venture Planning Form shown on p. 288.

2. Using sturdy dividers, create as many sections in your ring-binder as you have class sections. Label them clearly.

3. For each *activity* you plan for a given class section, include a Venture Planning Form in the ring-binder section you have created for that class. When a given activity is used in more than one class section, photocopy the Venture Planning Form so that one copy is filed for each class.

4. Immediately behind each divider (or taped directly on its front or back side) use a *Planning Record Grid* such as the one shown in Fig. A:3.

5. As you plan *lessons* by placing the Venture Planning Forms for each *activity* constituting the lesson in the appropriate section(s) of your ring-binder, enter the date and other information on the Planning Record Grid for the class section(s) involved. After a while, a Planning Record Grid might look like the one shown in Fig. A:4.

6. Each subsequent time you plan—planning for block of two weeks is often the most practical for ensuring unity and continuity—first study the Planning Record Grid for the class in question to get an impression of what your overall coverage of your curriculum has been to date. Then thumb through the most recent Venture Planning Forms for that class and note what you have most recently accomplished and whatever "future reminders" you have written to yourself as remedial or follow-up ideas. Include these as partial basis, at least, for the new activities you plan.

Fig. A:3

	Listening	Creating	Composing	Singing	Playing	Moving	Discussing	Other	U • F • P
Melody									
Harmony									
Rhythm/Meter									
Form									
Timbre									
Texture									
Style									
Other									

U = Understanding   F = Feeling Response   P = Performance Skills

Across the top, list your activities. Down the left side, list references to your curriculum outline. In its finished size, the Grid should be as large as you can make it in order to provide the most room in the squares for the relevant information.

Fig. A:4

	Listening	Creating	Composing	Singing	Playing	Moving	Discussing	Other	U • F • P
Melody	9/10	9/11	9/11	9/21			9/10 9/11		✓ ✓ ✓
Harmony	9/11 10/1 10/2	10/1 10/2			9/12				✓ ✓
Rhythm/ Meter				9/21	9/29	9/26 9/29	9/29	9/29	✓
Form		9/11	9/13				9/13	9/11	✓
Timbre	9/13 9/14 9/17		9/18 9/19 9/20		9/18 9/19 9/20		9/13 9/19 9/14 9/20 9/18	Film	✓ ✓
Texture	9/18 9/30 9/19 10/1 9/20 10/2 9/29	9/17	9/18 9/19 9/20		9/18 9/19 9/20		9/18 9/29 9/19 9/30 10/1 9/20 10/2		✓ ✓ ✓
Style	9/24 9/25 9/23	9/17	9/23 9/25	9/23 9/25			9/24 9/25 9/23		✓ ✓ ✓
Other						DANCING 10/3	MUSICAL CAREERS 9/21		✓ ✓

U = Understanding   F = Feeling Response   P = Performance Skills

Place in the appropriate square the date of each time you do an activity that features one or more aspects of your curriculum outline. Notice, for example, for 9/18-20 the activities recorded here emphasized listening, composing, playing and discussing. This is typical for sound compositions. In the far right vertical column keep a record of whether your activities involve understanding, feeling or playing. Just place a check in each column. Notice that this Grid shows at a glance that "form" and "singing" have been slighted.

7. And, of course, after you have planned new activities for your lessons, enter this information as you did for point 5 above.

This system of planning and record keeping is more difficult to explain than it is to use. Once the teacher has set up the ring-binder with a divider and a Record Planning Grid for each class section, it is only a matter of running off multiple copies of blank Venture Planning Forms, then of filling out these blank forms for daily planning. Each section of your ring-binder will have a complete record of every activity the class in question has accomplished, and the Record Planning Grid will give you an instant overview of how well you are using your curriculum as the basis for instruction. This process ensures a unified curriculum.

One warning: It is usually a good idea to notify building principals and other concerned administrators that you will be using this form of planning and record keeping rather than the typical "teacher plan book" with its 2″ squares for keeping class plans and records. To date, it is unheard of that any objection is ever made to this kind of extensive planning. Among other things, it has real advantages for substitute teachers who are far better able to teach from a Venture Planning Form than from a cryptic sentence in the traditional plan book.

ACTION EVALUATION

Finally, Action Learning has its own style of evaluation. It is predicated on the types of evaluation procedures used in businesses to evaluate employees according to prestated criteria. Thus, just as with Action Learning, Action Evaluation is oriented toward "real life" conditions and processes.

It must be noted, first of all, that evaluation, reporting and recording evaluations are three separate functions. An *evaluation* amounts to any *value judgment* made of a student, whether on the basis of prestated criteria or impressionistically. It is important to note that even when criteria are prestated, an evaluation is still inevitably subjective since few values in life, and perhaps even fewer in music, are 100 percent agreed upon by all.

An *evaluation* may be *reported* to a student, or to his or her parents, in any number of ways. Systems of anecdotal reports are increasingly being adopted for this purpose since they are most accurate and complete. An anecdotal report is simply a statement—anything from a sentence or two to a paragraph—summarizing the teacher's diagnosis of a student's accomplishments, shortcomings, and potential. Where this is impractical (as it often is when teachers have hundreds of students), two other formats are often used:

1. Various kinds of bar graphs that visually represent levels of accomplishments in prestated categories are becoming common. So on a 0-10 basis, the teacher rates the student's accomplishments for each curricular aspect.

2. Another means is for the teacher to make a numbered list of sentences that describe the most likely to occur conditions of achievement or weaknesses. The evaluation report, then, includes a copy of this list, with the items from the list that apply to the student in question, marked or noted in some manner. Such a process usually includes some space to note any qualities the student possesses that are not otherwise included in the listing of most common remarks.

An evaluation may be *recorded* in any number of ways. Perhaps the most direct and accurate means is simply to keep the evaluation *report* permanently on file. The traditional means of recording reports of students' achievements has been *grading*, but what this system gains in efficiency it loses in accuracy. A single letter or numerical grade, by itself, is almost meaningless, as has been demonstrated time and again by researchers. When a student gets a "B" or an "85" neither the student nor his or her parents are likely to know exactly what skills and what weaknesses are reflected in the grade. For example a "C" grade (or its numerical equivalent) can mean that the student is excellent in one-half of the learnings required and very poor in the other half. So, even when schools are still enamored of the use of grades, teachers should be aware that it is important to their curricular aims for students to be fully apprised of their accomplishments, of their individual strengths and weaknesses. Action Evaluation is a simple and effective way of conducting evaluation, of reporting it to students, and of recording it in an economical form.

It uses a standard form, illustrated in Fig. A:5. In Fig., A:5 the "Objectives" are keyed to the sample curriculum provided at the beginning of this Appendix. One word suffices to "key" the teacher and student to the relevant category of achievement. Additional categories can be created to reflect nonacademic variables such as "effort."

The column marked "WFI" involves "weighting for importance" the objectives involved. In simple terms this means that, as in any aspect of life or work, *no goals are equally important* even when all are important to some degree. Thus this column allows you to rate how important you regard the category of

Objectives	WFI	X Level	= Score	minus readi- ness	= Final Score	Comments
1. Melody						
2. Harmony						
3. Rhythm/Meter						
4. Form						
5. Timbre						
6. Texture						
7. Style						
8. Effort						
	Total			Total	Total	

$$\bigcirc \times 4 = \bigcirc \quad minus \quad \bigcirc = \bigcirc \Big/ \bigcirc \overset{\times 4}{\underset{}{}} = \bigcirc$$

TOTAL Possible WFI   TOTAL Readiness   TOTAL SCORE   Grade Point Average

Fig. A:5   Action Evaluation Form

accomplishment to be for a learner or class. This is done on a 1-through-4 basis, with 1 being less important and 4 being very important. It is often wise, say in high school theory class, to negotiate this column with each individual student. The idea is to rate categories in which the student most needs improvement higher than those in which the student is already amply accomplished. It can also be done to effect a balance between needed improvement and past accomplishment.

The idea is not necessarily that "melody" is somehow inherently more important that "harmony." Rather "WFI" establishes that for this student this marking period (or for this entire class for the marking period) "melody" will be rated higher because the student needs more work (or because the teacher is planning to emphasize it for the entire class). Whenever you negotiate the WFI column with each student, you must ensure that the total resulting from adding up the column is identical for all students in the class. This puts everyone on an equal footing. It does mean that you have to go through the categories on your own first and establish an "ideal" *total* weighting.

The column marked "x Level" rates the student's accomplishment in each category on a 0-to-4 basis with 0 meaning no accomplishment and 4 meaning maximum reasonable progress that could be expected. The "x" is a multiplication sign. In practice the WFI for a category is multiplied "times" the "Level" at which you have rated the student. This provides the number that is entered in the column below the equals sign (=).

That figure is usually regarded as a "subtotal" from which you deduct a certain number of points according to your estimate of a student's "readiness" (prior preparation, prior accomplishment, overall ability). From 0 to 2 points can be deducted from the subtotal; 2 points for students who have demonstrated the qualities described for Level III (pp. 262-264), 1 point for the students who exhibit the qualities described for Level II, and no (0) points for students whose readiness is that of a Level I student.

Once the "readiness' is subtracted from the subtotal, a "score" results. Teachers who prefer may eliminate the readiness factor and, instead, use the "subtotal" as the final "score" for a category. Whichever process is used, the score for each category is added to achieve a "Total Score" for the student's overall achievement. This by itself could be used as a record of overall achievement. But where grades are required, a grade can be derived from the Total Score by simple arithmetic.

1. Add up (if you haven't already) the total WFI used as the common basis for the class.

2. Multiply it by 4.

3. Divide the result into the Total Score.

4. Muitiply that result by 4. This results in a Grade Point Average.

Using a scale such as the one furnished below, the grade point average can be converted into letter or numerical grades.

A	A-	B+	B	B-	C+	C	C-	D+	D	D-	E
4.0	3.7	3.3	3.0	2.7	2.3	2.0	1.7	1.3	1.0	0.7	0.0
100	96	92	88	84	80	76	72	68	64	60	

A completely filled-out Action Evaluation Form resulting in a Grade might look like Fig. A:6. The teacher can keep a record of this form and submit only the grade to the administration. Thus the more detailed reporting of the evaluation is available for the teacher to use in discussing with the student (or the student's parents) the specifics of the overall evaluation.

One final word: you are urged to tremendously deemphasize grades altogether. Every class activity your students do should provide them with diagnostic evaluation, either spoken or written depending on the nature of the activity. If you grade each activity it is bound to destroy the Action Learning concept! If you use the Action Evaluation Format of evaluation and reporting, you might find, as have other teachers, that for one of the so-called special subjects in middle or junior high school the administration will allow you to "grade" on a Satisfactory/Unsatisfactory or Pass/Fail basis.

Some principals will want a category for high achievement (e.g., S+) but otherwise as long as they are assured that you are employing a regular and detailed evaluation process, they are often satisfied to dispense with traditional grades in recognition of the original purposes of these classes as exploratory surveys. Sadly, many principals feel they must require teachers to produce

Objectives	WFI	X Level	= Score	minus readi- ness	= Final Score	Comments
1. Melody	4	3	12	2	10	*melodic songwriting coming along*
2. Harmony	3	4	12	1	11	
3. Rhythm/Meter	2	4	8	1	7	
4. Form	3	2	6	1	5	*some progress over last marking period*
5. Timbre	3	1	3	1	2	*?*
6. Texture	2	2	4	0	4	*OK but needs more experience*
7. Style	1	0	0	0	0	
8. Effort	4	2	8	0	8	*Tries reasonably well most of the time*
	22			6	47	
	Total			Total	Total	

57 × 4

(22) × 4 = (88) minus (6) = (82) / (47) = (2.29)

TOTAL Possible WFI   TOTAL Readiness   TOTAL SCORE   Grade Point Average

Notice that this hypothetical student has done well in the first three objectives, fair in objectives 4, 6, and 8, and not very well in objectives 5 and 7. This is computed along with the teacher's estimation of readiness (2 = an objective for which a student has much readiness, 1 = average readiness, and 0 = no previous experience can be predicted). This student, thus, has been recorded as a little above average, but the more specific evaluations entering into this judgment are also reported. Thus this record can be explained to the student, his or her parents, or administrators, guidance counselors and the like.

Fig. A:6 Action Evaluation for a Hypothetical Student

frequent grades because this is the only way (they think) to ensure that the teachers are evaluating at all, and principals want evidence of evaluation in the event that parents complain. Thus the system recommended here may assist you in removing grades and all their negative effects from being a problem in your teaching.

Appendix B

The Progress of Musical Growth

A NATURAL MUSIC EDUCATION CURRICULUM FOR ACTION LEARNING

The typical preschool youngster has many contacts with music. All are important ingredients in nurturing musical abilities. For many reasons, however, some children do not have the advantage of very many such musical experiences in their formative years. Their preparation, and thus their readiness for musical instruction in school will be less rich. (See Fig. B:1)

The fundamental entrance to music for the largest number of children who *do* have significant preschool musical experience is *listening* (as shown in Fig. B:1). Children hear people around them sing or perform on instruments, and hear recordings and television music. As part of their physical development, expressive movement—not necessarily to music, but nonetheless rhythmic and organized—is predictable. When these movements are in some way a response to musical stimuli, the child once again is using listening as the major vehicle for musical growth. *Creative activities** and *performing*† are, of course, only improvisatory and spontaneous at this stage, but that should not minimize their importance any more than it is possible to deny musical validity to jazz and other similar kinds of musical improvisation.

If anything, it is the unfettered simplicity and authenticity of such creative efforts at this stage to which adults often wish to return. While the initial artistic

---

* For present purposes, *creative activities* should be understood as those exclusive of *composing* which are nonetheless "created" by young people through manipulating, arranging, or rearranging materials in an original manner (e.g., shining flashlights with colored cellophane over the lens on the walls of a darkened room in time with music).

† Singing, banging on a piano, playing toy instruments "expressively."

402

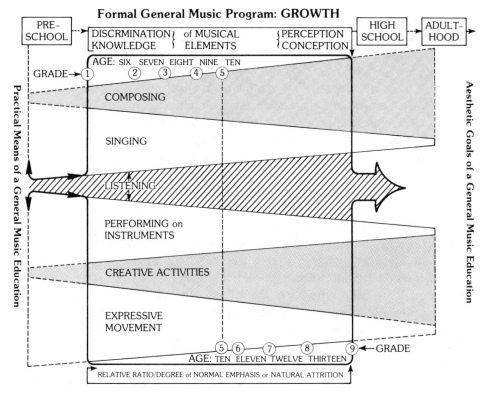

Fig. B:1

impulse or gesture always seems to have the "playful" nonplanned character of childhood, the "working out" of it by mature artists often seeks to conceal craftsmanship in an attempt to make the artwork *seem* "natural." Some artists go so far as to believe that if the handling of materials and craft draws attention to itself, then the artist has distracted the perceiver from the true intent of the artwork (which should not be obscured by bursts of technical virtuosity).

So it is through listening—and the central role of listening in singing, performing, composing, and creating—that the child comes to "know" music and to grow musically. With the onset of formal schooling, listening continues to play a clear role. But other means or methods are now employed. Singing, playing instruments, and expressively moving to music become major ways of actively involving the child with musical perception. Active involvement is absolutely required at this stage. In Piaget's terms this is the "preoperational" stage of development when the child requires much actual experience. This is organized inductively in order to serve increasingly as the basis for the "concrete operational stage" that begins around second grade (age seven).

The growing fund of perceptual experience, and the resulting though primitive concepts that are thus acquired, are also applied or related to listen-

403

ing, composing, and creating. These, in turn, become correspondingly more and more important as time moves the child through the elementary years.

Somewhere around fifth grade, or between the ages of nine and ten years, all six major means of a general-music education are perhaps in as much of a balance as they will ever be. This is the time at which the specialized functions of each brain hemisphere are established. The child is on the brink of a new life-stage. Through their provision of the "middle school," educational leaders seek to accommodate the new needs of children which arrive at this time. These have been explained at some length in the Introduction and in chapter 1 of this text.

After age nine to ten, listening becomes increasingly central. Compositional and creative activities will benefit students only to the degree that they can *hear* and understand the fruits of their own and others' activities. Singing, performing on instruments, and expressive movement (dance) are also entirely dependent upon listening for their success. These three means, however, begin their own inherent process of natural selectivity at this point. Such "performing arts" are not democratic: not all people will have either the inborn "talent" or enough significant musical accomplishment to profit from the increasing specialization of skill required by the performing arts.

Natural attrition results as fewer and fewer children develop the requisite skills for singing (e.g., sufficient development of the inner ear to match pitch and stay on one part of multiple-part music), for performing on instruments (this requires many of the same skills as singing, plus others), or for dance (especially concepts of rhythm and meter, and a kinesthetic appreciation of such concepts). The accomplishments and personal satisfaction of performing can lead some students into ever more specialized training, and chorus, band, and orchestra opportunities exist for *these students* for this reason (see Fig. B:2). But they have all the more need for the enriching effects of listening, composing, and creative activities. In this way they can avoid becoming so narrow in their musical involvements as to limit their musical contacts to only one major category (e.g., "liking" only band music, or only choral music, or only orchestra music, or only music for dancing).

In the meanwhile, the increasing numbers of otherwise intelligent and sensitive children who cannot or do not pursue the performance aspects of music* should have the benefit of an increasing emphasis on listening, composing, and creative activities. These are means through which a general musical growth can proceed. This will still allow them to reach aesthetic goals similar to the ones reached by those who have gone the performance route.

---

* It would seem that this attrition is to be expected, since it is natural for individuals to have a wide variety of interests and pursuits they find gratifying. What would *not* be expected or natural is for any person to have learned *no means* for being productively involved in music. Therefore no stigma should be attached to those who, for a variety of reasons, choose not to pursue musical performance separately outside of general music classes.

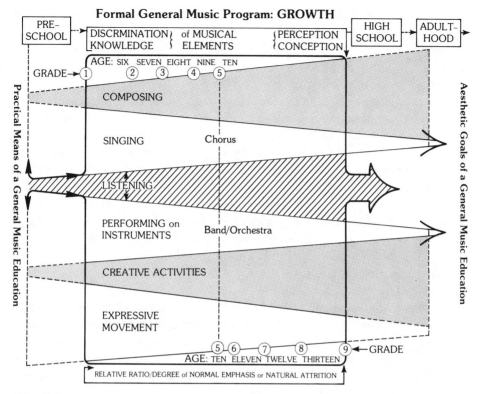

Fig. B:2

Listening is, again, the most central, however, for it is the musical action most accessible to all people, even long after they have left school.

As a result of this process of natural attrition, the performing aspects of the early elementary years of general music classes should gradually taper off as a main *formal* means of a *general music* education based on *Action Learning.* Correspondingly, composing and creative activities grow in importance and application. In the middle school years, these activities naturally constitute the largest portion of the formal program. Some smaller amounts of performance activities are still available in this later stage, though far fewer and fewer each year.† So the *general music program,* as such, generally deemphasizes these for everyone, while the few for whom musical performance is a realistic and satisfying experience are provided a *performance program* (chorus, band, orchestra) for such pursuits (see Fig. B:2).

Notice, however, that it is precisely the children with "talent" or interest in performing who can profit most from the type of general music-class emphasis intended mainly for the children not as able at, or interested in, performing. As Fig. B:2 shows, listening will still be a major vehicle for lifelong involvement

---

† Once again, you are reminded not to view such a natural thinning out in a negative way.

even for those children who are in school performance groups of one kind or another. Not all of these children can or will go on and perform music for the remainder of their lives. They will and can fulfill their musical interests and needs throughout their lifetimes as listeners, so the emphasis through the school years on listening is once again justified.

What is neither justified nor realistic is to expect *all* children to be gratified by (or good at) singing, playing instruments, or expressive movement. The circumstances of individual lives do not permit such uniformity. It is mistaken, therefore, to make these activities the *only* or *main* practical means of a general music education for *all children*. For children who have some potential and interest in performance it is just as unwarranted that performance should be *their* only or main musical diet. For both kinds of students much musical discrimination (perception) and knowledge (conception) is gained as inductive learning from compositional and other creative activities (which nonetheless also involve significant amounts of listening) and from activities whose major focus is listening.

This kind of learning enables all students to be intelligent *consumers* of music. It provides them with the bases for knowledgeable choice, and for personally valid musical values. On the other hand, an emphasis on creative listening activities serves two groups of students simultaneously. It serves the realistic needs of those who might someday have the opportunity or desire to resume or continue performing as well as those for whom performance was never a major avenue of musical involvement.

So as the inherent criteria surrounding the performance aspects of music slowly thin out the ranks of those who will remain to derive the joy and rewards of musical performance, there is a corresponding emphasis on composing and creating, and ultimately on listening in all its forms. This *decrease of performance-oriented class activities* (i.e., singing and performing on classroom instruments; but not a decrease in students' performances of their own compositions) and *increase of listening-oriented activities* (especially students' listening to their own creations) nurtures the musical growth of both kinds of students.

Indeed, it even allows the general music programs to produce three entirely different yet overlapping kinds of musical involvement:

1. *Listening:* this is suitable for *all* students, regardless of their other interests and accomplishments in music.

2. *Performing:* this is suitable for the decreasing number of students well suited by virtue of talent, inclination, or interest to the inherent demands of musical performance.

3. *Creating:* this is suitable for the relatively few students whose creativity is enhanced by these activities, and for students who are inclined toward listening and performing as well. Here "creating" need not be understood in its "in-

spired" sense as much as in the sense of "making something" and learning more about music as a result.

In sum, musical performance skills are inherently selective. Because of this inherent selectivity they are less and less suitable as the *sole or major emphases* in a program of *general* music education for *all* people. On the other hand, they are the major purpose of the performance ensemble program. As a general music education program progresses, the more general means (in comparison to the specific and selective performance areas) of composition, creative activities, and listening activities become increasingly important and thus more frequently used.

Finally, as the broken lines show on Fig. B:2 under the headings "high school" and "adulthood," any one or more of the means of a general music education *can become* for some people a rich source of musical involvement after leaving school. But the one route that is available to all people, regardless of other special interests, is listening. Thus listening is the major distinguishing characteristic of a general music program that intends to serve *all* students. Not coincidentally, listening is also the major raison d'être of the musical art; composing and performing exist to make possible the listening experience. Listening, then, is central to the goals of a music-education program seeking to nurture aesthetic goals.

Selected Bibliography

HANDLING ADOLESCENT BEHAVIOR PROBLEMS

*Alschuler, Alfred, and Shea, Joel V. "The Discipline Game: Playing Without Losers." *Learning*, vol. 3, no. 1 (Aug.-Sept. 1974), pp. 80-86.

Berger, Kathleen Stassen. "Adolescent Self-Charting and Change." Unpublished Ph.D. dissertation, Yeshiva University, New York, 1972 (University Microfilm no. 73-11, 982, 187 pp.).

Buckley, Nancy K., and Walker, Hill M. *Modifying Classroom Behavior: A Manual of Procedure for Classroom Teachers.* Champaign, Ill.: Research Press, n.d.

*Buxton, Claude E. *Adolescents in School.* New Haven, Conn.: Yale University Press, 1973.

Calvert, Barbara. *The Role of the Pupil.* Boston: Routledge & Kegan Paul, 1975.

Canter, Lee. *The Whys and Hows of Working with Behavior Problems.* San Rafael, Calif.: Academic Therapy Publications, 1974.

*Carter, Ronald D. *Help! These Kids Are Driving Me Crazy.* Champaign, Ill.: Research Press, n.d.

*Caspari, Irene E. *Troublesome Children in Class.* Boston: Routledge & Kegan Paul, 1975.

*Cultice, Wendell W. *Positive Discipline for a More Productive Educational Climate.* Englewood Cliffs, N.J.: Parker, 1975.

Dreikurs, Rudolf, and Grey, Loren. *A New Approach to Discipline: Logical Consequences.* New York: Hawthorne Books, 1968.

English, O. Spurgeon, and Finch, Stuart M. *Emotional Problems of Growing Up.* Chicago: Science Research Associates, 1972.

Emmer, Edmund T., and Evertson, Carolyn M., "Synthesis of Research in Classroom Management," *Educational Leadership*, vol. 38, no. 4 (January 1981), pp. 342-347.

* Recommended as especially useful.

*Ernst, Ken. *Games Students Play*. Millbrae, Calif.: Celestial Arts Publishing, 1974.

Fargo, G. A.; Behrns, C.; and Nolen, P., eds. *Behavior Modification in the Classroom*. Belmont, Calif.: Wadsworth Publishing Co., 1970.

Francis, Paul. *Beyond Control? A Study of Discipline in the Comprehensive School*. London: George Allen & Unwin, 1975; U.S. distribution, International Publishing Service, Collings, Inc. (114 E. 32nd St., New York, N.Y. 10016).

*Gammage, Philip. *Teacher and Pupil*. London: Routledge & Kegan Paul, 1971.

Genot, Hiam. *Teacher and Child*. New York: Macmillan, 1972.

*Glasser, William. *Schools Without Failure*. New York: Harper & Row, 1969.

*———. "A New Look at Discipline." *Learning*, vol. 3, no. 4 (Dec. 1974), pp. 6-11.

*Gruen, Arno. "Autonomy and Compliance: The Fundamental Antithesis." *Journal of Humanistic Psychology*, vol. 16, no. 3 (Summer 1976), p. 61.

Hargreaves, David H.; Hester, Stephen K.; and Mellor, Frank J. *Deviance in Classrooms*. Boston: Routledge & Kegan Paul, 1976.

Havis, Andrew Lee. "Alternatives for Breaking the 'Discipline Barrier' in Our Schools." *Education*, vol. 96 (Winter 1975), pp. 124-128.

Homme, Lloyd, et al. *How to Use Contingency Contracting in the Classroom*. Champaign, Ill.: Research Press, n.d.

Hoover, Kenneth. *Secondary/Middle School Teaching*. Boston: Allyn & Bacon, 1977. See chapter 4.

*Janov, Arthur. *The Feeling Child*. New York: Simon & Schuster, 1973.

Johnson, Eric W. *How to Live Through Junior High School*. New York: Lippincott, 1975.

*Konopka, Gisela. *Young Girls: A Portrait of Adolescence*. Englewood Cliffs, N.J.: Prentice-Hall, 1972.

Krumholtz, John D., and Krumholtz, Helen B. *Changing Children's Behavior*. Englewood Cliffs, N.J.: Prentice-Hall, 1972.

Laufer, Moses. *Adolescent Disturbance and Breakdown*. Baltimore: Penguin Books, 1975.

Martin, Reed, and Lauridsen, David. *Developing Student Discipline and Motivation*. Champaign, Ill.: Research Press, 1974.

Milson. Fred. *Youth in a Changing Society*. Boston: Routledge & Kegan Paul, 1975.

Muhgham, Geoff, and Peason, Geoff, eds. *Working Class Youth Culture*. Boston: Routledge & Kegan Paul, 1976.

O'Leary, K. D., and O'Leary, S. G. *The Successful Use of Behavior Modification*. Elmsford, N.Y.: Pergamon Press, 1973.

Pearson, Craig. *Resolving Classroom Conflict*. Lincoln, Neb.: Professional Educators Publications, 1975.

Peel, E. A. *The Nature of Adolescent Judgment*. Somerset, N.J.: John Wiley & Sons, 1972.

* Raffani, James P. *Discipline: Negotiating Conflicts with Today's Kids*. Englewood Cliffs, N.J.: Prentice-Hall, 1980.

Rikes-Inesta, E., and Bandura, A., eds. *Analysis of Delinquency Aggression*. New York: Halsted Press (A Lawrence Erekaum Associates Publication), 1976.

Shaw, Marilyn. "Uncooperative and Incorrigible." *Media and Methods*, vol. 12 (April 1976), pp. 43-45.

Sheldon, Rose. *Treating Children in Groups*. San Francisco: Jossey-Bass, 1972.

Sheppard, William C.; Shank, Steven B.; and Wilson, Darla. *Teaching Social Behavior to Young Children.* Champaign, Ill.: Research Press, n.d.

Sheviakov, George, and Redl, Fritz. New revision by Sybil K. Richardson. *Discipline for Today's Children and Youth.* Washington, D.C.: National Educators Association, 1956.

Shipman, Helen, and Foley, Elizabeth. *Any Teacher Can . . .* Chicago: Loyola University Press, 1973.

Smith, Othanel B., and Orlosky, Donald E. *Socialization and Schooling: The Basics of Reform.* Bloomington, Ind.: Phi Delta Kappa, 1975.

*Stradley, William E., and Aspinall, Richard D. *Discipline in the Junior High/Middle School: A Handbook for Teachers, Counselors, and Administrators.* New York: Center for Applied Research in Education, 1975.

Sullivan, Patricia. "Suicide by Mistake." *Psychology Today,* vol. 10, no. 5 (Oct. 1976).

Sulzer, B., and Mayer, G. R. *Behavior Modification Procedures for School Personnel.* Elk Grove, Ill.: Dryden Press, 1972.

Sweat, Clifford; Tink, A. Kerby; and Reedy, Lyle, eds. *Humanizing Instruction in the Junior High School.* Danville, Ill.: Interstate Printers and Publishers, 1974.

*Swift, Marshall S., and Spivak, George. *Alternative Teaching Strategies: Helping Behaviorally Troubled Children Achieve.* Champaign, Ill.: Research Press, n.d.

Tink, A. Kerby; White, Connie; Shields, Pat; and Wood, D. A., eds. *Junior High Pressure Points in the '70s.* Danville, Ill.: Interstate Printers and Publishers, 1973.

*Truesdell, Bill, and Newman, Jeff. "Can Jr. Highs Make It with the Wide Open Spaces?" *Learning,* vol. 4, no. 3 (Nov. 1975), pp. 74-77.

Whiteside, Marilyn. "School Discipline: The Ongoing Crisis." *The Clearing House,* vol. 49 (Dec. 1975), pp. 160-62.

*Wilson, P. S. *Interest and Discipline in Education.* Boston: Routledge & Kegan Paul, 1974.

INSTRUCTIONAL MEDIA

Baird, Jo Ann. *Using Media in the Music Program.* West Nyack, N.Y.: Center for Applied Research in Education, 1975.

Bottje, Will Gay. "Electronic Music—Creative Tool in the Classroom." *School Musician* (April 1970), p. 58.

Brown, James W.; Lewis, Richard B.; and Harcleroad, Fred F. *AV Instruction: Technology, Media and Methods.* 4th ed. New York: McGraw-Hill, 1973.

Burkhart, Arnold E. *Keeping Up with Experimental Music in Schools* (series). Muncie, Ind.: 1220 Ridge Rd. See especially vol. 2, no. 2 (Nov.-Dec. 1975), pp. 21, 24, 28-29.

Dale, Edgar. *Audiovisual Methods in Teaching.* 3rd ed. New York: Dryden Press/Holt, Rinehart & Winston, 1974.

Dunn, Rita, and Dunn, Kenneth. *Practical Approaches to Individualizing Instruction: Contracts and Other Effective Teaching Strategies.* West Nyack, N.Y.: Parker, 1972.

——. "Practical Questions Teachers Ask About Individualizing Instruction—and Some of the Answers." *Audiovisual Instruction* (Jan. 1972), pp. 47-50.

Dwyer, Terence. *Making Electronic Music.* Books 1 and 2; Source Material 1 and 2; Teacher's Book. London: Oxford University Press (44 Conduit St., WIR ODE), 1975.

Gerlach, Vernon S., and Ely, Ronald P. *Teaching and Media.* Englewood Cliffs, N.J.: Prentice-Hall, 1974.

Glogau, Lillian; Krause, Edmund; and Wexler, Miriam. *Developing a Successful Elementary School Media Center.* West Nyack, N.Y.: Parker, 1972.

Hagemann, Virginia S. "Are Junior High Students Ready for Electronic Music? Are Their Teachers?" *Music Educators Journal* (Dec. 1969), p. 35.

Klasek, Charles B. *Instructional Media in the Modern School.* Lincoln, Neb.: Professional Educators Publications, 1975.

Landon, Joseph W. *How to Write Learning Activity Packages for Music Education.* Costa Mesa, Calif.: Educational Media Press, 1973.

Langdon, Danny G. *Interactive Instructional Designs for Individualized Learning.* Englewood Cliffs, N.J.: Educational Technology Publications, 1973.

Lewis, James, Jr. *Administering the Individual Instruction Program.* West Nyack, N.Y.: Parker, 1971.

Meske, Eunice Boardman, and Rinehardt Caroll. *Individualized Instruction in Music.* Reston, Va.: Music Educators National Conference, 1975.

Modugno, Anne D. *Creating Music Through the Use of the Tape Recorder.* New Haven, Conn.: Keyboard Publications, 1975.

Mohan, Madan, and Hull, Ronald E., eds. *Individualized Instruction and Learning.* Chicago: Nelson-Hall Co., 1974.

Monsour, Sally. *Music in Open Education.* West Nyack, N.Y.: Center for Applied Research in Education, 1974.

"Music in Open Education." Entire issue, *Music Educators Journal,* vol. 60, no. 8 (April 1974).

Olmstead, Joseph A. *Small-Group Instruction—Theory and Practice.* Alexandria, Va.: Human Resources Research Organization, 1974.

Pearson, Neville P., and Butler, Lucius A., eds. *Learning Resource Centers.* Minneapolis: Burgess Publishing Co., 1973.

Tillman, Rix W. *Music Educator's Guide to Personalized Instruction.* West Nyack, N.Y.: Parker, 1975.

Index

Index

Index